# George Washington

# George Washington

## THE MAN BEHIND THE MYTHS

*William M. S. Rasmussen and Robert S. Tilton*

UNIVERSITY PRESS OF VIRGINIA

*Charlottesville & London*

The University Press of Virginia

© 1999 by the Rector and Visitors of the University of Virginia

Printed in Canada

*First published 1999*

∞The paper used in this publication meets the minimum requirements
of the American National Standard for Information Sciences—
Permanence of Paper for Printed Library Materials, ANSI Z39.48-1984.

Library of Congress Cataloging-in-Publication Data

Rasmussen, William M. S. (William Meade Stith), 1946–
    George Washington—the man behind the myths /
        William M.S. Rasmussen and Robert S. Tilton.
            p.        cm.
    Catalog of an exhibition held Feb. 1999 in Richmond, Va.
    Includes bibliographical references.
    ISBN 0-8139-1900-2 (pbk. : alk. paper
1. Washington, George, 1732–1799—Exhibitions.
2. Presidents—United States—Exhibitions. I. Tilton, Robert S. II. Title.
E312.17.R37 1999
973.4'1'092—dc21                                       98-31010
                                       CIP

Composition by Hillside Studio, Inc.

Printed and bound in Canada by Friesens Printers

*frontispiece:* Joseph Wright, *George Washington,* 1784, oil on panel, 14⅛×12 in
(Courtesy of Historical Society of Pennsylvania)

やや

# Contents

Forewords     *vii*

Acknowledgments     *ix*

やや *Introduction*     *xi*

*1 The Early Years: Washington's Youth (1732–1752)*     *3*

    Virginia: The Physical Landscape     *3*

    Washington's Boyhood     *9*

    Virginia: The Social Landscape     *18*

    Profiting from the Land: Washington as Surveyor     *28*

*2 The Virginia Soldier (1753–1758)*     *37*

    Peale's Washington     *37*

    The Making of a Virginia Officer     *45*

    Service with Braddock and the Defeat at Monongahela     *57*

    Defending the Frontier and the Capture of Fort Duquesne     *64*

*3 The Virginia Planter: Washington's First Retirement to Mount Vernon (1759–1775)*     *75*

    Preparing for Retirement     *75*

    Becoming a Planter     *88*

    "The Illustrious Couple": Washington's Marriage and Family Life     *93*

    Land in the West: Opportunity for Empire     *99*

    Farming under British Taxation     *105*

*4 The War Years (1775–1783)*     *111*

    An Unsought Honor     *111*

    Improving Mount Vernon     *114*

    Equal to the Command     *127*

    Return to Virginia     *140*

5 *The American Cincinnatus: Washington's Second Retirement to Mount Vernon (1783–1789)*    155

     The American Cincinnatus    155

     "Mount Vernon and Peace": Social Life after the War    167

     Renewed Family Life    178

     Improving Nature: Washington as Landscape Gardener    184

     The First Farmer in America    189

     What "Imperious Necessity Compels": Washington as a Slaveholder    197

6 *The First President of the United States (1789–1797)*    205

     "Concerned Spectator": Washington's Acceptance of the Presidency    205

     The Machine of Government    210

     The Image of the President    215

     The Accoutrements of the President    226

     Absentee Farmer    232

7 *Return to Virginia: Washington's Final Retirement to Mount Vernon (1797–1799)*    245

     "The Humble and Endearing Scenes of Private Life"    245

     The Pursuit of "Rural Amusements"    254

     The Death of Washington    258

     The Apotheosis of Washington    261

*Afterword: The Legacies of Washington*    275

     Mount Vernon and the Mount Vernon Ladies' Association    275

     Washington Academy (Washington and Lee University)    280

     The Virginia Historical Society    282

     Conclusion: "Below the clouds"    287

Notes    289

List of Illustrations    315

Index    321

# *Forewords*

ALTHOUGH THE LIFE OF George Washington has been abundantly chronicled, it remains an enigma. Throughout the nineteenth century historians and biographers who followed in the footsteps of Parson Weems were often careless about the facts of his life, to the point where Esmond Wright would note that the image of Washington presented by early writers was "carved in marble prose, lost to flesh and blood and temper." Twentieth-century historians have tended to portray Washington in more realistic terms, but their presentations have often alternated between idolatry and iconoclasm. To this day it is difficult to separate fact from myth. *George Washington: The Man behind the Myths* will allow visitors to consider many of the legends associated with Washington in the context of his own accounts and reports by his contemporaries, and will thereby equip them to decide for themselves what is to be believed.

This exhibition would not have been possible without the strong partnership we forged early on with Washington and Lee University and the Mount Vernon Ladies' Association. Through this cooperative effort we have brought together a remarkable collection of images and objects, many of which have never been on public display before. *George Washington: The Man behind the Myths* is the second collaborative project for the society of our cocurators, Dr. William M. S. Rasmussen, Curator of Art at the Virginia Historical Society, and Dr. Robert S. Tilton, Assistant Professor of English and Director of American Studies at the University of Connecticut. In 1994, their solid scholarship and creativity led to one of the most successful exhibitions we have ever mounted, *Pocahontas: Her Life and Legend*. We are fortunate that these two fine scholars have once again combined their talents. Thanks to their hard work and that of many members of our staff, we will all gain a fuller understanding of Washington, a person whose image we see daily on our currency and whom we recall fondly from childhood lessons, but about whom we actually know very little. I wish to take this opportunity to welcome visitors to the Virginia Historical Society, where I am confident that they will have an enlightening, and often surprising, experience.

Charles F. Bryan, Jr.
Director
Virginia Historical Society

IT IS PARTICULARLY FITTING that Washington and Lee University should join with its sister institutions, the Virginia Historical Society and the Mount Vernon Ladies' Association, to sponsor the exhibition, *George Washington: The Man behind the Myths*. On the occasion of the bicentennial of the death of Washington, we each have reason to honor his memory.

The exhibition affords the University yet another opportunity during its two hundred and fiftieth anniversary year to acknowledge the abiding gratitude we owe to the father of our country. Less than fifty years after its first beginnings in 1749, it was the generous and timely benefaction of George Washington that secured the future of Liberty Hall Academy, enabling an impoverished and struggling school "in the upper country" of Virginia to become a college and then a university that would bear his name and that of Robert E. Lee.

Long a repository for various family papers, paintings, and other Washington memorabilia, the University is pleased to share some of its most valued treasures, many of which are associated with Washington's private life in colonial Virginia. It is our hope that these and the other artifacts, images, and documents in this exhibition will acquaint visitors anew with George Washington by separating the man from the myths.

John W. Elrod
President
Washington and Lee
University

&

NOT TOO MANY YEARS AGO a portrait of George Washington presided over almost every classroom in the nation, reminding students that the character and leadership of a single man played a crucial role in the creation of the United States. But no longer. Today, Washington is fast disappearing from history textbooks and is seldom pointed out as a role model to young leaders-in-training. Each year, as mid-February approaches, Washington's image appears in a wide variety of advertisements and promotions keyed to President's Day, a sad remnant of what used to be a meaningful day of remembrance, George Washington's Birthday. We need to recognize that we are losing touch with our true heroes, and to address this problem in a determined and organized fashion. *George Washington: The Man behind the Myths* is a creative step in the right direction. By visiting the exhibit and spending time with this thought-provoking catalog, Americans will be encouraged to reestablish their connection to the "Father" of their country.

James C. Rees
Resident Director
Historic Mount Vernon

# Acknowledgments

Our previous exhibition, *Pocahontas: Her Life and Legend,* examined the historical record of Pocahontas's life and compared it to the works of writers and artists who had adapted it to their purposes. After that show we began to think about other historical figures whose real lives have been pushed into obscurity by the myths surrounding them. We agreed that there was no one about whom we assume so much but actually know so little than George Washington. Jim Kelly of the Virginia Historical Society encouraged us to pursue this idea and provided the intellectual support that got us started. Once we had decided to seek the support and collaboration of other institutions that honor Washington's memory, Tom Litzenburg (the Director of the Reeves Center at Washington and Lee University), and John Riley, the historian at Mount Vernon, offered useful advice and encouragement and helped to transform the exhibition from a lengthy set of plans into reality. Peter Agelasto, who served on an alumni committee charged to plan Washington and Lee's 250th-anniversary commemoration, and Clare Edwards, the Vice-Regent of the Mount Vernon Ladies' Association from Connecticut, heartened us with their enthusiasm at crucial stages of this undertaking.

This is an interdisciplinary project, in which the methodologies of historical research play a large role. We have benefited from the input of historians who have studied this subject for as many decades as we have years. We must first thank William Abbot and Dorothy Twohig, the two previous editors-in-chief of the monumental *Papers of George Washington* project, for agreeing to assist our efforts, as well as Philander D. Chase who has now assumed that mantle, Frank E. Grizzard Jr., Mark A. Mastromarino, Beverly H. Runge, and Jack D. Warren for the care that went into their reading of our manuscript. They provided a good deal of guidance and a number of excellent suggestions. Twohig and Chase should be singled out for allowing us to pester them about assorted minutiae concerning Washington. They were consistently patient about these queries and always succeeded in getting us back on the right track. A special mention must be made as well of the aid and encouragement provided by Don Higginbotham. Don's initial positive response, as well as his many comments and timely corrections, bolstered us throughout this undertaking. In all, we found our consultants to be extraordinarily generous and warmly supportive, and we owe to them a higher degree of thanks than can be registered here.

At the Virginia Historical Society, Bob Strohm and Lee Shepard directed us to significant books and manuscripts in the society's collection, Giles Cromwell answered our questions about arms, Stacy Gibford-Rusch conserved a number of the pieces that were loaned for the exhibition, Ron Jennings took most of the photographs of the objects owned by the society (as well as of many that we borrowed), and AnnMarie Price, Dale Kostelny, and Jeff Eastman arranged the shipping and installation of objects. We also thank Pam Seay, Pat Morris, Nadja Gutowski, and Doris Delk in the society's public affairs office and Bill Obrochta in the education department. Barbara Macmillan and King Laughlin guided us through the available holdings at Mount Vernon, and Karen Van Epps Peters provided many images from the picture collection. We have also been aided by the staffs at many museums, galleries, historical sites, libraries, and institutions. We are particularly indebted to Georgia Barnhill, Shirley Belkowitz, Jeanne M. Benas, Anne E. Bentley, Ellin Burke, Jean Collier, Jack Cowart, David Curry, Anne M. Decker, Karie Diethorn, John J. Donahue, Peter Drummey, Frank R. Dunaway Jr., Vernon Edenfield, Suzanne Foley, Debra Force, William M. Fowler Jr., Kristen Froehlich, Wayne Furman, Gerald Gawalt, Elizabeth Gordon, Lisa Kathleen Graddy, Elizabeth M. Gushee, Alan M. Hantman, Sarah Jeschke Harman, Jill Hartz, Robert E. Hawks, Melissa Heaver, William J. Hennessey, Joice Himawan, Larry Hinckler, Farris Hotchkiss, John K. Howat, James Hutson, Audrey C. Johnson, Catherine H. Jordan, Wayne L. Joyce, Peter M. Kenny, Dan Lewis, Tom Manley, Linda H. Mattingly, David Meschutt, Ellen Miles, Jim Monday, Stacia Norman, Ruth M. O'Brien, Susan Olsen, Michelle S. Peplin, Charles E. Pierce, Paul Provost, Jennie Rathbun, Harry Rubenstein, Andrew Schoelkopf, Bryan

Shaw, Nancy Rivard Shaw, Suzanne L. Shenton, Linda Simmons, Barbi Schecter Spieler, Lora Stowe, Louis Tucker, Craig Tuminaro, Dominique H. Vasseur, Lee Viverett, Celeste Walker, Jack Warner, Nancy Edelman Work, and David S. Zeidberg. We also thank E. Lisk Wyckoff Jr. of the Homeland Foundation and all of the private lenders to the show.

Others who have contributed, either through pointed questions or casual conversations, include W. Guthrie Sayen (who was kind enough to allow us to see his recently completed dissertation on Washington), Richard D. Brown, Caroline P. Sloat, Wayne Franklin, Jay Fliegelman, Laura Mills, David Rawson, and Fredrika Teute. Bob would also like to thank his colleagues in the English department at the University of Connecticut for their suggestions and notes especially the questions raised by Roger Wilkenfeld, Hap Fairbanks, Veronica Makowsky, and Lee Jacobus at a faculty seminar, which helped him to clarify a number of persistent vagaries. John Gatta and Michael Meyer also offered useful guidance along the way. Bob would also like to thank Steve Kruger and Betty Weidman of Queens College for their support and suggestions and Tom Moser Jr. and Cathy Bledsoe for their wisdom, accommodation, and fellowship.

The production of this catalog was underwritten by a generous contribution from Washington and Lee University. The costs of producing the transparencies for the illustrations and attaining the permissions to use these images were covered by a grant from the Research Foundation at the University of Connecticut. We would also like to acknowledge generous gifts from the E. Rhodes and Leona B. Carpenter Foundation, the Society of the Cincinnati in the State of Virginia, the Robins Foundation, the William H., John G., and Emma Scott Foundation, and Mrs. John H. Guy Jr. We thank Lora Robins for acquiring for the society's permanent collection fifteen of the paintings that are illustrated in this catalog, including the thirteen by J. L. G. Ferris.

At the University Press of Virginia, we wish to thank Nancy Essig for taking on this predictably troublesome project and Deborah A. Oliver, Janet Anderson, and Mary MacNeil for making sure that the various strands were pulled together in a cohesive manner. We must also thank Ed King of Hillside Studio for his wonderful design, creative suggestions, and extraordinary patience during this process, and Annette Wenda, whose masterful copyediting skills made this a far more readable and sensible book.

We should mention here that not every object in this catalog is included in the exhibition, nor is every exhibited object discussed.

Finally, Bill would like to thank Lin, Dru, and Marc, and Bob would like to thank Rita for putting up with us during this excruciatingly long process and for enduring more conversations about George Washington than anyone should have to abide.

William M. S. Rasmussen
Richmond, Virginia

Robert S. Tilton
Storrs, Connecticut

15 July 1998

# Introduction

And indeed, my dear General, it must be a pleasing reflection to you amid the tranquil walks of private life to find that history, poetry, painting, & sculpture will vye with each other in consigning your name to immortality.

David Humphreys to George Washington (17 July 1785)

First in war, first in peace, and first in the hearts of his countrymen, he was second to none in the humble and endearing scenes of private life. . . . The purity of his private character gave effulgence to his public virtues.

Henry "Light-Horse Harry" Lee (1799), *A Funeral Oration on the Death of General Washington*

Both of these well-known statements suggest a clear differentiation between the private and the public lives of the man who by the mid-1770s had already been christened "the Father of His Country."[1] In his musing upon Washington's sense of his own achievements, David Humphreys separates the public, soon to be "immortal," Washington from the private man, who presumably has the time and inclination to look back from Mount Vernon over his military career and ponder the idea that his accomplishments will encourage future authors and artists to perpetuate his memory. In the most famous tribute paid to Washington after his death, "Light-Horse Harry" Lee makes the point that it was not only in his public life that Washington excelled. Indeed, Lee reminds his listeners of the distinction of Washington's private life and suggests that this aspect provided the brilliance with which his public persona had been endowed. Ironically, the eloquence of "First in war, first in peace, first in the hearts of his countrymen" has caused most of us to forget the remainder of his statement.[2]

When commentators speak of Washington's private life, they refer either to some aspect of his domestic existence or to his years as a Virginia planter at Mount Vernon. The long periods when he was in residence, which have often been made subordinate to his life in the public sphere, will be emphasized in this study. We also focus on the experiences of his Virginia upbringing, which we believe greatly influenced his later demeanor and decisions. While by no means ignoring his crucial contributions during two wars and two terms as president, we are more interested in the man behind the office. His papers reveal that private concerns were often at the heart of his national policies and has brought to life the family man and Mount Vernon planter who existed behind the well-crafted public persona. By juxtaposing these documents with accounts by his contemporaries, with household and decorative objects, with visual images, and with the narratives of the first gener-

ation of Washington biographers, we have attempted to tell his story in an untraditional way and, we hope, to inspire our readers to reassess their beliefs about Washington. A further goal will be to demonstrate that Washington, in the views that he held, in the activities in which he engaged, and in the manner in which he maneuvered himself socially and used objects and territorial acquisitions to define his ever rising status, was a clear-cut product of Virginia's peculiar colonial society. His strong connection to his native land grounds Washington and sets the stage for his future successes; indeed, we believe that his unflinching "Virginian-ness" ultimately formed the basis for his various public personae. We look to the models of his youth—his father, Augustine; half brother Lawrence; and the men of the Fairfax family—and note how their influence stayed with Washington throughout his transformation from a young man in search of suitable models to the mature man who became the model for all Americans. Finally, throughout the course of our discussion we hope to elucidate the creation of the mythic Washington through an examination of the agendas and methods of the antebellum writers and artists who brought him to life.

Lawrence J. Friedman has pointed out that the full-scale mythologizing of Washington began almost immediately after his death. His public persona is now best remembered because of statements like that of Lee and other contemporary eulogists, and the efforts of early national historians and biographers who sought to immortalize Washington through renditions of his life that emphasized his leadership roles, thereby equating his history with that of the new nation. As John Marshall, who wrote the first authorized biography of Washington, put it: "[The] history of General Washington, during his military command and civil administration, is so much that of his country, that the work appeared to the author to be most sensibly incomplete and unsatisfactory, while unaccompanied by such a narrative of the principal events preceding our revolutionary war, as would make the reader acquainted with the genius, character, and resources of the people about to engage in that memorable contest."[3] To Marshall, the link between the man and his public endeavors is inseparable, to the point that he believes his readers must understand the nation's genesis before they can understand the life and accomplishments of its greatest hero.

Other than in relation to a specific collection of moral and physical attributes, the private Washington frequently fades from view in the early biographies by Marshall, Mason Locke Weems, Washington Irving, Jared Sparks, and James Kirke Paulding. These efforts, like the late portraits by Gilbert Stuart, were in many ways intended less to capture the actual man than what Washington had come to signify; we look especially to the popular biographies of Weems and Sparks, the first editor of Washington's papers, because these writers, while employing different strategies, both palpably participate in the idolization of Washington.[4] After the turn of the nineteenth century he quickly becomes nationalized (in that his life is rarely understood to be anything other than a series of remarkable contributions to the founding of the United States), sentimentalized (in that 14 December 1799, perhaps even more so than 1 January 1800, comes to be seen as the end of the first period of American national history), and mythologized (as can be seen in the proliferation of Washington apotheoses and parabolic tributes and the immediate popularization of his image and biography). The private Washington becomes almost inaccessible, hidden behind the mythic facade, and has remained so in the public consciousness. Our goal in 1999, the two-hundredth anniversary year of his death, is to return the actual man to the forefront and to argue for the importance of those segments of his life that quickly faded from consideration in the years following his death.

In our efforts to differentiate the myths about George Washington from the discernible facts of his life we are following in the footsteps of a number of studies, including Friedman's "The Flawless American," in his *Inventors of the Promised Land*, Barry Schwartz's *George Washington: The Making of an American Symbol*, Paul K. Longmore's *Invention of George Washington*, Richard Norton Smith's *Patriarch: Washington and the New American Nation*, and, most recently, Richard Brookhiser's *Founding Father: Rediscovering George Washington*. The emphasis in the Friedman and Schwartz texts is on the development of the myth and its legacy. Longmore and Smith discuss a number of the differences between the man and the public perception of him, but in each case the focus is on a discrete period in Washington's life. Brookhiser, in his "moral biography," often alludes to details of Washington's private life but only as "they relate to his public career." Our study is indebted to each of these efforts, and will have the advantage of including illustrations of the documents, objects, and visual images that make up the exhibition in our effort to encourage a new look at the totality of his life as well as to separate the man from the myths and the moral principles that he has come to represent. In this way our work actually comes closest to the efforts of Margaret Brown Klapthor and Howard Alexander Morrison in their *George Washington: A Figure upon the Stage*, which served as the catalog for an exhibition at the National Museum of American History that celebrated the 250th anniversary of his birth. We have also looked to such early studies as Paul Leland Haworth's *George Washington: Country Gentleman*, Charles Moore's *Family Life of George Washington*, William Alfred Bryan's *George Washington in American Literature, 1775–1865*, and to the Douglas Southall Freeman biography in our search for information about Washington's private life. Two dissertations that were especially helpful are W. Guthrie Sayen's "'A Compleat Gentleman': The Making of George Washington, 1732–1775" and Mark Edward Thistlethwaite's "The Image of George Washington: Studies in Mid-Nineteenth-Century American History Painting." We have been most dependent, however, on the work of William W. Abbot, Dorothy Twohig, Philander Chase, and their colleagues at the monumental *Papers of George Washington* project. Without these editors' careful scholarship, an exhibition of this type would not have been possible.[5]

Recent studies of antebellum representations of American mythic figures, which always tell us more about the literary and visual artists who constructed them than they do about the figures themselves, have also influenced this project. Our discussions of the cultural usefulness of the Washington myth and of the preoccupations that underlie such usages have literary ancestors in the work of Richard Slotkin, particularly his seminal study of the Daniel Boone myth, *Regeneration through Violence*, Nian-Sheng Huang's *Benjamin Franklin in American Thought and Culture, 1790–1990*, Robert S. Tilton's *Pocahontas: The Evolution of an American Narrative*, and our own *Pocahontas: Her Life and Legend*, the catalog for an exhibition at the Virginia Historical Society in 1994–95. Although it would be unreasonable to think that we could substantively demythologize our subject, it is inevitable that an examination of Washington's private life, coupled with a debunking of some aspects of his mythic persona, might undermine many prevailing opinions. Our hope is that by providing a more complete picture of Washington we will simultaneously encourage a new understanding of the well-known events of his life and promote further study of his domestic existence.

An inquiry of this type demands a careful examination of the estate at Mount Vernon. We discuss in detail Washington's additions to his house and properties and chronicle his attempts at agricultural reforms. We also point to his continued interest in the running of the plantation, even when pressed by the demands of his military command or the presidency, and argue that his feelings for his home, and his home state, actually provided much of the impetus for his participation in public affairs. We are fortunate to be able to include in the exhibition a number of documents pertaining to his attentions to Mount Vernon, and through them to point to Washington's unceasing concern for his plantation and to what life there had come to mean to him. Throughout his military career his heedful consideration of affairs at Mount Vernon helped to "fill his tank," to reaffirm his belief in what he was fighting for; while in residence, which he was for twenty-four of the forty years between 1759 and 1799, he sought to re-create and then maintain the gentility that he had experienced in his youth; and during the presidency, whether discussing the possibilities for trade on the Potomac, the potential of the "western lands," or the placement of the federal district, Washington consistently supported what he saw as best for the Old Dominion and yearned for the day when he could once again focus his energies on the management of his farms.

By his own admission, and as the compendious new edition of his papers attests, George Washington spent a great deal of his adult life writing. Indeed, much of our knowledge about Washington has become available because he was a prolific writer and because so many of his papers have survived. In some cases he wrote what were basically identical letters to a number of different correspondents, tailoring the letter for each recipient, but in others he wrote often quite personal, poignant letters to family members and close friends that belie the widely held belief in his steadfast stoicism. This constant flow of correspondence allowed Washington to maintain an amazing degree of control over both his public and his private affairs and, when necessary, to manage simultaneously a number of demanding tasks. Much of what we have to contribute in this exhibition is based on the often surprising results of our bringing the weight of this documentary evidence to bear on our own beliefs and preconceptions about him. We hope to enlighten, and occasionally surprise, our audience by introducing them to a Washington that we, until approximately two years ago, had never before encountered.

A number of scholars have commented on the importance of the young Washington's having copied out the "Rules of Civility."[6] In this exercise Washington acquired both a detailed knowledge of the particular model of social decorum that would remain with him throughout his life and a sense of the efficacy of copying what he thought might become useful to

him in the future, whether in print or in the skills or deportment of others. His early associations with the Fairfax family both provided Washington with economic and cultural goals and allowed him to witness the use and delegation of authority. The understanding he gained, for instance, of when the presence of the ultimate authority is necessary versus when the employment of a subordinate is appropriate would become extremely useful in his adult leadership roles. The effect of his exposure to the Fairfaxes and their milieu cannot be overestimated when one attempts to understand his emergence from relative obscurity to positions of command in the Virginia Regiment and the Continental Army, and his memories of William Fairfax remained with him even as he helped design the role of president. We therefore spend a great deal of time discussing Washington's youth and arguing for the continuing importance of his early influences.

Paul K. Longmore has identified a series of stratagems that date to the period preceding Washington's appointment as commander of the Virginia forces in 1755 that would serve him well throughout his public life: "Four tactics emerge here that would reappear in Washington's later, more sophisticated and subtle performances at the times of his appointment to command the Continental Army, his selection as a delegate to the Constitutional Convention, and his two elections to the presidency. He carefully regards appearances; how will his audience perceive and interpret his conduct? He protests his inadequacy. He avoids actively soliciting the job. And finally, by making the offer come to him, rather than promoting himself, he increases his influence and authority."[7] Longmore makes clear his subject's consistent attendance to matters of appearance and propriety; what is implicit is Washington's confidence that he is the man for the job and that others will ultimately concur. Throughout his life Washington put tremendous pressure on himself, in large part because he had greater faith in his own abilities than he did in those of his contemporaries and also, we believe, because of his consideration and understanding of the consequences of failure. When one looks for consistencies between his public and private careers, one notes his tendency to see himself as the person best qualified to carry out a required course of action. For instance, if he did not defend Virginia against the French and their Indian allies, then all that Belvoir represented, and all that he aspired to, might be lost; if he did not become financially successful as a farmer following his first return to Mount Vernon, then all his efforts toward becoming a full-fledged member of the gentry would have been for naught; if he did not become commander of the Continental forces, if he left it to someone less able, then all his youthful accomplishments might be at risk; if he did not follow through on his agricultural reforms, if his model farm failed, then he could see a sad future for American agricultural interests; and if he did not become the first president, then the country might not survive, and all that he had fought for, both nationally and personally, could be lost. Such resoluteness did not make for an easy existence, but it did provide Washington with the challenges he apparently needed to make life fulfilling.

Two aspirations inspired, one might say "drove," the young Washington: he wanted to become a great landowner and aristocrat, on the model of the Fairfax family, and he hoped to build a successful military career as had his brother Lawrence. In an amiable world the one avocation would have supported the other, but Washington learned early that his wealth would have to come from the land. He also came to see that a single, powerful force was hindering his success in either field. His goal of becoming a successful planter was continuously hampered by taxes and trade restrictions imposed by the British government. An arm of this entity, which he believed had no "Right to put their hands into my Pocket without my consent," had previously refused Washington a commission in the regular British army.[8] It is therefore not surprising that he would one day prove ready and willing to take the necessary measures to free himself, his colony, and his country from their colonial status. In his youth he had acquired the skills and the drive necessary to make himself a success. Those who would stand in his way, from the lowliest colonial bureaucrat to the British ruling powers, would eventually be forced to step aside.

The exhibition, and therefore this catalog, are ordered chronologically. While this approach might appear to compartmentalize Washington's biography into discrete units, our goal of finding the man behind the myths will be served by our paying particular attention not only to his domestic affairs but also to the transitional moments in his life. We argue that the persona Washington adopted during each period emerged naturally from its immediate predecessor and was ultimately rooted in the experiences of his youth; we further suggest that he was able to transform his public image when necessary because of the stability of his private life. We analyze selected nineteenth-century images in part because they are the only illustrations available for many of the events of his life, but more important because through them the Washington we know today was originally brought to life. Such works, which of necessity focused on a single occurrence, helped to create the impression that Washington's life was made up of a few momentous events separated by wide chasms about which we know comparatively little. An illumination of those spaces, we believe, is long overdue.

In chapter 1, "The Early Years: Washington's Youth (1732–1752)," we begin by focusing on the Virginia into which George Washington was born. We examine the physical landscape of his Westmoreland County birthplace and the eastern Virginia of his childhood, and the equally important social landscape, including his interactions with the Fairfax family of Belvoir through which the young Washington witnessed the society to which he would aspire. We also discuss his education and his years as a surveyor, which would serve him well during his military career. This chapter also includes an examination of many of the popular myths about Washington's youth.

Chapter 2, "The Virginia Soldier (1753–1758)," examines Washington's first experiences in the military. We discuss in detail his service as an officer in the Virginia Regiment during the French and Indian War, paying special attention to his journey to the French commandant at Lake Erie, the death of the sieur de Jumonville in the first engagement of the war, and his conduct at the defeat of General Braddock's forces and in other Ohio Valley campaigns. We also look closely at his interactions with his comrades in the colonial force, with representatives of the British army, and with Gov. Robert Dinwiddie, with whom Washington engaged in interesting and often forthright correspondence. We argue for the importance of both his early military successes and failures to the young Washington and discuss the long-term effects of his first experiences as a leader of men.

Following his contributions to the safety of the huge geographic entity known in the mid-eighteenth century as "Virginia," Washington retired for the first time to Mount Vernon. In our third chapter we discuss the estate, focusing on Washington's evolving ideas about his house and plantation during the seventeen years between his arrival home and his assumption of the command of the Revolutionary forces. During this period we see his earliest attempts as an amateur architect in the first of his major renovations to Mount Vernon and consider the results of his early career as a farmer. We also devote a good deal of time to the crucial personal event of this period, his courtship and marriage to the wealthy widow Martha Custis, through which Washington was elevated into the social and economic elite. During this time Washington also renewed what would be his lifelong interest in the "western lands," which, we argue, appear in the background of the 1772 portrait by Charles Willson Peale.

While we include analyses of some of the better-known images of Washington as general of the army in our study of the Revolutionary War years, in chapter 4 we again focus on his continuing interest in the domestic affairs at Mount Vernon. In his letters to his cousin Lund, who was managing the estate in his absence, Washington makes clear his attention to the details of running the plantation, even at times when he was under great duress in his role as commander of the colonial forces. Among his domestic interests was the second set of renovations to the house, which had been begun in 1773 but were largely carried out during the war years. Our argument is that it was as much this estate as the political entity that had been recently christened the "United States" that he was fighting for.

Washington's postwar retirement, which gained him the title "America's Cincinnatus," led to a period of great social activity. In chapter 5 we examine this rarely discussed period of his life. Although his long service had left him fatigued and in need of recuperation, he almost immediately began to recondition his house and grounds and to entertain a great many visitors, including domestic and European dignitaries. He also kept up-to-date on the political affairs of the new nation through his highly placed contacts in the recently formed government and was therefore ready when called upon to serve at the Constitutional Convention. During these years Washington also made a number of attempts to put into practice his often revolutionary ideas about farm and estate management. Our discussion of this phase of his life also allows us to examine Washington's status as a slaveholder and to point out the evolution of his ideas about the institution that provided the labor that created much of the wealth in colonial Virginia.

Chapter 6, "The First President of the United States (1789–1797)," includes discussions of the significant domestic and international events of Washington's presidency. However, a large part of our focus here, as previously, will be on his continued interest in Mount Vernon and his serving as a quiet but effective advocate for Virginia in the political discussions of the moment, including the selection of a site for the federal district. A study of his two terms in office also provides us with the opportunity to discuss his importance in the formulation of what the duties of a president should be, and to examine what have become the most popular images of Washington, the Gilbert Stuart portraits. Both the protocol and the paintings provide evidence of an aristocratic formality that, we argue, he adapted from his experiences in prewar Virginia society and brought to the presidency.

His final return to Mount Vernon is the subject of chapter 7. During his last years Washington was able to focus on family responsibilities and events, such as the marriage of Nelly Custis, and to once again direct his energies to the management of his beloved farm. However, Washington continued to stay abreast of the brewing international crisis of the moment and, in a final expression of his readiness to serve, was prepared to respond to a final "call to arms." We then discuss the reaction of the American public to his death in December 1799, and consider his apotheosis, the process that contributed to Washington's elevation to mythic status. He would come to epitomize the virtues that Americans perceived to be worthy, and to provide an untarnishable reminder of what sort of men the revolutionaries were and what they had achieved.[9] Washington's image would, in a sense, become their memorial. We also speculate here about the twentieth-century's interest in Jefferson and the lack of similar attention to Washington.

In *A Sacred Union of Citizens,* their book on the cultural importance of Washington's "Farewell Address," Matthew Spalding and Patrick J. Garrity open with a chapter titled "Remembering Washington's Legacy" in which they lay the groundwork for their useful discussion of Washington's effect on the American national character. We end our volume with a discussion of legacies as well, but rather than dealing with such intangibles as Washington's integrity or his other well-known virtues, we look instead at a few of his actual bequests and associations and thereby seek to remind our readers of the importance of Washington to the three sponsoring institutions. For instance, we discuss his contribution to Liberty Hall, the first incarnation of what is now Washington and Lee University. Our examination of the history of Mount Vernon concludes here with the Civil War years, by which time the Mount Vernon Ladies' Association had purchased the house and two hundred surrounding acres from John Augustine Washington Jr., the last family owner.

Bushrod Washington, who had inherited the estate after the death of his aunt Martha in 1802, asked John Marshall to write the authorized biography of his famous uncle. Marshall's having served as an officer under Washington during the Revolutionary War and his interest in the crucial figures and events of his home state of Virginia made him a logical choice for this endeavor and would later make him the obvious candidate to become the first president of the Virginia Historical Society, which was founded in December 1831, two months before the one-hundredth anniversary of Washington's birth. It is not surprising that the first book donated to the society's collection was one of Marshall's own copies of his *Life of George Washington.*

In the second quarter of the nineteenth century, John Gadsby Chapman, a young Virginia-born painter, began a series of subdued, almost pastoral images of places important in Washington's life. Although one might argue that his nostalgic depictions constitute an attempt to break from the larger-than-life literary portrayals by Marshall and Weems, Chapman's renditions of these sites contributed to the antebellum blurring of the distinction between the actual man and his burgeoning mythic presence. In our first chapter we bypass what was the most popular of these locations—Washington's burial site at Mount Vernon, which had become a popular destination for tourists by the early nineteenth century—and begin with Chapman's perhaps surprising rendition of his birthplace.

*George Washington*

1. John Gadsby Chapman, *View of the Birthplace of Washington,* 1834, oil on canvas, 21¾×29¼ in. (Courtesy of Homeland Foundation, Incorporated, New York)

# 1

## The Early Years: Washington's Youth
## 1732–1752

### Virginia: The Physical Landscape

AFTER COMPLETING an extended tour of Italy, during which he had honed his skills by copying old masters and sketching the traditional antiquities, John Gadsby Chapman returned to Virginia in 1831 in search of subjects that would allow him to make manifest his talents, and the commissions that would affirm his entry into the ranks of professional painters. Through his long friendship with the Lewis and Custis families the young Chapman was able to gain access to Arlington, Mount Vernon, and their environs, and to complete a number of studies of members of Washington's extended family; George Washington Parke Custis even allowed Chapman to copy the Charles Willson Peale portrait of Washington in the blue coat of the Virginia Regiment. It perhaps occurred to Chapman during this period that Mount Vernon itself would one day become an important American antiquity. This notion, coupled with the fact that the American public was still greatly interested in Washington, would have suggested that a concentration on this subject would be well worth an investment of his time.[1]

In the centennial decade of Washington's birth Chapman produced a dozen paintings that illustrate locations important in the life of the "Father of His Country." These efforts did enhance the reputation of the ambitious young painter, in that seven of them were exhibited in New York at the National Academy of Design in 1835, and ultimately provided an income, in that three served as models for engravings that were published that same year in a biography of Washington by James Kirke Paulding. That effort, which began as a quest for the truth about Washington's life—a truth, one might argue, that Paulding believed was not readily to be had—ultimately evolved into an exposition of his subject's moral qualities, directed, at least in part, to "pious mothers" for the use of their children.[2]

In his depiction of the birthplace of Washington Chapman emphasizes the emptiness that characterized much of Tide-water Virginia in the colonial and early national eras (fig. 1). Admittedly, there were people living near this spot in 1830—the region had been settled since the seventeenth century—but there were virtually no towns. Chapman emphasizes the solitude and tranquility of the site. He pictures a farm in the left background, but there is little activity. This picture actually suggests the lonely environment described in letters written in the 1680s by a neighbor of the earliest Virginia Washingtons, William Fitzhugh. Fitzhugh had complained that there was a scarcity of "good & ingenious" company in this "strange land," a "want of spiritual help & comforts" in the rural parishes, and an absence of schooling for the education of heirs.[3] During the colonial era, however, it must have seemed that newness and possibility were in the air as well. Fitzhugh chose to remain in this "strange" region, and the opportunity it afforded ultimately made him a wealthy man. This was a place of beginnings—for Fitzhugh, for George Washington, and in turn for America; accordingly Chapman depicts the glow of dawn to remind his viewers of the connection between this site and the birth of the nation.

The birthplace of Washington is near the Potomac River in Westmoreland County, about fifty miles downstream from Mount Vernon. The property fronts a tributary, Popes Creek, at its entry into the Potomac. From the birthplace there is a panoramic view across the wide creek and its picturesque marshes. Chapman gives us that scene. His distant farmhouse is not intended to represent Washington's birthplace, which had burned in 1779. Augustine Washington (ca. 1694–1743), George's father, had bequeathed the Popes Creek plantation to his second oldest son and namesake. A grandson, William Augustine, owned the plantation at the time of the fire. Rather than rebuild the house, William constructed a new home near the other end of his property, to the west of nearby Bridges Creek. Thus, little remained on the site when Chapman visited in the 1830s. Indeed, the plantation had so deteriorated that George Washington Parke Custis, George Washington's step-grandson, made a pilgrimage there in 1815 to mark the birth

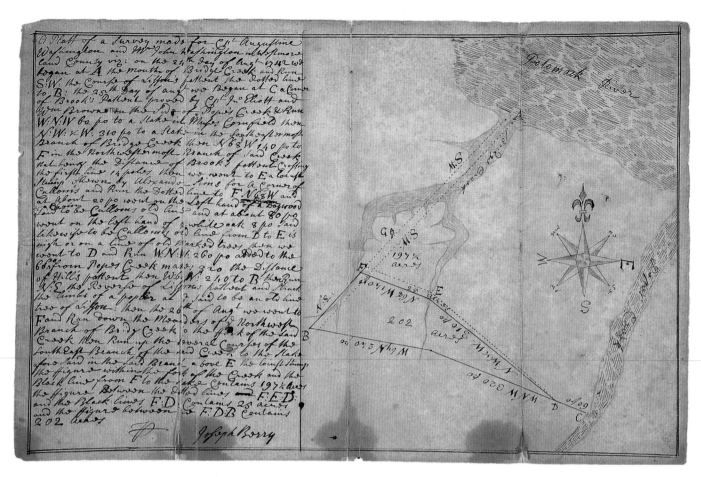

2. Joseph Berry, survey of Popes Creek Plantation, 24 August 1742. (Courtesy of Mount Vernon Ladies' Association, gift of Mrs. Arthur Newton Park, Vice Regent for Arizona, 1962–84)

site and thereby remind his countrymen of the sanctity of this spot. At Popes Creek he placed a freestone slab inscribed: "HERE THE 11TH OF FEBRUARY, 1732, GEORGE WASHINGTON WAS BORN." The chimney of a kitchen dependency was still standing, and the foundation lines of the main house were at least partially visible. Custis must have placed his tablet near those foundations, for he referred to the "scattered bricks" that had been gathered to form a pedestal for his stone.[4] Paulding had the Custis slab included in the foreground of the engraving. In the canvas, however, Chapman simply portrays the environment at Popes Creek as he imagined it might have been experienced by the young George Washington, who lived there during the first three years of his life and revisited it often during his childhood and adolescence.

The geography of the Popes Creek region is detailed in surveys, one of which was commissioned in 1742 to record a property settlement between Augustine Washington and his cousin, John Washington (fig. 2). The survey marked the last of several land acquisitions in the area by the father of George Washington. John Washington received the 197½ acres that are charted on the plat plus the portion of the adjoining 202 acres

that lie south of line FE. Augustine Washington received the land south of line ED and 100 acres to the west of Bridges Creek, which are not marked on the plat.[5] The only inaccuracy on the map is its simplified rendering of Popes Creek, which is not a straight channel at its juncture with the Potomac but widens considerably and feeds a marshland, as Chapman recorded in his landscape.

The 1742 plat shows much of the region that had been settled in the seventeenth century by the Washington family, as well as the extent of Augustine Washington's Popes Creek estate. In 1792 George Washington reported to Sir Isaac Heard, a British genealogist, that "In the year 1657 . . . John and Lawrence Washington, Brothers Emigrated from the north of England, and settled at Bridges Creek, on Potomac river, in the County of Westmoreland." The original Bridges Creek plantation, which was situated just east of the creek near its fork, was established by Col. John Washington seven years after he arrived in the region and six years after he married Anne Pope, the daughter of wealthy landowner Nathaniel Pope, whose family gave the name to the creek farther east. Colonel Washington was one of nearly a dozen settlers who in the 1650s and

3. Currier and Ives, *The Birth-Place of Washington,* ca. 1860, lithograph, 10×12⅜ in.
(Courtesy of Mount Vernon Ladies' Association, gift of Dr. and Mrs. Joseph E. Fields)

1660s divided this wilderness into small farms of fifty to one hundred acres each. His grandson Augustine (George Washington's father) was successful enough to buy out many of his immediate neighbors. He had inherited a large plot of land to the west of Bridges Creek, but in 1718 he purchased the more attractive site along Popes Creek where he built his house. During the next twenty-four years Augustine Washington methodically purchased tracts between Bridges Creek and Popes Creek so that his new lands would be linked to the ancestral property. He acquired much of the expanse shown in figure 2, except the portion covered by the surveyor's elaborate compass rose. These new holdings were appealing because they commanded a wide water frontage and the sweeping vista to the Potomac that attracted Chapman's eye.[6]

The birthplace of George Washington is located near point C on the 1742 plat. A dwelling of some sort existed there when Augustine acquired the property, but he chose to build a better one. The type of house that he erected in the mid-1720s tells us something about his aspirations and accomplishments;

this building would come to embody for his third son the sort of gentry lifestyle that was his birthright. Unfortunately, the truth about Washington's birthplace was long ago overshadowed by imaginative representations that for various reasons were deemed more appropriate to his memory.

Benson Lossing apparently created the image of the clapboard Dutch cottage that was widely published in the second half of the nineteenth century. He pictured this building, which is unlike any Virginia structure, in his volumes about Washington, and Currier and Ives perpetuated the fantasy in a sort of Hudson River–school scene (fig. 3). Lossing admitted that the house was gone in the nineteenth century, but he purported to have learned that it had four rooms on the first floor. He was quick to conclude that the plan must have been a simple rectangle.[7] In the inscription for the Currier and Ives lithograph, the inaccuracies are compounded because the immediate view is of Popes Creek, not Bridges Creek as stated, and the roofline would not have been the type shown.

George Washington described the structure where he was

born as "the ancient mansion seat." The house was, in fact, grander than Lossing's invention. Excavations at the site in 1936 uncovered the filled-up cellar that had been visible in its outline to Chapman and Custis a century earlier and provided a good deal of information about the house's structure (fig. 4). It had been a massive, slightly irregular, U-shaped building of brick, impressive for both its length of fifty-eight feet and its construction material. (Most Virginia houses of the early colonial period were small earth-fast or posthole buildings made of perishable wood.) Surrounding the house were a kitchen, a smokehouse, and other outbuildings, all evidence that this compound was, in fact, quite elaborate. Indeed, there were not many homes in the colony in 1726 that were so large or so grand. The "ancient mansion seat" had four large rooms downstairs, each with a chimney. The foundations of the nineteen-foot-deep center section (eighteen inches) were sufficient to support a second story. A nineteenth-century account by a man who had seen the house before it burned describes a hipped roof with dormer windows for the center section only and a one-story wing.[8] In its size and plan the Popes Creek mansion is best compared to houses such as Louis Burwell's Fairfield (in Gloucester County) or Robert "King" Carter's Corotoman (in Lancaster County), both of which were long brick structures that were single-pile, or one-room deep. Those mansions, which were not substantially larger than the Washington birthplace, were the best private buildings of their time and place.[9]

The house at Popes Creek was inherited by Augustine Washington Jr. in 1743 and inventoried at his death in 1762. It was well furnished then: there were nine beds and a couch, six rugs, fourteen tables, and more than fifty chairs, and wallpaper had been used in the house. The plantation itself was a large operation, for outside the house were more than one hundred farm animals and seventy-seven slaves. The entire estate was valued at the sizable sum of forty-six hundred pounds.[10] No doubt the son had improved the plantation, but the evidence of the foundations and this later inventory suggests that Augustine Washington, at a date that preceded the wave of Georgian mansion building, had established at Popes Creek an impressive seat. Despite the doubts of the later detractors of George Washington, or those who would have preferred that he arose from more humble beginnings and was therefore a suitable hero for the democratic fantasy that any American, even one from an impoverished childhood, could through hard work become president, the physical evidence at Popes Creek argues that he was born into a comparatively high level of the Virginia gentry.

It is a measure of the energy and ambition of George Washington's father that he was not content to farm at Popes Creek. He understood that under the best conditions he might turn a profit there through agriculture, but he could never build a fortune that way. Augustine was an entrepreneur who looked for every means to improve the status of his family. He saw great potential in the ownership of land, which he continued to acquire throughout his life; his holdings at his death totaled more than nine thousand acres. Despite the predominantly rural economy of the colony, he even pursued mining and manufacturing when he found rich deposits of iron ore on land that he had acquired in 1724 along Accokeek Creek, which empties into the Potomac River some thirty-five miles

4. Excavated ruins of the Washington family house at Popes Creek, Westmoreland County, 1936. (Courtesy of National Park Service)

5. John Gadsby Chapman, *View from the Old Mansion House of the Washington Family Near Fredericksburg, Va.,* 1833, oil on canvas, 21⅝×29 in. (Courtesy of Homeland Foundation, Incorporated, New York)

upstream from George Washington's birth site. To work the ore, he entered into a partnership with the Principio Iron Works in Maryland.[11]

In 1726, the year that his house at Popes Creek was at or near completion, Augustine Washington, for the modest price of £180, purchased from his sister Mildred and her second husband a twenty-five-hundred-acre tract named Little Hunting Creek, which was situated farther upstream on the Potomac.[12] This area would later be the core of George Washington's Mount Vernon estate. Augustine Washington moved the family to Little Hunting Creek in 1735, when George was three years old, no doubt in part to be closer to his mining operation, which had proved a sound investment. But Augustine was also motivated to move there so that he could develop the property in anticipation of turning it over to his oldest son; this transfer would occur some five years later, when the newly commissioned Lawrence Washington was about to embark on his military career. The Washingtons' next move, in 1738, brought them even closer to the Accokeek furnaces, as well as to some land that was inherited by Augustine Washington's second wife, Mary Ball, George's mother. This third site, Ferry Farm, was directly across the Rappahannock River from the town of Fredericksburg. The motivation behind this last relocation again reminds us of Augustine's entrepreneurial spirit, but it might also have had to do with his growing number of sons. In his apparent determination to provide a viable plantation for each of his oldest children, Augustine Washington was striving to achieve what only the wealthiest men of the colony, like "King" Carter, would even have considered attempting. Very few Virginians of this era were able to pass on working farms to three of their sons.

As at Popes Creek, the Washington house at Ferry Farm did not survive into the 1830s when Chapman visited; the artist similarly found there a prospect that had changed little in the century since the Washingtons' tenure. Chapman would have us believe that this Virginia landscape had much to do with the shaping of George Washington between the ages of six and sixteen. He presents the view from the site of the colonial house, looking to the west-northwest, across the river to Fredericksburg (fig. 5). It is an entrancing vista; the town beckons the viewer, and the ships on the river speak simultaneously of faraway places and adventure, and the commerce that could produce a young man's fortune. Chapman thus suggests that the horizons of the young George Washington were widened by the move from the remote Potomac River to the outskirts of a city. The ferry, which gave the farm its name (at an early but as yet undetermined date), was still in operation in 1833. By then the town had grown, but there was still in the landscape a mix of settlement and wilderness, development and opportunity.

Ferry Farm was a working plantation—it had most recently been the estate of the late William Strother—but Augustine Washington had been able to purchase it in 1738 for the relatively low price of £317. The house was advertised as "very handsome"; there were four rooms on the first floor with a passage between and two above. The ferry, which was free and operated from the Fredericksburg side of the river, was not included in this sum. (The ferry was never owned by the Washingtons; they at times even considered it a nuisance.) Nonetheless, there were economic possibilities at this location, which was described in a newspaper advertisement as not only "a beautiful Situation" but also "very commodious for Trade."[13] The inference was that produce from the farm, and from inland plantations with no water frontage, could be loaded onto

ships and marketed either across the river or ultimately carried as far away as England. However, Augustine would die less than five years after this move, and there is no evidence that Ferry Farm ever became a particularly profitable operation. The Rappahannock River was too narrow and shallow for Fredericksburg to have developed into a major trade center; consequently the city's growth was confined to the west side of the river. Even today Ferry Farm and the property surrounding it would not be considered an urban area (fig. 6).

Chapman wrote on the back of his canvas that the house had been torn down long ago. Only a cabin, presumably used by the ferryman, was standing in 1833. The artist uses the rubble of the house to establish the antiquity of the site and to suggest that he has located the exact spot where the young Washington lived. This first Washington house at Ferry Farm apparently burned on Christmas Eve 1741, as confirmed by documentary and archaeological evidence. However, the house must have been rebuilt because the family remained at Ferry Farm and was living there when Augustine died in 1743. Preliminary excavations have shown that at least the second building, if not both, had masonry foundations and was not an impermanent posthole structure. In any case, there can be no doubt that Augustine Washington had done well for his family. The inventory for the Ferry Farm estate reveals a relatively sizable house, twenty-seven slaves, and more than one hundred livestock.[14]

While Chapman implies that George Washington's environment may have encouraged his worldly ambitions, the inventory of his father's estate gives us a sense of the immediate surroundings that nurtured him. The house was large and

6. Ferry Farm, Stafford County. The farm is located on the left bank just beyond the rail bridge. The ferry that gave the property its name crossed the river at the middle of this view. (Courtesy of Ferry Farm and Kenmore Plantation)

double-pile, or two-rooms deep, which might well have established in the young Washington's mind that his father was indeed a member of the gentry. In addition to tobacco, the fields must also have produced enough grain crops to support the slaves and the livestock, so Washington would have seen the methods of cultivation of both the staple crop of the colony and some of the other plantings that he would later develop at Mount Vernon. Here, too, he may well have observed the treatment of slaves as less than human beings; Washington as a young adult viewed them with a crass insensitivity that only his own later experiences would temper into compassion. These early lessons about gentry life, the raising of crops and livestock, and the management of a black workforce must have been reinforced at Popes Creek and Mount Vernon when Washington visited those places during his childhood years. Perhaps most important, he had observed his father engage in the types of self-fashioning that would become an obsession throughout George's adult life. Although the inventory of Augustine's estate admittedly does not contain the sorts of items that one today might associate with colonial wealth, such trappings were not always deemed necessary in early Virginia. (For instance, although the widow Custis was far wealthier than George Washington, Mount Vernon was much better stocked with decorative objects than the White House in New Kent County in which she lived prior to their marriage.) Augustine had been successful, and he had raised himself almost to the level of the most wealthy and influential men in Virginia. He had built a number of homes, at least the first of which would have rivaled the great houses of its day; he had acquired enough property so that when three of his sons came of age they would each have a plantation from which to begin to build their own empires; and one can only imagine the satisfaction that he would have felt had he lived to see Lawrence marry into one of the wealthiest and most prominent families in Anglo-America only two months after his death. It is probably fair to say that Augustine expected dedication and hard work from all his children; his third son would not have been a disappointment.

## Washington's Boyhood

With the death of Augustine Washington on 12 April 1743 the life of his eleven-year-old son, George, was altered from its anticipated course. Washington would not be able to follow his father and his two older half brothers to Appleby School in Westmoreland, England, where he would have been educated beyond the rudiments, trained in the manners of the gentry, and introduced to a wider world. Instead he would learn from tutors and be subjected to the will of a somewhat domineering mother, who, it should be said, had every reason to be in-

secure. Mary Ball Washington (ca. 1708–1789) was an orphan who knew firsthand the instability of domestic arrangements in colonial Virginia. At Augustine's death she not only lost her husband; she also inherited only a portion of his estate, thus making it difficult to raise the five surviving children of his second marriage. It was Augustine's intention that within five years after his death she would relocate the family to the nearby Deep Run tract of land and thereby vacate Ferry Farm for George to develop, but she never did. Perhaps that decision was for the best, because it prompted the young Washington to pursue opportunities elsewhere and thereby position himself to fulfill a greater destiny. Mary Ball Washington's strong will and determination, which were perhaps bothersome to those around her and may explain why Washington was infrequently in her company in later years, were no doubt her legacy to a son who would eventually need those very qualities to win a desperate war and establish a nation. As a role model, she did not illustrate how to maneuver with social grace; rather, she was the embodiment of strength and endurance.

Augustine Washington's two best plantations, and the goods and holdings on them, were awarded to his first sons, born of his marriage to Jane Butler. Actually Lawrence, the oldest, already held title to Little Hunting Creek; it had been deeded to him during a settlement of his affairs before he left in 1740 for military service in the War of Jenkins' Ear in the Caribbean. Lawrence held a commission in the regular British army and commanded a company of one hundred Virginia troops who were part of the land force sent to support the Royal British Navy in its assault on Cartagena, a Spanish stronghold. The gift of Little Hunting Creek seems to have been a reward to Lawrence for earning so prestigious a position; at the very least, it was a vote of confidence in the son's newly proved abilities. George Washington surely noticed that land acquisition (and its attendant social advancement) could be the reward for distinguished military service. Lawrence ultimately renamed Little Hunting Creek "Mount Vernon" in honor of Adm. Edward Vernon, his British commander. Augustine Jr., who had returned from his schooling in England only a year prior to his father's death, inherited the Popes Creek plantation. The third son, George Washington, was awarded Ferry Farm and was to come into its ownership upon his maturity.[15]

We know comparatively little about the details of George Washington's day-to-day life during the next five years; he reemerges at the age of sixteen, when he first traveled to the frontier as a surveyor. But there is evidence of visits to Mount Vernon and Popes Creek in surveys that he made at those sites as study exercises. We can speculate that Washington spent as much time at these houses, and with cousins in the even closer Chotank area of Stafford County, as his mother would allow.[16] Augustine's legacy would have been visible to him in the accomplished manners of his older half brothers and in the physical presence of his father's plantations, which reminded the young Washington of the position of his family and encouraged him to seek his own place in Virginia society.

Of the sources that inform us about Washington's youth, the most significant are the documents in his own hand that make up his "School Exercise Book." These 218 pages of academic lessons and copy work are evidence of the type of education that Washington received. They were of sufficient value to him to be saved and now survive in three bound volumes, suggesting that the illustrators of Washington's youth would perhaps have been more accurate to depict him seated at a desk rather than active in a school yard.

According to a biographical sketch penned by his friend David Humphreys, Washington was instructed by a tutor. There is little evidence of who that man was or whether there was more than one teacher. Mason Locke Weems records in his *Life of Washington* that the future president attended a school run by a man named Hobby; a John Hobby did in fact operate a school near Fredericksburg. Weems also states that a "Mr. Williams, an excellent teacher," next instructed Washington in Westmoreland County, while George lived with his half brother Augustine; Williams did run such a school there. Weems's statements can be neither proved nor disproved. There is, however, no reason to doubt that Washington's formal education began around the age of six or seven, when instruction was generally undertaken. The earliest dated school papers bear a 1741 date, but these are the work of a boy who has already learned to read, write, and do basic arithmetic. To judge from other surviving papers, instruction was most intense in the years 1744 to 1748, when Washington was twelve to sixteen years old.[17]

The volumes of schoolwork record instruction that is almost entirely practical. Nearly half of the exercises are lessons in mathematics. There are studies in geometry and trigonometry that would prepare a pupil to understand the measurement of land, a relevant subject in a colony then still in the process of being surveyed and divided. Another fifty pages are given to the rudiments of surveying. There are also lessons in solid and liquid volumes, decimals, interest, and money conversion; these would prepare Washington to keep accounts in a cash-poor society that traded almost entirely by means of credit. Just as practical were the twenty-one pages of business and legal forms then used in the colony (fig. 7).[18] Washington was made to copy bills of sale and exchange, notes of release and conveyance, indentures, leases, contracts, deeds, and wills as a means to introduce him to the often complex and burdensome documents that made

transactions legal and binding in colonial Virginia. A member of the Virginia gentry might not understand the nuances of the law, but it was imperative that he at least comprehend its instruments. Here, as with his mathematical training, Washington was given a solid footing.

There is no evidence in the surviving papers of any significant instruction in the humanities. There are six pages about geography, two poems copied from issues of the *Gentleman's Magazine,* and a treatise on manners. There must have been reading assigned in history and classical literature because in the

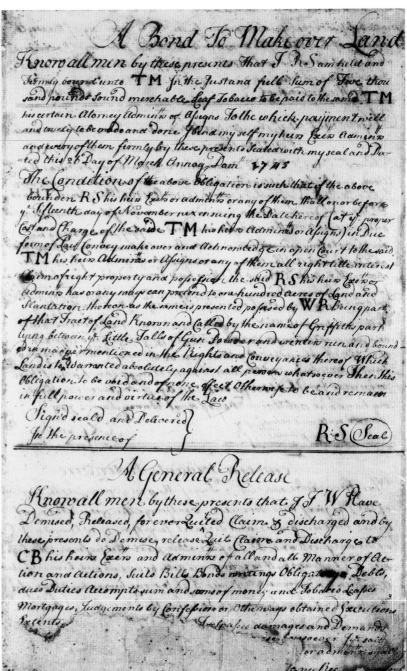

7. George Washington's *School Exercise Book,* legal forms, late 1740s. (Courtesy of Library of Congress)

eighteenth century the ancient world seemed the fountainhead of knowledge, but there is no record of such instruction. Nor was Washington trained in languages; he would find himself in the company of Frenchmen in two wars, but he never learned to speak or read their language. Because of these omissions, he would later describe his education as "defective."[19] By that time he had served in the Continental Congress and had interacted with some of the best minds in the colonies; however, their abilities reminded the ever self-conscious Washington that he had not been sent to England for quality schooling as his older brothers had been, nor had he been trained in the social graces as befitted a son of the gentry.

The most interesting of the documents in Washington's copy book are the pages that make up a book of manners called *Rules of Civility and Decent Behaviour in Company and Conversation* (fig. 8). Washington's education was "defective" not only because the range of his academic instruction was limited, but also because the schooling in England that he was denied would have provided him with training in manners. In early Virginia, such an omission would have to be addressed. It is telling evidence about the priorities in the colony that the instruction provided to the son of a planter would be both highly practical and focused on what is essentially etiquette. In fact, the appearance of being a cultivated man was as important, if not more so, than being educated as one.

This manual about gentlemanly behavior was derived from a treatise titled *Bienséance de la conversation entre les hommes,* which was prepared in 1595 at a Jesuit college in France. It was published in London about 1640 (and in eleven later editions) with the title *Youths Behaviour, or Decency in Conversation amongst Men.* George Washington's copy was shorter and had a different title; either he repeated the various maxims in abridged form or, more likely, his source was an intermediary copy.[20] The Jesuit origin of *Youths Behaviour* is surprising because it so closely resembles the popular courtesy books that were published in the 1640s by Richard Allestree and his contemporaries. Allestree's *Gentleman's Calling* and *Ladies Calling,* which went through multiple editions and were found in libraries in Virginia as well as in England, provided people on their way up in society with the information they needed to know about behavior in social situations. As readers endeavored to shed their coarse manners, they learned from Allestree what was proper in good company, from dress and deportment to the methods and patterns of social interaction. Admittedly, the courtesy books were of greater length than the Jesuit manual; they were infused with the tenets of the Church of England, warnings against idleness, and logical arguments intended to persuade the reader to prefer the merits of refinement over vulgarity. Still, they remain manuals of etiquette. What makes *Youths Behaviour* stand apart, as the title suggests, is that it was ostensibly written for young people.[21]

8. *Rules of Civility and Decent Behaviour in Company and Conversation,* as copied by George Washington, ca. 1744. (Courtesy of Library of Congress)

The first of the 110 maxims in Washington's *Rules* is typical in its directive that respect should guide social behavior: "Every Action done in Company, ought to be with Some Sign of Respect, to those that are Present." There is much in the manual about decorous interaction. For instance, you should not argue but submit judgment with modesty, without malice or envy or injurious words (nos. 40, 58, 65). Do not reprehend with cholar or with reproachful language, but with sweetness and mildness, and consider whether to do so in public or private (nos. 45, 49). When you reprove another, be unblamable yourself (no. 48). Such maxims would prove good advice for a man whose careers in the military and government would demand effective communication.

The manual seeks a middle ground between the extremes of crude behavior and pomposity. On the one hand, the prospective young gentleman must be steered from the ways of the rabble, who in early Virginia as in the Old World were considered to be uncouth. Readers were warned to keep their hands where they belonged and to keep them clean, not to spit in the fire or in another's face when speaking, not to speak or laugh loudly, not to kill fleas or lice in the sight of others, and not to scratch, spit, cough, or blow their noses at the table. On the other hand, the roughness of colonial life made pomposity even more inappropriate in the New World than in England, where it was scorned and had become a favorite target of the courtesy-book authors. If few Virginians needed the advice to "play not the peacock" (no. 54), rule 25 might have caught their attention: "Superfluous complements and all affectation of ceremonie are to be avoided, yet where due they are not to be neglected." This philosophy governed gentry life in Virginia and would ultimately define Washington's conduct during his presidencies.

Many of these rules ingrained in Washington the need to offer respect to people of higher rank, as they could block or allow his entry into their society. He learned how to approach them (not too closely), how to look at them (not too directly), and when to speak (not until questioned). He was to answer with few words. He should not utter frivolous things among grave and learned men or speak of doleful things in times of mirth. The *Rules of Civility* were therefore critically important to an aspiring but inexperienced Virginian who, until he was in the company of other members of the gentry on a regular basis and could observe their behavior, had no other practical means to learn the social graces. A knowledge of mathematics and accounting would be of limited value to him if he was denied entry into the right circles. He must look and behave in what William Fitzhugh two generations earlier had called a "creditable" manner.[22] Socially deprived while he lived with his widowed mother, Washington would learn how to play his part primarily from this manual.

The setting for much of Washington's tutoring was presumably Ferry Farm and the Fredericksburg vicinity. However, as mentioned above, among the twenty-two practice surveys in the exercise books are examples that were drawn at Mount Vernon and Popes Creek, apparently on extended visits to those plantations. One is a plat of "Major Law. Washington's Turnip Field as Survey'd by me." Another maps the land below Mount Vernon Hills that adjoins Little Hunting Creek. Those surveys are evidence that Washington was on occasion able to withdraw from the austere environment at Ferry Farm and retreat to Mount Vernon to the company of a brother whom he appears to have adulated as a father figure. The record of their relationship is sketchy because few of Washington's early papers survive, but Lawrence must have cared especially for George because he remembered him in his will with "love and affection," and it would be George who would eventually inherit Mount Vernon.[23]

Washington's schoolboy exercises in manners and his studies of surveying facilitated his passage out of Fredericksburg and into manhood. As Guthrie Sayen has recently stated, the *Rules* "gave George practical instruction in the self-control, composure, discretion, modesty, deference, and knowledge of place that were essential for a young man of uncertain prospects making his way in a hierarchical world."[24] They prepared him and gave him the confidence necessary to enter Belvoir, the Fairfax seat that was a center of culture in the colony, where at any time a sophisticated visitor from Williamsburg or London might be present. Once inside, Washington found countless opportunities to refine his behavior. His studies of surveying were similarly brought to fruition at Belvoir. By learning the rudiments of land measurement, Washington acquired a useful and ultimately profitable trade; he would soon be invited to join a Fairfax-sponsored surveying trip to the western lands of the proprietary. Once familiar with that land, he could build a career there in surveying and thus begin to acquire the wealth and property expected of a gentleman.

The school exercises also provided Washington with a methodology that would stay with him throughout his life. He learned not only manners and the language and structure of legal documents but also the usefulness of imitation. Whether it was his later rewriting of orders penned by a commander or his attention to presenting himself in a way that mirrored the deportment of his aristocratic acquaintances, Washington took any available opportunity to fill in what he saw as gaps in his education or experience by mimicking the behavior of his betters. The most important of such fortuities would be provided by the Fairfaxes, who had much to do with the fashioning of both the private and the public personae of the young George Washington.

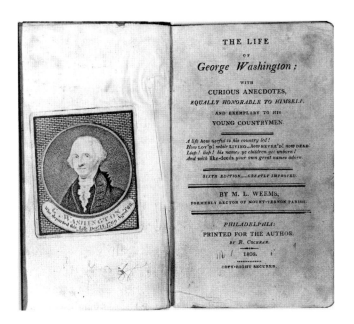

9. Mason Locke Weems, *The Life of Washington,* 6th ed. (Philadelphia, 1808). (Courtesy of Virginia Historical Society)

Although Washington apparently spent much of his youth at his studies, the mythmakers of the nineteenth century showed little interest in the processes by which he learned. Despite the critical importance of his taking advantage of every opportunity to learn from others, they instead depicted the young Washington as a teacher, a miraculous man-child who somehow already knew what other children had to be taught. The best known of the tales is, of course, Mason Locke Weems's account of a destructive little boy with a hatchet. Today, nearly two centuries after its invention, the cherry-tree story is so renowned that it is one of the few episodes about Washington that most Americans are able to recite. This fable did not appear in the first editions of Weems's *Life of Washington,* but once he presented it this engaging tale, only two pages long, became

the most memorable passage that Weems ever wrote (fig. 9).[25]

The "Revd. Mr. Weems" was acquainted with George Washington and visited him as early as 1787. Later, Weems sent Washington a moralizing pamphlet titled "The Philanthropist," and the president responded that he wished its sentiments were more prevalent in the new nation. This reply provided at least a partial basis for the author to introduce moralizing stories into his biography. He may have found corroboration for some of these tales by talking with people who had contact with Washington in his youth; Weems traveled frequently to Fredericksburg and the Northern Neck to research his subject. Also, he was related by marriage to James Craik, who was Washington's physician and close friend for forty years; from the doctor and other such sources Weems may have found a factual basis for some of what he wrote. We know that this happened in at least one instance, the case of George Washington's proposed naval career. For other accounts that are fantastic or exaggerated, such as the cherry-tree tale, we must credit Weems with becoming aware of the sorts of stories that his audience craved to read about Washington, and his giving the people what they wanted.[26]

The cherry-tree story is a parable about truth. Truth, George was supposedly told by his father, "is the loveliest quality of youth." When the boy "was about six years old, he was made the wealthy master of a hatchet" that "he unluckily tried . . . on the body of a beautiful young English cherry-tree." When George was confronted with the question of who had attacked the tree, he "staggered under it for a moment; but quickly recovered himself: and looking at his father, with the sweet face of youth brightened with the inexpressible charm of all-conquering truth, he bravely cried out, 'I can't tell a lie, Pa; you know I can't tell a lie. I did cut it with my hatchet.'" Augustine Washington responded, "Run to my arms, you dearest boy, . . . for you have paid me for it a thousand fold." Hon-

10. Augustus Köllner, *The Frank Confession,* lithograph, published in Anna C. Reed, *The Life of Washington* (Philadelphia, 1842). (Courtesy of Mount Vernon Ladies' Association)

*The Early Years: 1732–1752*

esty, that most crucial of virtues, is thus rewarded with a manifestation of paternal love.[27]

A number of graphic artists in the nineteenth century gave visual form to this popular episode. The anecdote continually found its way into books for children because of its ability to present clearly and simply the fruits of honesty. The story was illustrated for the first time in 1842 in Anna C. Reed's *Life of George Washington* (fig. 10); its immortality was secured when it was included in 1846 in *McGuffey's Eclectic Reader*.[28] The artist for Reed's volume was Augustus Köllner, a German immigrant who was a better landscapist than figure painter, but who had more innate ability than other nineteenth-century renderers of this scene. His image, which surprisingly includes other family members as witnesses to the climactic moment, is arguably the best of those that predate Grant Wood's memorable interpretation of 1939.

In an interview in 1940, Wood explained that his own generation was both the last to be taught the Weems story in school and the last to accept it as truth. The cherry-tree myth, he believed, was in danger of being lost due to the current generation of realist disbelievers. Wood saw this fable as a highlight of American folklore, and he triumphantly painted it as such (fig. 11). His goal was to help preserve the story in the American imagination.[29]

Wood created an image that is as memorable and appealing as Weems's story. His vision stands apart from those drawn by his predecessors because he introduces the figure, at once comical and charming, of a child Washington who has sprouted the head of the aging president as he was painted in the 1790s by Gilbert Stuart, which by 1939 had become trite from overuse in reproductions. Nathaniel Hawthorne had anticipated Wood when he quipped that Washington "was born with his clothes on, and his hair powdered, and made a stately bow on his first appearance in the world." In this humorous image Wood probes the issue of truth. The lack of documentation for Weems's account was jeopardizing its survival in the twentieth century, yet the virtue of truth is the very parable that Weems offers. Instantly, through the engaging figure of the child Washington, Wood admits that the Weems story is a falsehood. His picture, however, which presents Weems unveiling his invention as if he is pulling back a curtain to reveal the contrivances of his art, is itself truthful.[30] Wood tells us that Weems made up the anecdote, which we should accept without complaint, enjoying what the story has to offer and savoring it as a foundational American parable.

The artist provides an array of elements to pique the viewer's interest. For instance, the fringe of the curtain dangles like cherries from a tree. Not only is the figure of Washington droll, but Wood also wryly gives Weems a pose from an eighteenth-century portrait, one in which the sitter points to a scene that illustrates an episode in his biography.[31] A star is visible over the room where the child resides, which, reminiscent of the star over the manger at Bethlehem, suggests that this is where one might find America's savior; in this context, however, Wood seems to be pointing out that Americans have excessively deified Washington, to the point that we have lost the actual figure to such fabulous stories as those of Weems. Another effect of Wood's picture is to remind us that we know even less of George Washington's childhood appearance than we do of the events of his youth. He makes us recall that the earliest image we have, the Charles Willson Peale portrait (cover and fig. 35), depicts Washington at age forty. By humorously cleaning the slate of the popular, necessarily fraudulent, images of Washington's childhood, Wood suggests that his viewers need to rethink their understanding of the real man.

Another of the nineteenth-century images of the youthful George Washington, Henry Inman's *Early Days,* presents a figure who intervenes to prevent a school-yard brawl. Inman's painting, which was well known to contemporaries, is lost, but his conception survives in an engraving (fig. 12). Weems created the idea that as a child George Washington would never allow fighting: "He was never guilty of so brutish a practice as that of fighting himself; nor would he, when able to prevent it, allow [his classmates] to fight one another." Jared Sparks followed Weems's lead but further embellished the story so that Washington becomes not only a child policeman but judge and jury as well: "while at school his probity and demeanor were such, as to win the deference of the other boys, who were accustomed to make him arbiter of their disputes, and never failed to be satisfied with his judgment." According to the catalog of the 1846 Inman memorial exhibition, Sparks was indeed Inman's source.[32]

Some of Inman's contemporaries read so much into his image that they believed this childhood experience had a bearing on world history. *Godey's Lady's Book* commented on the air of "authority" given the figure of the boy Washington, who appropriately looks as though he "was born to command." In *The Gift* (1844), the boy on the left is seen to represent the Yankee backwoodsman, while the boy on the right is "the Saxon gentleman from the other side of the water." At the center "is the very look of Washington throughout the whole war"; he sees beyond passions to principles. These readings were probably in line with the artist's intentions. The child Washington has a powerful yet almost saintlike demeanor. In contrast, the figure on the right, who was said to represent England, is an overly civilized blond who is bound by his restrictive clothing, while the barefoot "Yankee" to our left is passionate but in need of a controlling hand. This illustration was so well received in mid-nineteenth-century America that it appeared in a series of publications.[33]

11. Grant Wood, *Cartoon for Parson Weems' Fable,* 1939, charcoal, pencil, and chalk on paper, 38¼×50 in. (Photograph courtesy of Christie's Images. ©Estate of Grant Wood/Licensed by VAGA, New York, N.Y.)

12. A. B. Walter, after Henry Inman, *Early Days of Washington,* ca. 1844, engraving, 16½×18¼ in. (Courtesy of Mount Vernon Ladies' Association, Stanley DeForest Scott Collection)

*The Early Years: 1732–1752*

13. Frank Schoonover, "*Now Boys, a Rush Forward and in We Go,*" *Shouted George,* 1924, oil on canvas, 36×30 in. Painted for an illustration in Lucy Foster Madison, *Washington* (New York, 1925). (Courtesy of Virginia Historical Society, Lora Robins Collection of Virginia Art)

Inman's scene is obviously fictional. The setting is inaccurate—mountains do not exist east of the Virginia Piedmont—and we have no evidence that this incident ever happened. As such, it tells us nothing about Washington's actual youth, other than that Americans enjoyed fantasizing about it. We can be sure, however, about one consequence of this type of imagery. Such scenes that portray a man-child actually deprive their viewers of the opportunity to consider Washington's actual boyhood. This is evident when one compares these depictions with contemporary portraits of colonial children, which often capture the frailty of youth.[34] It must have seemed safer, and more patriotic, to provide him with a parabolic childhood than to trust the scanty documentary evidence about his young life.

To Weems, brawling was irrational and brutish, but war games were a different matter, because war was seen as an activity guided by responsibility and valor. Thus, Weems reported a story about the eleven-year-old Washington dividing his playmates into two armies that would march or "fight their mimic battles, with great fury."[35] Admittedly, this tale could have had some sort of factual basis because of the military example of

Washington's half brother Lawrence during the War of Jenkins' Ear; that conflict must have been the talk of the colony between 1740 and 1742. Lawrence's role in the war was conspicuous both because he was a captain of a regiment and because he and his troops had served on Adm. Edward Vernon's flagship during the battle at Cartagena (in present-day Colombia). It seemed to matter little that the assault on this Spanish stronghold had failed and that Lawrence actually saw no action; Vernon had at least been successful in his earlier campaign to capture Porto Bello (in Panama). The failure at Cartagena could therefore be either conveniently forgotten or viewed in the context of other victories. During the duration of the war, when George was eight to ten years of age, it is entirely possible that he could have found in school-yard play a means to mimic his brother's imagined exploits.

The story about mock childhood battles must have seemed plausible enough to Sparks who repeated it, being sure to clarify that George Washington always led one of those armies: "Tradition reports, that . . . he formed his schoolmates into companies, who paraded, marched, and fought mimic battles, in which he was always the commander of one of the parties." A century later, author Lucy Madison perpetuated the legend, fleshed it out, and included an illustration of it in her biography of Washington. She chose Frank Schoonover to give visual form to the story (fig. 13). Madison's book is the life of Washington "retold for children." She felt compelled to justify the sort of mythmaking that Weems had begun, arguing that "to illustrate his resourcefulness and boyhood inclinations, some little license [can be] taken with history." Madison introduced a "battle in which apples were used" because "Washington was a normal boy" and "he did fight boyish battles at school, and apples might have been used."[36] Her invention of this secondary "fruit" story was perhaps a further tribute to Parson Weems. Madison provides her readers with the background of the war with Spain in which Lawrence Washington served. Excited by that news, the boys at the schoolhouse stage a mock battle. George leads the "English" contingent that captures the enemy fort of Cartagena. (The real one, it will be remembered, eluded English conquest.) To symbolize the victory, he removes the "Spanish" flag. This "born soldier" had diverted his opponents' attention with a shower of apples.

Weems may perhaps have uncovered some proof that the general's propensity for military leadership found expression early, but no documentary evidence for such games exists. There was, however, nearer the end of Washington's youth, an episode that would be depicted by artists for which we do have some corroboration. The viewer, however, would be hard-pressed to identify it as more or less credible than the events we have just examined. Indeed, at first encounter, it seems to be just as much the stuff of legend.

14. After Alonzo Chappel, *Washington's Interview with His Mother,* engraving, published in John Frederick Schroeder, *Life and Times of Washington* (New York, 1857). (Courtesy of Virginia Historical Society)

The example of his brother's service under Admiral Vernon nearly led George Washington to go to sea at age fourteen. The handsome military uniforms and stories from the war with Spain must have held an allure for the adolescent Washington and prompted his near enlistment into service either on a merchant vessel or in the Royal Navy itself. The documentary evidence for such a surmise consists of three surviving letters regarding this scheme: two written to Lawrence Washington, who had instigated it, and one written to Mary Ball Washington, who opposed it. In 1746 two of Lawrence's friends reported to him that his letters to his half brother and stepmother had been received and that Mary Ball Washington would probably never agree to his idea. The letter to Mrs. Washington, which is dated in the spring of 1747, is from her half brother Joseph Ball, a lawyer and patriarch of the family, who lived in England, supported by income from his Virginia estates. Ball strongly objected to George's career choice: "I think he had better be put apprentice to a Tinker; for a Common Sailor before the Mast, has by no means the Common Liberty of the Subject; for they will . . . cut him and staple him and use him like a Negro, or rather, like a dog." Ball went on to say that Washington would find no opportunity in the navy because "there are always too many grasping for it here"; instead he suggested for his half nephew the life of a planter.[37] This letter presumably ended the debate for good, although Mary Ball Washington's strong opposition may have settled the matter months earlier. Nothing more is known of the incident.

15. Jean Leon Gerome Ferris, *The Call of the Sea, 1747,* ca. 1921, oil on canvas, 35×24 in. (Courtesy of Virginia Historical Society, Lora Robins Collection of Virginia Art)

Weems learned the core of the story and then embellished it, introducing a waiting ship and a weeping mother. "The rank of midshipman was procured for him on board a British ship of war, then lying in our waters. . . . But when he came to take leave of his mother, she wept bitterly, and told him, she felt that her heart would break if he left her. George immediately got his trunk ashore! as he could not, for a moment, bear the idea of inflicting a wound on that dear life which had so long and so fondly sustained his own." In 1837 Sparks knew of the letter to Lawrence Washington that predicted little likelihood that Mary Ball Washington would consent to the plan, and he deduced simply that "she would not see him separated from her at so tender an age, exposed to the perils of accident and the world's rough usage." Sparks did not speculate about whether this strong-willed mother wept or issued a decree.[38]

The artist Alonzo Chappel had clearly read Weems, for the theme of his image is the compassion of George Washington, who would not "wound" his loving mother (fig. 14). But in this artist's scene virtually every detail is inaccurate, from the Victorian setting to figures that are the antithesis of what they should be. The athletic George Washington is shown to be less vigorous than the mother of six children.[39] The scene calls to mind the canvases by Hogarth and Greuze that it so vividly re-

*The Early Years: 1732–1752*

sembles, but there is none of the expected satire here nor a moral about the loss of virtue. The marine print on the wall is intended to inspire the viewer to imagine that a mother's judgment and pleading not only saved her son from a possible death at sea, but also changed the course of the history of two nations by preserving the leader who would win American independence. But this print within the print is high on the wall, small and barely visible. Its theme, however, would be brought to center stage in the twentieth century by Jean Leon Gerome Ferris, a Colonial Revival painter who had taken a special interest in the life of Washington (fig. 15).

Ferris had read Weems's account of a British ship waiting in Virginia waters at the moment when Washington was halted by his mother; the artist mentions such a ship in his notes about the painting of this subject. Ferris must also have consulted the Chappel engraving, since his canvas resembles it in its setting and composition. This artist, who was inclined to depict significant behind-the-scenes moments in history, valued the incident because he felt that it determined the course of the American Revolution. In his notes he argues that the war would have been lost if Washington had here been diverted from his destiny.[40] Thus we are no longer presented with the considerate George Washington, who is so concerned about the welfare and feelings of his mother that he relents. Rather, Ferris gives us an energetic and talented adolescent ready to achieve in whatever career he pursues. At this early age, however, he is fortunately steered from what would have been the wrong path by his determined mother. Because Ferris cites Ball's comments in his notes, we can assume that it is the letter of advice from her half brother that rests on the stool to the right, beside the figure of Mary Washington.

In Chappel and Ferris, as in Weems and Sparks, we are offered only speculation about George Washington's attitude and behavior during this incident. It would appear that none of the four knew of a letter to Lawrence from his father-in-law, William Fairfax, which is a particularly important document because it preserves an early statement by Washington. Fairfax reports that he had delivered Lawrence's two letters promoting the navy scheme to Fredericksburg and mentions that the fourteen-year-old George had said "he will be steady and thankfully follow [his brother's] advice as his best friend."[41] This lone sentence strongly suggests that George Washington respected the opinion of his much older, accomplished brother and reaffirms that Lawrence's military career was probably a major influence on the young man. Again and again in his youth, when George was contemplating his future Lawrence seems to have inspired and supported him. George would continually need his brother's assistance in his efforts to distinguish himself; at this point, however, Lawrence led him not into the navy but rather to the Fairfax family at Belvoir.

## Virginia: The Social Landscape

For a host of reasons, including the bond of life-sustaining trade with the mother country and a gentry tradition predating the arrival of cavaliers from puritan England, the sharp social divisions of the Old Country were in no way dulled in Virginia. George Washington was determined to establish himself as a viable member of the colony's gentry, and he did what he could to groom himself to fit into that elite society. This meant that he had to follow the prescribed patterns that were associated with refinement: he had to look, dress, and act the part; to display, without being ostentatious, the accoutrements of aristocratic life; to be ready to invoke a heritage worthy of respect; to offer public service; and to own and display sufficient property to suggest a fortune great enough to survive the vacillations of a colonial economy based on a single crop, tobacco.

Washington displayed his understanding of the importance of pedigree in his use of the family coat of arms. The Washington family arms can be dated to fourteenth-century England, where it was used on a deed of sale in 1376. The crest depicts a raven rising from a ducal crown. The inscription, drawn possibly from Ovid's *Heroides,* is "EXITUS ACTA PROBAT," which has been variously translated as "The Act Proves the Deed," "The Event Proves Well the Wisdom of Her Course," or, as Benson Lossing suggests, "The End Justifies the Means."[42] One could devise various meaningful explications of any of these choices in the light of Washington's later successes, but it seems more likely that having a coat of arms was more important to him than what the inscription actually meant.

Though he clearly displayed this emblem, Washington actually had little interest in family genealogy. He simply wanted to state, for any eyes that might look for the evidence, that a pedigree existed. He knew nothing about his English ancestry other than that his forebears came from Yorkshire in the north of England. Nor did Washington have any interest in learning about his distant cousins in America, the descendants of his great-grandfather's brother: "I have not the least Solicitude to trace our [Virginia] Ancestry," he wrote to his grandnephew, William Augustine Washington. George explained that "Sir Isaac Heard, Garter and principal King at Arms [of the College of Heraldry, London], wrote to me some years since enclosing our Armorial; and requesting a genealogical account of our progenitors since the first arrival of them in this country. I gave him the best information of which I was possessed. . . . If you are able to do it, trace the descendants of Lawrence Washington who came over with John, our Progenitor."[43] While one might argue that in this letter, written exactly one month before his death, Washington expresses a wish that he had learned more about his family, or perhaps felt that as a republican hero

16. Washington family coat of arms, ca. 1772, book-plate. (Courtesy of Virginia Historical Society)

17. Unidentified artist, copied by John Hesselius in 1751, *William Fitzhugh,* 1690s, oil on canvas, 30×25 in. (Courtesy of Virginia Historical Society)

he had a duty to feign disinterest in his family background, the simple fact is that Washington used what genealogy he knew about, as well as the family coat of arms, purely for social statement.

This emblem makes one of its earliest colonial appearances on a cruet stand ordered by Washington in 1757 (see fig. 80). In 1771 he ordered several hundred bookplates with this design (fig. 16).[44] Like the purchase of a portrait or an elaborate tombstone, this was not a sound financial investment. But in Washington's Virginia, a coat of arms answered a social need. It established the status of the owner before the eyes of those who might question whether he was their social peer. Washington would use such apparently extravagant objects throughout his life, especially when entertaining European visitors at Mount Vernon and during the presidency, in quiet attempts to reassert his worthiness. The obsessions of his youth did not disappear, even at the times of his greatest successes.

The aristocracy of colonial Virginia was made up of English men and women who sought no political or religious separation from the home country, but rather attempted to perpetuate a remembered lifestyle in a new land. Members of the gentry were highly conscious that a comfortable living was available to only a few. They were ever mindful to establish and maintain their status by separating themselves through their property, dress, manners, and public service. The young George Washington needed to look only at the accoutrements of his neighbors, such as their family silver and portrait galleries, to be reminded of the divisions even within the upper echelons of colonial society. Indeed, one could argue that what these objects represented to him ultimately determined what he would become.

Some of the peculiarities of gentry behavior in the colony had been documented a half century earlier by William Fitzhugh (fig. 17). The Fitzhugh dynasty was ensconced in King George County, only a short distance north of the Popes Creek plantation. William's descendants were neighbors and friends of the Washingtons; Martha Washington's grandson George Washington Parke Custis would later marry one of the fam-

18. William Fitzhugh to Dorothy Fitzhugh, 22 April 1686. (Courtesy of Virginia Historical Society)

ily. Fitzhugh identified a need to put forth a creditable facade, or to playact, in order to live comfortably in Virginia. In that way, a gentleman would enjoy the financial credit that was essential in a cash-poor society and would be accepted socially by the neighboring gentry. In a letter to his sister in England in advance of her emigration to Virginia, Fitzhugh explains how appearance determined an individual's reception in the colony (fig. 18). He wanted her to arrive "handsomely & gentelely & well cloathed, with a maid to wait on her, & both their passages paid there." This would "give us both credit & reputation, without which its uncomfortable living, & I am assured my Brother will both assist & direct you in it." By the time of Washington's birth, this social posturing was so established in the colony that a Philadelphian was warned to go "handsomely dressed" to Virginia because people there look "more at a man's outside than his inside."[45]

George Washington wished to avoid "uncomfortable living" and was therefore willing to play the role demanded of him.

19. Isaac Zane, Belvoir fireback with Fairfax family coat of arms, cast at Marlboro Furnace, Frederick County, Va., 1770, cast iron, 34½ × 31 in. Inscribed at bottom, "ZANE MARLBRO." (Courtesy of Fairfax Retirement Community)

He found models to follow and a means of introduction into the gentry at large in the Fairfaxes of Belvoir, the seat that was the immediate neighbor to the south of Mount Vernon. Indeed, perhaps the most revealing advice that George gave to his younger brother John Augustine Washington concerned their aristocratic neighbors: "Live in Harmony and good fellowship with the family at Belvoir, as it is in their power to be very serviceable upon many occasion's to us as young beginner's: I would advise your visiting often as one Step towards the rest, if any more is necessary, your own good sense will sufficient dictate; for to that Family I am under many obligation particularly to the old Gentleman."[46] If he was deferential and observant, John, too, could perhaps find the keys to success.

A massive fireback made for Belvoir, weighing nearly three hundred pounds, is a fitting symbol of the prominence and power of the Fairfax dynasty in Virginia (fig. 19).[47] The design of the coat of arms is an impressive display of heraldic art appropriate for an ancient English family that had been seated at Leeds Castle in Kent since the Middle Ages. The arms were also used to decorate silver, maps, and bookplates, but the cast-iron fireback captures especially well the power enjoyed by the Virginia Fairfaxes. Thomas, sixth Baron Fairfax of Cameron (1693–1781), was the rare peer of the realm to leave his ancestral lands in England and set up residence in an American colony. He came to Virginia in 1735 to control and administer the Northern Neck proprietary, a 5-million-acre tract of land situated between the Potomac and Rappahannock Rivers and stretching westward to their headwaters. This fief was granted in 1649 by the future Charles II to a group of loyalists to the House of Stuart and was inherited by Fairfax through a Culpeper ancestor. The Fairfaxes of Virginia were as close to medieval feudal lords as were ever seen in America, for the proprietor owned the land in perpetuity and could do with it as he pleased.

Thomas, Lord Fairfax, was born at Leeds Castle and educated at Oxford (fig. 20). After retiring to his birthplace, Fairfax found his leisurely life in Kent interrupted, at about the time of George Washington's birth, by challenges in the Virginia assembly to his claim to the proprietary. After positioning his cousin William in Virginia, Lord Fairfax traveled to the colony to defend his title to the Northern Neck lands and to arrange for surveyors to clearly define the area's western boundaries. On this visit Fairfax decided to settle in Virginia. Two years later, however, in 1737, he was back in England to defend his claims before the Privy Council, a process that took a decade. In the end, his legal efforts were successful and the proprietary lands became indisputably the possession of Fairfax, to sell or rent at his pleasure.[48]

Lord Fairfax is often described as a somewhat eccentric character, even a recluse and a misogynist. He eventually settled at Greenway Court, in what was then a frontier region of his proprietary, largely because there he could escape from both colonial society as a whole and women in particular. At Greenway Court he was said to dress as a frontiersman, eschewing the fashionable clothes he ordered in quantity each year from London. His portrait, which was painted in England before his return to Virginia, however, presents a different picture. We see a sensible man who is dressed in vogue, though without an ostentatious display of fine lace or embroidery. The fact that Fairfax commissioned this portrait and carried it to Virginia suggests that while he resided at Belvoir he chose to play the part of an English lord. In fact, it was the proprietor who set the standards of gentility at Belvoir that most influenced George Washington. At his death in 1781 Washington wrote, "altho' the good old Lord had lived to an advanced age, I feel a concern at his death."[49] If Thomas Fairfax had his eccentricities, and if in the comparative wilderness of Greenway Court he wore the clothing of a frontiersman, Washington saw in him a father figure who, as his portrait projects, was a model of dress and deportment. It is somewhat ironic that Washington, who would champion American independence and lead the army of rebellion, received his social rearing from the Fairfaxes, for they introduced him to an English lifestyle and point of view that was little tainted by the experience of colonial life. Of all the Virginia Georgian mansions, Belvoir was exceptional in that it was built and inhabited by English-born residents. The Fairfaxes were comparative newcomers to the colony and to visit them was nearly the same as visiting a family in Kent. Other prominent dynasties of Virginia, such as the Fitzhughs, the Carters, and the Randolphs, had been established in the seventeenth century, and though their members tried to mimic their English forebears, they were not unchanged by conditions on the Virginia frontier. It is also fair to surmise that although Washington probably already spoke with a modified British accent, he may well have adopted the speech patterns of the male members of the Fairfax family in his attempt to fashion himself into an appropriate candidate for inclusion in their circle.

When George Washington told his younger brother that he was particularly obligated to "the old Gentleman" at Belvoir, he was referring to William Fairfax (1691–1757), the patriarch

20. Unidentified artist, *Thomas, Sixth Lord Fairfax,* ca. 1735 or 1737–45, oil on canvas, 49¼×38½ in. (Courtesy of Alexandria-Washington Lodge no. 22, A.F. and A.M.)

of the family. William Fairfax's portrait does not survive, for, as Washington recorded, it was "left standing at Belvoir; and, unfortunately, perished with the house," which was lost to fire at the end of the Revolution.[50] A cousin of Thomas, the lord and proprietor, William Fairfax was born in Yorkshire, England, and served briefly in the British army before he received royal appointments in the Bahamas and then Massachusetts. When Lord Fairfax became dissatisfied with the string of local agents who administered the proprietary and collected his rents, William Fairfax was invited to accept that post. He moved to Virginia in 1734 and by the early 1740s was at Belvoir.

After first settling in King George County, William Fairfax began in 1736 to accumulate for himself choice tracts of land farther up the Potomac River, in the northern reaches of Prince William County, the same area where Augustine Washington a decade earlier had acquired acreage. There he would be closer to the center of the proprietary that his cousin had entrusted him to administer, and so it was there he would locate his Virginia seat. On one of those tracts, overlooking the Potomac River, and apparently with the input of Lord Fairfax, who for several years would reside there with him, he built

... &afsigns for ever; He the S. William H. Fairfax ... his heirs & afsigns
Yielding & Paying unto me my heirs & afsigns or to my certain Attorney or Attorney
Agent or Agents or to the certain Attorney or Attorneys of my heirs & afsigns Proprietors of the S. northern neck yearly & every year on the feast day of S. ...
Michael the Archangel the fee rent of one shilling sterling money for every ...
fifty acres of Land hereby granted & so proportionably for a greater or lefser ...
quanti... ...vided that if the the S. Will. H. Fairfax his heirs or afsigns ...
shall not pay the before reserved annual rent so that the same or any part th
shall be behind or unpaid by the space of two whole years after the same shall ...
become due if lawfully demanded. That then it shall & may be lawfull ...
for me my heirs or afsigns Proprietors as afores? my or their certain Attorney or ...
Attorneys Agent or Agents into the above granted premises to Reenter & hold ...
the same so as if this grant had never Pafsd. Given at my Office in the County
of Fairfax within my S? Proprietary under my seal. Witnefs my Agent &
Attorney fully authoriz'd thereto. Dated the fifteenth day of December in the
sixteenth year of the reign of our Sovereign Lord George the Second &c. A? One
thousand seven hundred & forty two
Mr William H.Fairfax's Deed
for 260 Acres of Land in Fairfax C?ty. —

W. Fairfax

21. Thomas, Lord Fairfax to William Fairfax, patent for 260 acres in Fairfax County, 1737. (Courtesy of Virginia Historical Society)

Belvoir. The Fairfax presence in this region caused it to be split apart from Prince William County in 1742 and named Fairfax County in honor of the proprietor. The patent displayed is William Fairfax's claim to a large tract in the vicinity of the future Belvoir (fig. 21). It provides evidence of how unclaimed lands in the proprietary were acquired. A claimant would commission a survey of the land that he sought, the plat of that survey would be deposited at the proprietor's office, and a patent granting the land to the claimant would be issued. Unsettled land was of little value to Lord Fairfax, who willingly granted most requests because the new owner would then owe him, as is stated in this patent, "rent" of "one shilling sterling money for every fifty acres of Land hereby granted."

The son and heir of William Fairfax was George William Fairfax (1724–87), who was George Washington's contemporary, friend, and the husband of a woman for whom the young Washington had strong feelings, Sally Cary Fairfax. George William had been born in the Bahamas but was educated in England. In 1746, after fifteen years of schooling, Fairfax rejoined the family at Belvoir and remained there for the subsequent years that Washington visited the house. To judge from the portrait that was commissioned on his return to England in 1773, George William was an amiable man who was entirely at ease with the dress and manners of the English gentry, exuding refinement without the slightest pretense (fig. 22). His appearance, manners, and intelligence had won him election to the House of Burgesses from Frederick, one of the western counties of the proprietary, the rank of colonel in the militia, and eventually the high honor of service on the Governor's

22. Unknown artist, *George William Fairfax*, ca. 1760, oil on canvas. (Photograph courtesy of Virginia Historical Society)

Council. In 1757 George William Fairfax inherited Belvoir from his father. Two years later he inherited from an uncle the estate of Toulston Manor in Yorkshire, a significant turn of fortune that would ultimately allow his return to England.[51]

As a boy of sixteen, George Washington became enamored with Sally Fairfax (ca. 1730–1811), the then eighteen-year-old wife of George William Fairfax. Her portrait was commissioned by a Fairfax descendant and is purported to be a copy of either a miniature or a lost oil (fig. 23). But this canvas may be a total fabrication; there apparently is no reliable visual record of Sally Fairfax's appearance.

On the eve of his marriage to Martha Custis, Washington's infatuation with Sally apparently remained. He wrote to her in September 1758:

> Tis true, I profess myself a Votary to Love—I acknowledge that a Lady is in the Case—and further I confess, that this Lady is known to you.—Yes Madam, as well as she is to one, who is too sensible of her Charms to deny the Power, whose Influence he feels and must ever Submit to. . . . You have drawn me my dear Madam, or rather have I drawn myself, into an honest confession of a Simple Fact—misconstrue not my meaning—'tis obvious—doubt it not, nor expose it,—the World has no business to know the object of my Love, declard in this manner to—you when I want to conceal it. . . . I dare believe you are as happy as you say—I wish I was happy also. (fig. 24)

23. Duncan Smith, *Sally Cary Fairfax*, ca. 1915, oil on canvas, 38×32 in. (Courtesy of Virginia Historical Society)

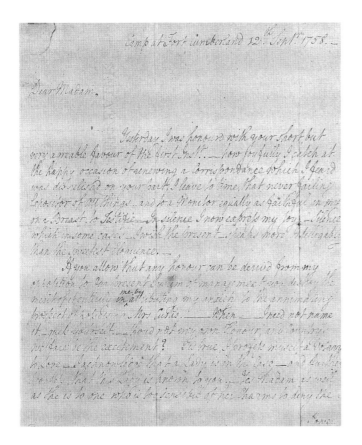
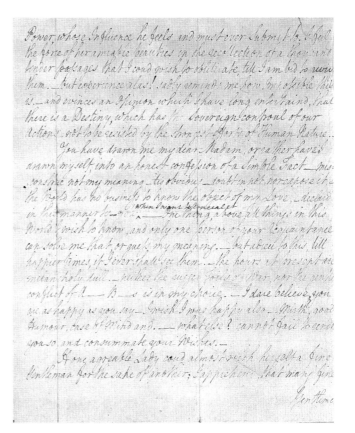

24. George Washington to Sarah Cary Fairfax, 12 September 1758. (Courtesy of Houghton Library, Harvard University)

This theme is continued in additional letters. Two weeks later he asks, "Do we still misunderstand the true meaning of each others Letters? I think it must appear so."[52]

Prudently, it would seem, Sally Fairfax did nothing to encourage Washington further, and there is no record that their relationship extended beyond public interactions and an exchange of letters. In a guest book kept at Belvoir during these years, Sally philosophized about misfortune and loss, which surely would have resulted from any indiscretion: "Un Malheur ne vient jamais seul. On n'estime jamais une Chose asser avant que nous l'avons perdu" ("A misfortune never comes alone. One never appreciates something enough until we have lost it") (fig. 25).[53] No doubt she specifically refers here to the loss of her father-in-law, William Fairfax, who had died four days earlier and was buried at just about the time she made this entry. However, one might infer that she would have been aware of the cost of an indiscretion with her youthful admirer a year later and might well have tried to dissuade him as gently as possible. This guest book, an unusual and interesting survival from the period, is simply a recycled volume from the Fairfax library; its several blank end pages served as a convenient place to record the names and visits of distinguished friends. In their signatures and inscriptions we find evidence of the erudition of the Northern Neck gentry and a suggestion of the ambiance at Belvoir, which had become a social and political center in a colony that had no major city.

In 1773, after leaving Belvoir and arriving in England, a land that she had never before visited, George William and Sally Fairfax settled into a country retirement near Bath, "in as perfect an Arcadia as ever Poet's fancy formed," as George William later wrote to Washington. "We live in an humble, neat and comfortable way," he added, "have a Chaise and pair, have only two Men and two Women Servants, have every necessary of Life brought to our door, our Garden produces the sweetest Vegitables I ever tasted, and the Flowers and Shrubs employ me, and delight my old Woman. In short We enjoy the constant feast of content, and would not change situations with any Crown'd head, upon earth." But, as Washington's friends, they had been "humbled" by their neighbors during the years of the Revolution, to be reconciled only afterward when opinions about Washington changed in England. They later remembered Belvoir with emotion: "Your pathetic discription of the Ruin of Belvoir House produced many tears & sighs from the former Mistress of it."[54]

It had been the presence of Sally Fairfax, as much as the fellowship and patronage that he found there, that made the young George Washington's visits to Belvoir so pleasurable. Late in his life, he wrote with fondness a discreet, yet telling, letter to his then long-widowed friend:

> None of [the past] events . . . have been able to eradicate from my mind, the recollection of those happy moments, the happiest in my life, which I have enjoyed in your company.
>
> Worn out in a manner by the toils of my past labour, I am again seated under my Vine and Fig tree. . . . It is matter of sore regret, when I cast my eyes towards Belvoir,

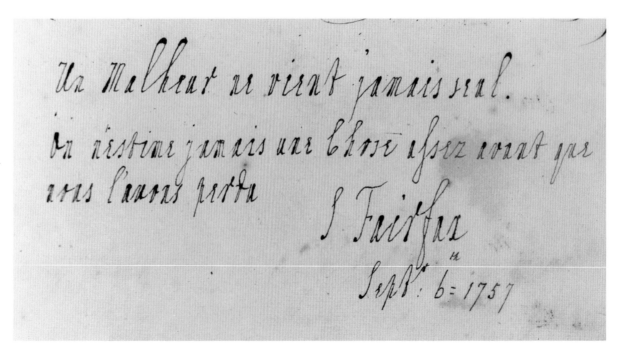

25. *Liber Amicorum* (or Belvoir house guest book), in a copy of Ralph Thoresby, *Ducatus Leodiensis: Or the Topography of . . . Leeds* (London, 1715). (Courtesy of Virginia Historical Society)

which I often do, to reflect that the former Inhabitants of it, with whom we lived in such harmony and friendship, no longer reside there; and that the ruins can only be viewed as the memento of former pleasures; and permit me to add, that I have wondered often, (your nearest relations being in this Country), that you should not prefer spending the evening of your life among them rather than close the sublunary Scene in a foreign Country, numerous as your acquaintances may be, and sincere, as the friendships you may have formed. . . .

Knowing that Mrs. Washington is about to give you account of the changes wch happened in the neighbourhood, and in our own family, I shall not trouble you with a repetition of them.

It is easy, but perhaps unfair, to suggest that the mature Washington speculated at that moment about what might have been as he passed this letter on to Martha. There can be no doubt, however, about his feelings for the woman who had apparently been the first object of his affections.[55]

What ruins of Belvoir remained standing after the fire of 1783 were, ironically, leveled by shells from British ships in 1814. However, the foundations were excavated in 1919, and, as is evident from the photographs taken then and from contemporary accounts, it must have been an extraordinary house (fig. 26). The exact appearance of the building is unknown, but it can be approximated. Belvoir was described in a rental advertisement placed in the *Virginia Gazette* when the Fairfaxes vacated it for England as made "of Brick, two Stories high, with four convenient Rooms and a large Passage on the lower Floor, five Rooms and a Passage on the Second."[56]

The designer of Belvoir is also unknown. Generally, Virginia houses of this scale were jointly created by the owner and a talented master craftsman. The owner would stipulate an approximate idea of what he wanted, and the builder would make his own suggestions and work out the innumerable details. In the case of Belvoir, help with the plan, which is not the

standard cross-passage Virginia type, may have come from England. In 1735 Lord Fairfax had sent a plea to Bryan Fairfax, his father's first cousin and the powerful British commissioner of customs, on this point: "When I can fix upon a proper Tract of Land for the Proprietor, a Plan for a House will be very acceptable, in which I shall beg your assistance."[57]

Archaeologists in 1919 found on one short side of the house foundations that were inadequate to hold a two-story structure; they identified these as belonging to a porch or piazza, 19½-by-35-feet long. These foundations are to the south, overlooking a bend in the Potomac River. If this was a porch, it could have been a model (possibly taken from the Bahamas where William Fairfax had been resident) for the piazza that George Washington would build at Mount Vernon. Indeed, the entire house, from the finery of its contents to the odd diagonal layout of its support buildings, must have influenced Washington's ideas about his estate, probably in more ways than can be determined today.

From an inventory that survives in a fragmentary state, it is possible to reconstruct much about the appearance of the interior of the house. This listing of the contents of the rooms was commissioned in advance of their sale after George William and Sally Fairfax left for England in 1773. Identified in the document are a passage below stairs and a wide entrance lobby, the latter a feature more English than Virginian, as well as eight of the house's nine rooms. There was a "Dining Room" and a "Parlor" (which also had chairs and tables for dining), both of which were certainly below stairs. The "Dres[s]ing Chamber" and "Colonel [George William] Fairfax's D[ressin]g Room" most likely were downstairs as well. The "Chintz Chamber," the "Red Chamber," "Mrs. Fairfax's Chamber," and the "Yellow Chamber" were all probably upstairs.

The quality of the furnishings in the house was extraordinary. What stands out in the inventory is not only the expense of the many objects but also the allocation of the money used

26. Excavated ruins of Belvoir, the Fairfax mansion of William Fairfax, Fairfax County, early twentieth century. (Courtesy of Virginia Historical Society)

to buy them. There were many fine mahogany tables and chairs (literally dozens of the latter), as could be found in other Virginia Georgian mansions, as well as highly expensive mirrors, "large" carpets, and seemingly countless yards of fine fabrics to serve as draperies and to cover furniture. The gilt looking glass in the dining room must have been large and elaborately crafted, for it was valued at the substantial sum of £15. The "Large Wilton Persian Carpet" was worth £9.15.0. In the bedchambers, if not in nearly all of the rooms, more money was spent on fabrics than on anything else. For example, the objects in "the Chintz Chamber" were valued at more than £50; fabrics accounted for more than 60 percent of that amount, of which the window and bed curtains alone made up £19.4.9.

In an inventory of "the Dres[s]ing Chamber" we see that sixty-seven yards of a blue damask fabric were used not only for curtains but also to cover an expensive sofa and the seats of eight mahogany chairs (fig. 27). The braid, fringe, tassels, and pins that are listed are the types of accessories used in the finest drapery treatments. In fact, all the material was so fashionable ("in the neatest manner") that the maker of the inventory felt compelled to make note of that quality. Also typical for Belvoir, this room boasted a particularly expensive carpet (valued at £12) and a "large" looking glass. It was a lushly furnished room, and since its fine contents were no doubt imported, the dressing chamber must have been virtually identical to its English models. To be sure, this was not a royal apartment, but it must have matched many gentry interiors in London. This inventory allows us to speculate about the effect that such affluence might have had on the young George Washington. It is fair to say that his early experiences at Belvoir helped to set his future course. He longed to emulate this style of living and possess the signifiers of aristocratic society. When the opportunity presented itself, he would use some of these very objects to achieve his goal.

When the furniture at Belvoir was sold in 1774, George Washington, who managed the sale, purchased much of it (fig. 28). He spent the ample sum of £169.12.6, which was three and a half times the amount of his nearest competitor, and more than half of the total receipts of £315.16.7. The timing of the sale was fortuitous, in that Washington had just begun to expand Mount Vernon to nearly twice its length and size, and would soon have new rooms to fill with additional furniture. But, more important, Belvoir had been for the young Washington a sort of stage where he had learned the intricacies of the gentry lifestyle that he was so determined to follow. If he could now own much of this "set," he could conceivably play out the remainder of his boyhood fantasy. What better way to reaffirm his position in the colonial aristocracy than to take possession of the accoutrements of those who had been his models.

Although Washington purchased from Belvoir an assortment of objects, ranging from farm animals to andirons, he focused on a number of the finest pieces of furniture, including an expensive mahogany desk and bookcase (£16.16) that had been kept in one of the bedchambers. He bought the best mirror in the house, apparently the large one in the dining room (£13.5.0). Nearly as expensive was the fine sideboard (£12.5.0), which had probably stood in the Belvoir parlor. (In this section the inventory is fragmentary.) The twelve chairs and three window curtains from the parlor no doubt were of fine quality for they too were highly valued (£31), as was the bed that he purchased (£11). The "Large Carpet in the Blue Room" (£11), which he also acquired, was either from the Dressing Chamber, which was blue, or perhaps from the unidentified ninth room of the house. Finally, Washington purchased the handsome mahogany double chest of drawers that had stood in the bedchamber of Sally Fairfax (£12.10).[58]

In terms of his penchant for decorative objects, George Washington was not particularly extravagant. He had assumed the tastes of a typical Virginian of the upper level of the gentry class. Accustomed to the frontier conditions of the colony, he did not pursue luxury with the immoderate inclinations of the nobility in England. In terms of clothing, he echoed the sentiments of many other Virginians of his stature when he told a merchant in 1761: "I want neither Lace nor Embroidery—plain Cloaths with a gold or Silver Button (if worn in genteel Dress) is all I desire."[59] It follows that in furniture he would have thought it inappropriate to pursue the equivalent of "lace and embroidery," those pieces that were excessively carved or even gilded. Some of the Belvoir furniture probably fell into the latter category, as surely did the fine fabrics that were there, but Washington acquired many of these objects also, perhaps because they had sentimental value to him, or because he had an appreciative eye for good design, which he no doubt found in these furnishings. The fact that he would have to transport his purchases only four miles was also certainly a factor. Here, as throughout his life, Washington would opportunistically bring whatever new objects and new ideas he could to what were ongoing renovations at Mount Vernon.

If Washington did not purchase every carpet, case piece, or bed in Belvoir, he did move a substantial part of that house to his estate. The presence of those objects in their new setting must have been startling to anyone who had known the Fairfax house, and their visual impact would hardly have been lost on their new owner. What he had acquired was more than just furnishings; Washington had purchased as well a house full of memories. The pieces must have brought remembrances to him on an almost daily basis. For instance, Sally Fairfax's tall, impressive chest on chest was so valuable and useful a furnishing that it almost certainly would have been placed in the

27. "The Dres[s]ing Chamber," from the "Inventory of the Furniture of the Several Rooms at Belvoir," ca. 1774. (Courtesy of Virginia Historical Society)

28. "Account of Sales at Belvoir," 15 August 1774. (Courtesy of Virginia Historical Society)

master bedroom. We know that it was in George Washington's bedroom at his death.[60] If it was indeed at hand throughout the last twenty-five years of his life, Washington's daily use of this piece could not have been matter-of-fact.

In the letter to the Fairfaxes that "produced many tears & sighs from the former Mistress of [Belvoir]," Washington had described the melancholy effect of seeing the remains of the house: "Alas! Belvoir is no more! I took a ride there the other day to visit the ruins—& ruins indeed they are. . . . When I considered that the happiest moments of my life had been spent there—when I could not trace a room in the house (now all rubbish) that did not bring to my mind the recollection of pleasing scenes; I was obliged to fly from them; & came home with painful sensations, & sorrowing for the contrast."[61] Belvoir was an arcadia that had disappeared, one that Washington would spend much of his life trying to recapture.

Although George William Fairfax had left Virginia, other members of the family remained. His younger brother Bryan, the namesake of the former commissioner of customs, had by the time of the Revolution become a loyalist. However, this future minister maintained a friendly relationship with Washington. They debated the question of independence in their correspondence, and Washington never faulted Bryan for

29. Unidentified artist, *Ferdinando Fairfax,* ca. 1800, oil on canvas, 18×14¾ in. (Courtesy of Virginia Historical Society)

presenting the opposing viewpoint. He wrote from Valley Forge, "The friendship I ever professed, and felt for you, met with no diminution from the difference in our political Sentiments."[62] George and Martha Washington ultimately became the godparents of Bryan's third son, Ferdinando Fairfax (1774–1820), who would later serve as a principal mourner at his godfather's funeral.

Ferdinando Fairfax was the heir to the sizable estates of his uncle, the childless George William Fairfax, in both Virginia and England (fig. 29). He lived on lands granted from the proprietary in Jefferson County (later West Virginia) and Fairfax County, and he spent his adult life disposing of his vast fortune. His obituary, printed in the *Washington Tri-Weekly Gazette* of 28 September 1820, states that "more money escaped from him than from any other man."[63] His fathering of sixteen children must certainly have put something of a drain on his resources, but the larger problem was his insistence on maintaining a lavish lifestyle.

By living and entertaining on a grand scale, in the manner once seen at Belvoir, Ferdinando Fairfax persisted in carrying on the type of existence that had so influenced the direction of his godfather's life. But times had changed. In figure 29 Ferdinando Fairfax wears an elegant cravat, but he also wears his own hair; some of the gentility—one might even say some of the confidence—manifested by previous generations of the Anglo-American gentry seems drained from his face. This is, in fact, the portrait of an American, a Virginian, of the new Republic. These heirs of both English nobility and the American Revolution faced a hard life as planters because the income generated from the exhausted soil was unpredictable at best. Fairfax could ride out the storm by spending his inheritance; a million other Virginians would migrate from the state during the first half of the nineteenth century. This agricultural crisis, which began late in the colonial era, would remain a challenge to George Washington throughout his life.[64]

*Profiting from the Land: Washington as Surveyor*

The 1743 inventory of Ferry Farm lists "1 sett Surveyors instruments," the property of Augustine Washington.[65] As a landowner and land speculator, surveying tools were a necessity to George Washington's father. He would have used them to examine the countryside and to determine the extent not only of tracts that he owned, but also of unsettled lands that he might wish to acquire. In the sparsely settled colony, surveying was one of those duties, like the practice of medicine or architecture, that a property owner might assume in the absence of a professional.

George Washington probably used his father's surveying instruments. Over the years he acquired a number of other sets, and he came to value surveying as a skill that was indispensable to a planter: "Nothing can be more essentially necessary to any man possessed of a large landed estate, the bounds of some part or other of which is always in controversy," he wrote in 1771 to the tutor of his stepson.[66] From 1748 to 1751 Washington was, for all intents and purposes, a professional surveyor. This vocation provided both an immediate income and the opportunity to visit unsettled western lands where he could acquire tracts at bargain prices. George Washington came to live at Ferry Farm because his father had pursued opportunity westward; he would do the same.

By midcentury, those who had prospered through land acquisition were looking west of the Blue Ridge, to the Shenandoah Valley and beyond. In 1744 the Treaty of Lancaster had opened the valley to increased settlement when the Indians of the Six Nations agreed to leave the region. By 1747 both Lawrence and Augustine Washington Jr. were involved with other Virginians in a project to settle a half-million acres west of the Allegheny Mountains by forming the Ohio Company.[67] This settlement, it was hoped, would both block French occupation from Canada and direct a portion of the fur trade to the Potomac.

It was apparently Lawrence who guided George into the profession of surveyor. Washington had learned the fundamentals of this field during his studies, and his brother's contacts with the Fairfaxes would present him with most of his surveying opportunities. In 1748 George William Fairfax, acting as Lord Fairfax's agent, went with a team of surveyors to the south branch of the Potomac River to explore the western boundary of the proprietary; George Washington, at sixteen, accompanied the group. He gained practical experience under the direction of James Genn, an accomplished professional who held the lucrative and coveted surveyorship of Prince William County.

John Gadsby Chapman provides an interesting depiction of Washington at this craft at about the time of the Genn expedition (fig. 30). An unusually capable but still young man, only recently groomed in the behavior of the English gentry, had been sent into the colonial backwoods, where he was appalled by the crude people he saw but taken by the beauty and potential of the landscape. Sensitive to the youth and fragility of Washington at this juncture, Chapman clothes him in gentry garb and in a marvelous pictorial invention juxtaposes the delicate hand of the young Washington against the wild roots and blasted trees of the mysterious and potentially dangerous wilderness. This is the youth who wrote memoranda to himself about the quantity and design of his waistcoats, who was accustomed to sleeping on clean sheets, and who in the valley was dismayed to find lice and fleas in his bed and a table set

30. John Gadsby Chapman, *George Washington as a Young Surveyor,* 1841, oil on canvas, 28×22 in. (Courtesy of New-York Historical Society)

without cloth or knives.[68] In the background of Chapman's portrait the Potomac River reaches westward, across the range of mountains at Harpers Ferry and beyond. A surveyor's tripod placed in the foreground explains Washington's presence in the region. This virtually untouched landscape awaits not only settlement by Anglo-Americans, but also the unfolding of the first adult years of the greatest figure the nation had produced.

Chapman's source is most probably Sparks, who emphasized Washington's first trip westward, describing it as a turning point in his life. The journey over the mountains, Sparks wrote, "inspired a confidence in himself, kindled fresh hopes, and prepared the way for new successes." Sparks explained that "the immense tracts of wild lands, belonging to Lord Fairfax in the rich valleys of the Allegany Mountains, had not been surveyed. Settlers were finding their way up the streams, selecting the fertile places, and securing an occupancy without warrant or license. To enable the proprietor to claim his quitrents and give legal titles, it was necessary that those lands should be . . . accurately measured."[69] Sparks was in error, however, when he stated that Lord Fairfax "entrusted to [Washington] this re-

31. John Rogers, after John McNevin, *Washington and Fairfax at a War Dance,* colored engraving, published in Benson Lossing, *Washington and the American Republic* (New York, 1857). The engravings in Lossing's bound volumes are not colored. (Courtesy of Mount Vernon Ladies' Association, gift of Mrs. John H. Guy Jr., Vice Regent for Virginia, 1963–95)

sponsible service" of leading the 1748 survey. In fact, Washington was there only to learn. This journey was comparatively brief, only four weeks long. It was during the following three years, when Washington returned to the western proprietary lands to run surveys independently, that he came to know well the country that would be the setting for his first military operations.

The most romantic episode of the journey over the mountains was the party's encounter with Indians. The surveyors had traveled uneventfully for nearly two weeks, but near the headwaters of the Potomac River, as Washington recorded, "We were agreeably surpris'd at the sight of thirty odd Indians coming from War with only one Scalp. We had some Liquor with us of which we gave them Part it elevating there Spirits put them in the Humour of Dauncing of whom we had a War Daunce."[70] Washington may or may not have seen Indians before, but we can conclude that this was probably his first encounter with a war party; the sight clearly impressed him. He left a full account of their formation around a fire and of the roles of their "Speaker" and musicians.

Lossing, who published a depiction of this episode in his *Washington and the American Republic* (fig. 31), commented that "it must have been a picturesque and striking sight amid those lonely old woods, to see the savages, in their wild costume, dancing, in the strong fire-light to the discordant music of their

war songs. To Washington it was a novelty."[71] This introduction would prove particularly significant because hostile Indians, directed by the French against Virginia settlers, would be the bane of Washington's existence during the next decade. On this journey Washington was "with the Indians" all of the following day. This experience, therefore, however brief, may have been helpful as he began to develop an understanding of Indian life and values. It should be noted that the eastern Indians had been driven far enough west by the year of Lossing's publication (1857) for his readers to look upon them more as curiosities than enemies.

Following the journey over the mountains, Washington could find little employment as a surveyor until the Fairfaxes intervened once again.[72] He was still young and inexperienced and by no means a likely appointee to one of the county surveyorships. Yet in July 1749 he was awarded the Culpeper County surveyorship, almost certainly through the influence of Lord Fairfax and the implementation of William Fairfax, then a member of the powerful Governor's Council. Two days later, Washington was in the field in Culpeper, surveying four hundred acres for Richard Barnes of Richmond County and signing the plat of his first professional survey with his full name and his new title (fig. 32).

The plats drawn by Washington show that he was a highly competent surveyor. If we compare the sheet that he prepared

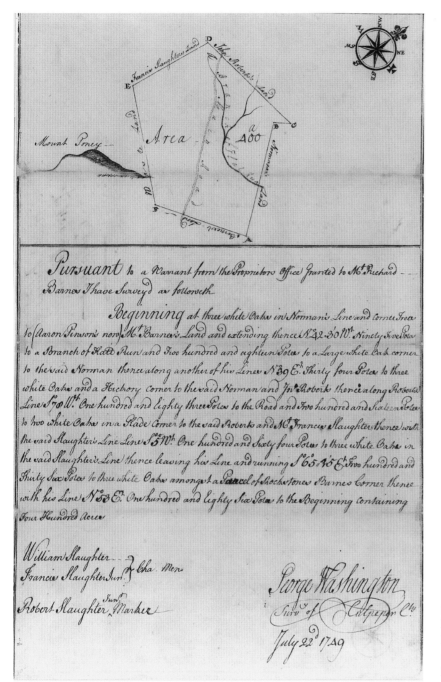

32. George Washington, survey for Richard Barnes for a tract of four hundred acres in Culpeper County, 1749. (Courtesy of Virginia Historical Society)

for Richard Barnes with the Joseph Berry plat of the Popes Creek region (see fig. 2), we find that Washington's narrative is much more carefully presented, giving the impression that the survey had been undertaken by an reliable, even experienced hand, belying its author's seventeen years. Every surveyor copied the narrative section of his plat from notes he had made in his field notebook, but Washington took the time to transcribe them with remarkable legibility. As we shall observe throughout this study, his attention to detail and his ability to present information succinctly and to formulate clear directives would allow Washington to maintain order during even the most chaotic periods of his public and private lives. This

Culpeper plat, however, is unusual for its detail. The nonessential elements—the elaborate compass card, the profile of a nearby mountain, the full signature of the surveyor—do not appear on later plats, as Washington learned to focus more on improving his earnings than on producing overly ornate results.

From 1749 to 1751, and for part of 1752, Washington turned his attention to less settled lands than those of Culpeper County. He worked on the frontier of Lord Fairfax's proprietary, running more than 190 surveys west of the Blue Ridge in the valleys of the Shenandoah and Cacapon Rivers of Frederick County. As before, the Fairfax family was responsible for Washington's employment. Lord Fairfax engaged him as one of a

*The Early Years: 1732–1752*

31

33. Frank Schoonover, *Whatever He Did He Did Well—So It Followed That His Surveys Were the Best That Could Be Made,* 1924, oil on canvas, 36×30 in. (Courtesy of Virginia Tech)

number of surveyors needed for so vast a region, but orders sent from Belvoir gave him profitable assignments on tracts that tended to be close together, uncomplicated, and situated in the most fertile regions. Typically, his instructions would be to carve out a specific acreage for a specific individual within a general location.[73]

Given the neatness of the draftsmanship in the individual plats, and a sense that these documents also measure Washington's intense motivation and precocity, it is no wonder that Lucy Madison would make the statement that "whatever [Washington] did he did well—so it followed that his surveys were the best that could be made."[74] This title was ultimately applied to another painting by Schoonover, who illustrates part of the fieldwork involved in making a survey (fig. 33). The surveyor determines the orientation of a tract's boundary lines through the use of a circumferentor or brass magnetic compass, which is pictured here with its sights open, mounted on a tripod. He then records the compass bearings for each of those

lines in a field book, as Schoonover suggests. Of course, the surveyor could not work alone; chain men were needed to determine the distance of each boundary line, which was ascertained with an iron-link surveying chain. Someone was also needed to notch trees and thereby mark the course of the lines. It was fitting for Schoonover to focus on the field book, however, because from its notes the surveyor later prepared the finished plats that he deposited at the proprietor's office. Through the steady pose and concentrated energy that the artist gives to his figure, Schoonover effectively illustrates the theme from Lucy Madison's text. He suggests that Washington made the best of surveys, and that this ambitious young man was capable of much greater accomplishments.

Schoonover pictures two Indian figures who examine a map but are bewildered by the strange process that engages Washington. The artist references a text that was fabricated by Madison: "[Washington] saw the Indians also in their native haunts, and learned to know their character. . . . He learned their method of warfare and how to meet it. Above all he learned how to conciliate the red men."[75] The historical record, however, provides no evidence that Washington enjoyed much contact with American Indians at this juncture. In 1748, when he had encountered the war party, Washington was at the far-western extremity of the proprietary. Indians came infrequently into the Shenandoah Valley until the mid-1750s, when the warring Frenchmen prompted them to cause havoc on the English frontier.

Schoonover's depiction of Washington clad in buckskins again follows Madison's text. She wrote erroneously that Washington "learned to know the frontiersmen, and wore their dress of hunting shirt, fringed leggins, and moccasions while in the woods. He shared their cabins that reeked of corn pone and bacon, and the odor of pelts, and often slept on their shakedowns. A mutual esteem and liking, founded upon respect for each other, sprang up between the intrepid youth and the trappers and pioneers that was of great value to him in after life." There is little documentation as to how Washington actually dressed while he ran the surveys. Presumably he wore more practical clothing than the type Chapman painted; after all, even Lord Fairfax at times assumed the attire of a frontiersman. But if Washington did make concessions to the ruggedness of the untouched landscape, he would not have been happy with the implication that he resembled a backwoodsman. Contrary to what Lucy Madison imagined, Washington was repulsed by the people and conditions he encountered on the frontier. In 1748 he had thought the valley inhabitants "to be as Ignorant a Set of People as the Indians." He later wrote to a friend that they were "a parcel of Barbarian's and an uncooth set of People" who slept "before the fire . . . with Man Wife and Children like a Parcel of Dogs or Catts." He added that "there's nothing would make it pass of tolerably but a good Reward and Dubbleloon [doubloon] is my constant gain every Day that the Weather will permit my going out." In other words, Washington was there only for the money he could earn by surveying land for others and to patent some acreage for himself. He left the valley with an attitude akin to that of Maj. Robert Fairfax, later seventh Baron Fairfax of Cameron, who visited his older brother Thomas in 1768 but soon returned permanently to England. The future Lord Fairfax found at Greenway Court "nothing but buckskins, viz., back-woodsmen and brutes . . . it is almost past description."[76]

At the time of the French and Indian War, Washington would encounter such people again. However, his job then, as a soldier, was to protect settlers rather than to displace squatters from land that they had failed to patent. In time he would come to see the inhabitants of the valley differently, as family men and, ultimately, as allies. His early exposure to Virginia's frontier population had at least introduced the haughty easterner to his western neighbors, who far outnumbered the colony's gentry and who, down the road, would help him to expel the French and eventually to found a new nation.

Schoonover introduces one final element into his painting, a spectacular landscape of the western mountains of the state. His Washington, enveloped in that scenery, is seemingly enraptured. The artist had instinctively hit upon the truth, for Washington, during the journey of 1748, had recorded a sensitive response to the area, noting in his diary that he had "spent the best part of the Day in admiring the Trees & richness of the Land."[77] The Virginian came to recognize that the views of the western lands were as handsome as the opportunities offered by them. Indeed, the two were intertwined; the views were in effect symbols of the potential rewards that lay to the west. His fondness for such scenes continually stoked Washington's interest in these lands, and led him in later life to become one of the first Americans to collect landscape paintings.

While Washington's experiences as a surveyor introduced him to new lands and the frontiersmen who lived on them, this trade also allowed him to meet the members of the gentry who paid him to measure their tracts. These new contacts with prominent Virginians helped Washington to make himself welcome at important houses throughout the region. He was fixed in the good graces of the powerful Fairfax family; the competency and reliability that he demonstrated as a surveyor made other powerful men aware of his gifts as well.

Washington had taken to the fields in search of contacts and opportunities for advancement. His other immediate goal, which was to accumulate cash and acreage, was also accomplished. It is estimated that in four years he earned nearly four hundred pounds, a sizable income that exceeded the earnings of most planters and tradesmen. In addition, through purchases and grants Washington acquired 2,315 acres in the Shenandoah Valley. These were choice lands that he had handpicked, and were of acreage equal to that of his brother's estate at Mount Vernon. Because he was thereby a landowner in Frederick County, Washington would later be elected to the House of Burgesses from that region.[78] Washington never gave up his surveying; he was always acquiring new lands both east and west of the mountains, and that acreage, like the tracts he already owned, was ever in need of definition. There were constant challenges to boundaries and a need to subdivide fields into workable units. Only a few weeks before his death Washington was running what would be his last survey at Difficult Run in northern Fairfax County.[79]

His experiences as a surveyor would ultimately benefit Washington the soldier, though not in the area of tactics. He learned nothing about warfare at this juncture, as would be proved by his blunders in the impending French and Indian War. But he did begin to learn how to decode the face of a

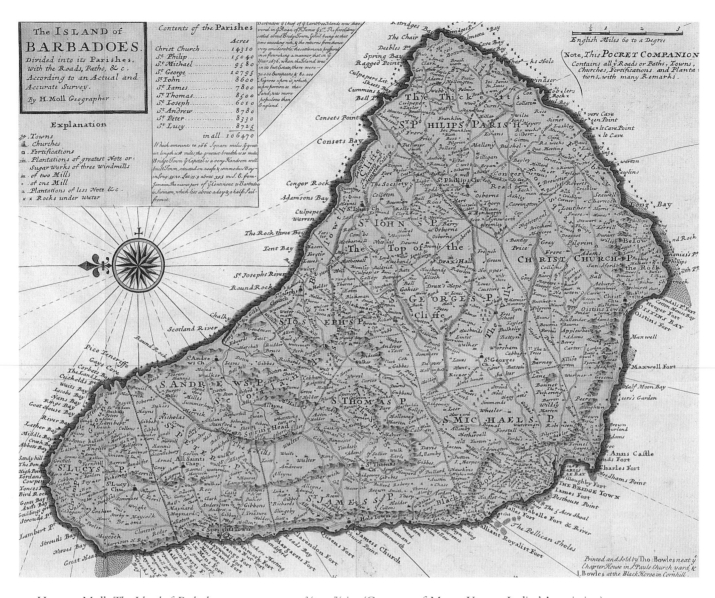

34. Herman Moll, *The Island of Barbados,* ca. 1735, map, 14⅜×15⅞ in. (Courtesy of Mount Vernon Ladies' Association)

landscape and to become aware of potential dangers. In his first journey over the mountains he had been introduced to the difficulties of travel over impassable roads and swollen rivers; he and George William Fairfax had even lost their way on the return trip. With experience, however, Washington became more and more comfortable about traversing the landscape and sanguine about his ability to find his way through it. He learned to navigate with accuracy by compass, and through his experiences as a surveyor was able to estimate distances of hundreds of yards. When he would need to decide how to move soldiers across various types of terrain, or where to engage an enemy, these would prove useful skills.

By 1752 much of the land in the lower Shenandoah Valley had been surveyed, and the opportunities there for a surveyor had greatly decreased. George Washington had earned income and acquired property in this occupation, but not enough to ensure his social status. The time was approaching for his career to take a turn.

Washington's activities as a professional surveyor were interrupted in the fall of 1751 by the illness of his brother Lawrence, who since at least 1749 had suffered from a lung condition, probably tuberculosis, that within a year would kill him.[80] It was thought that the warm climate of a Caribbean island might relieve this sickness, which had so weakened Lawrence that it was doubtful he could travel and convalesce by himself. Thus it was agreed that his younger brother would accompany him to Barbados (fig. 34). Lawrence had married Anne, the daughter of William and Deborah Clarke Fairfax of Belvoir, in 1743; Barbados was selected for this recuperative journey almost certainly because Deborah's brother Gedney Clarke was a merchant and planter on the island.

George did lose income during those weeks that he might have been surveying, but this travel to Barbados would prove both culturally and socially beneficial for Washington. The time that he spent with Lawrence also seems to have increased his enthusiasm for a military career. The exposure to ocean travel and the new, exotic setting might well have provided Washington with a different perspective about the world and the place of the American colonies in it. This experience diminished somewhat the provinciality of a nineteen year old who had been denied an education in England yet sought to match the social refinement of gentlemen who had spent years abroad.

The British had come to Barbados in the 1620s, not long after the settling of Jamestown, but the island had developed more quickly. Herman Moll's map is dense with the names of the "Roads or Paths, Towns, Churches, Fortifications, and Plantations"; the geographer states in his key that in 1676 the island, "in proportion to the land, was more populous than England." By 1735, the date of Moll's map, Barbados was a model, especially to the eyes of a colonial American, of the cultivated landscape. By comparison, Virginians had made little progress in wrestling order out of their wilderness. They had built few roads, kept close to the rivers, and planted little more than tobacco, a crop that ravaged the land. The Washingtons lodged southeast of Bridgetown, on the western coast.[81] Lawrence rented a substantial planter's house, and the brothers were welcomed as gentlemen by the best families on the island.

In Barbados, Washington "was strongly attacked with the smallPox." The illness left no lasting ill effects and seems instead to have implanted in Washington an immunity that later protected him. The fact that Washington produced no children of his own has led some to believe that this early episode made him sterile. However, Washington would later suggest that his wife was unable to conceive due to complications following the birth of her fourth Custis child.[82] (We will return to this subject in chapter 3.)

Upon viewing the landscape of Barbados, George Washington noted: "We . . . were perfectly enraptured with the beautiful prospects which every side presented to our view. The fields of Cain, Corn, Fruit-Trees, &c. in a delightful Green." The trees yielded "the greatest collection of Fruits I have yet seen set on the Table."[83] In an instant Washington was made aware that a well-ordered plantation could support a multitude of crops and could include vegetable gardens that would enhance the beauty of the landscape without depleting it. At least some of the species of tropical fruits that he saw could be grown in Virginia, if only in a greenhouse. Washington the soon-to-be farmer was enlightened by the visit to Barbados.

His ambition would be to achieve a measure of this agricultural diversity and fecundity at Mount Vernon.

Moll records the positions of a long succession of forts along the vulnerable western coast of Barbados. These gun emplacements and cannons no doubt brought back to Lawrence memories that he shared with his brother of his service with Admiral Vernon. In the environment of this fortified island, and through social interactions with Lawrence and the officers resident there, George Washington's interest in the military was revived. After several weeks and little change in his brother's condition, George returned home. Not surprisingly, on his way he stopped in Williamsburg to introduce himself to the Virginia governor, Robert Dinwiddie, who held the authority to make military appointments.[84] With this move Washington positioned himself to pursue a military career; he was ready and willing, if not particularly able, when the colony's militia was restructured only weeks after his brother's death.

Augustine Washington had toiled to acquire enough holdings to provide each of his oldest sons with a farm from which to begin his ascent into the highest levels of the aristocracy. Lawrence had rightfully taken the lead, becoming a success in the military and marrying into one of the most prominent families in Virginia. Further, he had served as young George's mentor and model through his difficult adolescent years. His death no doubt hit his younger brother hard. As Don Higginbotham puts it, "For Washington, the loss of his Fairfax-connected older half-brother Lawrence, who was moving rapidly into the squirearchy's inner circle, represented both a personal deprivation and a lost touchstone to preferment. Lawrence's death was more deeply disturbing to Washington than the passing of his father and the influence of his mother."[85] Lawrence had entered into the world that his father's ambition had unlocked; in so doing he had left the door open for his younger half brother, who was determined that he would not be denied entry.

While there is much that we do not know about Washington's youth, there is evidence of his skill, ambition, and good judgment, all of which would serve him well in the crises that he would face as an adult. When we look at how his youth has been represented, we perceive a need to fill in the blanks in the historical record and to accentuate his unique gifts while, as the pervasiveness of the image of the unimposing Dutch cottage suggests, making clear that this was a self-made individual who was able to rise above what has been widely believed to be his comparatively humble beginnings. Perhaps in this way his history could be more easily equated with that of the nation he would one day lead.

35. Charles Willson Peale, *Washington as Colonel of the Virginia Regiment,*, 1772, oil on canvas, 50½×41½ in.
Signed lower-right, "Chas: W Peale, pinxt:1772." (Courtesy of Washington and Lee University)

## 2

# The Virginia Soldier
# 1753–1758

*Peale's Washington*

IN 1772 Charles Willson Peale painted the only likeness of George Washington rendered prior to the Revolutionary War (fig. 35). Peale depicts an impressive and still young-looking man of forty, with reddish brown hair, gray-blue eyes, and a thick yet graceful nose. This is the figure who contemporaries said had a commanding presence because of his "six-foot height," his natural athleticism, and his admirable deportment.[1] Washington apparently had no inclination to commission such a portrait. Martha, however, wanted a canvas of her husband to hang beside the portraits of herself and her children in the west parlor at Mount Vernon (see figs. 74, 75). These had been painted by John Wollaston in 1757 when she was married to her first husband, Daniel Parke Custis, and transported to her new home after her marriage to Washington in January 1759. Peale would be called upon to paint a canvas of roughly the same size that would fill the glaring void in the family collection.

Peale's visit to Mount Vernon was actually serendipitous. In 1772, Martha Washington's son John Parke "Jacky" Custis was in Annapolis, under the academic tutelage of the Reverend Jonathan Boucher. Boucher was acquainted with Peale, who was also a resident of Annapolis. Peale at that moment was planning one of his tours of the neighboring colonies in search of portrait commissions. He particularly enjoyed visiting Virginia because there the hospitality of plantation hosts often saved him the expense of room and board.[2] Boucher introduced the artist to his future patron by letter, and on 18 May Washington recorded in his diary that "Mr. Peale and J. P. Custis came to Mount Vernon." On the nineteenth Peale may well have worked on the miniatures that he painted of Martha and the two children, because the master of the house was away for the day. It would be on 20 May that Washington "sat to have my Picture drawn." He wrote Boucher that, "inclination having yielded to Importunity, I am now, contrary to all expectation under the hands of Mr Peale."[3]

There is no record as to who decided that Washington should be pictured as a colonel of the Virginia Regiment, a position that he had retired from almost fourteen years earlier. Peale, however, did like to include whenever possible an unusual accessory or landscape motif that would differentiate a sitter. Washington was renowned for his service in the French and Indian War, rather than for being a simple planter, and so a military conception was logical for his portrait. This choice allowed the colonel to dress in the colorful uniform of the regiment, rather than be pictured in the more drab costume of the plantation owner, and would thereby serve as a reminder of the youthful George Washington of the 1750s, the soldier who had married the woman in the more fanciful Wollaston canvas.[4] Rather than including as a backdrop the spectacular panorama of the Potomac River that a visitor to Mount Vernon still enjoys today, or perhaps a view of the gardens of the estate, the subject stands before his earliest battleground. The mountains, woodland, Indian camp, river, and falls suggest the landscape of the Ohio Valley, the western empire that had been considered so crucial by the European powers that they had warred over it. By 1772 these lands represented to Washington both the past, where he had fought for his king and colony, and where the future greatness of Virginia might lie.

Washington may also have agreed to a military conception because an issue that lingered from the decade of his career in the Virginia Regiment was again at hand in 1772. He was in the midst of trying to resolve the patenting of two hundred thousand acres of Ohio lands that had been long ago promised to the earliest Virginia veterans of the French and Indian War, the very lands suggested in the background of Peale's portrait. These "Ohio bounty lands," as they came to be called, were to have been a compensation to Virginia soldiers for their service. As the former commander of the regiment, Washington was to receive one-tenth of the land, twenty thousand acres. By 1772 the matter was finally drawing to a conclusion, thanks largely to Washington's persistence. Two years earlier he had traveled to the Ohio country and spent several months locating the best tracts of land so that they could be surveyed and claimed. None of the land had been granted, however, because of the complexities of identifying tracts and then assigning them to individuals. While in the West, Washington was met by Indians who remembered him and rekindled his memories of an earlier time: "In the Person of Kiashuta I found an old acquaintance. He being one of the Indians that went with me to the French in 1753. He express'd a satisfaction in seeing me and treated us with great kindness." In March 1771 Washington had called a meeting of the officers of the Virginia Regiment to report his findings from the trip. In November he again failed to persuade the Governor's Council to divide the two hundred thousand acres in question into the small tracts that he suggested. A year later Washington was finally successful in winning the Council's approval of his plan, but at the time of the Peale portrait the matter remained unresolved.[5] Therefore, while he might have felt gratified that his former officers supported his plan and still held him in high esteem, as he posed he may well have doubted that they would ever receive their rewards. He had cause both to appreciate the loyalty of those he had commanded and to regret yet another disappointment that came with his service, the most important of which was his failure to gain a commission in the regular British army.

Almost from the start of his military duties Washington pursued such a commission. An officer of the provincial Virginia Regiment earned too little pay and received too little respect from the regulars, and one could hardly expect to build much of a career as a colonial commander. He soon complained to the governor about salary, adding, "I do not see why the lives of his Majesty's subjects in Virginia should be of less value, than of those in other parts of his American dominions," which suggests his sense that others in the military were receiving higher pay than those in the Virginia Regiment, but his harangue fell on deaf ears. In terms of status, those who shaped British military policy concluded shortly thereafter that colonial soldiers might be courageous but were untrained in the science of warfare and therefore undependable; accordingly, George II ruled that officers commissioned by colonial officials "shall have no rank with" officers bearing his commission.[6] Washington would eventually travel to Boston to pursue this issue with ranking British military officials, and a primary theme of his letters of the 1750s was the need to better the situation of the officers of the Virginia Regiment. Their second-class status would give him cause for complaint throughout the war. Washington could never be happy in the wake of failure. This is not to say that throughout the 1760s the retired colonel brooded over his unfulfilled military ambitions, but this experience, and his belief that he was denied a designation that he felt he had earned simply because he was a Virginian, would not be forgotten.

Interestingly enough, it may have been Washington himself who caused George II to limit the authority of colonial officers. This possibility is suggested by the timing of events in 1754. In previous years colonial officers had been granted commissions; in fact, Lawrence Washington had received one prior to his service in the War of Jenkins' Ear. In late May 1754 a troop under Washington's command attacked a French force, and an officer, the sieur de Jumonville, was killed; this engagement provoked a counterattack that led to Washington's defeat at Fort Necessity on 3 July. The news of these actions would have reached London during August, where it was soon realized that Washington had initiated what could become a major war between England and France. The young Virginian's actions became the topic of a great deal of conversation. For example, Dennys De Berdt, the London agent for the colonies of Massachusetts and Delaware, wrote on 7 September to an unidentified English nobleman, "I leave to your Excellency to Judge of Washington's conduct." Charles Cecil Wall suggests that "In England it was conceded Washington and his men had displayed courage and resolution, but their military competence was doubted." Wall then quotes the man who would have been one of the crucial figures in this discussion. "The earl of Albemarle, titular governor of Virginia in absentia and Ambassador to France, wrote 'Officers, and good ones, must be sent to discipline the militia and to lead them'"; the sense was that officers like Washington simply did not have the training to command troops in battle.[7] The king's decree was issued on 12 November 1754. It probably never occurred to the twenty-two-year-old Washington that his actions that summer may actually have inspired the decree that he found so unpalatable. Most Virginians saw no fault in his actions, however; rather, he was praised for his valor.

Washington would come to feel that he had spent the best years of his life with the Virginia Regiment, and had endangered his sturdy constitution by the trials that he had endured along the Ohio. His failed military career meant that the reward, which was possibly nothing if the land grants were never realized, hardly matched the expense; his years of greatest physical vigor had been wasted. As Washington put on the uniform for Peale, he no doubt worried, as many forty-year-old men do, that his physical powers had diminished. In fact, there is a record that he tested his constitution during the artist's visit. What might seem like a Weemsian fantasy appears to be rooted in fact, and is all the more believable because of the state of mind that apparently had been occasioned by the retrieval of his blue coat.

Charles Coleman Sellers, the generally reliable biographer of Peale, thinks it "most likely" that excerpts from the artist's lost account of his Washington portraits were sent by his son, Rembrandt Peale, to George Washington Parke Custis. Custis later published the following anecdote in his *Recollections and Private Memoirs of Washington* (1859): "While the late and venerable C. H. [*sic*] Peale was at Mount Vernon in 1772, engaged in painting the portrait of the provincial Colonel, some young men were contending in the exercise of pitching the bar. Washington looked on for a time, then grasping the missile in his master hand, whirled the iron through the air, which took the ground far, very far, beyond any of its former limits—the Colonel observing, with a smile, 'You perceive, young gentlemen, that my arm yet retains some portion of the vigor of my earlier days.'"[8] Custis's romantic belief that the colonel was still in his full powers aside, Washington at age forty felt that his physical prowess was slipping; his pose might well have made him again resent the British governmental policy that in his mind had wrongfully blocked his ambition. In a sense, that policy had stolen his youth.

Peale was apparently an engaging guest. He and Washington struck up a friendship that would last for decades, and would underlie Washington's willingness in later years to sit for Peale on six additional occasions. During this visit Washington "rid with him to [show Peale] my Mill." They "walked together to enjoy the evening breezes, and . . . danced to give exercise to Miss [Patsy] Custis, who did not enjoy a good state of health." Peale admired that the colonel was "uncommonly modest" and "avoided saying anything of the actions in which he was engaged in [the] last war." But the uniform may well have inspired a conversation about the injustice of colonials putting their lives on the line for George II without the honor of being commissioned in his army, as well as the current taxes and logistical problems that made it almost impossible for a planter to farm profitably. Such complaints may well have given rise to belligerent sentiments in Peale, which would emerge as Revolutionary fervor grew in the colonies over the next three years. Whatever the cause, Washington fell into a peculiar reverie, which the sitter admitted had overcome him. He told Boucher that he posed "in so grave—so sullen a mood—and now and then under the influence of Morpheus, when some critical strokes are making, that I fancy the skill of this Gentleman's Pencil, will be put to it, in describing to the World what manner of Man I am."[9] The artist pictures the colonel between thought and action, his eyes looking aside, his body almost in motion, as if he were about to turn toward the scene of his youthful exploits. The trace of melancholy and the averted gaze are not characteristic of Peale's portraits of this period and are absent in his later portraits of Washington. However, the combination of disparate elements actually go far toward capturing "what manner of Man" Washington was in 1772.

The artist pays a great deal of attention to the colonel's blue and red outfit, which we believe represents Washington's attempt to reconstruct as best he could his uniform of the Virginia Regiment; the handsome silver-braid trim, silver buttons, and hat medallion stand against the various colors and fabrics of the uniform and enhance the portrait's considerable visual appeal. The elegant lavender sash, an ornate version of a traditional element of an officer's uniform, is draped across the figure, accentuating the curved, almost pearlike, shape of the body.[10] The blue coat of the regiment had served as a badge of honor in the colony; many local soldiers who wore it had served with valor at Monongahela, the disastrous defeat of Braddock's army in 1755, as well as at other encounters of the French and Indian War. If Washington was disgruntled that he had been denied a career in the regular army, he could at least take satisfaction in having served with distinction as commander of the Virginia forces and therefore pose proudly wearing his blue coat.

At Washington's side is the English-made sword that he had ordered in 1757, which he would carry in 1783 when he resigned his commission as commander in chief of the American Revolutionary forces and in 1789 when he was inaugurated as president of the United States. It was made to be both decorative and functional, but the artist focuses on the former, painting only the elaborately crafted hilt. Peale's eye for detail also allows us to recognize a "fowler," a type of shoulder arm used by colonials for hunting, which during the past fourteen years Washington had no doubt aimed at wildfowl and the occasional fox. In the king's army, only an artillery officer, on rare occasions, would have carried any sort of long arm, and no soldier would have used such a hunting weapon; rather, a musket with attachable bayonet would have been standard in an era when such a gun would have been considered as much a hand-to-hand weapon as a firing piece. Don Higginbotham notes the significance of this detail when he asks why the artist might have added such a weapon: "Was it to signify the importance of firearms in this New World society for all men, both officers and the rank and file?"[11] Peale and his sitter might well be making such a point. By including any shoulder arm, much less this type of bizarre weapon, in a portrait of a uniformed officer, the artist calls attention to a different understanding of the role of the commander in this American setting. If officers carry the same arms as the men they command, you have a break from—some might say a breakdown of—accepted military procedure. This might be considered detrimental, until one remembers that accepted military procedure had gotten Braddock's army slaughtered.

Another of the focal points of the portrait is the gorget that hangs from Washington's neck. This piece of decorative armor, a remnant of the protective gear of medieval knights, was worn only by those in command as one means to differentiate themselves from their troops. Officers of the Virginia Regiment found that if they were to win the respect of their counterparts

*The Virginia Soldier: 1753–1758*

in the regular army then they, too, must wear gorgets; Capt. George Mercer said that it was as much a part of a "genteel Uniform" as was a colorful sash and "a Sword properly hung." In the following account he reports an encounter with British regulars to his no doubt approving commander, Colonel Washington:

> We have been told here by the [British regular] Officers that nothing ever gave them such Surprize as our Appearance . . . for expecting to see a Parcel of ragged disorderly Fellows headed by Officers of their own Stamp (like the rest of the Provincials they had seen) behold they saw Men properly disposed who made a good & Soldier like Appearance and performed in every Particular as well as could be expected from any Troops with Officers whom they found to be Gent[lemen]. to see a Sash & Gorget with a genteel Uniform, a Sword properly hung, a Hat cocked, Persons capable of holding Conversation where only common Sense was requisite to continue the Discourse, and a White Shirt, with any other than a black Leather Stock, were Matters of great Surprize and Admiration & which engaged Them all to give Us a polite Invitation to spend the Evening, & after to agree to keep Us Company which they had determined before not to do—agreeable to what they had practised with the other Provincial Troops. We have lost the common Appellation of Provincials, & are known here by the Style & Title of the Detachment of the Virga Regiment.[12]

The gorget in Peale's painting, the details of which are difficult to discern, has long been thought to be the one illustrated in figure 36, for which the provenance is impeccable. This gorget descended in the Washington family and was given by Martha's granddaughter Martha Custis Peter in 1813 to the Washington Benevolent Society of Massachusetts, from which it passed to the Massachusetts Historical Society.[13] It displays

the Virginia coat of arms, which dates back to 1619 and the reign of James Stuart, who claimed dominion over England, France, Scotland, and Ireland. Those four kingdoms were originally depicted by four crowned shields, set within a larger field, flanked by human support figures, and surmounted by the half figure of a maiden queen (fig. 37). When England and Scotland were united as one kingdom in 1707, and with the accession of the Hanoverians in 1714, the imagery of the shields was altered to the form seen on this gorget. A united England is suggested by the shield at the top left, France by the shield at the top right, Ireland by the lower-left shield, and Hanover, which is not technically one of the applicable domains, by the lower right. The phrase "En Dat Virginia Quartum" ("Virginia

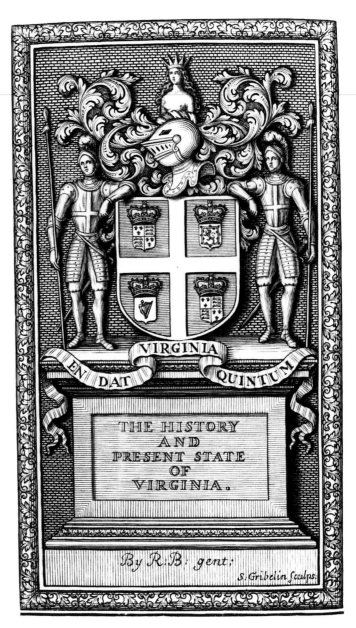

37. Early "Stuart" Virginia coat of arms, from Robert Beverley, *The History and Present State of Virginia* (London, 1705). Here, Virginia supplies the "Fifth" of the British Kingdoms. (Courtesy of Virginia Historical Society)

36. Gorget with the Virginia coat of arms, ca. 1750, gilded brass. (Courtesy of Massachusetts Historical Society, Boston)

*The Virginia Soldier: 1753–1758*

Supplies the Fourth") refers to Virginia as the fourth of the British kingdoms.[14]

Like the blue coat of the militia, the Virginia "coat" of arms was a badge of pride in the colony. It purported to equate Virginia with Ireland, France, and even with England itself, and suggested that all British citizens, no matter what realm they inhabited, had equal status. In the first decades of the eighteenth century this seal was printed on official publications and displayed prominently at Williamsburg. In the late-colonial era, as the British policy of discrimination against her colonies became more focused, the seal appeared more frequently, most notably on coins and banknotes. It came to serve as a reminder of the promised standing within the realm of British citizens who lived overseas, which by the 1760s had apparently been forgotten by the decision makers at home.

The gorget with the Virginia seal makes a clear statement about what were believed to be the rights of colonials. While it has long been assumed that this accoutrement was acquired during the French and Indian War and worn by Washington in his role as colonel of the Virginia Regiment, evidence suggests it was purchased only months prior to the outbreak of the Revolution when he put together a uniform to wear in service with the Fairfax Independent Company of volunteers. In November 1774 and January 1775, Washington exchanged letters with a Philadelphia agent, William Milnor, who had a gorget made for the colonel, along with four additional gorgets "having the Virginia arms engraved; but some what smaller than the last"[15] The four gorgets were for officers of the neighboring Prince William Independent Company who had looked to Washington for guidance in military matters. Washington's comment about the size of "the last" gorget suggests that it is probably the large one that we illustrate as figure 36, which was apparently created by a provincial silversmith unfamiliar with British military ornamentation. These officers of the Fairfax and Prince William companies felt the need to acquire such gorgets, as well as sashes and epaulettes, in order to boast their rightful claim as well-dressed commanders and to assert their status as equal to any British officer.

The gorget in the Peale painting is rendered in enough detail that the engraved heraldic seal is recognizable (fig. 38). The center emblem is divided into four sections, with an inscribed pendant beneath. It is flanked on the right by what is unmistakably a unicorn and on the left by what appears to be a lion. Those royal beasts were well known to colonial Virginians from the examples at the Governor's Palace and elsewhere in Williamsburg and to soldiers from the gorgets worn by British army officers (fig. 39). This is the coat of arms of George II,

38. Detail of gorget in Charles Willson Peale, *Washington as Colonel of the Virginia Regiment,* 1772. Either a silver or a gold gorget was considered acceptable attire. (Courtesy of Washington and Lee University)

39. Gorget with the royal coat of arms, ca. 1750–75, gilded brass. (Courtesy of Jay Fliegelman and Renee Santifaller, Palo Alto, Calif.)

*The Virginia Soldier: 1753–1758*

bearing the good news. Five hundred pounds was the traditional gift for such a courier, but Parke had shrewdly asked instead for his flattered monarch's likeness. With it came a gold locket set with diamonds, a thousand guineas, and widespread acclaim, which the ambitious Parke believed would be worth more to him than money.[19]

Probably little was said by Washington or the Custis descendants about Parke's dark side. It would have been easy for the family to forget how he had first scorned Virginia's provincial society and then shocked it, particularly when in 1692 he brought from London a married woman he called "cousin Brown" and their illegitimate son, and then placed that child with his wife, Jane Ludwell, to be raised in Tidewater Virginia with their legitimate daughters, Frances and Lucy. Even more distressing were the circumstances of Parke's death in Antigua. As governor of the Leeward Islands since 1706 he had debauched a number of the wives and daughters of the settlers, who were consistently frustrated in their efforts to remove him from office. They ultimately formed a mob that brutally murdered him on the steps of the statehouse.[20]

Ever enamored with the prospect of a successful military life, George Washington must have envied Parke's successes, which had been earned comparatively quickly and with seemingly less effort than the colonel had expended against the French and Indian forces. But Parke's story also provided unmistakable evidence that British inequity in the treatment of colonials was long-lived. He had been able to work his way into Marlborough's army and good graces during a residency in England, but he could never rid himself of the stigma of being a colonial. For that reason he was unable to extract from the queen, who so favored him, the governorship he longed for, that of Virginia. He settled instead for a much lesser position in the Leeward Islands. Parke was disgruntled by this rejection, and he took up residence in Antigua with a poor attitude, which perhaps explains the behavior that ultimately ignited his downfall. Having been to Barbados, Washington could easily reconstruct Parke's denouement in his mind. In the early 1770s, when he considered the subject of British discrimination, Washington saw a consistent policy that extended for generations and had even touched his stepchildren's family. This was all the more reason for the colonial to ultimately conclude that nothing short of independence would allow someone in his position to attain the respect he had earned.

If Parke had won a governorship, albeit far from home, Washington had nothing to show for his efforts. Eventually he became sullen about his rejection by the British army. We can assume that his pose for Peale, and the portrait itself, served to remind him of his curt treatment and thereby helped shape his mood on the eve of the Revolution. Only three years after this portrait was painted the disgruntled British subject pictured here would appear in Philadelphia, at the gathering of the Second Continental Congress, in uniform.[21] Fortunately, Peale left us a visual record of the impressive figure to whom the delegates there would award command of the Revolutionary forces.

In the Peale portrait we are reminded of Washington's first military experience, which is important because of its relevance to his later command successes, its provision of one possible basis for his willingness to entertain ideas about independence, and his commitment to the concept of westward expansion. After choosing the martial road toward social advancement Washington had endured severe physical hardships in the Ohio Valley; indeed, he nearly lost his life there, and so his disappointment at the failure of his military career was particularly keen.

Washington had served his monarch in the field, but since his retirement he had been fighting the economic battles necessary to run his estate. By 1772 he had emerged from his various trials with a family and a large, if not particularly profitable, plantation, which one might argue had been his goal twenty years earlier, as well as with the respect of his peers. In Peale's effort we see a man on the prelude of motion, perhaps, as we look back on it, into a new epoch in his life. As a colonel in the Virginia Regiment, Washington had gained more military experience than any other officer in the colonies, which would weigh heavily on his behalf when the command of the Revolutionary forces was being decided. He had also discovered the beauty and value of the Ohio lands and gained a financial interest in their settlement when he was ultimately granted the thousands of acres there that were his due. This appreciation of the "West" would later shape the imagination of the first president and make him among the earliest to envision a grand national destiny intertwined with westward expansion and development.

While Peale might well have made suggestions concerning what type of costume and accoutrements to include, Washington, who always paid a great deal of attention to detail, would have made the final decisions. This is the picture that he wanted hanging in his parlor, visible to the "world" that he inhabited in 1772. As far as he knew this would be his one and only portrait, and so we should not think of it only as his first; we must also consider that from Washington's perspective it was most probably his last. He would have made sure that the artist got it right. Washington would have wanted visitors to his house to remember that he had once had a promising military career, only to be denied its fruition by small-minded bureaucrats. If his days on the frontier had cost him his best years, he had since enjoyed a happy domestic life, built a large plantation, and found some degree of usefulness as a farmer, minor politician, and member of the Virginia gentry. Perhaps the point was also being made that after a decade of family felicity the old fires still burned.

42. Charles Willson Peale, *George Washington,* 1772 and later, oil on canvas, 17¼×14⅞ in. (Courtesy of Historical Society of Pennsylvania)

The status of "gentleman" had traditionally been a function of birth. In the colonies, a land with few titles, a man could presumably become a gentleman through his acquisition of the requisite wealth and social position. For such individuals, however, the behavior expected of a gentleman would have to be consistently exemplified. The portrait's military conception, which invoked one of the last strongholds of rigid hierarchy, offers Washington in a guise where his rank, and therefore his class, are evident. The Peale portrait of 1772 should be seen as a composite, a conglomeration of disparate elements that speak to Washington's successes both as an officer and as a member of the gentry. In this family painting, which we must remember was meant to hang in his home, the sitter, with a subtlety that suggests the "becoming Modesty" for which he was known, illustrates the whole history of his life and makes clear the connection between the soldier of the 1750s and the planter of the present; both would have been recognized to be gentlemen. The social status so clearly defined in the 1757 Wollaston portrait of Martha is reasserted here, thereby making it a worthy companion piece, which in the end was all it was ever meant to be.

Before Charles Willson Peale left Mount Vernon in 1772 he painted a head-and-shoulders version of the larger portrait of Washington (fig. 42). It has never been clear why he produced this second canvas. We might think that it was the artist's first attempt, a study of the head that was a test before beginning his large canvas, except that Peale is not known to have made preliminary studies. Perhaps he wanted a model in case the family ordered another likeness. It is even possible that Peale sensed he might paint again the youthful image of this unusual man who already was an American hero. As it turned out, when producing his later efforts, such as the wonderful miniature of 1776 or the full-size portraits of the late 1770s and 1780s, Peale would have access to the man himself and therefore not need to refer to this model. The artist took the smaller painting home with him, and it remained in his studio for decades until one of his sons, apparently, finished the canvas by sketching in a uniform below the existing head.[22] By that time Washington had achieved international fame as commander of the victorious Continental Army, and consequently the uniform that was added to the canvas was the Revolutionary War type. The Virginia blue coat, the British army gorget, and the unrecognized service to George II that they signified were no longer important. This is the Washington that nineteenth-century Americans wanted to remember.

### The Making of a Virginia Officer

The story of George Washington's exploits in the French and Indian War is still exciting, as it must have been at the time for those who followed the episodes from the safety of their plantations in the Tidewater. Washington perhaps first became enamored with the idea of being a soldier when his half brother Lawrence set out for Cartagena in 1741. Lawrence served with distinction; upon his return he was appointed adjutant of the colony, a post that held the rank of major. His job was to train the county militias, which he did until he fell fatally ill nearly a decade later. Lawrence had been his young brother's friend and role model, and George wanted nothing more than to emulate him; the allure of the military that had so appealed to the elder brother not surprisingly attracted the younger. George Washington would later write to Col. William Fitzhugh that "my inclinations are strongly bent to arms"; after his first combat experience he reported that he "heard Bulletts whistle and believe me there was something charming in the sound."[23]

Life on an isolated Virginia plantation was in its pace and concerns the opposite of service in the military. This contrast was emphasized in a 1758 letter to Washington from John Kirkpatrick, a neighbor in Alexandria. Kirkpatrick complained, "to tell you our Domestick occurrances woud look silly—& ill sute your time to peruse—We have dull Barbecues—and yet Duller Dances—An Election causes a Hubub for a Week or so—& then we are dead a While."[24] Upon his first retirement from the military Washington would learn to savor the tranquility of the planter's domestic existence, which he had ex-

*The Virginia Soldier: 1753–1758*

Horses." The distance, according to Jared Sparks, whose account Chappel would almost certainly have read, was some 560 miles, "in great part over lofty and rugged mountains."[29] The artist depicts a foreboding sky, a portent of the violent weather that the party would encounter upon its return.

Dinwiddie had instructed Washington to "address Yourself to the Half King . . . & other the Sachems of the Six Nations; acquainting them with Your Orders to visit & deliver my Letter to the French commanding Officer." Accordingly, when the party arrived at Logstown in what is now Pennsylvania, Washington engaged an Indian interpreter, John Davison, and then met with the Half King, Tanacharison, to confirm the Seneca chief's allegiance. The Half King had recently visited the commandant of Duquesne's expeditionary force and had told the Frenchman that "the [Ohio] Land does not belong either to one or the other [of the white nations]; but the GREAT BEING above allow'd it to be a Place of residence for us; so Fathers, I desire you to withdraw." According to what Washington recorded in his journal, which would eventually be published and thereby contribute to the clamor for war, the commandant had responded, "I am not affraid of Flies or Musquito's; for Indians are such as those; I tell you down that River I will go, & will build upon it according to my Command."[30]

On the next day Washington addressed a council of the Six Nations, telling them of the governor's "Important" letter and requesting their "Advice & Assistance" in leading his party to the French. He apparently succeeded in renewing their allegiance. Frank Schoonover re-creates this moment in his illustration for Lucy Madison's biography of Washington (fig. 45). The author draws from Washington's journal, which accounts for what accuracy there is in Schoonover's depiction. The setting of "the Long House" at Logstown is probably a fair approximation, as is, in all probability, the mood of the picture. If Washington wears the uniform of the Continental Army that did not yet exist, at least the youthful expression that Schoonover gives the twenty-one-year-old emissary is convincing. Sparks, writing in 1834, had nothing to say about Washington's particular influence over the Indians. Instead, he condemned the way they had been treated by both the French and the English. This historian saw "no difference between [the] professed friends and open enemies" of the Half King, and he criticized "the prerogative of civilization to prey upon the ignorant and defenceless." Washington, who would state that in frontier warfare Indians were worth double their number of whites, would never have called them defenseless. He did, however, think they were ignorant and so "naturally suspicious" that every promise made to them had to be kept, as he told Dinwiddie. Washington exhibited nothing like Sparks's retroactive remorse about the removal of Indians from lands that white men could develop, but in most cases he did want them to be treated honorably. His ambivalent feelings concerning the native population would stay with him throughout his life; during the first presidency, when deciding what should be done with "a small refugee banditti of Cherokees and Shawanese, who can be easily chastised or even extirpated," Washington chose to back off. He wrote Lafayette that "the basis of our proceedings with the Indian Nations has been, and shall be, justice, during the period in which I may have any thing to do in the administration of this government."[31]

The subject of Washington's encounter with Indians in 1753 appealed to artists and writers of the mid-nineteenth century because the displacement of Native Americans from their lands had again become a national issue.[32] The point of interest, presumably, was that the "Father of His Country" had been able to negotiate successfully with the Indians and thereby keep them in line. Here was an example that might well be followed in nineteenth-century America, although the demands of Anglo-America's "Manifest Destiny" would often relegate sincere diplomacy to an inconsequential place in Red/White interactions.

In answer to Dinwiddie's request for their "Advice & Assistance," the Half King and three others from the Six Nations alliance joined Washington's party at Logstown. The group then

45. Frank Schoonover, *The Sachems Sat in Silence After He Had Made an End of Speaking to Consider the Discourse. Then the Half-King Got Up and Spoke,* 1924, published in Lucy Foster Madison, *Washington* (New York, 1925). (Courtesy of Virginia Historical Society)

46. Augustus G. Heaton, *Washington Presenting Governor Dinwiddie's Letter to Jacques Le Gardeur, sieur de Saint-Pierre, 1753,* ca. 1890, oil on canvas, 42×50 in. (Courtesy of Union League of Philadelphia)

traveled some fifty miles north to the French outpost at Venango. Four French officers accompanied them on the final thirty miles to Fort Le Boeuf. Their progress was impeded by "excessive rains, Snows, & bad traveling"; some of the rivers were "so high & rapid" as to be "impassible." Washington's reception by the French commandant is re-created in a canvas painted at the end of the nineteenth century by the Philadelphia artist Augustus Heaton (fig. 46). He depicts the moment when the young Virginian "acquainted [the commandant] with [his] Business, & offer'd [his] Commission & Letter."[33] Van Braam is at Washington's left hand; the Half King is the Indian figure to the rear. Washington confronts an experienced soldier in Jacques Le Gardeur (1701–55), sieur de Saint-Pierre, a man twice his age whose title alone—"Knight of the Military Order of St. Lewis"—impressed Dinwiddie's young emissary. Saint-Pierre had, in fact, arrived at his command only a week before Washington's visit.

As the French officers translated the letter and composed their response, Washington seized the "Opportunity of taking the Dimensions of the Fort, & making what Observations I cou'd." He sketched a plan and described in his journal the various buildings placed within the walls of the fort, in answer to Dinwiddie's instructions that he "diligently . . . enquire into the Numbers & Force of the French on the Ohio, . . . what Forts the French have erected, & where; How they are Garrison'd & appointed." Heaton shows what Washington described as one of the "4 Houses [that] compose the Sides" of the fort. Out-side this house he depicts the "Bastions . . . made of Piles drove into the Ground, & about 12 Feet above" and a few of the more than one hundred soldiers that Washington had estimated were in residence as a reduced winter force; presumably this number would double or triple in the spring.[34] Saint-Pierre, pictured with his secretaries busily at work before him, is shown to be entirely at ease, in full control of the situation and, by extension, his seasoned army. Heaton presents Washington as a figure who is tentative in his action because of his inexperience, yet at this early age already in possession of the qualities that destined him for future greatness.

As much as any single episode of this mission, Washington's survival of the long trip back to Williamsburg earned him the respect of his contemporaries, many of whom eagerly read his published journal. According to that account, while the French commandant pondered Dinwiddie's letter, "the Snow increased very fast, & our Horses daily got weaker," so Washington sent them ahead and decided to travel by canoe. The river meandered and was partly frozen, making the passage to Venango "tedious and very fatiguing." Then "the Cold increas'd very fast, & the Roads were geting much worse by a deep Snow continually Freezing." Anxious to report to the governor, Washington and Gist set out "through the Woods on Foot," only to be forced to walk "all the remaining Part of the Night" to escape "a Party of French Indians." When they reached the Allegheny River, "there was no way for us to get over but upon a Raft."[35]

*The Virginia Soldier: 1753–1758*

The crossing of the Allegheny was a climactic event. At one point Washington even fell into the icy torrent: "We were jamed in the Ice in such a Manner, that we expected every Moment our Raft wou'd sink, & we Perish; I put out my setting Pole, to try to stop the Raft, that the Ice might pass by, when the Rapidity of the Stream through it with so much Violence against the Pole, that it Jirk'd me into 10 Feet Water, but I fortunately saved my Self by catching hold of one of the Raft Logs." Readers of this account could only marvel at how Washington endured cold "so extream severe, that Mr. Gist got all his Fingers, & some of his Toes Froze." In the mid-nineteenth century the episode on the Allegheny River was remembered both because Washington almost perished there and because the crossing of the Allegheny seemed to prefigure the more famous crossing of the Delaware. Each was at Christmastime, in the worst of weather, and was a desperate and heroic act that carried the day. Among the artists who painted this episode was Daniel Huntington, whose canvas was exhibited at the Pennsylvania Academy in 1843 and then published as an engraving in at least five books (fig. 47).[36] Huntington gives us figures who look rather like Roman statues, which was how many Americans in the nineteenth century wanted to remember the Revolutionaries, and especially Washington. For the reader of Washington's journal, the artist provides elements that carry the story of the raft ride from beginning to end. At the left is the single hatchet (always a resonant symbol where Washington is concerned) with which the raft was completed after an entire day's work. The valuable papers (the commandant's letter of response and the two journals) are stored in knapsacks lying on the raft. Washington holds the pole by which he was catapulted into the freezing river. To the right is the island where the pair was forced to camp for the night until they could cross the next morning, on what would become a frozen mass of ice.

Mason Locke Weems had said that "there was a hand unseen that effected [Washington's] escape" from "perishing in the ice" of the Allegheny. In the *Columbian Magazine,* one of the many periodicals where Huntington's image appeared, the reader was asked to consider that Washington might have drowned during this crossing: "What a change might have been wrought, by the event of a few minutes, in the whole destinies of this republic."[37] As Heaton had done with the scene at Fort Le Boeuf, Huntington looks at the return from the Ohio with confident hindsight and reminds his viewers of what could have happened to their eventual leader. In the 1750s, however, these episodes were significant only in the way that Washington had hoped for when he first volunteered; his successful completion of his assignment, and his reconnoitering of the French forces

47. D. Kimberly, after Daniel Huntington, *Washington Crossing the Allegheny River,* ca. 1844, engraving, 7⅛×6¾ in. (Courtesy of Mount Vernon Ladies' Association, Willard-Budd Collection)

and works, would cause the enemy incursions into the Ohio Valley to be taken all the more seriously by the Virginia politicians back home. As important, on this journey he established his reputation for reliability and launched a promising military career.

Soon after crossing the Allegheny, Washington was safe at Christopher Gist's house near the Monongahela River. The remainder of the trip to Williamsburg was without incident. The tenor of the letter from the French commandant to Governor Dinwiddie was disappointing but not unexpected. The French would not retreat. Saint-Pierre even suggested that Washington's trip was pointless, because he should have been ordered "to proceed to Canada" to confer with the governor, Duquesne, whose orders "I have a firm resolution to follow."[38] But the mission was as much about reconnaissance as diplomacy. Washington brought back in his journal evidence that incriminated the French. Dinwiddie immediately published his account in Williamsburg, and soon it was reprinted in newspapers throughout the colonies.

To the reader of Washington's journal there could be little doubt about the intentions of the French in the Ohio Valley. The frontispiece to the London edition is a "Map of the West-

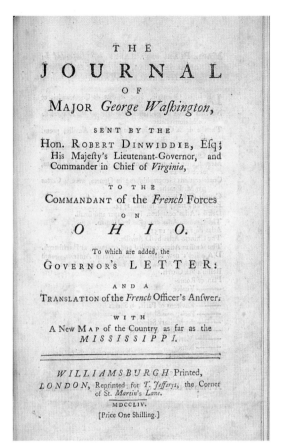

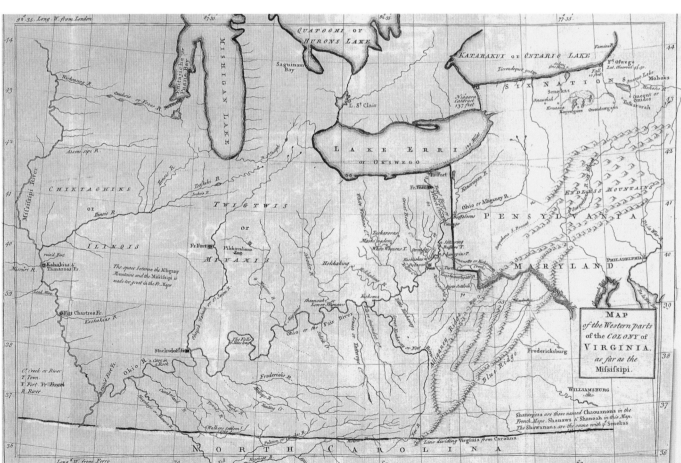

48. *The Journal of Major George Washington* (London, 1754). Below is the "map" that was included as the frontispiece. (Courtesy of Virginia Historical Society)

*The Virginia Soldier: 1753–1758*

ern parts of the Colony of Virginia as far as the Mississippi" (fig. 48). We are thereby reminded of the English sense of the perimeter of their huge colony; within the borders are plotted the forts that had been erected by the encroaching French. More evidence of their machinations is found in the text, which includes such stories as that of the Seneca chief Monacatoocha, who had reported to Washington that the French had boasted to "assuredly expect them [back] in the Spring, with a far greater Number" and that they "expected to fight the English three Years, (as they suppos'd there would be some Attempts made to stop them) in which Time they shou'd Conquer." Washington himself recounted how the French officers at Venango, after "they dos'd themselves pretty plentifully with [wine]," admitted their intention to take the Ohio. Even the careful Saint-Pierre "told me the Country belong'd to them, that no English Man had a right to trade upon them Waters; & that he had Orders to make every Person Prisoner that attempted it on the Ohio or the Waters of it." Washington concluded the journal with typical understatement. The trip was "as fatiguing a Journey as it is possible to conceive, rendered so by excessive bad Weather." Those severe conditions, however, were what made his effort especially heroic. In response, the House of Burgesses awarded him fifty pounds "to testify our Approbation of his Proceedings on his Journey to the Ohio."[39] With so good a record of conduct, Washington could well expect to be awarded a prominent position in the colony's retaliatory forces.

Dinwiddie moved quickly into action, spurred by the report that only the cold of winter was holding back a massive French incursion into the Ohio. He sent the journal, along with Washington's map of the Ohio region and plan of Fort Le Boeuf, to the Board of Trade in London as evidence that accounts of French encroachment were accurate and that further intrusion was imminent and must be met. He persuaded his own Council to recommend the raising of troops from the Shenandoah Valley counties of Augusta and Frederick. Dinwiddie was soon authorized by the crown to build a militia, but to meet this crisis the burgesses provided only ten thousand pounds, which was insufficient to supply an army. Consequently, recruiting efforts met resistance from Virginia farmers who had little interest in challenging a distant enemy in lands where only the Ohio Company had a vested interest. In addition, militia units were not traditionally empowered to leave the colony, even to pursue a French army into unsurveyed regions that might belong to Pennsylvania. Dinwiddie solved this dilemma by forming a volunteer army, which he believed would be more than a match for the smaller French force, even though that unit was made up of regulars. To encourage enlistments he promised recruits a grant of two hundred thousand acres—the same size parcel set aside for the Ohio Company only five years before—

on the eastern side of the Ohio River, to be divided among them at the conclusion of their successful service. Thus began the Virginia Regiment and Washington's lengthy involvement with the so-called Ohio bounty lands.

Here also was the start of Washington's dissatisfaction with both his low pay and his low rank; his pay was too little to advance him economically, and as a colonial he was subordinate in rank to all regular British officers. The former is a subject that occupies much of his correspondence with Dinwiddie in 1754; the latter surfaced when an independent company of the British army from South Carolina, commanded by Capt. James Mackay, arrived in June to join Dinwiddie's forces and serve beside Washington's Virginia Regiment. Washington would continue to be annoyed by such circumstances throughout the war. Both represented bad situations that even his best efforts could not entirely rectify.

Because of Washington's youth, command of the Virginia forces was initially given to Joshua Fry, a fifty-four-year-old veteran of varied service in the colony, including surveying and mapmaking. But in late May 1754, en route to his command, Fry fell from his horse and died of his injuries. The authority over the Virginia Regiment then passed to Washington, who had already been in the region two months. While Washington had been anxiously awaiting Fry's arrival, however, the French had taken dramatic action. They had seized the "Forks of the Ohio" (where the Monongahela and Allegheny Rivers meet to form the Ohio River, the site of present-day Pittsburgh) and established a fort there that they named for Governor Duquesne.[40] The French detachment at the Forks was described to Washington as made up of "upwards of one Thousand Men, who came from Vena[n]go with Eighteen pieces of Cannon, Sixty Battoes, and three Hundred Canoes." This was the army that had been anticipated on the Ohio in the spring. Dinwiddie had directed Washington "to act on the Difensive," though he could "kill & destroy" any who obstructed his work or interrupted "our Settlemts."[41] But in the wake of the French advance, Washington would feel compelled to take the offensive if his troops were to survive against such overwhelming odds.

The year 1754 is remembered for two major events in the Ohio Valley. The first occurred when Washington's force attacked a French party and killed its commanding officer, the sieur de Jumonville. This initial combat between French and English forces, more than any other incident in America or abroad, initiated the Seven Years' War. It also brought about, within a month, a French retaliatory strike that forced Washington to surrender to his enemies at the outpost he had aptly named Fort Necessity, which was located at Great Meadows in what is now southwestern Pennsylvania. Today these events are generally seen as the nadir of Washington's military career.

But at the time, and to the nineteenth-century chroniclers of Washington's life, both were viewed differently; Washington somehow escaped fault for both of these incidents.

In a long letter to Dinwiddie following the first incident, Washington devotes the opening four pages to his complaints about low pay. Only then does he mention what Horace Walpole in England would describe as "the volley of a young Virginian in the backwoods of America [that] set the world on fire" (fig. 49).[42] His defeat of a small detachment of French troops, whose commander, Joseph Coulon de Villiers, sieur de Jumonville, was killed in a skirmish that lasted only fifteen minutes, would have wide repercussions. The French were quick to point out that the English had been the aggressors in what turned out to be the first clash of a lengthy, costly war.

For the previous six weeks the Indian allies of the English had pestered Washington to join them in attacking the French. In mid-April the Half King told Washington, "We are now ready to fall upon them. . . . If you do not come to our Assistance now, we are intirely undone, and imagine we shall never meet together again." Four days before the fateful encounter with Jumonville the Half King had again agitated Washington, advising that "the French Army is set out to meet M. George Washington, I exhort you, my Brethren, to guard against them; for they intend to fall on the first English they meet." Ultimately the Virginian was persuaded that if he did not take the initiative, he would lose both his Indian allies and a strategic advantage in an inevitable battle. As Washington explained to Dinwiddie, "I thereupon in conjunction with the Half King & Monacatoocha, formd a disposion to attack [them] on all sides, which we accordingly did and after an Engagement of abt 15 Minutes we killd 10, wounded one and took 21 Prisoner's, amongst those that were killd was Monsieur De Jumonville the Commander." He added, "these Officers pretend they were coming on an Embassy, but the absurdity of this pretext is too glaring."[43]

The French claimed that Jumonville had left Fort Duquesne as an ambassador. He was to deliver a "summons" directing the English to vacate the Ohio Valley, much as Washington had done

49. George Washington to Robert Dinwiddie, 29 May 1754. (Courtesy of Virginia Historical Society)

*The Virginia Soldier: 1753–1758*

with his letter from Dinwiddie six months earlier. The English viewpoint, as recorded by Washington, was that Jumonville's mission was "to get intelligence." He had "sent Spies to Reconnoitre our Camp," and so large a party as "36 Men" would have been unnecessary for a diplomatic mission. Jumonville had encamped "within 5 Miles of us witht delivering his Ambassy, or acquainting me with it." And the Half King believed that "they never designd to have come to us but in a hostile manner, and if we were so foolish as to let them go again, he never would assist us in taking another of them."[44] Of course, Washington's ostensibly diplomatic mission of six months earlier had also been "to get intelligence." The other points were perhaps better taken.

If Washington's judgment in attacking Jumonville's party would be questioned years later, nothing of the sort happened at the time, at least not in Virginia or the other American colonies. Like his trip to the French commandant, this was viewed as a heroic accomplishment that enhanced the young colonel's reputation. Dinwiddie immediately applauded the action in a letter to Washington of 1 June: "Mr Gist brot Yr Letter & the very agreeable Acct of Yr Killing [Jumonville] & taking Monsr Le Force & his whole Party of 35 Men on wch Success I heartily congratulate You, as it may give a Testimony to the Inds. that the French are not invincible wn fairly engagd with the English; but hope the good Spirits of Yr Soldiers will not tempt You to make any hazardous Attempts agst a too numerous Enemy" (fig. 50). Washington's first biographers were little troubled by the political implications of the episode. John Marshall pointed out that Washington meant to anticipate a possible attack by the French and mentions that Indians had served as his guides through a "dark and rainy night." Weems dismissed the violence of the encounter in a sentence, saying only, "This officer was killed, and all his men taken prisoners." He looked beyond the brief skirmish to the larger campaign, where Washington demonstrated exceptional fortitude: "From these prisoners, he obtained undoubted intelligence, that the French troops on the Ohio, consisted of upwards of a thousand regulars, and many hundreds of Indians. But notwithstanding

this disheartening intelligence, he still pressed on undauntedly against the enemy, and, at a place called the Great Meadows, built a fort, which he called Fort Necessity." Jared Sparks would later follow in the same vein, editorializing about both the incident and the way it was interpreted abroad:

> No transaction in the life of Washington has been so much misrepresented, or so little understood, as this skirmish with Jumonville. It being the first conflict of arms in the war, a notoriety was given to it, particularly in Europe, altogether disproportioned to its importance. When the intelligence of the skirmish with Jumonville got to Paris, it was officially published by the government, in connexion with a memoir and various papers, and his death was called a murder. It was said, that, while bearing a summons as a civil messenger, without any hostile intentions, he was waylaid and assassinated.

It should be pointed out that Sparks had traveled to England to examine Dinwiddie's papers and satisfy himself as to the truth of the matter. He triumphantly announced that the documents "afford not only a complete vindication of the conduct of Colonel Washington in this affair, but show that it met with the unqualified approbation of the governor and legislature of Virginia, and of the British ministry." Recounting the same arguments that Washington had recorded in his diary and offered to Dinwiddie, Sparks concluded that any competent officer would have taken the same action: "The mode in which [Jumonville] approached the English camp [does not] indicate that he came on an errand of peace. He was at the head of an armed force, he sent out spies in advance, concealed himself and his party two days in an obscure place near the camp, and despatched messengers with intelligence to his commander at the fort. These were strong evidences of a hostile intention; and, had Colonel Washington not regarded them in that light, he would have been justly censurable for ignorance or neglect of duty."[45]

As Washington had anticipated, the skirmish with Jumonville brought about a reprisal from the French army stationed at Fort Duquesne. The combined forces of Washington and James Mackay were defeated by that larger company at Fort Neces-

50. Robert Dinwiddie to George Washington, 1 June 1754. (Courtesy of Virginia Historical Society)

sity. This battle, however, lasted all day, under a driving rain, during which the colonial troops exchanged fire with the French and Indian forces and repelled their repeated attacks. At eight in the evening, the French commander, Louis Coulon de Villiers, the brother of the slain Jumonville, allowed the besieged colonial forces to surrender. Greatly outnumbered and exhausted, with their little remaining powder wet, their food supply depleted, and no hope of reinforcement, Washington and Mackay had little choice but to accept the conditions offered by the French.

The terms of surrender were highly favorable to the colonials in all respects but one. The army was allowed to leave the fort honorably, "with our Drums beating and our Colours flying," but Washington and Mackay were compelled to sign a document of capitulation wherein they admitted that Jumonville had been "assassinated." In the opening paragraph the French state that their only intention in taking Fort Necessity was "to revenge the Assassination of one of our Officers, who with his Guard were Bearers of a Sumons," and "to prevent any Settlements being made on the Lands" of the Ohio, which belonged to the French king. In an English copy, the word *assassination* was begun but then replaced by the word *Killing* (fig. 51). With little understanding of French vocabulary, and perhaps misguided by an inept translator, Washington possibly had no idea that his signature could one day be misrepresented as a confession that he had murdered a diplomatic emissary.

Upon their return to Williamsburg, Washington and Mackay explained their actions to the governor; an account of this engagement was soon published in the *Virginia Gazette*. The commanders reported that "from the Numbers of the Enemy, and our Situation, we could not hope for Victory." This explanation was never doubted. Two months later, the pair was honored by the House of Burgesses: "Ordered, That the Thanks of this House be given to Colo. George Washington, Captn Mackay of his Majesty's independent company, and the Officers under his Command . . . for their late gallant and brave Behaviour in the Defense of their Country."[46] Some historians have cited the defeat at Fort Necessity as evidence of ineptitude and argued that Washington's qualifications to command the Continental Army were, in fact, unimpressive, although they were admittedly better than anyone else's in the colonies. To his contemporaries, however, as well as to observers in the nineteenth century, this

stand against the French only enhanced Washington's reputation.

Weems ranked the heroic defense at Fort Necessity as one of the great moments in the entire history of warfare: "Never did the true Virginia valour shine more gloriously than on this trying occasion—to see 300 young fellows—commanded by a smooth-faced boy—all unaccustomed to the terrors of war—far from home—and from all hope of help—shut up in a dreary wilderness—and surrounded by five times their num-

51. Capitulation at Fort Necessity (surrender document), 3 July 1754. (Courtesy of the Library of Virginia)

*The Virginia Soldier: 1753–1758*

ber of savage foes, yet without sign of fear, preparing for mortal combat! Scarcely since the days of Leonidas and his three hundred deathless Spartans, had the sun beheld its equal." Weems was even able to transform what was clearly a defeat for Washington into a kind of heroic victory: "For nine glorious hours, salamander-like, enveloped in smoke and flames, they sustained the attack of the enemy's whole force, and laid two hundred of them dead on the spot! Discouraged by such desperate resistance, the French general, the Count de Villiers, sent in a flag to Washington, highly extolling his gallantry, and offering him the most honourable terms. It was stipulated, that Washington and his little band of heroes, should march away with all the honours of war, and carry with them their military stores and baggage." If less effusive, Sparks was just as commendatory: "Although as yet a youth, with small experience, unskilled in war, and relying on his own resources, [Washington] had behaved with the prudence, address, courage, and firmness of a veteran commander. Rigid in discipline, but sharing the hardships and solicitous for the welfare of his soldiers, he had secured their obedience and won their esteem amidst privations, sufferings, and perils, that have seldom been surpassed."[47] Sparks was apparently the source John Gadsby Chapman consulted in 1842 when he depicted an episode from the Fort Necessity campaign. This was soon after Chapman had painted his large mural of *The Baptism of Pocahontas* for the rotunda of the U.S. Capitol. In that room hang several Revolutionary War scenes devised by John Trumbull, who had recreated most of Washington's memorable victories with the Continental Army and had, in effect, closed those subjects to other artists. Trumbull's monopoly may have inspired Chapman to consider the engagement at Fort Necessity, and Sparks's detailed account of the episode provided him with sufficient background information.

Chapman's *Retreat to Fort Necessity, June 1754* was a large canvas (33½ by 48 inches), which he exhibited at the National Academy of Design in New York in 1843. It apparently was never reproduced as a print, and the canvas is now lost. One critic who saw the painting at the National Academy exhibition called it Chapman's masterpiece in the "historical landscape" genre; another praised the artist's fidelity, especially in his ability to capture the green foliage of June.[48] The Fort Necessity canvas was a major painting for Chapman; it was ultimately sold to the American Art Union in 1848 for the large sum of three hundred dollars. We can assume that Chapman would not have undertaken such a piece had he not viewed the episode as a particularly heroic event in the life of Washington.

Chapman chose not to show the defeat nor even the battle at Fort Necessity, but rather the gallant retreat to that spot. After the French had seized the Forks of the Ohio, Washington decided to advance only as far as Redstone Creek where it meets the Monongahela River thirty-seven miles to the south,

and there raise a fort. On the way to Redstone Creek he had passed Great Meadows and selected it as a site where he might choose to encounter the French. On 27 May he wrote to Dinwiddie, "we have with Natures assistance made a good Intrenchment and by clearing the Bushes out of these Meadows prepar'd a charming field for an Encounter." Following the skirmish with Jumonville the fort was built.[49]

As the French seemed to delay their reprisal, Washington renewed the offensive to Redstone Creek, only to stop short and return to Fort Necessity when Monacatoocha reported what he had learned from French deserters: the French would soon attack the colonial forces with eight hundred of their own men and four hundred Indians. Washington's native allies demanded that he fall back to the defensible position of the fort at Great Meadows. And so began a heroic retreat, as described by Sparks, over a twelve-mile stretch of rough and mountainous terrain: "The horses were few and weak, and a severe service was imposed on the men, who were obliged to bear heavy burdens, and drag nine swivels [artillery pieces] over a broken road. Colonel Washington set a worthy example to his officers, by lading his horse with public stores, [and] going on foot, and paying the soldiers a reward for carrying his baggage." We know that Chapman focused on the column of soldiers led by Washington, for in his journal he refers to the painting not as the "retreat" but pointedly as the "march" to Fort Necessity. He must have also taken the setting from Sparks, who offered both a map and a written account (fig. 52). "Fort Necessity was situate in a level meadow, above two hundred and fifty yards broad, and covered with long grass and low bushes. The foot of the nearest hills came within one hundred yards of the fort, and at one place within sixty yards. The space between the fort and hills was open and smooth, the bushes having been cleared away. The fort itself was an irregular square, each side measuring thirty-five yards, with a trench partly finished on two sides. The entrances were guarded by three bastions." Chapman no doubt would have followed Sparks's error with regard to the shape of the fort, which was not square but circular, with a small house at the center in which to store provisions. (Sparks was clearly unaware of contemporary accounts of the site, which in 1952 were confirmed by archaeologists.)[50] In any case, he would have emphasized the heroism of the still youthful colonel, who would again make the most of a bad situation.

A little more than a decade after the event, Washington was able to "recapture" this territory and thereby assuage, if only symbolically, any regrets he might have had about the surrender of Fort Necessity. In 1767, in advance of the settlement of the Ohio bounty lands, he acquired title to more than two hundred acres around Great Meadows, including the site of his famous encampment.[51] Never comfortable with failure, he bought this ground and thereby, in the only way possible, erased from the ledger his less than successful adventures there.

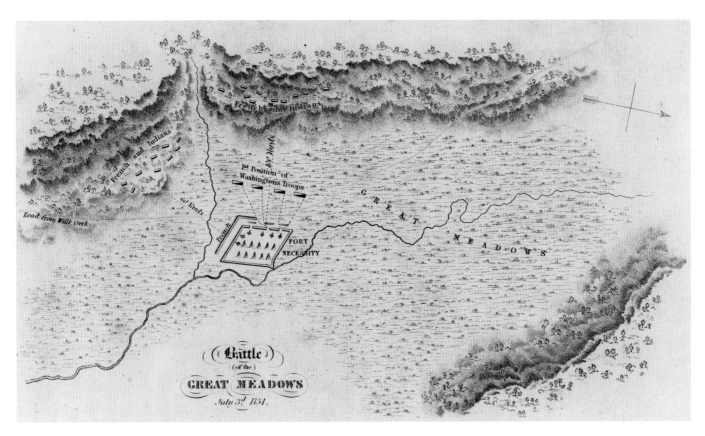

52. G. W. Boynton, *Battle of the Great Meadows, July 3rd, 1754,* engraving, published in Jared Sparks, *The Writings of George Washington* (Boston, 1837). (Courtesy of Virginia Historical Society)

## Service with Braddock and the Defeat at Monongahela

Undaunted by the rout of his inadequate army at Fort Necessity, Dinwiddie within weeks resolved "that the Forces shou'd immediately march over the Allegany Mountains, either to disposses the French of their Fort, or build a Fort." The governor ordered Washington to "get Your regiment compleated to 300 Men" and "march directly" to the north, before the winter season. Washington could only respond, perhaps with a degree of sarcasm, that "no more than ten Men" would follow him and that "soldier's are deserting constantly." When the governor decided to enlarge the army to ten companies, each to be commanded by a captain, Washington's patience was finally exhausted. Such a reorganization would actually reduce his rank and influence. This was unacceptable, and he resigned from the military. However, no such army was ever raised, and the Ohio Valley remained silent for nearly a year, until a sizable British army under the command of Maj. Gen. Edward Braddock arrived in the colony in the spring of 1755. Washington "wrote a congratulatory Letter" to Braddock upon his "safe arrival," and the general—who was informed of the events at Forts Le Boeuf and Necessity—invited the Virginian to join his expedition and share his knowledge of "the Country, Indians, &ca." To circumvent problems of rank, Braddock placed the colonial on his immediate staff; as an aide to the general he could command the British regulars. (This, presumably, is when Washington acquired the gorget worn in the 1772 Peale portrait.) Washington served Braddock without pay and with no immediate hope of a commission. He told Robert Orme, another of the general's aides, that his goal was "to attain a small degree of knowledge in the Military Art." He spoke of earning "regard & esteem" when he explained this move to powerful political figures in the colony such as John Robinson and Carter Burwell, who had taken an interest in his military career. Washington was more clear to his brother, writing that this was an opportunity to form "an acquaintance which may be serviceable hereafter, if I can find it worth while pushing my Fortune in the Military way." In the end, Washington's experiences of 1755 would advance his military career, although of course differently than he expected since no one anticipated that the Braddock expedition would end in disaster for the army and the death of the general, or provide a new means of glorification for the young and rising Virginian.[52]

Jared Sparks described the defeat of Braddock's army as "one of the most remarkable events in American history," because "there was the most sanguine anticipation . . . of its entire success." Accordingly, "the effect produced on the public mind was like the shock of an earthquake, unexpected and astounding."[53]

*The Virginia Soldier: 1753–1758*

He would have been more precise if he had added that even Washington did not imagine this possibility. Later analysts would come to blame Braddock not as much for his stupidity in marching into a trap as for his ignoring the warnings of his young Virginian aide. But, in fact, there was no critical advice offered by Washington at this juncture. No one, including Washington, who had been defeated by a larger force at Fort Necessity, anticipated that it would not be the size and might of an army that would be the crucial factors in this particular wilderness engagement. Although this expedition was a costly learning experience for the Anglo-Americans, Washington gained a great deal, and, unlike Braddock, he and his reputation survived it.

Midway on the march toward Fort Duquesne, which was Braddock's objective, Washington became so severely ill with a fever that he was incapacitated for two weeks. He managed to proceed, however, with the rear guard of the army. Before his illness he had been able to confer with Braddock, and in fact the two had "frequent disputes" about the "Honour and Honesty" of Virginians. Washington was more than annoyed that the general blamed the entire colony for the failure of individual agents to provide the army with a sufficient number of wagons and horses. Indeed, Braddock took the opportunity to praise Pennsylvanians for helping in this regard. The general had asked the Virginian his "prive Opinn" about the expedition and in turn was "urgd . . . in the warmest terms . . . to push on" with all speed, carrying from the general's slow and unwieldy baggage train only the equipment that was absolutely necessary. Washington's reasoning was that "if we cd credt our Intelligence, the French were weak at the Forks but hourly expectd reinfts" of some nine hundred men. Braddock heeded the advice: "This was a Scheme that took, & it was detd that the Genl, with 1200 Chosen Men and Officers of all the difffert Corps, . . . with such a certain number of Wagons as the Train wd absolutely require, should March as soon as things could be got in readiness." Washington was ultimately discouraged, however, "when I found, that instead of pushing on with vigour, . . . they were halting to Level every Mold Hill, & to erect Bridges over every brook." In the end those delays made little difference, and Washington's advice, though in this case sound, proved insignificant. It was not the anticipated large French force that would defeat the British.[54]

The point to be made today, which was often steadfastly denied in the nineteenth century, was that Braddock followed what counsel Washington was able to offer. Also, to the general's credit, he regularly sent out flanking parties to protect the army as it marched. Washington himself recorded that there had been occasional Indian attacks ("several Men [were] Scalp'd") that were done "to retard the March," but, like Braddock, he was "certain they have not sufficient strength to make

head against the whole [army]." Washington's sense that these peripheral Indian attacks could not slow down, much less defeat, such a large, well-equipped force was, as it turned out, entirely wrong. Years later, in an apparent effort to control how history would remember his role in this disaster, Washington spoke of his attempt "to impress the General, & the principal Officers around him, with the necessity of opposing the nature of his defence, to the mode of attack which, more than probably, he would experience from the *Canadian* French, and their *Indians* on his March through the Mountains & covered Country." It is at this point, in 1786, that we learn of his wise tactical advice, and that the British commanders were "so prepossessed . . . in favor of *regularity & discipline* and in such absolute contempt were *these people held,* that the admonition was suggested in vain." At the time, however, Washington seems to have held the Indians in as much contempt as did Braddock and his staff, and we have no evidence that he advised anything but more speed in their march toward Fort Duquesne. At best, he did not press the issue of tactics because he, too, felt that Braddock's army could not be defeated, regardless of how it maneuvered.[55]

Braddock's biggest problem was that his large force of more than two thousand men (of which some fourteen hundred pushed ahead), which was accompanied by heavy artillery pulled by teams of as many as nine horses to each piece, could stretch to a length of four to five miles as it made its way through the Ohio wilderness. With good timing and the right terrain, a smaller force could attack and obliterate one end of the army before the other end could come to its defense. This is what would happen at the Monongahela River; to the surprise of all on the British side, it was the enemy who chose to initiate an early engagement and thereby prevent Braddock from ever reaching Fort Duquesne and deploying his full force and its powerful artillery.

In the mid-nineteenth century Junius Brutus Stearns, as Chapman had before him, painted a series of canvases celebrating Washington's life. Stearns re-created Washington's military and political careers, alluded to his devotion to his family and interest in farming, and depicted the scene of Washington's death, all as a means to commemorate a life lived long and well. For his picture of Washington as a soldier Stearns did not select an episode from the Revolutionary War, but instead, perhaps surprisingly, depicted the defeat of Braddock's forces at the Monongahela River (fig. 53). Stearns may have been drawn to this subject from the French and Indian War because its centennial was fast approaching, and because other artists had tended to overlook it.

In his attempt to familiarize himself with the episode of Braddock's defeat, Stearns would have found little help in Weems's *Life of Washington;* this account is incomplete as well

53. Junius Brutus Stearns, *Washington as a Captain in the French and Indian War*, 1849–56, oil on canvas, 37½×54 in. (Courtesy of Virginia Museum of Fine Arts, Richmond, Va., gift of Edgar William and Bernice Chrysler Garbisch)

as incorrect. Weems called Braddock an "epauletted madman" because he failed to heed Washington's advice about the tactics of Indian warfare. (We note here the pervasiveness of Washington's 1786 version of events.) He then fabricated that Washington's rangers "flew each to his tree, like the Indians" and engaged in a tomahawk fight.[56] In contrast, Jared Sparks researched the battle in considerable detail, even traveling to the site and to the war department in Paris to locate French records of the episode. Sparks presents a much fuller account, complete with a map of the battleground.

Both Sparks and Stearns saw Monongahela as a critical episode in American history because it established a crucial element of Washington's reputation. Admittedly, the Braddock enterprise was "almost unparalleled for its disasters, and the universal disappointment and consternation it occasioned," Sparks wrote, "yet the fame and character of Washington were greatly enhanced" by his valorous performance and his survival of so bloody a battle. The defeat of Braddock was, to Sparks, tantamount to a victory for Washington: "His intrepidity and good conduct were lauded by his companions in arms, and

proclaimed from province to province. Contrary to his will, and in spite of his efforts, he had gathered laurels from the defeat and ruin of others." Sparks's point was that this personal success positioned Washington where he could advance to even greater achievements. To this interpretation Sparks tied a second notion that would have made even less sense to colonial Virginians; he suggested that the outcome of the battle was influenced by intervention from above. Washington was somehow divinely favored and therefore protected in battle because he was predestined to be the protagonist of future world-historical events: "Had the expedition been successful, these laurels would have adorned the brow of his superiors. . . . For himself, for his country, for mankind, therefore, this catastrophe, in appearance so calamitous and so deeply deplored at the time, should unquestionably be considered as a wise and beneficent dispensation of Providence." Washington himself may have even believed that he had been spared through "the miraculous care of Providence," as he wrote to his brother John Augustine after the battle.[57] For Stearns and his audience, such a sanctified event was a worthy subject for a painting.

*The Virginia Soldier: 1753–1758*

Before Sparks compiled his account, no one on the English side understood how Braddock's seemingly invincible force had been defeated. Washington had always thought that the enemy numbered only about three hundred, but Sparks found that there were in fact almost nine hundred men, most of whom were Indians.[58] It was widely reported after the battle that the French and Indian force was largely invisible to the English because they were hidden, but the manner of their hiding, and how they came to be there at all, was not known. Sparks uncovered in France several accounts of how the attack actually unfolded.

The initiative originated with a captain at Fort Duquesne, a M. de Beaujeu, who challenged his Indian allies to join in attacking the huge English army before it reached the Forks of the Ohio and could set in place its artillery. Beaujeu's intention was to strike the English as they forded the Monongahela, but as he approached his scouts discovered that Braddock's army was nearly there. The French and Indians then decided instead to lay in wait just beyond the river. This, by chance, proved a better site because of the peculiar lay of the land. When Sparks visited the battlefield he discovered what no one had previously reported: the English army's path was flanked by long, parallel ravines, each eight to ten feet deep and hidden by trees and long grass. In these the enemy force had been able to hide and protect themselves from both sight and gunfire. Granted, the element of surprise was the most important factor in the battle, but a critical advantage was also afforded by the terrain. After hiding themselves in the available ravines, the Indians and French quickly found that they might be more successful than they had imagined would be possible. The topography of the Monongahela delta contributed to the panic that caused the English soldiers to kill many of their own in the ensuing cross fire. As Washington reported to Dinwiddie, "it is supposed that we left 300 or more dead in the Field; abt that number we brought of[f] wounded; and it is imagin'd (I believe with great justice too) that two thirds of both those number's receiv'd their shott from our own cowardly dogs of Soldier's, who gatherd themselves into a body contrary to orders 10 or 12 deep, woud then level, Fire, & shoot down the Men before them." Washington's estimate was low, for in all more than nine hundred of the fourteen hundred English and colonial soldiers were killed or wounded.[59]

In addition to his narrative, Sparks provided his readers with a map or "Plan" that delineated how the battle was fought (fig. 54). Stearns no doubt consulted these sources; in turn, they allow the modern viewer to make sense of his painting (see fig. 53). We stand before the canvas as if we are members of the Anglo-American forces, whose advance party of three hundred soldiers has moved into the distance, up a wooded incline. The entire army has crossed the river. It is one o'clock in the af-

ternoon. Suddenly, the enemy attacks from the front and then from both flanks. The first action brings about such panic among the advance party that no efforts can rally the soldiers to order. Sparks described a scene of "carnage almost unparalleled in the annals of modern warfare." Braddock, according to Sparks, had five horses shot from under him and then was severely wounded, as were all his aides-de-camp, except one. It fell to Washington to distribute the general's orders. According to Capt. Robert Orme's account, Washington behaved with "the greatest courage and resolution" throughout the ordeal. Stearns shows him directing his Virginia soldiers, who are dressed in buckskins, to return fire to the viewer's left. These are the men who fought valiantly against a hidden enemy for nearly three hours and were therefore unlike their British counterparts, whose training made them virtually useless in this conflict. Sparks said that the latter were marched in "platoons and columns, as if they had been manoeuvring on the plains of Flanders," as is shown at the right. Washington made the contrast between corps even more vivid. He reported that the British regulars "behaved with more cowardice than it is possible to conceive" and ran "as Sheep pursued by dogs," while "the Virginia Troops shewd a good deal of Bravery, & were near all killd." Stearns also reminds his viewers that not all the Indians stayed invisible, as evidenced by the two fallen figures in the left foreground. In Sparks's words, some "were killed in venturing out [from the ravines] to take scalps." But for the most part the enemy stayed out of sight; like the British soldiers, we cannot see them, and we, too, are confounded and frightened by their invisibility.[60]

Fifteen years after the battle, when Washington revisited the vicinity to investigate the promised Ohio bounty lands, he was met by an Indian who had fought against the British at Monongahela and had become convinced during the battle that Washington was invincible. This report was apparently first mentioned by Weems and then was popularized by George Washington Parke Custis in his 1827 play *The Indian Prophecy*. Custis wrote that Dr. James Craik, Washington's companion on a later trip to the Ohio and longtime physician and friend, told him the story of how an aged chief, on hearing of Washington's return to the region, traveled many miles to see again the soldier who could not be killed. Sparks also recounts the incident with the then "aged and venerable chief": "During the battle of the Monongahela, he [the chief] had singled him [Washington] out as a conspicuous object, fired his rifle at him many times, and directed his young warriors to do the same, but to his utter astonishment none of their balls took effect. He was then persuaded, that the youthful hero was under the special guardianship of the Great Spirit, and ceased to fire at him any longer. He was now come to pay homage to the man, who was the particular favorite of Heaven, and who could never die

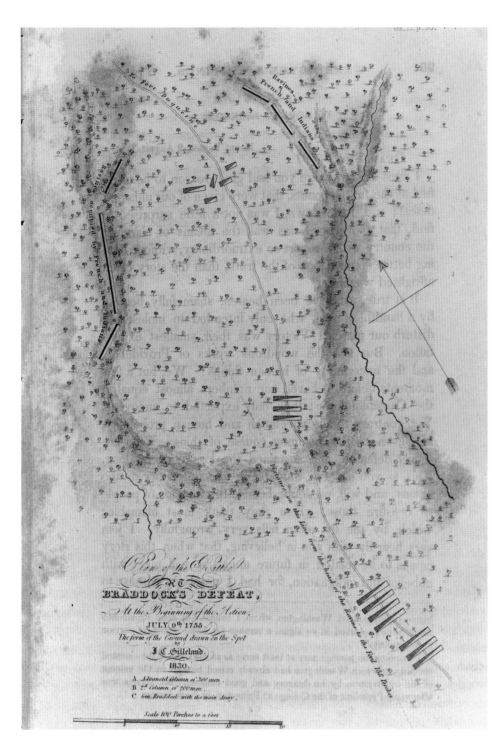

Plan of the Battle
of
BRADDOCK'S DEFEAT,
At the Beginning of the Action,
JULY 9th 1755.
The form of the Ground drawn on the Spot
by
J. C. Gilleland.
1830.

A Advanced column of 300 men.
B 2d Column of 200 men.
C Gen. Braddock with the main Army.

Scale 100 Perches to a Inch

54. *Plan of the Battle, Braddock's Defeat, at the Beginning of the Action, July 9th, 1755, the Form of the Ground Drawn on the Spot by J. C. Gilleland, 1830,* engraving, published in Jared Sparks, *The Writings of George Washington* (Boston, 1837). (Courtesy of Virginia Historical Society)

in battle." Weems even specified the number of shots fired at Washington—seventeen—and concluded that "there was some invisible hand that turned aside the bullets."[61] Many mid-nineteenth-century viewers of Stearns's painting would have known this myth and would have appreciated the conspicuous pose given to the mounted figure of Washington. Stearns was probably accurate, however, in depicting Washington in this way. As one of the few unwounded officers it would have been his duty to lead by example and to place himself where he could be seen by his troops, even if it put him in peril.

Washington's survival at Monongahela was in fact remarkable. First of all, there was the matter of his illness: "I was not half recoverd from a violent illness that [had] confin'd me to my Bed, and a Waggon, for above 10 Days; I am still in a weak and Feeble cond[itio]n," he wrote to his mother after the battle. He later recounted that he was so weak and sore that he had "mounted his horse on cushions." He calmly added, "I luckily escapd witht a wound, tho' I had four Bullets through my Coat, and two Horses shot under me." Washington had escaped at least six bullets, each of which had nearly found its mark.[62]

*The Virginia Soldier: 1753–1758*

57. Robert Dinwiddie to George Washington, 26 July 1755. (Courtesy of Virginia Historical Society)

Wound after Yr gallant Behavr on wch I congratulate You. . . . But pray Sr wth the Numbr of Men remaining is there no Possibility of doing somethg the other Side of the Mounts. before the Winter Mos" (fig. 57).[67] Such recognition, which one might argue was offered to encourage the colonel to go back into the field, probably allowed Washington to keep his military dreams alive, even during the long postwar hiatus at Mount Vernon, and consequently to pose for Peale years later in his uniform coat and to appear at the Second Continental Congress in attire that served as a reminder of his prowess as a leader who could be counted on in even the most dire of circumstances. Dinwiddie's letter also makes clear that in the governor's opinion the French and Indian War was far from over.

## Defending the Frontier and the Capture of Fort Duquesne

In August, only a month after the debacle at Monongahela, George Washington wrote a series of letters in which he professed "a determination not to offer my Services" to the Virginia Regiment because "I coud not get a command upon such terms as I should care to accept." Just as clear from these letters is that Washington was actually interested in the job, difficult as it would be in the wake of Braddock's defeat. As before, he was jockeying with influential members of the assembly in an effort to win acceptable "terms," meaning the rank of colonel and full command of the new Virginia Regiment, which Dinwiddie soon awarded to him (fig. 58):

I reposg especial Trust in Yr Loyalty Courage & good Conduct, do by these Presents appoint You Colonel of the Virga Regimt & Comdr in Chief of all the Forces now rais'd & to be rais'd for the Defence of [this] H: [Majesty's] Colony; & for repellg the unjust & hostile Invasions of the Fr. & their Indn Allies—And You are hereby charg'd with full Power and Authority to act defensively & Offensively as You shall think for the good & Wellfare of the Service. And I do hereby strictly charge & require all Officers and Soldiers under Yr Comd to be obedient to Yr Orders & diligent in the Exercise of [Their] several Duties. And I do also strongly enjoin & require You to be Careful in executg the great Trust & Confidence [that] is repos'd in Yr Managemt by seeing [that] strict Discipline & Order is carefully observe'd in the army & [that] the Soldiers are duly exercis'd & provided with all convenient Necessaries.[68]

If Washington's return to command had begun on a hopeful note, he was soon discouraged by the impossibility of the task at hand and by the ever dim prospects for the sort of advancement through the military that he had always envisioned. His job was to defend Virginia's vast frontier with a force too small to adequately protect against Indian incursions, much less steal the offensive and assault Fort Duquesne. Over the next three years, when the war was so unpopular in the colony that little money was appropriated for the building of an effective army, Washington's motivation seems to have been at least in part his sense of honor, coupled with his acceptance of the obligation to try to protect the settlers whose lives were in almost constant jeopardy.

When he took command of the new Virginia Regiment, Washington was already anticipating further chaos on the frontier. A month earlier he had written to Dinwiddie, "I Tremble at the consequences that this defeat [of Braddock] may have upon our back setlers, who I suppose will all leave their habitation's unless their are prper measures taken for their security." Many of the settlers did in fact flee. Weems would tell his readers that "heart-sickening terrors, as of a woman in labour, seized upon all families," and that "the roads were filled with thousands of distracted parents, with their weeping little ones, flying from their homes."[69] If melodramatic, Weems does convey the passions that were recurrently aroused. To judge from Washington's letters to Dinwiddie, the frontier settlements were

58. Commission for George Washington, awarded by Robert Dinwiddie, 14 August 1755. (Courtesy of Virginia Historical Society)

periodically disrupted by intruding Indians sent by the French, and the situation often became as grim as Weems suggests.

Less than a year after the reversal at Monongahela, the frontier of the Virginia colony had receded to the Shenandoah Valley. The volatility in that region presented the Virginia burgesses with a problem akin to the one that had sparked Bacon's Rebellion in the preceding century; they would have to defend the valley settlers from Indian attack or risk internal consequences. James Titus has pointed out in *The Old Dominion at War* that the Williamsburg government rejected a full-scale mobilization and deployment of the colony's manpower in the valley because the burgesses dared not expose the eastern counties to the threat of a slave uprising, would not sabotage the colony's agriculture by pulling farmers from their fields, and were reluctant to draft from the middle class, members of which might refuse induction and thereby disrupt the status quo. The solution was to develop the Virginia Regiment into a more effective force than it had been at Fort Necessity and Monongahela.[70] This new policy set the stage for Washington to learn the military and political skills that would later serve him well as commander of the Continental Army.

Most nineteenth-century chroniclers of Washington's life failed to recognize the significance of his administrative du-

ties as commander of the revived Virginia Regiment. Instead, Weems and his followers seized upon the more dramatic theme of Washington as the people's deliverer from "those blood-thirsty savages" who would "surprise and murder the frontier inhabitants." One of Washington's letters, which contains a poignant account of the plight of frontier settlers, was frequently cited:

> I *see* their situation, *know* their danger, and participate in their *Sufferings;* without having it in my power to give them further relief, than uncertain promises. In short; I see inevitable destruction in so clear a light, that, unless vigorous measures are taken by the Assembly, . . . the poor Inhabitants that are now in Forts, must unavoidably fall; while the remainder of the County are flying before the barbarous Foe. . . .
>
> The supplicating tears of the women; and moving petitions from the men, melt me into such deadly sorrow, that I solemnly declare, if I know my own mind—I could offer myself a willing Sacrifice to the butchering Enemy, provided that would contribute to the peoples ease. . . .
>
> . . . The woods appear to be alive with Indians, who feast upon the Fat of the Land.

Washington Irving in his biography quotes two passages from this letter and then describes a scene that a number of artists

*The Virginia Soldier: 1753–1758*

would illustrate (fig. 59): "The terrors of the people rose to agony. They now turned to Washington as their main hope. The women surrounded him, holding up their children, and imploring him with tears and cries to save them from the savages." Felix Darley's drawing references this text through the peculiar image of a woman holding high her infant. Seeking to provide more pathos in his picture than Irving had suggested, Darley turned to Weems and found there the motifs of the burning house, the silent man, and the woman fallen to her knees. Weems even provided what he purported to be Washington's very words:

> The poor creatures would run to meet us, like persons half distracted with joy—and then with looks blank with terror, would tell that such or such a neighbour's family, perhaps the very night before, was murdered!—and that they heard their cries!—and saw the flames that devoured their houses! . . . But when we came to take our leave of these wretched families, my God! what were our feelings! to see the deep, silent grief of the men; and the looks of the poor women and children, as, falling upon their knees, with piercing screams, and eyes wild with terror, they seized our hands, or hung to our clothes, intreating us, for God's sake, and for mercy sake, not to leave them.[71]

Washington wrote several desperate letters to Dinwiddie in the spring of 1756 when the French and Indian invasion reached south into the Virginia valley and threatened the town of Winchester. The situation was then particularly bleak. During April Washington reported, "three families were murdered the night before last at the distance of less than twelve miles from this place"; the roads were "so infested that none but Hunters who travel the Woods by Night, can pass in Safety"; and "the people in general are [so] greatly intimidated" that he feared "the blue ridge Mountains will in a little time become the Frontiers of Virginia." There seemed to be "no prospects of Relief," and Washington even worried that his own Fairfax County would next be invaded.[72] Then, just as suddenly as the Indians had appeared, to the colonel's surprise and relief they retreated in May to the Ohio.

Washington had been busily supervising the erection of some eighty-one forts that stretched nearly four hundred miles down the Shenandoah Valley. These fortifications, which often were little more than blockhouses, had been ordered by the burgesses in March 1756. In most cases they were too far apart to seal the border effectively. But, as Washington pointed out, they at least provided places of refuge for the settlers and thus prevented a widespread evacuation of the backcountry.[73] One was a particularly large structure that served almost as a British counterpart to Fort Duquesne. Erected outside of Winchester and named for the new British military commander in North America, Fort Loudoun was intended to be impregnable, and, though never entirely completed, it may well have dissuaded the French and Indians from escalating the war in the valley (fig. 60). The design and building of so large a strong-

59. G. R. Hall, after Felix Darley, *The People of Winchester Appealing to Washington,* 1856, engraving, published in the centennial edition of Washington Irving, *The Life of George Washington* (New York and London, 1889). (Courtesy of Virginia Historical Society)

*The Virginia Soldier: 1753–1758*

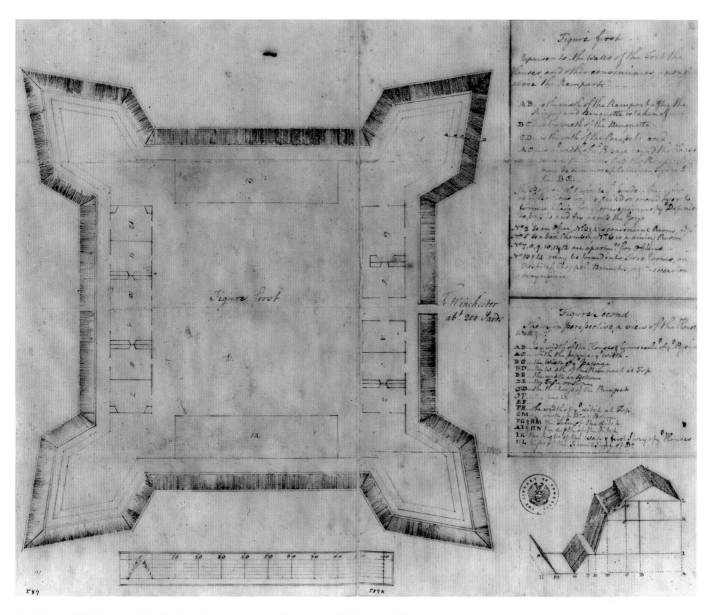

60. George Washington, *Plan for Fort Loudoun*, 1756. (Courtesy of Library of Congress)

hold was no easy undertaking. Fortunately, Washington had seen forts in Barbados and had taken notes about the French outpost when he delivered Dinwiddie's letter; however, he still felt compelled to write to his mentor William Fairfax, whose military service had carried him to Spain, for advice about the plan he had conceived. Washington's drawing depicts a massive structure that would cover half an acre, with four bastions holding fourteen cannons, barracks to house several hundred men, and a well sunk 103 feet into limestone. Fairfax thought it would be large enough to provide safe refuge for the inhabitants of a town, and he consoled the young colonel for having to devote so "much Thought and Fatigue" to what was "the Duty and Employment of an Engineer" rather than a soldier. In 1760, when the traveler Andrew Barnaby visited this site, he saw twenty-four cannons mounted on the four bastions, with

barracks for 450 men. Barnaby explained that a planned surround ditch (the dry moat suggested in Washington's sketch) had necessarily been abandoned because of the difficulty of digging through rock.[74]

Knowledge about fortification architecture did not prove critical to Washington during the Revolutionary War because the principal strategy of the Continental army then would not be to defend positions, but rather to outlast the enemy. However, a host of other skills learned during these years would later prove invaluable. Don Higginbotham has pointed out that Washington's service in command of the Virginia Regiment from 1755 to 1758 provided him with the military experiences that would best prepare him for his leadership role during the Revolution. In both wars his ultimate task was to hold together an army in the face of great adversity, including low enlistments

*The Virginia Soldier: 1753–1758*

and desertion, inadequate political support and funding, and the problems of intercolonial cooperation. One letter by Washington to Dinwiddie during the dismal month of April 1756 makes this point (fig. 61). Writing from Winchester, the colonel explains how his recent attempts at "raising a Number of Men to scour the adjacent Mountains" for Indians has "vanished into Nothing" and how he had to struggle continuously to placate the civilians, who were not only understandably frightened but also critical of the disorderly behavior of his soldiers. "I have done every Thing in my Power, to quiet the Minds of the Inhabitants, by detaching all the Men that I have any Command over, to the Places, which are most exposed." Eventually, because of the protection he awarded them and his skills at diplomacy, the colonel would win the support of the citizens in and around Winchester, but at this juncture the minds of the frontiersmen and their families were far from "quiet." Washington's recruiting efforts, like those of the governor and the burgesses, had failed to fill the army to its authorized size, which left them all to conclude, as Washington wrote to Dinwiddie, that "no other Method can be used to raise 2000 Men, but by draughting." However, if they had to draft men for this unpopular war, many of the draftees would necessarily come from the lower classes and would therefore lack the requisite skills. "The manifest Inferiority of inactive Persons, unused to Arms, in this Kind of Service . . . is inconceivable," Washington wrote; he further adjured Dinwiddie that "great Care should be observed in choosing active Marksmen." Many of these conscripts would also lack discipline, already a problem in the Virginia Regiment, and would be prone to desertion, which had risen to staggering numbers. Deserters and other serious transgressors had to be routinely hanged; "otherwise," Washington explained, "all the Draughts quit the Service, as soon or before they are brought into it."[75]

Many of the Virginia Regiment's problems stemmed from its inadequate funding, and so Washington also had to concern himself with the politics of financing the war. He mentioned to Dinwiddie that an unnamed "Gent. in WmsBurg" had advised him "that the Assembly have generously given the further Sum of £20,000, and voted the augmenting our Forces to 2000 Men."[76] This information prompted Washington's suggestion "to have the whole 2000 formed into one Regiment," modeled "after the British manner," all of whom would be under his command, which would lower the expense of maintaining the troops.

From the evidence of this letter we can surmise that Washington devoted much of his time and energy not only to fighting the enemy but also to keeping his army together and in the field. He was also conducting the sort of community relations that are warranted in a war zone, which include pleading with the regional governments for funds and recruits (as he would

with the many state governments two decades later), and disciplining his often disorganized army. All the while, his task was made more difficult because the geographical boundaries of the colonies, which by tradition governed his deployment of the Virginia Regiment, were not visible to his enemy. Working under that burden prepared Washington to recognize the autonomy of state governments and their inclination to influence the furnishing and deployment of troops.

The Indian incursions into the valley had generally been seasonal, beginning in the spring and lasting into the fall. In October 1757 Washington reported, almost routinely, that "the enemy continue their horrid devastations in this settlement." He pleaded with Dinwiddie, to no avail, that only by attacking Fort Duquesne could the valley be returned to the settlers:

> The raising a company of Rangers, or augmenting our strength in some other manner, is so far necessary, that *without* it, the remaining inhabitants of this (once fertile and populous valley) will scarcely be detained at their dwellings 'till the Spring. And, if there is no Expedition to the westward then—nor a force more considerable than Virginia can support, posted on our frontiers (if we still adhere to our destructive, defensive schemes) there will not, next campaign . . . , be one soul living on this side the Blue-Ridge the ensuing autumn; unless it be the Troops in Garrison, and a few inhabitants of this town, who may shelter themselves under the protection of this fort.[77]

In the winter of 1757–58 a severe illness forced Washington to return to Mount Vernon. While there he could await the shipment of goods due to arrive shortly from London, tend to the many aspects of farm operation and maintenance that he had long neglected, and consider a courtship of the newly widowed Martha Custis. In the spring he was back in the field, but by the following September he had lost the will to command. In the absence of Dinwiddie, who had left the governorship, a dispirited Washington reported to the Speaker of the House of Burgesses the dismal state of the army's morale: "We are still Incampd here [Fort Cumberland]—very sickly—and quite dispirited at the prospect before Us—That appearance of Glory once in view—that hope—that laudable Ambition of Serving Our Country, and meriting its applause, is now no more! Tis dwindled into ease—Sloth—and fatal inactivity—and in a Word, All is lost." But while attempting to defend the frontier, Washington had won friends and support in the valley. It was therefore not surprising when the people of Winchester and the surrounding Frederick County elected him to the House of Burgesses. In the summer of 1758 Washington won a decisive political victory, which made his decision to quit the military that same year much easier. The officers under his command lauded this triumph as a great "honour" to the man who "so long Commanded the whole of that Country in the worst of times."[78]

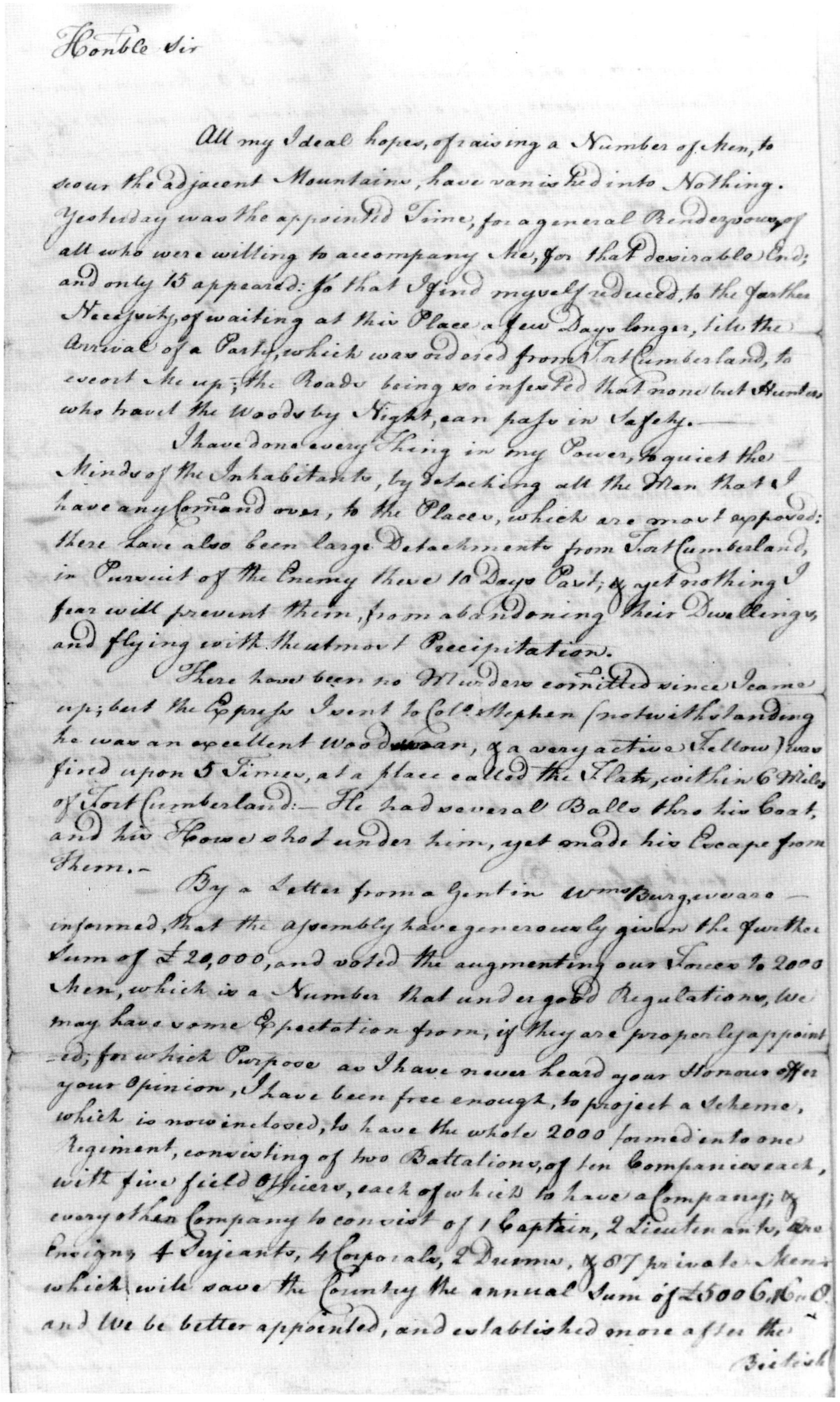

*Honble Sir*

All my Ideal hopes, of raising a Number of Men, to scour the adjacent Mountains, have vanished into Nothing. Yesterday was the appointed Time, for a general Rendezvous of all who were willing to accompany Me, for that desirable End; and only 15 appeared: So that I find myself reduced to the farther Necessity, of waiting at this Place a few Days longer, till the Arrival of a Party, which was ordered from Fort Cumberland, to escort Me up; the Roads being so infested that none but Hunters who travel the Woods by Night, can pass in Safety.—

I have done every Thing in my Power, to quiet the Minds of the Inhabitants, by detaching all the Men that I have any Command over, to the Places, which are most opposed: there have also been large Detachments from Fort Cumberland, in Pursuit of the Enemy these 10 Days past; & yet nothing I fear will prevent them, from abandoning their Dwellings, and flying with the utmost Precipitation.

There have been no Murders committed since I came up; but the Express I sent to Coll: Stephen (notwithstanding he was an excellent Woodsman, & a very active Fellow) was fired upon 5 Times, at a place called the Flats, within 6 Miles of Fort Cumberland:— He had several Balls thro' his Coat, and his Horse shot under him, yet made his Escape from them.—

By a Letter from a Gentln Wm Burges,was informed, that the assembly have generously given the further Sum of £20,000, and voted the augmenting our Forces to 2000 Men, which is a Number that under good Regulations, We may have some Expectation from; if they are properly appointed; for which Purpose as I have never heard your Honours offer your Opinion, I have been free enough, to project a Scheme, which is now inclosed, to have the whole 2000 formed into one Regiment, consisting of two Battalions, of ten Companies each, with five field Officers, each of which to have a Company; & every other Company to consist of 1 Captain, 2 Lieutenants, one Ensign, 4 Sarjeants, 4 Corporals, 2 Drums, & 87 private Men: which will save the Country the annual Sum of £5006 & & & and We be better appointed, and established on one after the

*British*

61. George Washington to Robert Dinwiddie, 16 April 1756. (Courtesy of Virginia Historical Society)

The disparity between the king's regular army and his loyal colonial forces had become apparent to Washington early in the conflict and was reemphasized when he accompanied Braddock in 1755. At Monongahela he had served beside regular British officers who were respected and in turn projected self-confidence and dignity. No less important to Washington was that they were positioned in careers that would advance them socially and financially. The combination of physical strain, danger, (in most cases) defeat in battle, the drain that he had put on his own resources, and his failure to become a regular officer was devastating to Washington. Soon after Monongahela he recounted to his brother his tale of two years of frustrations:

> I was employ'd to go a journey in the Winter (when I believe few or none woud have undertaken it) and what did I get by it? my expences borne! I then was appointed with trifling Pay to conduct an handful of Men to the Ohio. What did I get by this? Why, after putting myself to a considerable expence in equipping and providing Necessarys for the Campaigne—I went out, was soundly beaten, lost them all—came in, and had . . . my Comd reduced. . . . I then went out a volunteer with Genl Braddock and lost all my Horses and many other things. . . . I have been upon the loosing order ever since I enter'd the Service.

Robert Orme understood that Washington would have to be "very lucky" to win a commission from the British. He advised his friend to resign from the military because "Mount Vernon would afford you more Happyness." Orme could say only that "American Affairs are not very well understood at Home."[79]

On no less than seven occasions Washington would threaten to "obey the call of Honour" and resign. But he understood that his presence was needed on the Virginia frontier, and he continued to cling to the hope that a just king would right this wrong. In this persistence he was following the advice of his brother Augustine, who had reminded him of his duty in 1756: "You ought not to give up yr commission, as your country never stood more in need of yr assistance. . . . I am very desirous of your holding yr Commission till you see Lord Louden then you will know what prospect you stand to be put on the British establishment & you Ought to wait at lest 'till we have some acct from home how our address to his majesty in favr of the Virga Regiment was received." In 1757 Washington pleaded to the governor the same arguments he had raised years before:

> We cant conceive, that being Americans shoud deprive us of the Benefits of British Subjects; nor lessen our claim to preferment: and we are very certain, that no Body of regular Troops ever before Servd 3 Bloody Campaigns without attracting Royal Notice. . . .
>
> . . . There can be no Sufficient reason given why we, who spend our blood and Treasure in Defence of the Country are not entitled to equal prefermt. . . .

> . . . We want nothing but Commissions from His Majesty to make us as regular a Corps as any upon the Continent.
> . . .
> . . . It being the General Opinion, that our Services are slighted, or have not been properly represented to His Majesty: otherwise the best of Kings woud have graciously taken Notice of Us.[80]

Finally, in 1758, Washington accepted the reality of British prejudice, gave up his quest, and resigned, but not before taking part in one final and, for a change, successful campaign.

For three years Washington had advocated an expedition to the Forks of the Ohio "to remove the cause of our groundless Fears [by] the Reduction of the Place—Fort Duquesne."[81] In 1758 a new prime minister of Great Britain, the energetic William Pitt, reached the same conclusion. He formulated a plan to end the conflict in North America, beginning with the capture of this French stronghold. By September 1758, when Washington wrote so despondently from Fort Cumberland, Pitt had ordered the assembly of some six thousand men—more than three times the size of Braddock's army—to attack Fort Duquesne. The commander was John Forbes, an experienced British general. Two Virginia regiments (one commanded by Washington and the other by William Byrd III), along with soldiers from Pennsylvania, would be included in this force. To Washington's gratification, Pitt granted the provincial officers equal status with their British counterparts of the same rank. Possibly haunted by the specter of Braddock, Forbes ignored Washington's repeated objections and reversed his initial intention to follow his predecessor's road. Rather, he set aside precious time, late in the season, to build a new road to the Forks through western Pennsylvania. But, perhaps because of Washington's presence at Braddock's debacle, Forbes did listen to his ideas about positioning soldiers defensively as they marched through the wilderness, where they would be vulnerable to an Indian attack.

Forbes had requested that his officers make suggestions as to how the components of his army should be arranged as it advanced to the Ohio. In response Washington penned a letter, complete with an illustration (fig. 62A and B). He gave his "thoughts on a Line of March through a Country covered with wood, & how that Line of March may be formd, in an Instant, into an Order of Battle." In Washington's drawing, where the army is shown moving from right to left, the "First Plan" depicts the "Line of March," wherein "A" is a vanguard force that will draw the enemy's attack; "B" is a thousand "Pickd Men" formed into three divisions; "C" is two brigades of twenty-five hundred men, of whom six hundred are deployed on the flanks "for [the] safety of them"; and "D" is the rear guard. The "Second Plan" depicts the formation that the army is to assume if it is attacked. The three divisions of one thou-

The Plan of ye Line of March, and Order of Battle on the other side
is calculated for a Forced March with field pieces only unincum-
berd with Waggon's, — It Represents; first a Line of March, and
secondly how that line of March may in an Instant, be thrown
into an Order of Battle in the Woods,

This Plan supposes 1000 Privates 1000 of which —
(Picke'd Men) are to March in the Front, in Three Divisions — each
Division besides the Comman-
der of the whole and to be in readiness to oppose the Enemy's Attack, if the necessary precautions are observed, must be a front.

The First Division must, as the 2d & 3d ought likewise, be divided
for ye Captains; these again for the Subalterns, and ye Subalterns, for the
Sergeants & Corporals, by which means every Non Commission'd Officer
will have a Party to command under the Eye of a Subaltern, as the
Subalterns will have under the direction of a Captain &c.—

N.B. I shall, tho I believe it unnecessary, remark here that the
Captains when their Divisions are divided take no part of it
acting as Commandant of the Division he is
appointed to, visiting & encouraging all parts & keeping ye Soldiers to ye Duty

This being done the first Division is, so soon as the Van g'd
is attack'd (if that give the first notice of ye Enemy's approach) to file off
to the Right & left and Trees as described in Plan the 2d.— The Flank
Guards on the Right which belong to ye 2d Division are immediately
to extend to the Right follow'd by that Division and to form as described
in the aforesaid Plan.— The Rear Grand Division is to follow the
left Flankers in the same manner, in order if possible to Encompass
the Enemy, which being a practice different from any thing they
have ever yet experienc'd from Us, I think may be accomplish'd.—

What Indians we have shou'd be Order'd to get round unperceiv-
d & fall upon the Enemy rear at the same time

The Front & Rear being thus Secured, their remains a body of
2500 Men to form two Brigades on the Flanks of wch 600 Men must
March for safety of them; in such Order as to form a Rank entire by
only Marching ye Captrs & Subaltrs Guards into ye Intervals between ye
Sergeants Parties, as may be seen by ye 2 Plan.—

The main body will now be reduced to 1900 Men — which sh'd be
kept as a Corps de reserve to support any part that shall be f'rc'd
or forc'd. The whole is Submitted to the Correction of with the utmost Candour by Sir Yr most Obed:
& most Hble Serv. G Washington

62-A. George Washington, *Line of March and Order of Battle,* (Explanation of a line of March)
8 October 1758. (Courtesy of The Pierpont Morgan Library)

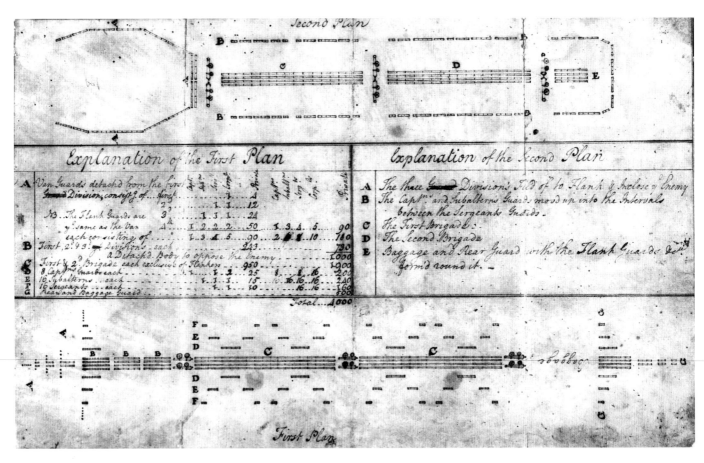

62-B. George Washington, *Line of March and Order of Battle,* (Plan of a Line of March)
8 October 1758. (Courtesy of The Pierpont Morgan Library)

sand soldiers ("A") "file of[f] to the Right & left and take to Tree's—gaining the enemies flanks and surrounding of them." The first and second brigades ("C" and "D") are protected by the lines formed by the soldiers who flank them ("B"), in the same way the rear guard ("E") is protected. Any Indians supporting Forbes's army "shoud be Order'd to get round unperceived & fall upon the Enemy Rear at the same time." Washington argued that this "being a practice different from any thing they have ever yet experienc'd from Us, I think may be accomplish'd"; Forbes agreed. Washington's plan, which was devised "For a Forced March with field pieces only" and no wagon train, was in fact utilized when Forbes's army hastened its progress to Fort Duquesne after learning through intelligence that the French had left the outpost virtually defenseless. In advance of Forbes's arrival, the small French force remaining at the fort quickly abandoned it. As Pitt had anticipated, a show of might by itself won the day. Just as Daniel Parke II no doubt enjoyed reporting the news of Blenheim to Queen Anne, Washington could take some gratification from informing the new Virginia governor, Francis Fauquier, that a longstanding goal had finally been achieved: "I have the pleasure to inform you, that Fort du Quesne—or the ground rather on which it stood—was possessed by His Majestys troops on the 25th instant. The Enemy, after letting us get within a days march of the place, burned the fort, and ran away . . . at night, going down the Ohio by water, to the number of about 5,00 men, from our best information."[82] During the Forbes campaign Washington learned much about British military procedure that would be useful to him two decades later. But because his leadership role in this campaign was minor, later authors and artists gave scant attention to an episode that seemed to have little importance to the greater story of Washington as the "Father of His Country." To nineteenth-century eyes, the Forbes expedition was like the Braddock campaign would have been had Braddock won and thereby overshadowed Washington. Just as they misunderstood Washington's tenure at Winchester, many later commentators missed the point at Fort Duquesne by looking for drama and valor when instead valuable lessons were being learned about command and tactics, as well as about British military capabilities and limitations. Since Washington was sick during much of the Braddock campaign, it was probably with Forbes that he gained his most intimate understanding of the workings of a British army; such a force would become his enemy two decades later.

*The Virginia Soldier: 1753–1758*

However, even Washington downplayed this experience. By late 1758 his thoughts were less directed to military matters and increasingly focused on personal ones. His letters show new fixations: on his relationships with Sally Fairfax and Martha Custis, on his service as a burgess, and on the potential upshot of his retirement to Mount Vernon.

As with all his military experiences, the campaign with Forbes served to enhance Washington's reputation. At his resignation from the Virginia Regiment his officers drafted a resolution that commended him: "Judge then, how sensibly we must be Affected with the loss of such an excellent Commander, such a sincere Friend, and so affable a Companion. How rare is it to find those amiable Qualifications blended together in one Man?" Just as important, because of its potential to effect positively his social status, the prestigious Virginia burgesses did the same: "The Thanks of this House be given to *George Washington . . .* late Colonel of the first *Virginia* Regiment, for his faithful Services . . . and for his brave and steady Behaviour, from the first Encroachments and Hostilities of the *French* and their *Indians,* to his Resignation, after the happy Reduction of Fort *Du Quesne:* And accordingly Mr *Speaker,* from the Chair, returned him (he standing in his Place) the Thanks of the House." Washington emerged from the French and Indian War with a reputation as a dependable leader of men, which was remarkable given the unpopularity of the later years of the war and the harsh criticisms leveled against nearly everyone but Washington.[83] He had dealt with all types of people, from Indians and frontiersmen to politicians and regular army officers and had seen firsthand the intransigence and, to his thinking, obtuseness of British authorities. He had also viewed many more of the "Western Lands" for himself and learned the tactics of New World fighting. Finally, he had earned the respect of his countrymen as the most important defender of the huge entity known as "Virginia," the bounds of which had been confirmed by the map appended to his published journal.

It is no surprise that a great future was predicted for Washington as early as August 1755, only months after the disaster at Monongahela. The Presbyterian evangelist Samuel Davies, who has been called the most effective pulpit orator of his generation in America, pointed to the now celebrated Virginian on an occasion when he addressed a body of Christian soldiers that had been recruited just north of Richmond to combat the increased French and Indian threat to the colony (fig. 63). Davies first recounts the "Perfidy of France," the devastation wrought on the frontier by the "merciless Savages," and the "mortyfying Thought!" of the rout at Monongahela. He sees, however, a "happy, encouraging Prospect [in the volunteers]

now before [him]" and was thankful that "God has been pleased to diffuse some Sparks of . . . Martial Fire through our Country." Davies then felt compelled to single out the hero of Monongahela: "As a remarkable Instance of this, I may point out to the Public that heroic Youth Col. Washington, whom I cannot but hope Providence has hitherto preserved in so signal a Manner, for some important Service to his Country."[84] These words would of course prove prophetic, but it would be some years before Washington would again find himself in need of this type of providential dispensation.

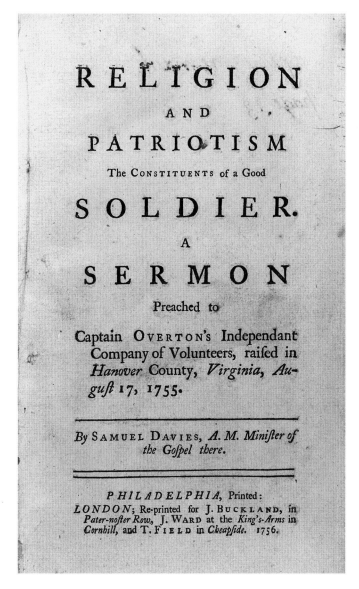

63. Samuel Davies, *Religion and Patriotism, The Constituents of a Good Soldier: A Sermon Preached to Captain Overton's Independent Company of Volunteers, raised in Hanover County, Virginia, August 17, 1755* (London, 1756). (Courtesy of Virginia Historical Society)

64. Junius Brutus Stearns, *The Marriage of Washington to Martha Custis,* 1849, oil on canvas, 40½×55 in.
(Courtesy of Virginia Museum of Fine Arts, Richmond, Va., gift of Edgar William and Bernice Chrysler Garbisch)

# 3

## The Virginia Planter: Washington's First Retirement to Mount Vernon
### 1759–1775

### Preparing for Retirement

THE VICTORY at Fort Duquesne brought about the close of George Washington's first military career, during which he had made both strategic and judgmental errors, but had also manifested his abilities in difficult circumstances and gained the respect of his soldiers and his political superiors in Williamsburg. The taking of Fort Duquesne allowed him to step down with honor; the mission to drive the French from the Ohio had been accomplished. Apparently, however, Washington had decided to retire to the life of a Virginia planter much earlier, for he came home in December 1758 to an entirely rebuilt Mount Vernon, the house that he had leased since 1754 from the widow of his brother Lawrence and would inherit upon her death in 1761. The necessary building materials had been ordered from London in the spring of 1757, and construction was proceeding while he was still in the field. During the closing days of his service Washington's courtship of the young widow Martha Custis was already well under way, and they married only weeks after his return, on 6 January 1759. His courtship and wedding were among the few private episodes from Washington's life that were often reproduced in the nineteenth century; artists such as Stearns believed there was an audience for representations of the tall, handsome officer's union with the attractive young widow (fig. 64).

Washington's ultimate dissatisfaction with his role as guardian of the Virginia frontier, coupled with his annoyance at his treatment by his better-connected comrades, prompted his resignation. One episode that particularly galled him concerned John Dagworthy, the captain of the Maryland Company at Fort Cumberland. During the winter of 1755–56 Dagworthy had claimed rank over all the colonial officers because he held an old but still sustainable commission from the king. Washington was so outraged that he journeyed to Boston to contest Dagworthy's claim with Gov. William Shirley, commander in chief of His Majesty's forces in North America. Shirley ultimately ruled in Washington's favor, and the Virginian was able to return home and report to Governor Dinwiddie with some degree of satisfaction.

During this trip Washington was introduced to the urban centers of Philadelphia, New York, New London, Newport, and Boston. On his trip north as well as on his return, Washington remained for at least four days in Philadelphia, and he made similar stops in New York. A year later, in February and March 1757, Washington was once more in Philadelphia, this time to attend a conference with Lord Loudoun and the provincial governors. In what was the grandest colonial city, which was even then being compared to London, Washington spent nearly three weeks awaiting the arrival of this newest governor and commander in chief of the colonial forces.

During these travels, which immediately preceded the first major renovations to what would become his lifelong house, Washington saw much of the significant architecture in the American colonies. No diary has survived from these years, but his journal from his 1789 trip through New England gives abundant evidence that he was observant about architecture; in these later notes he regularly identifies the types of houses built in various regions, their materials, and their floor plans. On his earlier excursions, which occurred during the period when he was leaning toward a return to Mount Vernon, Washington was overwhelmed with evidence that his own house was both out of style and far too small.

This was no revelation to Washington. He had spent much time during his formative years at Belvoir, which was a newer house and a model of architectural grandeur for its time and place. He had also seen a good deal of the Georgian architecture that had been introduced into Virginia about the year he was born; those mansions had been visible on his trips back and forth to Mount Vernon from the frontier as well as on his missions to Williamsburg. He had also made a point of being cordial to influential members of the Rappahannock River gentry such as Landon Carter of Sabine Hall and John Tayloe II of Mount Airy, and his acquaintances along the James River included such prominent people as William Byrd III of Westover. Washington knew their houses well; he now began to compare such homes to his own, with the buildings he had seen in the northern colonies and earlier in Barbados adding weight to his sense that he needed to attend to his outmoded seat. He would also have to deal with the fact that Mount Vernon had been less than effectively managed while he was in service and that, as Freeman put it, "everything needed for good [estate] management was worn out or lacking all together."[1]

Although he would never travel to England or the Continent, Washington was exposed to an astonishing variety of building types, which accounts, at least to some extent, for his willingness over the years to mix materials and motifs freely at Mount Vernon and in the process create a unique house. We know little about the exact appearance of Mount Vernon after the first remodeling because much of the building underwent further change during the Revolutionary War years. But from the documentary evidence, it seems clear that the house would have been considered a peculiar mix as soon as the first renovations were completed in 1758. Highly fashionable London wallpapers were displayed within, yet the exterior remained basically a wooden box with a cross passage so much off-center that the land facade of the house could never be brought into perfect symmetry (see figs. 67, 102). Through several building campaigns Washington tried to mask this problem, which violates the regularity that was a cardinal principle of Georgian design. The asymmetry of Mount Vernon is perhaps the primary reason that his considerable talents as an amateur architect have been little appreciated. Had Washington owned Mount Vernon in 1757, he might well have torn down the old house and started from scratch.

In April 1757, the month after his return from the three-week stay in Philadelphia, Washington sent to a London merchant the first of a series of orders that provide early evidence of the changes he would make to Mount Vernon in the following year. The house that Lawrence Washington had lived in was only one and a half stories, but it was double-pile, or two rooms deep. This was not grand enough to suit the elevated tastes of its new tenant, however. Washington would raise the structure to a full two and a half stories, and spend much time and money embellishing its interior. The expensive wallpapers he ordered were of the type perhaps best known to him from the colorful interior of Belvoir, though he no doubt saw similar decorations in his wider travels. He seemed to believe that Mount Vernon, at least in its interior, could be made to look like the great houses of the day.

From his outpost at Fort Loudoun near Winchester, Virginia, Washington drafted the early invoice of what were primarily architectural materials that he wanted shipped to Mount Vernon. It is clear that he knew at this point what he wanted to do to the house, for he ordered enough glass (250 panes) to build some twenty windows for the second and attic floors. He was also able to envision the rooms of the expanded second floor, although in the end they would be built differently than his original conceptions. Washington provided the dimensions of seven redesigned rooms. Six were to be papered, in different colors. Five of those six would be on the second floor ("all 8 feet pitch"), where Washington planned a layout akin to that at Belvoir. Also on the invoice were a dozen locks and hinges for the new doors on the second floor.[2]

The two large lower rooms on the west side would have papier-mâché decoration on their ceilings (fig. 65). The best room, however, the west parlor, would be paneled rather than papered as would the southeast room, which now became a bedchamber. (Downstairs bedchambers were common in colonial Virginia, partly because they are cooler in the summer.)

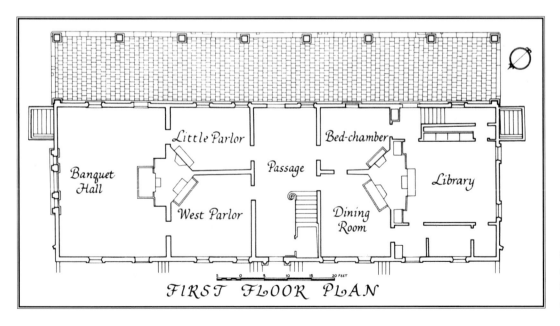

65. *Ground Floor Plan, Mount Vernon.* (Courtesy of Mount Vernon Ladies' Association)

Prior to 1757 this space had been "the little dining Room" that was used for informal dining.[3] Incorporated into the chimneypiece in the west parlor would be a "Neat Landskip" about two by three feet in size, which remains in place today (fig. 66). The "Marble Chimney piece" (a simple slab and plinths), which would have served as a focal point, is also, presumably, the one found today in this room. Washington also ordered "Two neat Mahogany tables 4½ feet square when spread and to join occasionally" plus a dozen "neat and strong Mahogany Chairs." A decade or so earlier in Virginia such items would have been kept primarily in the parlor, the room that was traditionally given the most ornate woodwork, which would have served simultaneously as a place for both sitting and formal dining. At dinnertime, drop-leaf tables would be set up and then later taken down by the servants. Some of the new London pieces may have been ordered for the west parlor; most, however, were probably put in the other large room ("18 by 16" feet) on the ground floor. This was described on the invoice as a "Dining Room," which was to have "paper of a very good kind and colour" above the chair rail. A room for formal dining only was a new idea in 1757. Washington, from the evidence of this order, clearly intended to be on the cutting edge of fashion.

The wallpapers that arrived in the spring of 1758 no doubt pleased their buyer, for they must have been striking. Each came with a matching border, and the solid-color papers were embossed. One wallpaper was blue, with a mosaic design. Another was green, and a third was yellow. The "India figurd Paper" (that is, inspired by Eastern designs) would probably have been what we think of as the Chinese style, while the "Chintz paper" (from the Hindustani word for painted or stained calico) would have had India-inspired floral designs. The paper for the dining room was also embossed, "Crimson" in color, with a mosaic design. Washington's plans for the second floor of the house were changed during construction, and the wallpapers must have been deployed in at least a slightly different manner than he had originally conceived. Wherever they were hung, though, they must have brought to mind those at Belvoir. Admittedly, this comparison can be carried only so far because noticeably absent from Washington's order were the expensive matching draperies that the Fairfaxes, and few others, could afford.

The chairs, too, were highly fashionable, in the Chippendale Gothic style. Some even had upholstered seats ("6 Mahagony Chairs, Gothick Archd Backs & Seats of Ditto" and "12 Mahay best gothick Chairs, wt. Pincushion Seats stufft in the best manner & coverd with horse hair"). These chairs and the two tables were part of Washington's order that included the wall-

66. The west-parlor chimneypiece, incorporating the "Neat Landskip" ordered by Washington in 1757 from London. (Courtesy of Mount Vernon Ladies' Association)

papers and had specifically to do with room definition; a second order was placed for him at about the same time, apparently by Alexandria merchant John Carlyle, for decorative items whose placement was perhaps less carefully defined at this juncture. The goods requested in the two orders were sent from London in two intermixed shipments. The first of the wallpapers ("9 ps. fine Crimson and yellow Papers") was included with the August shipment but was only enough to begin the redecorating process; the bulk of the paper followed in November. A sword that Washington had ordered earlier also arrived in the November shipment. This was "a fine strong Silver pierced, Boat Shell two edgd Sword Silver & gold gripe, spare & false Scabbard &ca." (This is apparently the sword depicted in the 1772 Peale portrait, fig. 35). The colonel was hedging his bets: if his military career took an unexpected turn for the better, he would be well equipped.[4]

In terms of the chronology of rebuilding the house, stocking it, and finding a wife to live there with him, Washington's plans progressed on schedule during the fifteen months following the spring of 1757. In January 1758 he ordered additional decorative objects. Two months later he visited Martha Custis, apparently for the first time. Before another month had passed he ordered velvet for a "Coat, Waistcoat & Breeches" that may have been intended for his wedding suit, although the material arrived months too late to be used for that purpose. By July he had won election to the House of Burgesses, and a work crew, assisted by a team of Washington's slaves, was in place at Mount Vernon. They removed and rebuilt the roof and began to underpin the house with sixteen thousand bricks for a foundation that could withstand the increased weight of the additional floor. George William Fairfax sent congratulations on Washington's victory in the polls: "You may add Sprigs to your Laurels, and sit down quiet and easy for the future on the banks of Potomack."[5] But Washington was still in the field, and it would have to be Fairfax, his friend and neighbor, who would ride to the building site and make the decisions that were too difficult for the workmen.

In June 1758, John Patterson, a local carpenter, wrote that he was ready to "take the Roof off the House." When he went on to say that he was in need of "two inch plank for to Cover the Balusterade," he left the only evidence that Washington had ordered at this date so fashionable a feature for the Mount Vernon exterior (fig. 67). In his travels north the colonel had seen roof balustrades at a number of public buildings, such as Christ Church in Philadelphia and the Old Colony House in Newport; these elements apparently struck Washington as a way of ensuring that the visitor to his newly designed home would immediately see the affluence and social position of the master of Mount Vernon.[6]

By mid-July "the Great house was Raisd" to its new height of two and a half stories, covered, and "the bricks [for the underpinning were] all burnt." The brickwork and the interior plastering were undertaken by William Triplett, who lived only four miles away but was much in demand in the neighborhood as a builder. Other commitments forced Triplett to delay until 1760 his work on a string of dependencies (now gone) that ran at forty-five-degree angles from the house, much like the ones at Belvoir. Triplett would "build the two houses in the Front of my House (plastering them also) and running Walls for the Palisades to them from the Great house & from the Great House to the Wash House and Kitchen also." Presumably, it was mainly for these dependencies that Washington ordered additional glass ("150 Squares best London Crown Glass") in the spring of 1759.[7]

By mid-August, Patterson had "got the outside of the House finishd, the Closets excepted."[8] This is the only mention of an exterior feature that was removed two decades later; lean-to closets added to the side of the house may have been inspired by New England examples. There, no doubt, Washington also saw the American version of "rustication," whereby wooden clapboards are sawed in such a way that they take the shape of finely cut blocks of stone and then are painted with sand in the mix so that their surfaces resemble the texture of stone. The rustication at Mount Vernon, which was one of the devices that Washington employed in his attempts to make his simple farmhouse resemble something that it was not, apparently dates to this period and presumably was the work of Patterson.

When it came to the rebuilding of the interior of the second floor, George William Fairfax was often obliged to stand in for the colonel. On the first of September he assured Washington that "Mr Patterson shall have all the Assistance I am able to give him." Patterson soon needed answers to two crucial questions. He had not been instructed as to whether he should replace the "upper Floors," the boards of which were "very un-

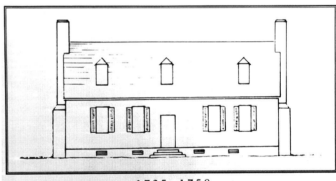

c. 1735–1758

1759–1774

67. *Conjectural Drawings of the Appearance of Mount Vernon Before and After the Rebuilding of 1758.* The earlier house is the simple building that Washington inherited. By 1774 he had increased the size of the house to the structure shown at the bottom here; in the mid-1770s he initiated yet another renovation to produce the structure that survives today. (Courtesy of Mount Vernon Ladies' Association)

even" and, at least in the passage, marred with "Nail marks," nor had Washington remembered to select a location for the attic stairs. The colonel encouraged Fairfax to have new floorboards installed; as to the stairs, Fairfax had little choice but to place them where they are today, in the middle of the house, on the river side. That space used to be the "old Store room."[9] In this process the fifth upstairs bedroom would lose half of its space. As mentioned, when the upper bedrooms were ultimately constructed, they did not match the dimensions that Washington had sent to London with his order for wallpapers. The evidence of the "Nail marks" suggests that some of the earliest walls may have been removed. In fact, the upper floor became as much the plan of Fairfax as of Washington, but how could the colonel go wrong with the most prominent member of the Fairfax County aristocracy as his design consultant? Washington wanted Mount Vernon to be a house worthy of his new social position; with his neighbor's input, this would ultimately be accomplished.

The best craftsmanship performed during this first remodeling of Mount Vernon was the work of the joiner Gawan Langfier, who Washington would invite back in 1774 to help with the next phase of construction.[10] Langfier apparently installed the paneling in the passage, the west parlor, and the downstairs bedroom. The colonel's order in 1759 for six busts of historical figures "to fill up broken pediments over doors" and "to stand on each end of a pediment" is evidence that the passage paneling, with its pedimented door surrounds, and the west parlor chimneypiece, with its swan's-neck pediment on which Washington wished to place two busts, were then finished or at least nearing completion. Langfier also put in the present staircase, although he did not finish all its detailed carving until after Washington had brought his bride home. Only in August 1759 did the colonel pay "Going Lamphire in full for Turnery 7.14.7½."[11]

Marriage was the other matter that needed attention as Washington prepared for his first retirement. If he was to retreat to the gentry life he would need a wife. As a teenager he had been ready to surrender to "cupids feather'd Dart," but as an adult he wanted a woman who was not only attractive and agreeable, but wealthy as well.[12] A solid financial footing was needed for the maintenance of his estate, and this would be most easily gained through marriage. In a matter of months the colonel would simultaneously build a relationship with his new bride-to-be and the new Mount Vernon.

Although Washington was young, handsome enough, and renowned for his military exploits, he had known only rejection from the wealthy women to whom he was attracted. Among those who refused his advances were the Virginian Betsy Fauntleroy and Mary Eliza Philipse of New York. And,

of course, Sally Fairfax, the wife of his close friend, was in no position to do anything but deny him, despite his heartfelt passion for her. In early September 1758, as George William Fairfax was riding back and forth to supervise the building of Mount Vernon's second floor, Washington wrote a letter to Sally Fairfax that contains his first reference to Martha Custis that survives; it also, perhaps not surprisingly, records one of the last statements of his intense feeling for his friend's wife: "If you allow that any honour can be derivd from my opposition to Our present System of management [that is, Forbes's handling of the Ohio military campaign], you destroy the merit of it entirely in me by attributing my anxiety to the annimating prospect of possessing Mrs Custis." (Sally Fairfax had apparently been encouraging the colonel to pursue Martha.) In the next lines, however, Washington "confesses" himself to be "a Votary to Love" and makes it clear enough that the "lady" who he loves is the recipient of his letter. There can be little doubt that he would rather have made Sally Fairfax his life companion, but he here seems to concede that he must look elsewhere.[13] Since Martha met other important criteria, this alternative to his hopeless passion for Sally would have seemed worth his best effort.

Six months earlier, in March 1758, Washington had paid the first of his three known visits to Martha Custis of New Kent County, Virginia. (The second visit was later that March, and the third was in the first week of June.) It is generally presumed that Washington's proposal was made to her and accepted in March, because the next month he ordered the material for a suit of clothes that would have been elaborate enough to serve as a wedding costume. One might think it surprising that in the following September he wrote such a passionate letter to Sally Fairfax, especially given the evidence of Washington's genuine affection for his wife after they were wed. We might see the correspondence of September as both his last, necessarily futile effort to bring about the impossible and a presumably welcomed admission to Sally that his attentions had found another outlet.

A discussion of his courtship and marriage to Martha Custis is vital to the story of Washington's private life. However, comparatively little is known about these events because Martha Washington, late in her life, destroyed nearly all her correspondence with her husband. We can only speculate as to what was said in their letters; however, the very destruction of so much paper, which must have been a laborious process given the penchant of the colonel toward correspondence, when coupled with his outpourings to Sally Fairfax, might be thought of as signals of something amiss. It is possible that there was only a modicum of passion in the relationship of George and Martha, and that one, or perhaps both, was not deeply in love with the other when they wed; it is also possible that Martha simply did not want posterity to analyze her letters to and from George, which might well have been appropriately passionate. (A newly discovered note written to "My love" in Martha's hand in 1777 suggests that a close bond did exist.) The dearth of evidence of this sort may explain why two of Washington's early biographers, John Marshall and Jared Sparks, each give the courtship and marriage only one sentence.[14]

Even Mason Locke Weems, who was inclined to see gaps in the historical record as opportunities to mythologize, had little to offer his readers on this subject. He concocted a tale of their infatuation that both flattered Washington and put the young couple in a church, where Weems believed his readers wanted to find them. There "the eyes of beauty would sometimes wander from the cold reading preacher" to catch a glimpse of the colonel: "At the head of all these stood the accomplished Mrs. Martha Custis, the beautiful and wealthy widow of Mr. John Custis [actually Daniel Parke Custis]. Her wealth was equal at least, to one hundred thousand dollars! But her beauty was a sum far larger still. It was not the shallow boast of a fine skin, which time so quickly tarnishes. . . . But it sprung from the heart." Weems concluded that "for two such kindred souls to love, it was only necessary that they should meet." Perhaps it was because he knew the widowed Martha Washington personally ("I preached in her parish") that Weems tempered his account of her courtship.[15] Or perhaps it was because readers in the first part of the nineteenth century were simply more interested in those events in Washington's life that led to his transformation into a national figure.

Midcentury Americans looked for assurances that in his private life the "Father of His Country" shared their Victorian values. These would have included a steadfast appreciation of religion and the family as cornerstones of social order. Accordingly, there was a good deal of interest in Washington's courtship of a widow with two children, because the marriage that followed made him an actual "father." Who was this woman, and how was it that she had won the heart of the man who would become the greatest of American patriots?

The status of Martha Dandridge, the daughter of John and Frances Jones Dandridge of New Kent, had been ensured when she married into the wealthy Custis family in 1750. Her own family was respectable; her father was a deputy clerk of the county and a vestryman, and her uncle, William Dandridge (d. 1743), had achieved appointment to the Governor's Council and had served in the British navy as captain of a forty-gun ship that saw action at Cartagena. (The latter was no doubt a point of interest to George Washington and a topic of conversation with Martha, since his brother Lawrence had also distinguished himself in the War of Jenkins' Ear.) But the Dandridge family had no fortune to match that which John Custis, the father of Martha's first husband, had accumulated through inheritance, good agricultural management, and the avoidance of debt.

To understand Martha's attitude as she contemplated a second marriage we must look first at her less than tranquil relationship with the Custises. We pick up the story in 1749. Martha Dandridge had known Daniel Parke Custis nearly all her eighteen years, for he was a vestryman at St. Peter's, the church she attended in New Kent County. At thirty-nine he was still a bachelor, presumably because of the failed marriages

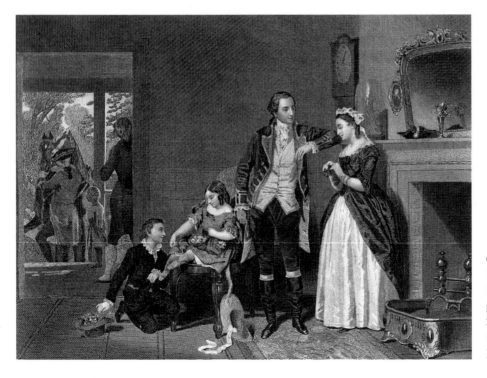

68. John Halpin, after Alonzo Chappel, *Washington's First Interview with Mrs. Custis, Afterwards Mrs. Washington,* engraving, published in John Frederick Schroeder, *Life and Times of Washington* (New York, 1857). (Courtesy of Virginia Historical Society)

of his parents and sister, and his father's domineering and eccentric nature. Their love blossomed, however, and soon Daniel and young Martha were married.

John Custis, Martha's new father-in-law, was an accomplished member of the colonial aristocracy. He served on the Governor's Council and was a talented horticulturist, whose garden in Williamsburg was known even in London. At his death in 1749 he bequeathed a huge estate to his son. But he also left other legacies that embarrassed his heir and new wife. John Custis had fathered a son by one of his slaves, and in his will he burdened Daniel with the illegitimate son's care. More important, although at one point he had called Martha "beautifull & sweet temper'd" and said that he preferred her over "any Lady in Virginia," John Custis apparently opposed his son's marriage to a woman he considered "much inferior"; indeed, he gave silver engraved with the Custis arms to Mrs. Anne Moody so that it would not fall into the hands of "any Dandridge's daughter." Mrs. Moody displayed it publicly in her tavern in Williamsburg, which could not have pleased Martha.[16] Although John Custis did grant permission for the marriage a few months before his death, the young wife must have despised her ambivalent father-in-law, and she was probably happy to leave the lower Tidewater to begin marriage in a different county. Their first two children, Daniel Parke and Frances, died young; however, with the births of John Parke "Jacky" and Martha Parke "Patsy" Custis, the family seemed to be happy and prosperous until Daniel's death on 8 July 1757. Early the following year Washington would begin to take serious notice of the still young Martha Custis. Douglas Southall Freeman suggests that in the small world of the colony the colonel had probably met both of the Custises, perhaps in Williamsburg where they owned a small house; Washington visited the capital frequently in the 1750s. He at least would have known by 1758 of both the Custis wealth and Martha's eligibility as a widow. It is not unfair to say that this information would have made a short stopover in New Kent County seem a prudent investment of his time.

In the space of a decade during the mid-nineteenth century at least three engravings of Washington's first interview with Martha Custis were published (figs. 68, 69, 70), and an account of the incident was offered by her grandson, George Washington Parke Custis, in his *Recollections and Private Memoirs of Washington*.[17] These scenes and the Custis account confirmed the sanctity of George and Martha's relationship and suggested his appropriateness for the paternal roles he would assume in his public and private lives.

According to Custis, who presumably was told the gist of this story by his grandmother, the colonel was traveling to Williamsburg when he "fell in with P. Chamberlayne, Esq., one of the ancient aristocracy of Virginia." Washington probably would have been on his way to confer with members of the Council or with the burgesses about conditions on the frontier. Richard Chamberlayne's home, Poplar Grove in New Kent County, near the ferry that ran across the Pamunkey River, was most likely "P." Chamberlayne's destination.[18] Chamberlayne, Custis tells us, introduced Washington to a "fine, young, and handsome widow, who was spending some days at his house." Custis then fleshed out, as much as he could, the few facts of the story:

69. John C. McRae, *The Courtship of Washington,* 1860, engraving, 15×21⅜ in. (Courtesy of Virginia Historical Society)

*The Virginia Planter: 1759–1775*

70. G. R. Hall, after J. W. Ehninger, *Washington's First Interview with His Wife*, 1863, engraving, 17×22 in. (Courtesy of Virginia Historical Society)

Fate destined this interview to produce the long and happy union which soon followed the first meeting and mutual attachment of the parties: for the enamoured Colonel, making duty, for this time only, to yield to love, permitted the sun to set and rise again upon him, the guest of Chamberlayne, while Bishop, his old soldier and body servant, tall as his chief, and in this one instance more punctilious, had, in obeying his orders of haste, long stood at his master's stirrup, 'ready, aye, ready for the field.' The ensuing evening the Colonel departed, 'nothing loth' to accept the kind bidding of his hospitable host to call again.[19]

Custis, perhaps not surprisingly, gives no indication of whether Martha's two young children, then aged four and two, were with her at Poplar Grove.

Alonzo Chappel, in an engraving for John Frederick Schroeder's *Life and Times of Washington* (1857), uses Custis's account (see fig. 68). This is apparent from his inclusion of the colonel's tall attendant who holds their two horses, and the way that the principal figures are shown to be "enamored" with one another. Schroeder repeats Custis's story in his text, embellishing it with suggestions of the couple's conversation. If the furnishings are a century out of date, at least the artist modeled the clothing for George Washington and Martha Custis on the widely reproduced Peale and Wollaston portraits (see figs. 35, 74).

Chappel also provides what is probably a fairly accurate architectural setting. Poplar Grove does not survive nor does the "White House" where Martha Custis lived. But an old photograph of Rockohoc, which was part of the White House estate, shows a single-pile structure akin to what Chappel drew (fig. 71). The White House, even if it was double-pile, which it probably was, would not likely have been grand, because few houses in early New Kent County were. The point, which is

rarely considered today, is that despite her late husband's considerable wealth, Martha Custis did not live in a Georgian mansion. Washington could offer his bride a house that was at least as large and certainly more fashionably furnished than her Tidewater residence. Therefore, although her large fortune dwarfed Washington's financial resources, Martha Custis would not have appeared to have suffered a loss in social status by marrying the young colonel.

While Chappel devised a credible setting, his competitors in the midcentury print market did not make such an effort. To modern eyes the interiors presented by two New York engravers, John C. McRae and George R. Hall, are too inaccurate to be taken seriously (see figs. 69, 70). Both scenes are significant, however, for the question they raise about George and Martha's early relationship. Unlike Chappel, both McRae

71. Rockohoc, New Kent County. (Courtesy of Virginia Historical Society)

and Hall suggest that the courtship was more formal than warm. They were influenced, no doubt, by the widely reproduced Gilbert Stuart portraits of the president, which showed Washington to be composed, placid, and somewhat aloof. The Stuart images, coupled with Washington's reputation for dignity and deportment, suggested that he was probably always in control of his passionate side. While there is a validity to the Stuart portraits because Washington, in the manner in which he received most visitors in the 1790s, had established such a reputation, McRae and Hall project the coldness of the elderly head of state backward in time to his courtship forty years earlier. These printmakers, however, may well have been closer to the truth than Chappel; the formality of Washington's later years was certainly present to some degree in Martha's suitor. More probably, however, they were simply manifesting their sense of the Washington that their midcentury customers wanted to see.

Decorum governed gentry living in early Virginia because it separated members of that class from their inferiors. This emphasis on behavior, carriage, and dress, which originated in British courtesy books, suggests that formality may well have been a dominant characteristic of not a few gentry marriages in the colony, where pedigree and appearance were judged to be at least as important as feeling. Propriety no doubt guided Washington and Custis's behavior during their courtship, perhaps especially because Martha's husband was so recently deceased. This emphasis on protocol, which was present at Mount Vernon throughout their life there, would ultimately be adapted to fit the needs of the new president and his first lady. It is fair to say that the manners displayed in the original president's house, which would influence the behavior of all of his successors, came from the Virginia gentry mansions, as McRae and Hall, perhaps inadvertently, imply.

Nearly seventy years later, Jean Leon Gerome Ferris imagined the courtship entirely differently; he saw it as a great romance (fig. 72). Ferris tended to view history through rose-colored glasses, seeing the good and noble in the past while ignoring the bad or mundane. Here, appropriately enough, he places the couple in a rose garden. The widow's young children, who might have been a hindrance to their courtship, are only suggested. Martha Custis is presented as a vibrant young woman who is totally enthralled by the handsome and gallant officer who courts her.

These varying depictions of the courtship suggest different answers to the question of how George Washington and Martha Custis might have reacted to each other in the spring of 1758. While we do not have many available facts, a consideration of this episode does shed light on both Washington's ambitions and his sense of what an appropriate private life should be like. Washington's heart may well have remained with Sally Fairfax months after his meeting with Martha in New Kent County, and it seems likely that the colonel pursued

72. Jean Leon Gerome Ferris, *The Courtship of Washington, 1758,* ca. 1917, oil on canvas, 25×32 in. (Courtesy of Virginia Historical Society, Lora Robins Collection of Virginia Art)

*The Virginia Planter: 1759–1775*

Martha Custis with propriety, as McRae and Hall depict, rather than with the passion Ferris imagines. Within that prescribed manner of behavior, however, there would have been room for the sort of tempered infatuation that Chappel suggests. In the final analysis, we have no way of knowing what actually occurred. If there was what to modern eyes might seem a shortage of passion, the formality would only have made the courtship easier; they would have understood their respective roles in the ritual that they were to perform.

How did Martha Custis view the vigorous young colonel? Had he appeared ten years earlier, before she married at eighteen a man more than twice her age, she might have reacted with the ardor that Ferris suggests. But in 1758 she was a twenty-seven-year-old widow who had given birth to four children, only two of whom survived. She had lost her father unexpectedly in the summer of 1756, and a year later had buried her husband. She may well have been a more sober and mature person than Ferris would have us believe; it is hard to imagine that her losses would not have exacted some toll, even in a world where the death of a loved one was not an unexpected occurrence. George Hall is probably closer to the truth in presenting a tired and almost dowdy woman, who seems a bit surprised at the interest of so gallant a suitor. Martha Custis was, however, in a position to pick and choose among the men

that her money and position would lure. No doubt there were many scions of the colonial aristocracy who would have been willing and able to administer the plantations and estate of Daniel Parke Custis. She could look further, for an affectionate companion and a caring father for her children. If that was indeed her purpose, she selected well. The courtship was the beginning of a successful relationship that lasted until the general's death in 1799. There is abundant evidence that as head of his household Washington proved a paragon. He was a loving stepfather to her children until their untimely deaths, and was just as able a grandfather. Washington was a pragmatic person, and both he and Martha Custis were mature enough by 1758 to follow the instinct of practicality. In many ways, each was a perfect match for the other, and through their prenuptial meetings they must have come to such a realization. Their marriage, then, at least by modern standards, might possibly have been based more on sense than on sensibility.

Little more than a year prior to Washington's courtship of Martha Custis, she had had her portrait made by John Wollaston, a London painter who made a tour of the American colonies at midcentury and completed some five dozen canvases in Virginia alone (fig. 74). The artist was also commissioned to paint companion canvases of her husband, Daniel Parke Custis, and their two children (figs. 73, 75). These por-

73. John Wollaston, *Daniel Parke Custis*, 1757, oil on canvas, 50×40 in. (Courtesy of Washington and Lee University)

74. John Wollaston, *Martha Custis*, 1757, oil on canvas, 50×40 in. (Courtesy of Washington and Lee University)

*The Virginia Planter: 1759–1775*

76. John Wollaston, *Mrs. William Randolph III (Anne Harrison Randolph),* ca. 1755, oil on canvas, 36×29½ in. (Courtesy of Virginia Historical Society)

75. John Wollaston, *John Parke (Jacky) Custis and Martha Parke (Patsy) Custis,* 1757, oil on canvas, 49×35 in. (Courtesy of Washington and Lee University)

traits, as far as we can tell, were at least begun prior to Daniel's death in late July. However, the artist was not paid for his work until 21 October 1757 when he wrote a receipt to "Mrs. Custis" for having received "the Sum of fifty pistoles for three pictures." With Martha's remarriage, the painting of Daniel Parke Custis most probably went into storage. We would surmise, however, that the Closterman portrait of Daniel Parke II, because of its quality, value, and reference to a martial theme, would have been kept on view in the colonel's house (see fig. 41). The portraits of Martha and the children were hung in the west parlor at Mount Vernon. The Peale portrait of Washington would join them there more than a decade later (see fig. 35).[20]

Wollaston's portrait is the only known image of the young Martha Custis; this is the woman who was courted by Washington. As a life portrait, it is a record both of her actual physical appearance at age twenty-six and of how she wanted to be perceived. The artist supplies evidence of unusually delicate features in her youthful face and captures in her look and pose an appealing young woman. Portraits were commissioned in colonial Virginia primarily to announce gentry status, and John Wollaston was popular in the colony because his canvases projected such a message at a glance. For this reason, however, portraits by Wollaston often prove ambivalent documents. His gentry sitters tend to look remarkably alike in costume, pose, and facial structure. When Martha Custis's portrait is compared to other such works, we see that neither her gown nor her deportment reveal anything about her as an individual. They serve only as signs of her wealth and social rank.

Though slightly larger, because it was the most expensive type to be commissioned from Wollaston, the image of Martha Custis closely resembles the same artist's portrait of Mrs. William Randolph III of Wilton on the James River (fig. 76). While the artist was aware that the paths of the sitters would inevitably cross, he was just as sure that the two paintings would not be placed in close proximity to each other as we have done here, and thereby display similarities that are almost uncanny.[21] Anne Randolph was born ca. 1724, seven years earlier than Martha Custis, but she sat for the artist at about the same time. In their portraits, both women are made to play the same role. They wear nearly identical costumes, and the rigid posture of each is governed by strict British rules of deportment. Wollaston often gave his sitters similar facial features, most notably

*The Virginia Planter: 1759–1775*

in the Tidewater in a most enviable social and economic position. Although Jacky's name is not mentioned in the document, Washington acted for him in good faith. Part of this property had been owned by the late Speaker of the House, John Robinson. In fact, the document is filled with the names of both established Tidewater families and future luminaries, including Edmund Pendleton, Carter Braxton, and Thomas Jefferson, all of whom had been involved in previous indentures that transferred titles of these various lands. On examining the deed today one is struck by the fact that through such purchases George Washington inserted himself, through his ward, into the hierarchy of the old Virginia gentry, which had been for him a primary life goal. Only a matter of months after this sale, however, he would risk all that he had achieved in the effort to gain political independence.

Washington's strong feelings of love for his stepchildren are evident in his letters and diaries. In the process of his participation in the raising of Jacky and Patsy Custis, he in turn earned their affection. In 1774, when Jacky was twenty and studying at King's College in New York City, he had occasion to remember his youth, which inspired him to record the sentiments and respect he held for his stepfather: "How to express fully my Thankfulness, for the many kind Offers you have lately made Nelly & myself; I find great Loss of Words. . . . The only returns required, were Effection and regard—both of which did not I posses in the highest Degree for You; I should look upon myself to be the most insensible & Ungrateful Being on Earth; and shall strenuously endeavour by my future Conduct, to merit a Continuance of your regard and Esteem."[45] Their relationship remained on affectionate terms until Jacky's death seven years later.

In 1757, when John Wollaston painted the portraits of Daniel Parke Custis and his wife, he was commissioned at the same time to record the likenesses of their two surviving children (see fig. 75). Artists were available so infrequently in colonial Virginia that commissions had to be awarded when the opportunity arose, not when the circumstances were best for the sitters. In this instance Jacky Custis was but three years of age, and Patsy Custis (whose exact birth date is unknown) was only one or two. The problem was that Wollaston's mannered style had been developed to record the deportment and likenesses of adults; he was ill equipped to respond to either the disposition or the more delicate features of children. Such a task is particularly difficult when the children are infants. Wollaston could produce only a highly formal image of young Jacky and Patsy Custis. Admittedly, however, this canvas successfully defines the gentry status of the young heirs. Such works served both to instruct the children as to what was expected of them in terms of dress, deportment, and behavior and to assure their parents that the family dynasties would be perpetuated by worthy offspring. That said, this is a poor likeness of the Custis

children. If a portrait is to be successful it should bring the sitter to life and, especially where children are concerned, enhance feelings of familial affection. Perhaps to make up for such shortcomings, a second portrait of the Custis children was later commissioned.

By family tradition, the "Matthew Pratt" painting presents the Custis children at a slightly later age, when their identifying features are more recognizable (fig. 87). The faces in this portrait resemble those in the miniatures painted by Charles Willson Peale in 1772 (figs. 88, 89). This is a loving portrait of children who are presented as paragons of innocence and sweetness. As such, it can be read as a valuable representation of the domestic bliss that the Washington family often enjoyed during the 1760s.[46]

This painting has been attributed to Pratt because it is reminiscent of his distinct style. But Pratt's first known visit to Virginia was in 1773, by which time the Custis children were well into their teens.[47] This evidence raises questions about the portrait. If it is by Pratt and if it depicts Jacky and Patsy Custis, then it was not painted from life. In 1773 Jacky Custis was in school in New York City; Patsy, who had been ill for many years, died unexpectedly that June. The painting owes enough in composition to the Wollaston canvas to suggest that the ear-

87. Unidentified artist (possibly Matthew Pratt), *The Custis Children*, n.d., oil on canvas, 30×24½ in. (Courtesy of Virginia Historical Society)

*The Virginia Planter: 1759–1775*

88. Charles Willson Peale, *Martha Parke Custis*, 1772, miniature. (Private collection)

89. James Peale, after Charles Willson Peale, *John Parke Custis*, after 1772, miniature. (Courtesy of Virginia Museum of Fine Arts, Richmond, Va., gift of Mrs. A. Smith Bowman and her brother Robert E. Lee IV)

lier portrait could have served as a model, used in conjunction with the recent Peale miniatures, which were also at Mount Vernon. If so, this would have been a most unusual commission, a posthumous work that looks back a decade to the happy childhood years of the Custis children. In this scenario, Patsy's tragic death from epilepsy makes the portrait a particularly poignant image.[48] Although both of the children's lives ended tragically in untimely death, this narrative of paternal devotion is at the same time heartwarming because of the bonds that were formed in the family. Two decades later Washington would give the same fatherly affection and guidance to Martha's grandchildren, the children of Jacky Custis. The "illustrious couple" came to be thought of having raised two families in an environment of bliss and love. For that reason, the story of Washington's marriage and domestic life offered a "salutary influence" for the average American family.

In the early summer of 1773 Patsy Custis was seized with a particularly violent epileptic fit and died. Washington had grown to love the girl whom he called his "innocent" stepdaughter. His account books for the last years of her life are poignant in their record of expenditures for medicines interspersed with those for the clothing and the types of accessories that a father enjoys buying for a daughter. Listed, for instance, are medicines purchased and visits from Dr. William Rumney, as well as a trip to the springs in an attempt to find an effective treatment for Patsy's epilepsy. In Williamsburg Washington bought her gold earrings and a tortoiseshell comb. In Fredericksburg he found her silk and more earrings. In 1770 he kept on the margins of the calendar pages of his almanac a record of Patsy's seizures. During a period of eighty-six days, she had "fits" on twenty-six.[49]

Premature death was not uncommon in colonial America. This was well known to the Washington family. In the spring of 1773 Betsy, the fourteen-year-old daughter of Martha's brother-in-law Burwell Bassett, had died. The death of the seventeen-

or eighteen-year-old Patsy Custis followed only a few months later. Washington had to convey the news to the still grieving Bassett:

> It is an easier matter to conceive, than to describe, the distress of this Family; especially that of the unhappy Parent of our Dear Patcy Custis, when I inform you that yesterday removd the Sweet Innocent Girl into a more happy, & peaceful abode than any she has met with, in the afflicted Path she hitherto has trod. . . .
>
> . . . This Sudden, and unexpected blow, I scarce need add has almost reduced my poor Wife to the lowest ebb of Misery; which is encreas'd by the absence of her Son (whom I have just fixed at the College in New York, from whence I returnd the 8th Instt) and want of the balmy Consolation of her Relations.[50]

The tragic, if not unexpected, death of his stepdaughter did not alter Washington's attentions toward Jacky. From the start Washington was fond of his "amiable" stepson. As a young man of considerable, if not consistently manifested, talents whose wealth would position him to become a prominent figure in Virginia society, Jacky could look ahead to a rewarding career. "He is a promising boy," Washington wrote, "the last of his Family—& will possess a very large Fortune." But Custis would have to be well educated in order to manage successfully his network of complex plantation operations, and he was not by nature a scholar. This gave "anxiety" to his guardian, who expended considerable energy in his attempt to mold a boy who was a hunter by nature into something of a student. Washington was determined to "make him fit more useful purposes, than a horse Racer," but he was at best only partly successful.[51]

At various points during his education Jacky Custis would return home from boarding school with "His Mind a good deal relaxed from Study, & more than ever turnd to Dogs Horses & Guns." Often he would make such "trifling" progress in his study of "Classical knowledge" that his guardian was al-

& innocent amusements than in preparing implements, & exercising them for the destruction of the human race. Rather than quarrel abt territory, let the poor, the needy, & oppressed of the Earth; and those who want Land, resort to the fertile plains of our Western country, to the second Land of promise, & there dwell in peace, fulfilling the first & great Commandment." Like most Anglo-Americans of this period, Washington does not seem to have remembered that the "fertile plains" were already populated. To him they represent what Emma Lazarus would later describe as the sanctuary existing behind the "Golden door" through which the oppressed of the Old World could enter.[58]

It was surely because Leutze was painting during a time of heightened sectional sentiments that he chose to include in his canvas the prominent figure of Washington's personal slave. On the eve of the Civil War, southern slavery was a topic of intense debate, particularly as it related to the settlement of the western states. The artist seems to offer no editorial statement other than to point to the paradox that Washington, and by implication other champions of American freedom, were slaveholders. In planning the nation's future, this was one problem the Founding Fathers had left unsolved.

The subjects of slavery and the western lands were tied together in Washington's mind at the end of his life in a surprising way. He did not see the Ohio as a place for the settlement of emancipated slaves, as some Americans did. Rather, Washington looked to the sale of his own western lands as a means to raise the funds that would free him to survive economically without slaves. He makes this clear to his secretary, Tobias Lear, in 1794, during the second presidency:

> My wish . . . is, to dispose of . . . my settled lands in the Western parts of this State [Pennsylvania]. . . .
>
> . . . My motives to these sales . . . are to reduce my income . . . that the remainder of my days may, thereby, be more tranquil and freer from cares; . . . for although, in the estimation of the world I possess a good, and clear estate, yet, so unproductive is it, that I am oftentimes ashamed to refuse [requests for] aids which I cannot afford unless I was to sell part of it to answer the purpose. (Private) Besides these, I have another motive which makes me earnestly wish for the accomplishment of these things, it is indeed more powerful than all the rest. namely to liberate a certain species of property [slaves] which I possess, very repugnant to my own feelings; but which imperious necessity compels; and until I can substitute some other expedient, by which expences not in my power to avoid (however well disposed I may be to do it) can be defrayed.[59]

Washington, at least at this late point in his life, was an unwilling slaveholder, but he could find no economic alternative to the use of slaves. His idea of freeing them was then so volatile that the Virginian felt compelled to label this part of his letter "private."

Washington's older half brothers had envisioned Virginia's next development in the far-western frontier of the colony. They had invested in the Ohio Company as early as the 1740s. In 1754, when Gov. Robert Dinwiddie challenged the French for ownership of the Ohio Valley, he promised the soldiers who served in his army the gift of two hundred thousand acres of land there. The grant of the "Ohio bounty lands" was delayed by the length of the Seven Years' War, by the problems inherent in dividing such a huge territory accurately and fairly, and by the subsequent hostility of the Indians displaced by European settlement. Their unrest caused passage of the Proclamation of 1763, which prohibited settlement west of the Appalachian Mountains. Washington would champion the cause of the bounty-land grantees in the late 1760s and early 1770s, and only by his laborious work was the grant eventually realized.

The story of the Ohio bounty lands extended across a period of more than forty years and thereby encompassed most of Washington's adult life. Initially, the prospect of owning large expanses of land in the western reaches of the colony stirred in him considerable interest and expectation. To the young Washington's thinking, the bounty lands would provide a means for his social ascent. They would earn income, either from rent or from sale after they had appreciated in value. And they would bring prestige. Washington talked of putting together parcels of this land to form a tract of "great dignity."[60] It seemed initially that one would not need to become a resident on the faraway Ohio River to reap financial benefits, but as it turned out the bounty lands were assets only for those owners who settled on them.

In 1769, once peace was restored with the Indian populations, Washington prepared a list of all the claims for land that had been made by the veterans (fig. 91). He then persuaded the new governor, Norborne Berkeley, baron de Botetourt, that the acreage to be given to the soldiers by Dinwiddie's proclamation should "be allotted them . . . On the Monongahela . . . On the New River or great Canhawa [Kanawha] . . . And on Sandy Creek." During the following year Washington traveled to western Pennsylvania and the Ohio country to select some of the best tracts for himself and to help supervise the surveying of the entire acreage.[61]

Washington spent considerable time and effort to gain ownership of some twenty thousand acres of bounty lands to which he was entitled. He soon added more acreage through purchases. In order to keep title to the Ohio tracts, however, owners were required to "seat" them within three years. This meant that Washington would have to construct at least a few buildings on each tract and clear and plant a minimum of one out of every five hundred acres. The easiest way to meet that requirement was to lease the lands. In 1773 Washington printed a broadside announcing the availability of leases to no avail.[62] He also failed to attract German, Irish, or Scottish settlers to the

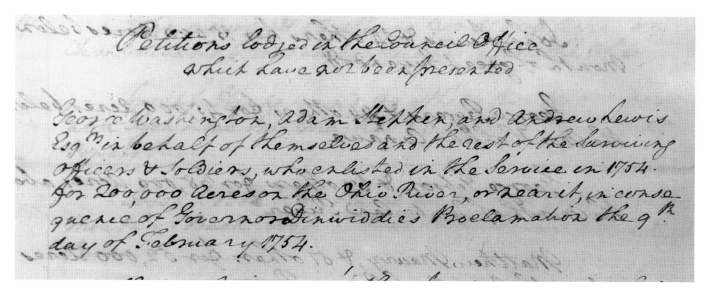

91. Washington's copy of the list of Ohio land petitions, 1769. (Courtesy of Mount Vernon Ladies' Association)

land, as he thought he might. Next he tried to buy indentured servants and to hire carpenters to settle and develop the various tracts, only to have those plans interrupted by the outbreak of Dunmore's War between the settlers and the Indians. A second attempt to seat artisans and laborers was interrupted by Washington's appointment to command the Continental Army in 1775. During the war he came to view the Ohio lands differently, as "an asylum" where he might hide from the British "in the worst event."[63]

Following independence, Washington found that his path to ownership on the Ohio was still blocked, this time by the resident Indians. He was angry when stating the problem to Lafayette, because like every Anglo-Virginian before him Washington had never seen landownership from the Indians' perspective. Also, he knew only too well their capability for violence: "The Indians on the Frontiers of Virginia and Pensylvania have lately committed Acts of hostility, murdering and Scalping many of the innocent Settlers. . . . It is much to be doubted whether these wretches will ever suffer our Frontiers to enjoy tranquility till they are either exterminated, or removed to a much greater distance from us than they now are."[64] These troubles passed quickly enough, however, and by the next year, 1784, the way was clear to try again to seat his property. It is interesting, however, that at this early date Washington invokes the idea of removal, which would come to define the policy of the U.S. government toward native peoples in the early decades of the nineteenth century.

At this point Washington remained optimistic about his project. After all, he believed that his Ohio and Great Kanawha property was "rich bottom land, beautifully situated on these rivers and abounding plentiously in Fish, wild fowl, and Game of all kinds." He even imagined that perhaps some religious sects might settle these lands with their pastors and thereby provide ready-made, stable, rent-paying communities, but he was unable to entice any such flocks to migrate to his properties.[65] In the fall of 1784 Washington traveled west to reexamine his lands and to look beyond them to the farthest reaches of the American empire that the Revolution had brought into being. In that way he could better assess the new importance that he believed his lands had assumed following independence. Unfortunately, he encountered tenants who paid little rent as well as squatters who paid none. "I found part of my property in possession of others," he wrote, "and myself under the necessity of bringing ejectments for the recovery of it." While we rarely think of Washington as an "absentee landlord," the courts ultimately returned verdicts in his favor, and what squatters he could find were summarily evicted.[66]

Exasperated by these experiences, Washington was ready by the mid-1780s to sell some parcels of land. As he put it to Charles Simms, "My Lands in Pennsylvania (west of the Laurel-hill) have been so unproductive of every thing but vexation and trouble, that I am resolved to sell them." He had finally realized that the western tracts might be "valuable and productive" to residents, but they were only "an incumbrance to me." He would complain in 1789 and 1790 that what rents he was receiving were too low to recoup his expenses or even to pay his land taxes.[67]

Washington persevered a few years longer with the western lands, ever thinking they would "fast increase in value."[68] But in 1794, as he prepared to leave the presidency, he was in need of funds "to defray the expences of my station" and to supplement the income of the Mount Vernon agricultural operation, which by then barely broke even. He was therefore forced to sell his "two very valuable tracts of land" in western

*The Virginia Planter: 1759–1775*

Pennsylvania.[69] In three years the money from that sale was gone, but in December 1797 it seemed that Washington had finally resolved his perpetual financial crisis when he arranged a thirty-year lease of his Kanawha lands, on "advantageous" terms, to James Welch. As it turned out, Welch was never able to fulfill his part of the bargain. In February 1799, the year he died, Washington wrote in vain to Welch, "The first of January is past . . . without my receiving any Money from you. . . . I am in real want of it."[70] Neither Washington nor his estate ever received any rents or other remuneration from Welch. The failure of this lease, which Washington entered into with such high expectations, was a fitting conclusion to what must have seemed like a lifelong struggle.

One manifestation of Washington's interest in the western lands was his patronage of artists who painted it. He was one of the first Americans to collect and display scenes of his native landscape. This interest began in Philadelphia in 1793, when for the considerable sum of $140 the president purchased two scenes of the Hudson River by William Winstanley, an English artist who had emigrated to New York. Nearly forty years earlier Washington had ordered for the west parlor at Mount Vernon an imaginary, or at least contrived, English landscape (see fig. 66); by the 1790s he chose instead imagery that spoke of America's destiny. Washington rated Winstanley "a celebrated Landskp Painter" and encouraged him to come to Virginia. "I have suggested," Washington wrote, that he paint "the Great and little Falls [of the Potomac River]; the passage of the River Potomac through the Blue [Ridge] Mountains, the Natural bridge, &c. as grand objects."[71] There is no evidence that Winstanley ever traveled as far south as the Natural Bridge, but he did traverse the Potomac and Shenandoah Rivers. Among the Virginia scenes that the artist exhibited in

92. George Beck, *The Great Falls of the Potomac*, ca. 1796–97, oil on canvas, 38⅞×50¹⁄₁₆ in. (Courtesy of Mount Vernon Ladies' Association)

London in 1806 were *View on the Shenandoah in Virginia* and *View from a Sketch Taken on the Potomac in Virginia, North America* (both unlocated). In 1794 the president bought a second pair of landscapes from Winstanley. One was *Falls of the Genessee;* the other may have been *Meeting of the Waters,* which is generally regarded as an idealized depiction of the Shenandoah and Potomac Rivers at their juncture.[72]

From George Beck, another English landscapist, who emigrated to Norfolk and then Baltimore, Washington acquired two canvases, *The Great Falls of the Potomac* (fig. 92) and *The Potomac River Breaking through the Blue Ridge.* These paintings, both circa 1796–97, are at Mount Vernon today. Washington actually hung seven large landscapes in the "New Room," or banquet hall, that he had built after the war. Four were the works by Winstanley, two were the Becks, and there was one European moonlight scene. The inventory taken after Washington's death lists "2 large Gilt frame Pictures representing falls of Rivers" (the Genessee and the Potomac), valued at $160; "4 d[itt]o. representing water Courses" (two of the Hudson and two more of the Potomac), valued at $240; and "1 Painting 'Moon light[']," valued at $60.[73] Six of the seven paintings, then, are evidence of the nationalistic perspective borne of his wartime experiences and his explorations of the Ohio Valley. Two are of the Hudson where he had campaigned for years, and four are of the Potomac, which he perceived to be the gateway to the western empire. These river landscapes served to define visually the potential of the new American nation; they celebrated its beauty and, by pointing to the available means for commerce, symbolized its ultimate greatness.

*The Great Falls of the Potomac* gives visual form to the idea that the western lands at the source of the river would be at the core of an expanding and divinely favored American nation. The extent of the western empire is manifested in the magnitude and force of the water that crashes over the falls.[74] The canvas thereby actually depicts a natural barrier to navigation—the falls—that become a symbol not only of the vitality of this natural wilderness but also of the efforts that will be required to bring it under control. It was fitting that Washington came to own multiple views of the Potomac, not only because this waterway served Mount Vernon but also because his efforts to make the river navigable to its sources consumed more than three decades of his life.

In 1770, when he was petitioning the governor for the bounty lands, Washington became one of the earliest proponents of a scheme to open the inland navigation of the Potomac River by means of a canal. Indeed, he had talked about this idea as early as 1762. In 1774 he was one of 337 trustees of the Potomac River Canal Company; after the interruption caused by the war he was made a director. By 1785, after public subscriptions had "filled very fast," Washington could write

to George William Fairfax in England that the work would soon begin.[75]

Washington could never put aside for long his schemes about the Ohio lands or inland navigation of the Potomac. While in New York at the conclusion of the war he toured that state. The experience inspired him to bring his thoughts about empire and destiny into clearer focus, the fulfillment of which he linked to the improvement of the inland waterways of the nation: "Prompted by these actual observations, I could not help taking a more contemplative and extensive view of the vast inland navigation of these United States, . . . and could not but be struck with the immense diffusion and importance of it; and with the goodness of that Providence which has dealt her favors to us with so profuse a hand. Would to God we may have wisdom enough to improve them. I shall not rest contented 'till I have explored the Western Country, and traversed those lines (or a great part of them) which have given bounds to a New Empire."[76] Washington's 1784 reexamination of his Ohio lands and exploration of the western reaches of the new nation confirmed his commitment to the Potomac-canal project. On this trip he thought about the produce of the farms that would soon proliferate in the West, the markets they would need, and the ways such commodities could be transported to consumers. He worried that the harvest of the western lands could be lost to the British in the North or the Spanish in the South if their markets proved easier to reach than the American settlements on the East Coast. By inactivity, he reasoned, the vast lands of the frontier might themselves be lost. Washington vented his concerns in a long entry in his diary: "I am well pleased with my journey, as it has been the means of my obtaining a knowledge of facts—coming at the temper & disposition of the Western Inhabitants. . . . The more then the Navigation of Potomack is investigated, . . . the greater the advantages arising from them appear. . . . The Ohio River embraces this Commonwealth [Virginia] from its Northern, almost to its Southern limits. It is now, our western boundary & lyes nearly parallel to our exterior, & thickest settled Country." He then drew in the diary a chart of the distances to market cities and concluded that the best route for western produce would be the Potomac:

> Let us open a good communication with the Settlemts. west of us—extend the inland Navigation as far as it can be done with convenience and shew them by this means, how easy it is to bring the produce of their Lands to our Markets, and see how astonishingly our exports will be encreased. . . .
>
> No well informed Mind need be told, that the flanks and rear of the United territory are possessed by other powers, and formidable ones too—nor how necessary it is to apply the cement of interest to bind all parts of it together, by one indissolvable band—particularly the Middle States with the

Country immediately back of them. For what ties let me ask, should we have upon those people; and how entirely unconnected shod. we be with them if the Spaniards on their right, or Great Britain on their left, instead of throwing stumbling blocks in their way as they now do, should envite their trade and seek alliances with them? . . .

The Western Settlers—from my own observation—stand as it were on a pivet—the touch of a feather would almost incline them any way. . . .

. . . The expence, comparitively speaking deserves not a thought, so great would be the prize. . . .

The way [to embrace these people] . . . is to open a wide door, and make a smooth way for the produce of that Country to pass to our Markets before the trade may get into another channel.[77]

A week after he wrote this nationalistic passage Washington advised the president of Congress that the central government should reserve "for special sale, all Mines, minerals and Salt springs in the general Grants of Land" in the West so that "the Public" would "derive the benefits which would result from the sale of them." Admittedly, Washington now envisioned an American rather than a Virginian empire, but it was primarily as a Virginian that he had become almost obsessed with extending the navigation of the Potomac. In 1785, when he explained that his "attention is more immediately engaged in a project which is big with great political, as well as Commercial consequences to these [United] States," he added, "especially the middle ones."[78]

By 1786 Washington was "divid[ing his] time between the superintendence of opening the navigations of our rivers & attention to my private concerns"; in 1793 he wrote that the project was "far advanced." But the canal was so great an undertaking and so slow in its progress that its funding would become increasingly difficult in the 1790s. Washington's dream of a navigation corridor to the West was not destined to be completed in his lifetime.[79]

Both the effort to develop or sell his Ohio lands and the attempt to build a Potomac canal frustrated Washington. He wrote in 1794 that his western holdings brought him "more plague than profit."[80] He might well have said the same about the canal were he not also interested in the growth of the new federal city. A canal would link what came to be called "Washington City" to the Ohio lands. The creation of the district in the 1790s was a new component in the equation. If troublesome, his western undertakings had provided Washington with a national perspective that made him a Federalist politician with a mission. His presidencies were governed by his strong determination to shape and hold together an American nation that stretched from the colonial seaboard to the West.

Like his experiences among the Virginia aristocracy, Washington's near obsession with the subject of inland navigation helped to prepare him for the presidency, when his duty would

be to think far beyond the confines of Fairfax County. In this way his admittedly provincial interest in Virginia would ultimately serve all the citizens of the United States. He would see in his Potomac River landscape paintings representations of untapped potential. For the president, any scene of this watercourse was as well a look farther westward, to the present and future settlements on the frontiers. He could turn to the canvas of the falls and envision the canal that would one day carry commerce around them and then to market along the Potomac.

It is fair to say that Washington's conception of America evolved from his Virginia background and was rooted in the history of his home colony. As defined in the original grant from James I, Virginia was a vast domain extending both far to the west and north to the Great Lakes. It encompassed much of the land that after 1776 would become the new nation. The property that Washington owned in what is now Ohio, West Virginia, and the far reaches of Pennsylvania was all Virginia land. The amassing of such extensive holdings on the colony's western frontier perpetuated a Virginia tradition dating back to the previous century. To look west, see what it had to offer, and try to figure out the best way to make use of it was, on a much grander scale, a repetition of what Augustine Washington had attempted during George's boyhood.

Washington also looked to the untapped regions of his home state. The promise of large tracts of Ohio land had helped induce him to serve with the Virginia Regiment. But the dispersement of the Ohio lands took nearly two decades to resolve. In the meantime, Washington looked for other opportunities. He invested in the Mississippi Land Company in 1763, only to write off the money as a loss nine years later. In the same year he helped to form the Dismal Swamp Land Company, which failed either to yield a return on his money or to reclaim land from the swamp, as was the intention.[81]

In 1763 Washington had explored the Dismal Swamp in order to assess the land's potential. A century later the Brooklyn illustrator John McNevin conceived a romantic image of the retired colonel at Lake Drummond alone with his thoughts, which was published in the 1889 edition of Washington Irving's *Life of Washington* (fig. 93). In this strange scene, a bird hovers above Washington like the dove of the Holy Ghost in religious paintings of the European Renaissance. This bird serves effectively to transform the entire picture, making Washington's presence at the otherwise gloomy swamp seem, if not sanctified, at least inspired. McNevin seems to tell us that his mission to the Dismal Swamp was spiritually if not practically important, although we are hard-pressed to figure out what he might have gained.

Swamps appealed to nineteenth-century Americans because they were mysterious and evocative. Here was nature in an enigmatic rhythm of decay, seemingly impervious to man's cul-

93. Samuel Valentine Hunt, after John McNevin, *Washington at Lake Drummond, Dismal Swamp*, n.d., engraving, 6¾×4⅜ in. (Courtesy of Mount Vernon Ladies' Association, gift of Mrs. John H. Guy Jr., Vice Regent for Virginia, 1963–95)

tivation efforts. The idea that the man who would become our first president had traversed these famous "dark and gloomy woods" with that very thought in mind, making his way "over a quaking bog that shook beneath his tread" and even camping there overnight, caused Irving to discuss in more detail than his predecessors the subject of the Dismal Swamp Land Company. His conclusion was that Washington contributed to "the subsequent improvement and prosperity of that once desolate region."[82]

In fact, Washington was at best only moderately successful with his efforts at the Dismal Swamp. He wrote that he had explored the area of Lake Drummond "for the purpose of reclaiming the Lands." He thought they could be "easily drained; and when drained [would be] equal to the richest rice land of So. Carolina." Washington told Patrick Henry that the "sunken Lands" would "in time become the most valuable property in this Country." All this, of course, proved untrue. Thirty years after exploring Dismal Swamp, Washington gave up on its investment potential and disposed of his interest in the gloomy recesses.[83]

His early efforts in Dismal Swamp were not entirely wasted, however. In the 1780s Washington recognized that there was a "practicability of opening a communication between the rivers which empty into Albemarle Sound [of North Carolina] . . . and the waters of Elizabeth or Nansemond Rivers." A canal, begun in his lifetime, was built through Lake Drummond to connect those waters. In helping to initiate that improvement, Washington earned the credit that Irving and McNevin gave him.[84]

## Farming under British Taxation

During each of the three lengthy periods of his life when Washington was able to retire from public duty to Mount Vernon, the greatest quantity of his time was consumed by the business of farming. Determined to excel in this endeavor in the same way that he was driven to succeed at everything that he attempted, Washington soon began to educate himself in the science of agriculture, while continuing to add arable acreage to his estate and involving himself in the daily activities of his

*The Virginia Planter: 1759–1775*

97. John Trumbull, *George Washington,* 1780, oil on canvas, 36×28 in. (Courtesy of
Metropolitan Museum of Art, bequest of Charles Allen Munn, 1924)

4

## The War Years
## 1775–1783

*An Unsought Honor*

WASHINGTON WAS CHOSEN to be the commander of the Continental Army on 15 June 1775. He had appeared at the Second Continental Congress in Philadelphia in uniform— most probably that of the Fairfax Independent Company— which demonstrated to his peers, as it does to us today, that no matter what he might have said on the subject he wanted the job.[1] For Washington the Revolutionary War would provide an unanticipated opportunity to fulfill his longstanding ambition of a successful military career while at the same time giving him the chance to humiliate the very army that had unreasonably denied him advancement. Washington made clear to a number of his contemporaries, however, that the decision to accept this post was extremely difficult for him to make. As would be the case regarding the presidency years later, Washington was pulled in different directions by what he perceived as conflicting public and private obligations and interests. When Trumbull presents him in 1780, however, he had already survived the worst of his command ordeals, and his coolness under adversity had become the stuff of legend (fig. 97).

After accepting the commission, Washington wrote a series of letters to family and friends explaining his decision. In every communication he states clearly that he did not want, and thought himself unworthy of, this exalted position. He had settled into the gentry life of a planter and had little desire to give up the felicity that he enjoyed with Martha at Mount Vernon. Washington also had a real concern that it might simply be impossible for untrained American militiamen to defeat the powerful British armed forces. By accepting this commission he could be putting himself and his reputation in a no-win situation. That being said, this possibility was undoubtedly exciting. As Thomas Fleming points out, "Here was an opportunity to serve his country, on a scale beyond the imagination of his brother Lawrence or the Fairfaxes."[2] He would have the chance to prove himself in what would be the most important events to take place in the Western Hemisphere, and he would again hear the "charming" sound of bullets "whistling" around

his head as he had in 1754. Although his first experience had ended disappointingly, Washington still loved the military, and vestiges of his once-driving ambition to succeed in arms were revived in the early 1770s.

In a letter to his stepson, Jacky Custis, the newly appointed general included many of the same phrases used in his correspondence with other family members, including his brother-in-law Burwell Bassett and a favorite brother, John Augustine Washington (fig. 98). In each case Washington denies interest in the position and questions his ability to succeed, but then refers to the convincing weight of his public obligation. This letter is particularly moving because Washington adds his concern that Jacky look after Martha:

> I have been called upon by the unanimous voice of the Colonies to take command of the Continental Army—It is an honour I neither sought after, or was by any means fond of accepting, from a consciousness of my own inexperience, and inability to discharge the duties of so important a Trust. However, as the partiality of the Congress have placed me in this distinguished point of view, I can make them no other return. . . . My great concern upon this occasion, is the thought of leaving your Mother under the uneasiness which I know this affair will throw her into; I therefore hope, expect, & indeed have no doubt, of your using every means in your power to keep up her Spirits, by doing every thing in your power, to promote her quiet.

In explaining to his wife his choice to return to duty, a decision that might cost him his life and lead to the loss of their property, Washington emphasized that he had "used every endeavor in my power to avoid it," but then pointed to what, for him, would have been the disastrous result of refusal: "I should enjoy more real happiness and felicity in one month with you, at home, than I have the most distant prospect of reaping abroad, if my stay was to be Seven times Seven years. . . . It was utterly out of my power to refuse this appointment, with out exposing my Character to such censures as would have reflected dishonour upon myself, and given pain to my friends."[3] Included with this letter was Washington's newly written will, which must have brought his wife as much distress as his words of affection had attempted to bring her comfort.

In his reply to Congress Washington accepted the appointment reluctantly, stating that he did not think himself "equal to the Command." He spoke with humility and, as he put it, "with the utmost sincerity," for he was truly concerned that success might well be beyond his reach. In his letters to Bassett and John Augustine the former colonel used the metaphor of the sea, describing his assumption of command as the beginning of a journey on a "tempestuous" and "wide" ocean, from which, perhaps, "no friendly" or "safe harbour" would be found. In such admissions he was trying to express eloquently his genuine fear. Benjamin Rush later recorded a story in his autobiography that enlightens us beyond Washington's own statements: "I saw Patrick Henry at his lodgings, who told me that General Washington had been with him, and informed him that he was unequal to the station in which his country had placed him, and then added with tears in his eyes 'Remember, Mr. Henry, what I now tell you: From the day I enter upon the command of the American armies, I date my fall, and the ruin of my reputation.'" In fact, he enhanced his already distinguished reputation not only by accepting the job but also by refusing a salary: "I do not wish to make any proffit from it: I will keep an exact Account of my expences."[4] This stance tells us much about his sense of duty to the evolving nation and in part explains why he was thought of so highly by his peers.

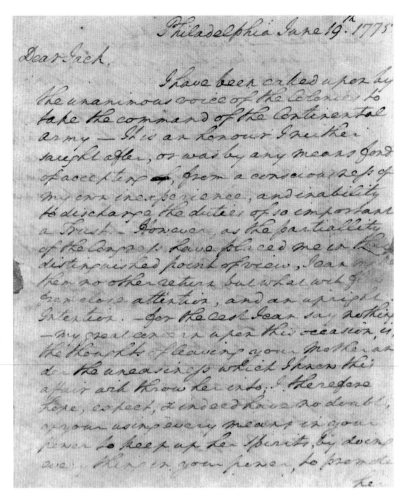

98. George Washington to John Parke Custis, 19 June 1775. (Courtesy of Virginia Historical Society)

Washington would not only have to command the Continental Army. It would also fall to him to shape this new entity, to make the best use of men with widely different training, experience, and ability, and to find a way to sustain it through what would clearly be difficult times. The army that awaited him outside Boston was composed of line regiments supplied by each of the states, thus recalling the Virginia Regiment that Washington had helped to build twenty years earlier. His task was to organize brigades and divisions as well as to make certain that the regiments were properly manned. These units were infrequently filled to their quotas, and so throughout the war, more like a politician than a military commander, Washington had to write what must have seemed like endless correspondence to state governors, strongly petitioning them to provide the promised manpower.

At least to some extent, the army's identity also came from Washington. His personal standards became a model and an inspiration for those who served under him. His manner of behavior with his officers involved a mix of formality and courteousness, what Abigail Adams would later describe as "a dignity that forbids familiarity, mixed with an easy affability that creates love and reverence."[5] His manner and civility became a standard of military propriety for his often quarrelsome, largely inexperienced officers, a number of whom were volunteers from Europe. This demeanor and his apparently natural ability to understand when to command directly and when to delegate authority were clearly rooted in the dignity and decorum of the Virginia gentry that he had witnessed nearly all his life. In ways that perhaps he did not immediately recognize, his years away from the service had helped to prepare him for his dual roles of autocrat and exemplar.

As much as anything else, Washington's character and patriotism sustained the army, and the nation as a whole, through eight years of war. He remained steady during even the most trying of times, although on occasion he privately despaired that the cause might be lost. However, everyone, including the

British, eventually concluded that Washington, because of his innate talent and fierce determination, would somehow endure. By his own example he held the army together, in the same way that as president Washington would later give cohesion to the disparate states that had formed an uncomfortable union.

Unlike politicians, military leaders do not exert their influence as much through the spoken word as through visual means; most of their soldiers know them only from a distance, and there is generally little opportunity for conversation. Washington's success in inspiring his regiments owed much to the fact that he looked the part of a general. He was an impressive physical specimen, skilled as a horseman, and impeccable in his military dress. There are a number of written accounts of his striking appearance; for example, Samuel Curwen, a loyalist who dined with Washington in Philadelphia in 1775, described him as having a "fine figure" with a "most easy and agreeable address."[6] Both Peale and Trumbull provide visual evidence of such opinions (see figs. 35, 97). They portray a tall and impressive figure who is somehow comfortable even in the contrived poses of the time, which were rooted in Old World ideals of deportment. No doubt the general at times assumed exaggerated poses like these because they would have looked appropriate to contemporary eyes. In chapter 2 we saw the word *easy* used in the description of a "gentleman" in *The Rudiments of Genteel Behavior.* By nature Washington seems to have been well suited to make this formal manner seem graceful rather than stilted, as it might appear to us.

Washington's impressive appearance on horseback apparently set him even further apart from his contemporaries. Again, Washington's size was a factor, as he seemed to tower above his similarly seated companions; just as important, however, were his natural equestrian talents, which had been developed through years in the saddle with the Virginia Regiment and in his more recent pursuit of foxes. Thomas Jefferson described Washington as "the best horseman of his age, and the most graceful figure that could be seen on horseback." A French officer, the marquis de Chastellux, noted that Washington "breaks in all his own horses; and . . . is a very excellent and bold horseman, leaping the highest fences, and going extremely quick." Such an accomplished horseman would have been inspirational at the head of an army. In fact, according to George Washington Parke Custis's account of a story told by Lafayette, the general was such a figure at the battle of Monmouth: "I was a very young major-general on that memorable day, and had a great deal to do, but took time, amid the heat and fury of the fight, to gaze upon and admire Washington, as, mounted on a splendid charger covered with foam, he rallied our line with words never to be forgotten: 'Stand fast, my boys, and receive your enemy; the southern troops are advancing to support you!' I thought then, as I do now," continued the good Lafayette, "that never have I seen so superb a man."[7]

Washington was certainly conscious of his appearance on horseback; he once went so far as to write that he had a predilection for the color of his mount. He "would prefer a *perfect* White, a dapple grey, a deep bay, a chestnut, a black, in the order they are mentioned." But, at the same time, he was less concerned about the horse's height and appearance than its strength and ability to carry him. "Being long legged, or tall, would be no recommendation," he wrote, "as it adds nothing to strength, but a good deal to the inconvenience in mounting."[8] Trumbull would later confirm the president's still graceful carriage on horseback (see fig. 139).

Washington also paid careful attention to the design of his uniform. He had learned early on that the proper clothing can convey status and power. As a civilian he had been inclined to be somewhat sartorially conservative, as were most members of the Virginia gentry. In such circles audacious displays were generally condemned. At one point Washington advised Bushrod, a favorite nephew, not to wear lace and embroidery because "fine Clothes [do not] make fine Men, any more than fine feathers make fine Birds." But the military was a different matter for there were troops to inspire and well-dressed enemies to impress. In arms, colorful fabrics and trim were not only appropriate but also necessary. In his 1780 study of the general Trumbull's purpose was to convince a European audience that Washington was a heroic leader, which was the message Washington himself hoped to convey to his counterparts in the British army (see fig. 97). When Washington had served with Braddock and Forbes during the French and Indian War he had seen that fine uniforms were one way officers differentiated themselves from their troops. This lesson no doubt encouraged him to specify every detail of his Revolutionary War uniform, from the number of silver stars on a gold epaulet to the various colors of sashes that would differentiate his officers by rank, to the summer and winter colors of vests and breeches. If the troops were discouraged, as they had to be by the often inadequate supplies of food, clothing, and ammunition, at least they would be inspired by the appearance of their officers. In 1798, when a war with an overturned France threatened, Washington would describe specifications for the uniform of his country's commanding general. At that point he would call for even more flair, presumably because the former president saw the American nation as the equal of any country in Europe. Embroidery and plumes now enter the picture: "The Uniform of the Commander in Chief to be a blue coat, with yellow buttons and gold epaulets (each having three silver stars) linings cape and cuffs of buff, in Winter, buff vest and breeches, in

The north addition would be given in its entirety to a banquet hall. He would decorate both the facades of the house and its interiors with classical detailing because it was in vogue and because examples were easily found in the new wave of architectural pattern books, a few of which were apparently owned by the craftsmen he engaged. This adaptation of a public model to the private sphere was an innovative move because the reverse was the norm, but it was typical of Washington's boldness as an amateur architect. We also see here another example of his lifelong tendency to make use of public "types" in his private life, as he would borrow elements from his private life for his public personae.

Washington's plan also involved physically connecting the house to its flanking dependencies, as was the fashion in the Palladian or Mid-Georgian style. He had seen this carried out nearby in Virginia at Mannsfield and Mount Airy. His willingness to be different would be manifested, however, when he dared to open up those connectors so that the site's spectacular view of the Potomac River would not be concealed. The dependencies would be rebuilt and better positioned (since the house would be much wider), and not appear at the end of a diagonal but rather terminate in a more graceful quarter circle. The structure to the south would be a kitchen, that to the north a servants' hall. (In later years this building would serve to house conveniently the many "strangers" who would visit.) Also, Washington would take the low "piazza," or river porch, of his Virginia neighbors at Belvoir and Sabine Hall and risk building it to a full two stories, as only Roger Morris and a few other colonial Americans had done to that date. And he would start the process of transforming the landscape, planting to the east irregular groves overlooking the river. Eventually, on the land side, he would install a modified English garden made up of a bowling green within a serpentine walk, with the obligatory utilitarian structures screened from sight.

Shortly after his return from New York, and apparently inspired by that trip, Washington began planning the changes to his home. Only a few months later, in October 1773, he was working with a master carpenter and ordering huge quantities of materials both locally and from London.[14] The carpenter was Gawan Langfier of Alexandria, who had constructed the staircase at Mount Vernon and put in wall paneling on the first floor in the late 1750s. By the spring of 1774 Langfier was at work again. The timing was fortuitous because only months later came the sale at Belvoir, where Washington bought much of the furniture he would use to fill his expanded house.

By the end of 1775, after the war had begun and Washington was in the field, the south end of the house and the new dependencies were nearly completed, as was much of the lavish decoration that was added to the interior of the existing house. In 1776 the general wrote to encourage Langfier to close the north wing to the coming winter weather. By the end of 1778 construction of the covered ways had begun. Then work slowed, however; the war, even though it was seemingly being fought at a distance, caused building supplies to be in short supply. As the conflict moved into a primarily southern theater, British ships began to raid seaports in earnest and threaten river plantations. Three more years would pass before the covered ways would be completed. The piazza was begun when the roofs to the new north and south ends of the house were built in 1775 and 1776, but Washington had to inquire about its pavement in the spring of 1781, just prior to Yorktown; that work would not be finished until 1786, three years after his return from the military. The interior finishing of the north banquet hall would also await his return. The windows there were not even glassed in until 1787, when the room was finally completed. The exterior shutters of the house were an even later addition; they would not be in place until 1796.[15]

Washington developed a philosophy of architecture that underlies the second renovation of Mount Vernon. He put into writing some of his ideas on this subject late in life, when he designed a pair of houses in the new federal city named in his honor. In a 1798 letter to William Thornton, Washington argues that the rules of architecture can be bent, because most people will neither care nor notice: "Small departures from *strict* rules are discoverable only by skilful Architects, or by the eye of criticism; while ninety nine of a hundred, deficient of their knowledge, might be pleased with things not quite orthodox."[16] Such a philosophy was useful, if only to excuse the many features at Mount Vernon that are "not quite orthodox." The most visible of these—and three of the most successful elements of the house—are the pierced covered ways, the oversized pediment that lacks a supporting pavilion, and the giant piazza.

Washington came to understand that a successful building combines "Grandeur, Simplicity and Convenience," to borrow the phrase he used to endorse Thornton's design for the Capitol. The same could be said about Mount Vernon. He also believed that a "plain and dead Surface" on a building needed some sort of embellishment. For that reason he added an elaborate west doorway and a Palladian window to his home, and rusticated its dull clapboarding. He also understood that while the "Rules of Architecture are calculated . . . to give Symmetry, and just proportion to all the Orders, and parts of [a] building," the purpose is simply "to please the eye." The eye should govern design, more so than a rigid set of principles. Washington actually described himself as "a person who avows his ignorance of Architectural principles, and who has no other guide but his eye, to direct his choice."[17]

Throughout his life, once he decided upon a plan, whether military or political, architectural or agricultural, Washington was eager to move quickly to execute it. Even in his last years, when he had worked out his conception for the town houses, he wanted an undertaker to "dig the Cellars and lay the foundation" quickly, before the coming winter. Once construction began, if he could be there, the then elderly general placed himself in the thick of the work. His step-grandson, George Washington Parke Custis, wrote that Washington "was his own architect and builder, laying off everything himself." John Hughes, a visitor to Mount Vernon, noted in his diary, "It is astonishing with what niceness he directs everything in the building way, condescending even to measure the things himself, that all may be perfectly uniform." There was a definite method in his obsessiveness, however; after the construction of the south addition was under way in 1774, a perhaps bemused Washington wrote, "I think (perhaps it is fancy) [that the work] goes on better whilst I am present, than in my absence from the workmen." His presence would, no doubt, have caused most workmen to attend more assiduously to their appointed tasks. Inevitably, there were laborers who failed to fulfill their commitments. When this happened Washington had no qualms about complaining that his high standards had not been met, as he would do in 1787 when "Mr. Tharp," a plasterer, disappointed him.[18] If such behavior continued, he would eventually discipline or dismiss the offending party.

As Washington planned the rebuilding of Mount Vernon he turned again to the best of the carpenters who had served him fifteen years earlier. This was easy enough to arrange because Langfier was then employed only a few miles away at the nearly completed Pohick Church. A second craftsman there, the carver William Bernard Sears, whose skills apparently surpassed even those of Langfier, followed him to Mount Vernon. A third master workman, whose name is not known, was a plasterer. He was an indentured servant who was brought to this country jointly by Washington and his brother-in-law Fielding Lewis. This "stucco man" had worked first at Lewis's house, Kenmore, in Fredericksburg before coming to Mount Vernon. Washington would also put together a team of itinerant bricklayers, carpenters, and painters. Some of the names of these other workers are known; others were indentured servants, some of whom worked off their debt and some of whom ran away. In addition, a group of Washington's slaves also assisted on this massive project.[19]

Before construction could begin, Washington and Langfier had to confer not only about the materials to be ordered for the rebuilding but also about what the owner envisioned for his house. Langfier or Sears must have owned some pattern books; one volume, Batty Langley's popular *Treasury of Designs,*

provided a number of the motifs that soon appeared at Mount Vernon. The two craftsmen may well have used that book at Pohick, the interior of which was destroyed during the Civil War. Other volumes, including Abraham Swan's *British Architect* and William Pain's *Practical Builder,* probably made their way to Mount Vernon in the same way. At least a half dozen of the design details applied to the facades and interior of the expanded Mount Vernon can be found in *A Treasury of Designs.* To be sure, some of these motifs can be located in other pattern books as well, but the sequence of so many that may have come from Langley enhances the probability that his book was the source of them all.

If we look at Washington's simplistic sketch of the land facade we find an outline of the basic configuration he would give to the house along with the features he wanted to develop (see fig. 99). Those elements, the cupola and the central pediment with an ocular window, are drawn darker and in more detail. Washington's idea was to follow the current Mid-Georgian fashion for defining the center axis. The tall cupola would make up for the absence of a projecting central pavilion, which would have been troublesome to build on the existing rusticated structure. To further emphasize the center axis, Washington had Langfier embellish the main doorway.

The purpose of the drawing was to allow Washington to determine the proportions of the cupola and pediment, as well as the length of the expanded house, and then to see what all these changes would ultimately look like. As was more usual than not with important Virginia architecture of this period, he would rely on the geometry of simple mathematical proportions. He drew the pediment to be one-third the length of the house. Its height from the ground is also one-third of this length, as is the distance from where the roof (and pediment) begin to the top of cupola. A vane would run up a bit higher, upon which Washington would eventually place a dove of peace ("a bird . . . with an olive branch in its Mouth") in celebration of the end of the long war for independence.[20]

The next step was to turn to the pattern books to find prototypes for the elements of the facade that were to be featured. Washington and his team needed a design for a modillioned cornice to emphasize the large pediment, which could have come from almost any of the books, including *A Treasury of Designs.*[21] Although Langley provides several choices for an ocular window, his elliptical design was selected because it would work best with the expansive length of the house (figs. 102, 103). He provided no designs for cupolas because they were no longer the fashion in England, but a profile of a pulpit and its sounding board may have been enough of a guide for Washington's creative craftsmen (fig. 104). Like most pattern-book authors, Langley offered a number of choices for doorways.

102. *West (land) Facade,* Mount Vernon. (Courtesy of Richard Bryant, Arcaid)

One Doric design seems the probable source used at Mount Vernon because of its unusual element of a resting block that raises each pilaster a foot above the ground (fig. 105).

Just as visible as these prominent features, and a key to the success of Mount Vernon's design, is the rustication that made the wood clapboards of the house resemble not just stone, but stone neatly dressed in the manner in which the ancient Romans had learned to present it. This feature, which was introduced to the house in 1758, contributes considerably to the "grandeur" that Washington wanted in a building. He had seen genuine rustication—actual stone with its edges beveled—at neighboring plantations such as Sabine Hall and Mount Airy,

and on his northern travels he had observed how others had adapted this European tradition to the wooden architecture of America. The always enterprising Washington ordered bushels of white sand to be shipped from Point Comfort on Chesapeake Bay. He then developed a novel technique for applying sand and paint. Onto a second fresh, thick coat, sand was thrown "as long as [it] will stick, and till every part of the paint is well covered." This peculiar coating, he wrote, "is designed to answer two purposes, durability, and presentation of Stone." It was, in fact, surprisingly long lasting; years later, in the 1790s, Washington was considering "Sanding my houses anew," with the implication that the original coat of sand (although cer-

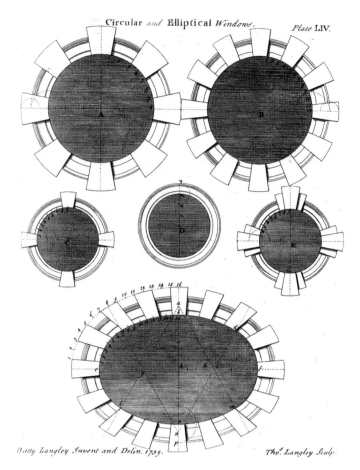

103. Batty Langley, *A Treasury of Designs* (London, 1740), plate LIV. (Courtesy of Virginia Historical Society)

104. Batty Langley, *A Treasury of Designs* (London, 1740), plate CXII. (Courtesy of Virginia Historical Society)

tainly not the outer paint) had survived. At that date he experimented with replacing the sand with pounded stone that, logically, would look even more like whole stone.[22]

A final distinguishing feature, which is visible on all the facades, is the unusual use of red on the roof shingles, which effectively complements the green of the grass and shutters. In November 1773, in the midst of the new construction, Washington visited Westover plantation and then "Rid with Colo. Byrd to see Shirly," where the idea for red shingles may have originated. Shirley had been inherited in 1770 by Charles Carter, who thereby became one of the richest men in the colony. He soon undertook a major renovation of the house and its dependencies. Shirley does not have red tile shingles today, but it did in the eighteenth century, as archaeologists in recent years have discovered. Washington may have been struck by the way that a solid field of red could pull what otherwise might seem to be disparate architectural elements into a well-proportioned whole, especially when seen from a distance across a green lawn. This was the illusion he hoped to create for visitors to Mount Vernon.[23]

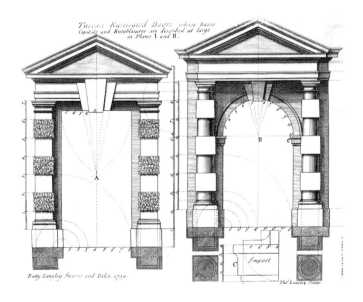

105. Batty Langley, *A Treasury of Designs* (London, 1740), plate XXXIII. (Courtesy of Virginia Historical Society

*The War Years: 1775–1783*

rather flamboyant chimneypiece (fig. 110) is so distinct that it can be firmly tied to a specific pattern book, Abraham Swan's *British Architect* (fig. 111). This book, which was published in London in 1745, had been used sixteen years earlier for the west-parlor chimneypiece (figs. 112, 113); plate LI provided a convenient frame for the "Neat Landskip" that Washington had ordered from London on the eve of his marriage. The book was brought back in 1775 when Washington or one of his craftsmen decided to coordinate the designs for the west-parlor and dining-room chimneys, which are located opposite one another and are both visible from the passage. The west-parlor chimneypiece is a composite, taken primarily from Swan's plate LI, with its pediment borrowed from plate L. The scheme decided upon in 1775 was to introduce the remainder of plate L into the dining room. This novel idea may well have been Washington's because in August 1775 the general wrote from New England to his plantation manager, his cousin Lund Washington, to "quicken Lanphire & Sears about the Dining Room Chimney Piece (to be executed as mentioned in one of my last Letters)."[26] (That entire letter is lost.)

The pediment from plate L calls for an ornate decorative element; this provided a convenient setting for a carved family coat of arms, which was introduced there no doubt at Washington's direction. In 1787 Washington purchased in Philadelphia an iron fireback with the family arms on it for this opening, thereby mimicking what he had seen at Belvoir (see fig. 19). It is possible that the Fairfax arms were also carved on a chimneypiece at Belvoir, which would have been unusual for a Virginia mansion. At Shirley there remains today in the large hall a pair of hatchments that display the family arms, but these are in fact mourning pieces that predate the Carter side of the family.[27] A more probable influence was the Governor's

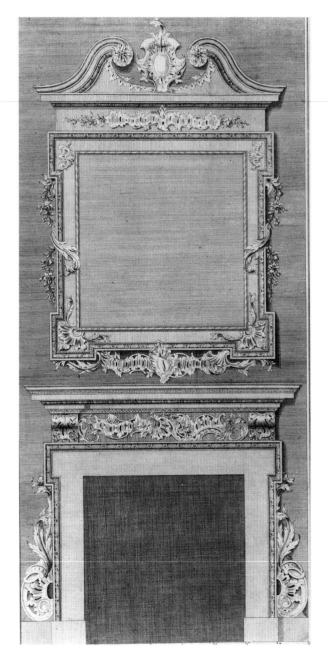

110. Dining room and chimneypiece. (Courtesy of Mount Vernon Ladies' Association)

111. Abraham Swan, *The British Architect* (London, 1745), plate L. (Courtesy of Virginia Historical Society)

*The War Years: 1775–1783*

112. West parlor and chimneypiece. (Courtesy of Mount Vernon Ladies' Association)

Palace in Williamsburg, where George I's coat of arms was believed to have been carved above the fireplace in the entrance hall, as it has now been reconstructed. If visitors to Mount Vernon were reminded of that decoration when they saw the Washington coat of arms displayed in a similar manner, then the colonel would have successfully made an unusually bold social statement, which was in particularly good taste because of the quality of the workmanship.

The question of whether this coat of arms was carved in 1759 or 1775 is not easily answered. Washington's conception may date to 1759 and thereby account for his peculiar idea of placing sculpted busts at the ends rather than in the center of this pediment; in this scenario he was saving the center for the family arms. On the other hand, the cartouche is so elaborately worked as to suggest that the skills of a carver were required for its execution. Either it is the work of the carver William Bernard Sears in 1775, or Gawan Langfier was a more able craftsman than has been generally believed.

Coats of arms and family lineage resonate in other elements of the west parlor as well. In this room the 1772 Peale portrait, which pictures the king's seal on the gorget, was hung to complete the Custis family group (see fig. 35). Here also, a few years later, Peale's portrait of Lafayette would be added (see fig. 130). This Frenchman came from so noble a lineage that his image

113. Abraham Swan, *The British Architect* (London, 1745), plate LI. (Courtesy of Virginia Historical Society)

114. West-parlor doorway, looking into the passage. (Courtesy of Richard Bryant, Arcaid)

alone would have suggested distinguished ancestry to American eyes. Perhaps Washington, by placing his coat of arms in such elevated company, was looking ahead to a time when his family would take its rightful place in an American aristocracy.

In 1787, when Washington returned with the fireback from Philadelphia, he introduced Prussian blue into this and other rooms and verdigris green into the dining room. These brilliant hues not only brightened his candlelit chambers but were also part of the neoclassical vogue and as such served to mask rococo designs that by then were thirty years out of date. His wish to keep up with current fashion had made Washington consider ripping out the work of Langfier and Sears in 1784, but he halted, partly because of the expense but also because his eye could identify quality workmanship: "When I came to examine the Chimney pieces in this House, I found them so interwoven with the other parts of the Work and so good of their kind, as to induce me to lay aside all thoughts of taking any of them down."[28] A new coat of paint was a less radical solution to the problem.

The details of the doorway surrounds in the west parlor—from the full Ionic entablature that surmounts each door to the elaborately carved capitals and the fluting of the pilasters—are so close to examples in Langley's *Treasury of Designs* as to suggest that this source, which was used for the exterior of the house, provided the motifs here as well (figs. 114, 115, 116, 117). Again there is no documentation as to whether Langfier or

116. Batty Langley, *A Treasury of Designs* (London, 1740), plate VIII. (Courtesy of Virginia Historical Society)

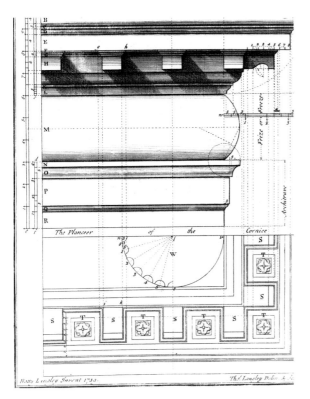

115. Batty Langley, *A Treasury of Designs* (London, 1740), plate VI. (Courtesy of Virginia Historical Society)

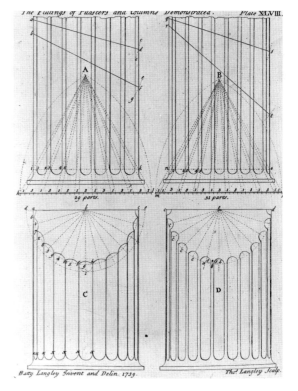

117. Batty Langley, *A Treasury of Designs* (London, 1740), plate XLVIII. (Courtesy of Virginia Historical Society)

*The War Years: 1775–1783*

Sears, in 1759 or 1775, carved these surrounds.[29] If Washington himself was not involved in the selection of the specific plates, which he may or not have been if they were chosen in late 1775 when he was in the field, at least his craftsmen knew that this was the type of design he favored. The doorways provided the mix of grandeur and simplicity considered appropriate by Washington.

As handsome as the dining-room chimneypiece, and just as well executed, is the stucco ceiling that was part of the "other" work to which Washington referred in 1784 (fig. 118). The "stucco man" turned out to be everything Washington and Lewis could have expected in an indentured craftsman. His series of ceilings at Kenmore helped to transform that house into an important American building, and both he and Lund Washington thought the ceiling he executed at Mount Vernon was "a handsomer one than any of Colonel Lewis." His talent greatly impressed Washington, who later called him "as ac-

complished a workman as ever came to this Country." (It should be added that Washington made this statement when considering the much higher price he was later forced to pay the craftsman who did his banquet room.) The "stucco man" and Sears worked side by side as they did their tedious work of molding plaster and carving wood. Lund Washington reported their progress to the general in the fall of 1775: "The Stoco Man is still about the Dineg Room & will I fear be for some time, Sears is still here about the Chimney piece, I suppose he will finish it next week you no doubt think him long about it, so do I, but I can assure you he is Constantly at worck—I think you never Intended such a one & must have been mistaken in the look of the Draught of the Chimney piece."[30] With this last statement Lund answered the general's complaint of a month earlier to "quicken" the completion of the chimneypiece; he further suggests that Washington did not understand just how much time it would take for a carver to execute properly the lavish detail that is suggested in Swan's plates, and he points to a fundamental difference between the chimneypieces in the west parlor and the dining room that is immediately visible today. The former had been finished simplistically by the joiner Langfier; it lacks the detailed carving that Washington ordered in 1775 for his dining room when he set both

118. Dining room ceiling. (Courtesy of Mount Vernon Ladies' Association)

119. William Pain, *Practical Builder* (London, 1774), plate LXII. (Courtesy of Virginia Historical Society)

*The War Years: 1775–1783*

a joiner and a carver, Langfier and Sears, to work on it. As always, Washington hoped he could obtain this labor at the lowest possible cost, but, no matter what the expense in time or capital, he had to be pleased with the quality of the work in the dining room, the details of which would be on view to his aristocratic visitors during the many intimate dinners held at Mount Vernon in later years.

The general's cousin thought the ceiling work was "light and handsome" and "very pretty"; interestingly, he reported that the specific design had been "recommended by Sears" (fig. 119).[31] Here, at least, is evidence that Washington did not make every selection, although he did make many decisions about the house during the years he was absent from Mount Vernon. This plan was based on a plate taken from William Pain's *Practical Builder* of 1774, a newly published book that either Sears owned or the "stucco man" brought with him. Pain's designs incorporated some of the lightness and delicacy of the Adam style, so Lund Washington was accurate in his description, even if he did not know what name to put to these new forms.

The banquet hall, which Washington referred to first as the "new room" and later as his "large dining room," provided the sizable hall for entertaining that was denied him by the narrowness of Mount Vernon's passage. Throughout the history of the Virginia colony, hospitality had been a characteristic of the lifestyle of the gentry, whose members were isolated on rural plantations and accordingly liked to congregate to enjoy festive events. A large room for entertaining was a feature of such houses as Stratford Hall and Sabine Hall, whose very names allude to the dominant feature of their floor plan. The "new room" was Washington's logical solution to meet what he saw as a pressing need. If Mount Vernon did not have a wide center hall, he would simply add one to the side of the house. Again making use of the prevailing belief that visual harmony is rooted in simple mathematical proportions, Washington designed the room to be thirty-two-by-twenty-four feet, with a sixteen-foot ceiling.[32] This made a handsome space that was slightly wider than a double cube, although it meant lowering the ceiling behind the false second-floor windows.

The north addition was under construction in 1776, with Langfier basically following what little design information was provided by the elevation of the facade (see fig. 99). Apparently not even the simplest floor plan had been drawn, because Washington had to inform his cousin that "the chimney in the new room should be exactly in the middle of it"; it was not to invade the adjoining rooms, and there should be a small cellar window below the Palladian window. In 1776 the room was roughed in, but ten years would pass before it was completed or before a door was even broken through into the existing house.[33] Washington's attentions and energies would be diverted elsewhere from 1775 to 1783, and most of his great

plans for the house either would have to be executed without his direct supervision or would have to wait until his second retirement.

## Equal to the Command

SIR.

I Have taken the freedom to address your Excellency in the enclosed poem, and entreat your acceptance, though I am not insensible of its inaccuracies. Your being appointed by the Grand Continental Congress to be Generalissimo of the armies of North America, together with the fame of your virtues, excite sensations not easy to suppress. Your generosity, therefore, I presume, will pardon the attempt. Wishing your Excellency all possible success in the great cause you are so generously engaged in. I am

Your Excellency's most obedient humble servant,

PHILLIS WHEATLEY

Wheatley's dedication, which reminds us of Washington's reputation at the beginning of the war, is dated 26 October 1775. At that point the general was debating how best to launch a campaign against the British in her home state of Massachusetts. He would not find time to respond until 28 February 1776 and apologized for the delay, which was based on "a variety of important occurrences, continually interposing to distract the mind and withdraw the attention."[34] Such interpositions would soon evolve into strategies meant to ensure the very survival, if not success, of his force.

While Washington initially meant to strike a decisive blow before British reinforcements could arrive, by 1776 success for the general and his newly organized Continental Army often meant surviving to fight another day. Their goal was to stay in the field, to outlast the will of the British government to expand from the pockets of territory under its control and regain dominion over the vast expanse of America's eastern seaboard; if the Continental Army could endure, the cost of maintaining the British armies in America might eventually become prohibitive. Given that objective, Washington had been surprisingly successful in the years leading up to 1780, when John Trumbull, in London, painted a full-length portrait of him (see fig. 97). Washington's survival, not to mention his occasional victories, had excited the imaginations of Europeans such as the Dutch banker De Neufville, Trumbull's patron. Even some English sympathizers had become interested in the remarkable if exasperating colonial general. While in London Trumbull had settled into the studio of his compatriot Benjamin West, where he quickly assimilated the latest fashions in English portraiture. His image of Washington would have seemed appropriate to European eyes. The general stands with his horse and servant, like the subjects in a succession of portraits dating back

122. Paul Girardet, after Emanuel Leutze, *Washington Crossing the Delaware,* 1853, engraving, 24½×38½ in. (Courtesy of Mount Vernon Ladies' Association, Willard-Budd Collection)

appear until four hours after the crossing was completed; the costumes and flag are inaccurate as are the boats, which were a flat-bottomed type built to carry heavy iron ore; and the horses and artillery were transported separately and last. One must also admit that Washington's pose is perhaps too theatrical (and open to enemy snipers) to be real, but he probably was near the front of his boat, scouting out a good landing site and encouraging his more timid companions onward. Rather than engage such issues, however, contemporary critics pointed instead to the inspirational qualities of this monumental canvas. "You feel embued [*sic*] with its spirit, animated by its impulse, and flushed with its excitement, ere you have time to break it up into groups or scan its details," reported the *Albion* in 1851. A second critic, writing at the same time in the *Bulletin of the American Art-Union,* called Marshall's biography of Washington "tame" and less instructional than this painting. Marshall gives ample space to the logistics of the strike at Trenton but only a bland sentence to the crossing.[47] At midcentury, when the United States was concurrently expanding westward and hurtling toward the most costly conflagration in its history, all that Washington had meant to the founding of the nation seemed embodied in this remarkable painting. At a time when Abra-

ham Lincoln was a little-known Illinois congressman, it seemed impossible to imagine that there could ever be another American as great as Washington. Leutze, in his powerful figure in the midst of, and perhaps subduing by his very presence, a tempestuous scene, rendered that belief for his audience better than has any painter, before or since.

Foolishly as it turned out, George Caleb Bingham tried in 1855 to paint a better version of Leutze's already famous painting (fig. 123). He labored for fifteen years before he was finally satisfied. The public, predictably, never embraced this work because the image is not as inspirational as Leutze's conception, nor is it as strong a demonstration of the evocative possibilities of history painting. But if we look beyond Bingham's preposterous suggestion that some of the officers were mounted in this situation and that their boats were crowded together on a wide river, we find that this artist's different focus is not without merit. He may have been responding to those critics who found Leutze's conception to be "too melodramatic in its character," with "too little reliance upon the expression or countenance which the manly souls and patriotic hearts of those brave men must have carried into that hour of might import."[48] Leutze's painting is an image of such exuberant

123. George Caleb Bingham, *Washington Crossing the Delaware*, 1856–71, 36⅝×57½ in. (Courtesy of Chrysler Museum of Art, gift of Walter P. Chrysler Jr. in honor of Walter P. Chrysler Sr.)

movement that it almost suggests the crossing was rapid. In Bingham's effort the movement is slowed almost to a stop; attention is instead directed to the face of Washington, who exhibits a good deal of concern. In this respect Bingham is probably closer to the truth, because the general had much to worry about as he neared the Jersey shore.

The crossing, which was a logistical nightmare made worse by deteriorating weather, had taken so much time that the army could not possibly reach Trenton before daybreak. The element of surprise would be lost, it seemed, and in daylight the Hessians could turn the tables and attack Washington. Because there were additional Germans encamped not far from Trenton, the enemy might even outflank him. The original plan had been to press onward after Trenton to Princeton to engage the British forces there. As dawn turned to morning, that seemed less and less possible. Washington was faced with the decision of whether he should even continue to Trenton. The reason for the crossing had been to win victories at Trenton and Princeton and thereby restore dwindling public support for the American cause. A disastrous mission would do the opposite, as Washington would later warn Lafayette: "*No rational person will condemn you for not fighting* with the odds against [you]

and while so much is depending on it; but all will censure a rash step if it is not attended with success."[49] Washington's force finally reached Trenton at approximately eight in the morning on 26 December, an hour after daylight. The general had divided his army into two units, which had marched the nine-mile distance along different routes. Progress was difficult because the weather had suddenly worsened. Washington later referred to "the Severities of rain, & Storm" that followed the crossing.[50] This mix of snow, sleet, and rain made footing difficult, but at the same time the storm had discouraged most of the Hessians from even venturing outdoors and brought decreased visibility for those who did. Washington's desired element of surprise remained intact. His two forces arrived at different parts of Trenton at about the same time, advanced through streets and amid houses with little opposition, positioned their artillery, and began firing.

Initially Washington could not follow the progress of the battle at Trenton. Eventually he moved to a high position and observed with his field glass. At this vantage point he received the news that his formidable enemy had surrendered. He responded to the messenger, Maj. James Wilkinson, "this is a glorious day for our country."[51] This moment of victory is what

John Trumbull celebrates in his life-size canvas, *General Washington at Trenton,* which was painted in 1792 (fig. 124). Four years later Trumbull's image was reproduced in an engraving (fig. 125), which was the source that Nora Mahoney, a Richmond schoolgirl, used in 1860 to weave a sizable needlework picture (fig. 126). Many of Miss Mahoney's schoolmates, to judge from their works that survive, illustrated scenes from the Bible. This great event from the life of Washington, apparently, was deemed comparable.

Trumbull's canvas was commissioned by the city of Charleston, South Carolina, which ultimately rejected it. This highly romantic image was simply ahead of its time. There is little wonder that it came into favor in the mid-nineteenth century, for it is almost as inspirational as Leutze's giant painting. The picture begs for comparison with Trumbull's depiction of the same subject twelve years earlier (see fig. 97). By 1792 the artist had sketched Washington from life, so the general's figure could be made more accurate in terms of his physiognomy. While abroad Trumbull had both developed his skills as a painter and learned much about high-style European art. He could now compete with Sir Joshua Reynolds as a portraitist and, like his better-known European contemporaries, could borrow ideas from the great artistic creations of the past. Trumbull's 1792 rendering of the then president portrays him as a magnificent and heroic general who had projected nobility and power. The superb white horse behind Washington rears like those carved on friezes of the Parthenon. Only the general can control him, like Alexander with Bucephalus, and there is no doubt about his similar ability to control the situation before him.

Trumbull skillfully used all the artistic means at his disposal to create a spectacular image. If he exaggerated the poses and lighting for dramatic effect, he was justified because the victory at Trenton was in fact a "glorious" day in American history, and Washington, according to his own statement, felt heroic at the time. Admittedly, the general held back his men from advancing to Princeton that same day because they were exhausted from their exertions of the previous twenty-four hours, but his success at Trenton, and the capture of 917 Hessians without a single American loss, was enough to change the course of the war. Not only were the British shocked at the daring and the fortitude of the colonials, but the morale of the American army was also restored, as was Washington's confidence and Congress's resolve to continue the struggle.

The survival of Washington's army a year later at Valley Forge would become as famous as his crossing the Delaware. In the intervening months Washington had advanced to Princeton where he defeated part of Cornwallis's army within sight of the college. But later, in September 1777, Sir William Howe finally captured Philadelphia. His advance was part of a two-pronged, though uncoordinated, British initiative: Howe would act in the middle colonies and perhaps move south as well,

124. John Trumbull, *General Washington at Trenton,* 1792, oil on canvas, 92½×63 in. (Courtesy of Yale University Art Gallery)

while Gen. John Burgoyne would march from Canada to New York, his purpose being to isolate the rebellious forces in New England.[52] Washington could only slow Howe's progress at Brandywine Creek and then attack him, valiantly but in vain, at Germantown. The Americans would retreat and winter nearby at Valley Forge, to answer Congress's concern that eastern Pennsylvania not be undefended. Before the autumn closed, in October 1777, Horatio Gates forced Burgoyne's army of five thousand soldiers to surrender at Saratoga. Although this proved one of the most significant single events of the war because it did much to encourage France to join in the conflict against its hereditary enemy, Saratoga did little at the time to encourage Washington's dispirited and poorly supplied army.

From Valley Forge Washington sent a desperate plea to Congress: "This Army must inevitably be reduced to one or other of these three things. Starve, dissolve, or disperse, in order to obtain subsistence in the best manner they can; rest assured Sir this is not an exaggerated picture, but that I have abundant reason to support what I say."[53] Not only were his soldiers demoralized by the inadequacy of their supplies and the power of their enemy, which was entrenched comfortably in nearby

125. Thomas Cheesman, after John Trumbull, *General Washington,* 1796, engraving, 29¾×19⅝ in. (Courtesy of Yale Center for British Art, Yale University Art Gallery Collection, the Mabel Brady Garvan Collection)

126. Nora T. Mahoney, after John Trumbull, *General Washington at Trenton,* 1860, needlework, 48×38½ in. Reverse-glass inscription, "St. Joseph's Academy, Nora T. Mahoney, Richmond, Va., 1860." (Courtesy of Virginia Historical Society)

Philadelphia, but there was also no assurance that Congress would ever adequately support the American forces. Here, perhaps more than at any other time during the war, the Revolution would have to be sustained by the example of Washington's character and unfailing patriotism.

The day-to-day conditions at Valley Forge are recorded in an order book kept by one of the officers under Washington's command, Col. James Meriwether from the Virginia Piedmont. His entry for 6 January 1778 (the Washingtons' nineteenth wedding anniversary), written in the dead of that terrible winter, records a series of incidents that in their number and variety well represent the adverse conditions (fig. 127). In the course of this one day, Washington ordered his officers to "part with" their horses because of the "difficulty of providing forrage" for them (the next day's entry mentions the burying of dead horses); a few "Iron ovens" arrived to help combat the cold; log "huts" were being built to shelter the troops; Washington (a property owner

127. Col. James Meriwether of Louisa County, Va., order book (kept at Valley Forge), 1777–78. (Courtesy of Virginia Historical Society)

*The War Years: 1775–1783*

135

himself) acted to protect a nearby private estate that already had been "nearly ruined by the Enemy" ("the Commander in Chief forbids the least Injury to be Done to the walls & Chimnies of Col. Devease's buildings"); the regimental surgeons called for a survey of all men who had had smallpox; Ens. Benjamin Arnold was court-martialed and dismissed from the army for "geting Drunk & behaving In an unsoldier Like manner"; and a regular in the Virginia Regiment named John Ryley, "Charged with Desertion from his guard and taking with him two prisoners In Irons," was sentenced "to suffer death." Washington approved both sentences and ordered Ryley to be executed the next Friday "near the grand parade [ground]." Such experiences gave renewed meaning to Thomas Paine's statements of a year earlier, during the crisis before Trenton, that "these are the times that try men's souls" and "it would be strange indeed, if so celestial an article as *Freedom* should not be highly rated."[54] By the spring Washington's army of nine thousand would be reduced by a third through sickness and desertion, and the remaining soldiers would hardly be in any condition to strike fear into the hearts of their enemy.

In the end, the majority of Washington's troops did somehow make it through the winter, but Weems reasoned that the general's faith in himself and in his maker must have been challenged at Valley Forge. He concluded that Washington must have prayed for help and guidance. From 1809, when Weems first published this incident, through the 1980s, when Ronald Reagan made reference to the purported prayer in his second inaugural address, many Americans have believed he did. Artists for more than a century have depicted the episode (fig. 128).[55]

In this obsession we see another instance of Americans looking to Washington's biography for values that match their own.

Weems concocted a simple-enough story but one that cannot be dismissed because his conclusion, perhaps surprising to some modern eyes, is one that Washington himself would not have denied.

In the winter of '77, while Washington, with the American army, lay encamped at Valley Forge, a certain good old friend, of the respectable family and name of Potts, if I mistake not, had occasion to pass through the woods near head quarters. Treading in his way along the venerable grove, suddenly he heard the sound of a human voice, which, as he advanced, increased on his ear: and at length became like the voice of one speaking much in earnest. As he approached the spot with a cautious step, whom should he behold, in a dark natural bower of ancient oaks, but the commander in chief of the American armies on his knees at prayer! Motionless with surprise, friend Potts continued on the place till the general, having ended his devotions, arose; and, with a countenance of angelic serenity, retired to headquarters. Friend Potts then went home, and on entering his parlour called out to his wife, "Sarah! my dear Sarah! all's well! all's well! George Washington will yet prevail!"

"What's the matter, Isaac?" replied she, "thee seems moved."

"Well, if I seem moved, 'tis no more than what I really am. I have this day seen what I never expected. Thee knows that I always thought that the sword and the gospel were utterly inconsistent; and that no man could be a soldier and a christian at the same time. But George Washington has this day convinced me of my mistake."

128. John C. McRae, after Henry Brueckner, *The Prayer at Valley Forge (March 1778)*, 1889, engraving, 15×21½ in. (Courtesy of Mount Vernon Ladies' Association)

He then related what he had seen, and concluded with this prophetical remark—"If George Washington be not a man of God, I am greatly deceived—and still more shall I be deceived, if God do not, through him, work out a great salvation for America."

There is no evidence that Washington prayed for divine assistance at Valley Forge, but there is little reason to doubt that he did; the general had little else to fall back on. Before the war Washington had learned to compare the "justice" of Providence to the "shallow eye of humanity"; this philosophy helped him and his contemporaries to accept the high premature death rate in the colony.[56] Later in his life he would posit that God had had a hand in American independence and had protected him so that he could fulfill an important role in that drama.

The survival of Washington's army at Valley Forge spurred the American resolve to persist in the struggle for independence. To sustain his own spirits during that difficult winter, the general's mind turned to the recent developments at Mount Vernon and to his eventual return home. As he explained to his cousin Lund, during that most difficult February 1778: "To go on in the improvement of my Estate . . . fulfilling my plans, and keeping my property together, are the principal objects I have in view during these troubles."[57] Washington was determined to again enjoy the gentry life that Mount Vernon had come to embody; indeed, he had gone to war to secure the political and economic means to do so. Martha's presence, which had helped him to survive the burdens of command during the arduous winter of 1777–78, had also reminded him of the joys of his private life, which a successful campaign against the British might allow him to again experience. The house had to be maintained, and if possible improved, so as to be adequate for the future he imagined. It is perhaps fitting that the most monumental of the renovations made to the house, which had been begun on the eve of the war, were largely carried out during his eight-year absence.

Washington, who was recognized as the inspiration for his army's endurance, came to be seen as a leader of extraordinary capabilities. Such a man, an officer of unquestionable ability and integrity, would be needed to impress favorably the French ambassador to the colonies. Conrad-Alexandre Gérard's opinions about Washington and the American cause would influence decisions made in Paris as to how seriously the French should participate in the war as an ally against Britain. France had signed a treaty of alliance with the Americans early in 1778, which to Washington immediately reversed the dire situation endured by his troops at Valley Forge: "the distress and perilous situation of this army in the course of last winter, for want of cloaths, provisions, and almost every other necessary, essential to the well-being, (I may say existence,) of an army"

had changed and "our prospects have so miraculously brightened."[58] But the French would be tentative in their support, even after Saratoga, until Washington could convince them that he could hold up his end of the bargain and persevere against the British. If the alliance was to survive, Washington would have to become a diplomat.

In the summer of 1778 the Admiral the comte d'Estaing cautiously approached the British-held city of New York; he soon retired to Boston, however, where his men were clearly uncomfortable, and soon became involved in various duels and brawls. Ambassador Gérard held long interviews with Washington on this and other subjects, during which the general convinced the Frenchman of his honesty, his character, and his indomitable purpose. To borrow the words of the marquis de Barbé-Marbois, who was secretary to Gérard's successor, the French saw a "noble, modest and gentlemanly urbanity . . . and graciousness" in Washington. They approved of the way he "carrie[d] himself freely and with a sort of military grace" and was "masculine looking, without his features being less gentle on that account."[59] The secretary, one might argue, saw Washington much as did the artists who painted him in uniform.

Gérard was himself painted by Charles Willson Peale; this image was copied, in all probability, by his son Rembrandt

129. Possibly Rembrandt Peale, after Charles Willson Peale, *Conrad-Alexandre Gérard,* after 1779, oil on canvas, 26×21¾ in. (Courtesy of Virginia Historical Society)

*The War Years: 1775–1783*

137. John Gadsby Chapman, *View of the House at Yorktown in which the Capitulation Was Signed,* 1834, oil on panel, 6¼×9½ in. (Courtesy of Homeland Foundation, Incorporated, New York)

U.S. Capitol between 1817 and 1824 (figs. 139, 140). Trumbull's idea to do a series of American history paintings originated in the 1780s, a few years after Yorktown, when the artist was in London with Benjamin West. His mentor had revolutionized that genre with his rendering of a modern event, *The Death of General Wolfe.* In 1787 Trumbull began a thirty-inch version of the Yorktown surrender, which he worked on intermittently over the next four decades. One of several oil sketches for the painting shows his progress toward the final composition. As was true of West's history paintings, the point of Trumbull's canvases was to memorialize a great event by re-creating the scene more or less as it happened but in such a way as to evoke the appropriate emotions that an episode of this magnitude would warrant.

Trumbull later visited Yorktown to see firsthand the site of the surrender. As a result, the finished version of the scene has a credible, if marginal, backdrop, in which the large Nelson House is visible far in the distance. Trumbull also went to great

lengths to sketch portraits of the thirty-four figures he would place in the final painting. He traveled to various states and even to Paris to track down the figures who were present. There were numerous accounts of the surrender that he could consult, and he could interview all the figures whose portraits he was taking. Included in that group was his brother Jonathan Trumbull Jr., who was Washington's secretary at Yorktown.

According to many of the surviving reports, the surrender documents were signed on the morning of 19 October. At two in the afternoon the British filed out of town, along a half-mile stretch of road lined with French soldiers on one side and Americans on the other. By Washington's estimate, these prisoners numbered "7,000, exclusive of the Seamen." They "march'd out with Colours Cased, and drums beating a British march." At the head of the column was not Cornwallis, who professed to be ill, but Brig. Gen. Charles O'Hara. Washington directed this subordinate to another subordinate, General Lincoln, who as commanding officer at the fall of

138. John Gadsby Chapman, *View of Yorktown, Virginia, and of the Spot Where Cornwallis Laid Down His Arms,* 1834, oil on panel, 6¼×9½ in. (Courtesy of Homeland Foundation, Incorporated, New York)

139. John Trumbull, sketch for *The Surrender of Lord Cornwallis at Yorktown,* 1787, oil on canvas, 13⅞×21 in. (Courtesy of Detroit Institute of Arts, gift of Dexter M. Ferry Jr.)

often the unavoidable fact that he would eventually succumb to the ravages of age. He made repeated references during this period to having passed the "noon-tide of life" and "mov[ing] gently down the stream of life, until I sleep with my Fathers." Perhaps the most telling evidence of his new state of mind is his candid statement to Lafayette that "I am not only retired from all public employments, but I am retireing within myself." Washington was trying, as he put it, to "tread the paths of private life with heartfelt satisfaction." He comments to Rochambeau that "the tranquil walks of domestic life are now unfolding to my view; & promise a rich harvest of pleasing contemplation." His stated goal was to "glide silently and unnoticed through the remainder of life."[27] But he must certainly have realized that there would be little silence. Washington was the most famous man in the world; never again would he go unnoticed.

In 1758 Washington had been able to set about getting his domestic affairs in order with little interference from the outside world. The constant attention he would receive during his second retirement, however, would make it far different from the first. As an international celebrity, Washington would be visited by travelers on an almost daily basis. He would have to allow for these intrusions and learn to approach his private projects and concerns differently. Most of the renovations to Mount Vernon were completed, or at least well under way, by the mid-1780s. The grounds, however, would demand his constant attention if he was to achieve his goal of becoming a model farmer. In his mind, the many visitors to Mount Vernon would expect only the highest standards in whatever he attempted, and he was determined not to disappoint them.

The general's daily routine evolved all too quickly to the point where he was spending much of the day indoors, corresponding and entertaining. Such activities had occupied some of his time before the war, but now the percentages shifted. Washington admitted to Benjamin Franklin that "retirement from the public walks of life has not been so productive of the leisure & ease as might have been expected." More than anything else, it was the increase in paperwork that displeased Washington. He would "not conceal" from Lafayette that "my numerous correspondencies are daily becoming irksome to me." There were "the numberless applications from Officers of the several lines of the Army for Certificates of Service—recommendations—Copies of Orders—references of old matters." Then there were "Enquiries, which would employ the pen of a historian to satisfy." There were "Letters of compliment, as unmeaning perhaps as they are troublesome, but which must be attended to." And finally, there was "the commonplace business, which employs my pen & my time; often disagreeably." Washington complained that these duties "confine me more to my writing Desk than I ever was at any period of my life; and deprives me of necessary exercise."[28]

What must have seemed like an endless stream of visitors journeyed to Mount Vernon to see the American Cincinnatus, and the entertaining of guests became an almost daily voca-

157. Jean Leon Gerome Ferris, *Washington's Silver Wedding Anniversary, 1784,* ca. 1913, oil on canvas, 25×35 in. (Courtesy of Virginia Historical Society, Lora Robins Collection of Virginia Art)

*The American Cincinnatus: 1783–1789*

tion. Two of the more formal gatherings at Mount Vernon were thought by Ferris to be important enough to merit reproduction; one looks at a special occasion, the silver-anniversary party that George and Martha Washington may or may not have staged (fig. 157), while the other celebrates the most famous visit by a European dignitary, that in 1784 by Lafayette (fig. 158).

There is no diary entry for 6 January 1784. Washington's correspondence at the time makes no reference to an anniversary party; therefore, there is no reason to believe that this event took place, particularly since the idea of such a gathering never occurred even to such nineteenth-century writers as Weems and Sparks. However, Washington no doubt did receive his neighbors in the manner Ferris suggests because gatherings of this nature at Mount Vernon and other gentry seats are documented.[29] The artist's depiction of so many guests crowding into the south end of Mount Vernon points to the general's pressing need to complete his new banquet hall.

Ferris, typically, is not accurate in many details of the painting, but the spirit is right. It is highly doubtful that captured Hessian and British flags were displayed in the Mount Vernon passage, and only in Ferris's own Colonial Revival era were Oriental rugs used as he suggests. But these elements bring welcome touches of color that help to convey the festive mood that no doubt was often experienced at Mount Vernon after Washington's triumphant return. Whether by chance or intention, the artist was right to emphasize silver decorative ob-jects because Washington would soon build his collection of hollowware. And the general did dress his ranking household slaves in livery, which he ordered from England, so Ferris's depiction of Billy Lee at the far left is appropriate. The inclusion of the livery in this image reminds us that after his return from the war Washington remained as predisposed as any member of the Virginia gentry to carry formality to an extreme and to use appropriate accoutrements to manifest one's social status.

Washington's day-to-day entertaining at times involved fewer guests, but some of the visits were of long duration, and he was often seating a dozen or more for dinner. If Washington could not always say with certainty who would arrive each day, he came to feel confident that someone would appear; a diary entry for June 1785 identifies the first day since his retirement that he had no visitors. The stream of pilgrims never ran dry, and in 1797 Washington would look back over the two decades after the war and comment that he and Martha had not once "set down to dinner by ourselves."[30]

Two of the many guests who came from afar were the English historian Mrs. Macaulay Graham and her husband, who visited for ten days in June 1785. The general, who "wish[ed] to shew them all the respect I can," extended an invitation to the family of David Stuart, the new husband of Eleanor, John Parke Custis's widow, to "come . . . dine with us." He admitted that "a Visit from a Lady so celebrated in the Literary world could not but be very flattering to me."[31] Washington no doubt enjoyed the attentions of his many important guests, especially

158. Jean Leon Gerome Ferris, *Mount Vernon and Peace, 1784,* ca. 1930, oil on canvas, 25×30 in. (Courtesy of Virginia Historical Society, Lora Robins Collection of Virginia Art)

*The American Cincinnatus: 1783–1789*

during the years immediately following the war, in part because such visits constantly reconfirmed his position in the social hierarchy. It might surprise those of us who have seen the countless "Washington Slept Here" advertisements throughout the mid-Atlantic states that his preference was to entertain guests as opposed to being himself the visitor. This predilection reminds us of his consistent strategy of making others come to him when his presence or services were deemed necessary.

The most famous visitor to Mount Vernon was Lafayette, who was exceptional both in that he was actually invited and in that Washington thoroughly enjoyed his company. From Valley Forge, where the Frenchman had shared in the "misfortunes" of the winter of 1777, the general had written, "in the end . . . My Dear Marquis, if you will give me your Company in Virginia, we will laugh at our past difficulties and the folly of others." Two years later, as their friendship matured, Washington made the invitation more definite: "I shall welcome you in all the warmth of friendship to . . . my rural Cottage, where homely fare and a cordial reception shall be substituted for delicacies and costly living." In this letter he makes clear the feelings he had developed for the young man who came to view himself as Washington's adopted son: "Your ardent and persevering efforts, not only in America but since your return to France to serve the United States; Your polite attention to Americans, and your strict and uniform friendship for *me,* has ripened the first impressions of esteem and attachment which I imbibed for you into such perfect love and gratitude that neither time nor absence can impair."[32] In August 1784 the invitation was accepted. However, Washington was absent for the month of September on a tour of his western lands, which he had not seen during the war years. While Washington traveled through the West, Lafayette toured the East, where the American people welcomed him. In November the pair met at Richmond and were honored by the state's House of Delegates, the body that had commissioned their statues for the statehouse. Washington brought Lafayette back to Mount Vernon in mid-November, and for the next three weeks they enjoyed each other's company.

The subject of how they spent their time together has interested artists more than authors. Weems, writing before Lafayette's even more triumphal tour of 1824–25 that forever enshrined the Frenchman in the American consciousness, does not even mention the visit. Sparks states simply, "Washington had the satisfaction of receiving at Mount Vernon the Marquis de Lafayette." There is little documentation about their activities, although Lafayette later wrote that he felt "Perfectly at Home . . . in Your family." We know that Washington invited Henry Lee to join them for dinner on at least one occasion. Ferris imagines that they played cards, which is plausible because Washington's account books over the years document minor gains and losses at this diversion. This is not to say that the general was a gambler; he denounced gaming as "a vice which is productive of every possible evil." But Washington enjoyed an innocent game of cards, and enjoyment is the theme of Ferris's painting. In *Mount Vernon and Peace* the artist effectively uses light to create the warm, protective environment that is the reward of victory and the very antithesis of the conditions that the pair had endured in the field, particularly at Valley Forge. Martha Washington sits with her back to the viewer, whose eye is drawn to two alluring women whose attentions are directed toward the general. Indeed, everyone in this scene is attractive. If we overlook the obvious inaccuracies, including the inappropriate Victorian furnishings (the lantern, after all, provides the light that makes the painting work), we can appreciate Ferris's accomplishment of successfully celebrating a relaxing episode in Washington's life.[33]

The reunion was also re-created by the figure painter Thomas P. Rossiter and the landscapist Louis Remy Mignot, who combined their skills to produce a massive twelve-foot canvas that was reproduced for popular consumption as a lithograph (fig. 159). As with the Ferris painting, there are anachronistic elements, such as the furniture and the dress of the grandchildren, which might have seemed familiar to the artists' mid-nineteenth-century audience. At this time the Mount Vernon Ladies' Association was being created, and Rossiter even wrote an article to help that effort. To go with the canvas he wrote a brochure, in which he states that in the painting, where Washington and Lafayette are shown "in colloquy," "the discourse is a topic of the times."[34] Given the idealism of the young Frenchman, who through years of correspondence with Washington inspired philosophical speculations on the part of the general, it is unthinkable that they did not converse about such notions as liberty, freedom, and the relationship between the aristocracy and the common citizenry during Lafayette's visit.

Other topics of conversation at Mount Vernon can be imagined partly from the record of the subjects that engaged the Frenchman's attention during the 1780s: he was constantly working on increasing trade between the two nations; on his tour of 1784 he repeated Washington's call for a stronger union of the American states; and he pursued the social issues of religious toleration in France as well as the abolition of slavery and the slave trade everywhere. At the end of the decade Lafayette would be influential in reshaping the French government (by changing the French Assembly of Notables into a National Assembly), and he would draft a French Declaration of the Rights of Man, which returned to French soil, where it had originated, the enlightened rhetoric of the American Founding Fathers. By 1784 Lafayette was already envisioning all that he wanted to achieve in his life, and there was no better mentor with whom to discuss such subjects than the man who had liberated a nation.

159. Thomas Oldham Barlow, after Thomas P. Rossiter and Louis Remy Mignot, *The Home of Washington*, 1860, lithograph, 18½×29¾ in. (Courtesy of Mount Vernon Ladies' Association)

In early December Washington escorted Lafayette to Annapolis. Upon his return to Mount Vernon, the general, in his own words, felt "love, respect and attachment" for the marquis and wondered "whether that was the last sight, I ever should have of you." Ever conscious of his age, perhaps especially in contrast to the youth of his guest, Washington worried again about "now descending the hill" and soon being "entombed in the dreary mansions of my father's." The two never met again, but they corresponded regularly, and Washington followed with interest and concern Lafayette's progression through the tumultuous events of the French Revolution. The day after the Bastille fell in 1789, the Frenchman was named commander of the Paris National Guard. He sent Washington the "main key of the fortress of despotism," and the Bastille key remains today in the passage at Mount Vernon. It came, in Lafayette's words, as a tribute from "A missionary of liberty to its patriarch."[35]

In 1792, when Louis XVI was deposed, Lafayette was forced to flee across the border, where he was captured and held in Austrian and Prussian jails for five years. During that time he entrusted the care of his son, George Washington Motier Lafayette, to the general. On Lafayette's release in 1797, Washington wrote to his friend: "Your son . . . is highly deserving of such Parents as you and your amiable Lady. He can relate,

much better than I can describe, my participation in your sufferings, my solicitude for your relief, the measures I adopted (though ineffectually) to facilitate your liberation from an unjust and cruel imprisonment, and the joy I experienced at the news of its accomplishment." Though finally free, Lafayette was not allowed to return to France until 1800, the year after Washington's death. Nor could he seek asylum at Mount Vernon because of the threatened war between his country and the United States. The general did not live long enough to know that Lafayette would triumphantly tour the United States on the invitation of President James Monroe and would regain political prominence in France during both the Restoration era and the Revolution of 1830. Washington would die with only a hope that "the differences between this Country and France [would be] adjusted and harmony between the nations . . . again restored."[36]

Not all of his callers would be from the Continent or the cosmopolitan centers of the new nation. Washington found that he would be in demand in terms of his Virginia neighbors as well, many of whom wished to renew their acquaintance with the general. In his response to a letter from Lee Massey, the rector of Truro Parish, Washington asserts that he is still haunted by his days in the military and makes clear how he has had to

*The American Cincinnatus: 1783–1789*

compartmentalize his day in order to find the time to attend to his affairs (fig. 160): "Business, & old concerns of the war, with which I have now nothing to do, are still pressed upon me.... I mean to devote my forenoons to business, while I give the afterpart of the day to my friends, 'til I can (if that should ever be) bring my affairs into order again."[37] The attempt to establish order, even when success was doubtful, was important to Washington, as he purposefully set out to put his military career behind him and reassert himself as a Virginia planter.

Even before the peace of 1783 had been finalized, Washington had determined that after the war he would entertain his guests lavishly. At his camp he had begun to seat a constant stream of visitors at his table, and he anticipated a continuation of this flattering yet often bothersome task at Mount Vernon. Three months before he returned to Virginia Washington began to look for a cook who could prepare dinner "to any Company which shall be named to him to the amount of 30."[38] Writing from the field outside of New York City, he also began a determined search for the sorts of decorative objects that would enable him to accommodate larger numbers of guests than he had previously known; the general realized that he would need more chairs, more china, and more silver. As we examine examples of the decorative objects that Washington sought versus what he eventually purchased, we will see that his concern was not only with fashion, as we have learned by now to expect, but also with quantity.

In the fall of 1783 Bushrod Washington was in Philadelphia studying law. The general sought his help to "make enquiry of some of the best Cabinet Makers" in the city and find "two dozen strong, neat and plain, but fashionable Table chairs (I mean chairs for a dining room)." Soon, Samuel Powel, Washington's wealthy and socially prominent friend in that city, was involved in the search, and Martha Washington was able to buy "on her way home" a set of handsome Chippendale ladder-back side chairs.[39] Nine of these chairs, which may have been intended initially for the large dining room, only to be replaced there by neoclassical chairs that better fit the evolving decor of the room, survive to this day in the small dining room at Mount Vernon. The increase in seating capacity gained by this purchase was notable and a harbinger of things to come.

The general next asked Bushrod to inquire about sets of "blue and white table china." He engaged Daniel Parker in New York City to look for the same, and he was specific to Parker as to the large quantity that he wanted: "Not less than 6 or 8 dozn. Shallow and a proportionable number of Deep and other Plates, Butter Boats, Dishes and Tureens, will suffice." Washington

wanted to be able to seat as many as several dozen guests. Parker, a merchant who had supplied the Continental army, turned to Samuel Fraunces, a New York tavern keeper, who found for Washington 205 pieces, though he had to mix sets to assemble such a collection. This ware, with its appealing Chinese scenes and motifs, was the type most consistently used at Mount Vernon from the early 1760s through the 1790s (see fig. 81). A year earlier, Washington had received as a gift the handsome Niderviller porcelain that carries a "GW" monogram in tooled gold on a cloud beneath a wreath of roses (fig. 161), but this was only a tea-and-coffee service. The Niderviller porcelain factory, near Strasbourg, had been purchased a decade earlier by Adam Philibert, Count de Custine-Sarreck, who was a colonel in the French army. The count had arrived in America with his regiment in 1780 and the next year was present at Yorktown. Custine presented the service to Martha Washington at Mount Vernon in the summer of 1782.[40]

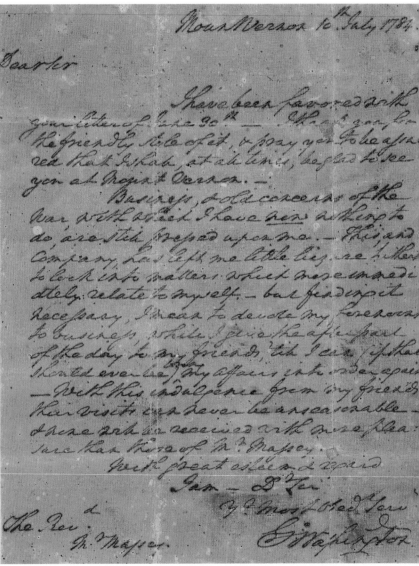

160. George Washington to Lee Massey, 10 July 1784. (Private collection)

161. Niderviller teacup and saucer, ca. 1779–80, porcelain. (Courtesy of Mount Vernon Ladies' Association)

The last of the decorative objects that Bushrod Washington was asked to locate in Philadelphia was French silver. The French, after all, were Washington's allies, while the English were still, technically, his enemies. He asked his nephew "whether French plate is fashionable and much used in genteel houses in France and England." He wanted to know if much of it could be found in Philadelphia and if there were "Tea urns, Coffee pots, Tea pots, and other equipage for a tea table, with a tea board, Candlesticks and waiters large and small." The Niderviller tea-and-coffee service was attractive, and Washington was grateful to Custine for the gesture, but at the same time he was set on acquiring large pieces of silver. He admitted to Lafayette, "I am not much of a connoisseur in, and trouble my head very little with these matters."[41] But he had learned that large silver services make an impression unlike anything else, so he had to have one. His visitors would expect as much.

What Washington meant when he said he was not a connoisseur of silver was only that he did not care much about specific designs in the new style; any design would probably do for him. But he knew enough about the various pieces of a fashionable set to be able to discuss them. He contacted Lafayette after having little success in Philadelphia and asked the Frenchman to find him "every thing proper for a tea-table." Lafayette apparently complied as well as he could. In the meantime, Washington had grown impatient and had purchased in New York "so many pieces of the plated Ware" that he then tried, unsuccessfully, to cancel the order from Lafayette (fig. 162). Finally, in 1784, after having told Lafayette that he did "not incline to send to England" for anything that could be found elsewhere, Washington gave in and ordered Sheffield plated silver from London. Among the items he received from the English firm of Joy and Hopkins were "4 plain beaded Waiters"

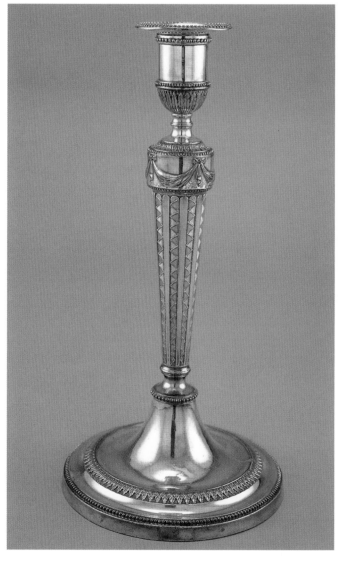

162. Candlestick of "Sheffield Plate," possibly made in New York City, 1783. (Courtesy of National Museum of American History)

*The American Cincinnatus: 1783–1789*

163. Armorial waiter of "Sheffield Plate," probably made by Joy and Hopkins, London, 1784. (Courtesy of National Museum of American History)

engraved "with crests & Arms" (fig. 163).[42] He picked up additional silver in Philadelphia, where the original search had begun. By their form, the large pieces would display the newest fashion, while the engraved Washington family crest would not too subtly remind his guests of both his long (if not particularly distinguished) lineage and his self-achieved status. No other decorative objects functioned so well as silver in answering such coincidentally practical and social needs.

The general concurrently set about to complete the renovations to his house. In January 1784, only a few weeks after his return to Mount Vernon, Washington followed up in writing a discussion he had had in Philadelphia with Samuel Vaughan, the wealthy English merchant who had supported American independence and whose friendship the general found irresistible. Vaughan told him that stucco was "the present taste in England," lent him a new book on the subject (Benjamin Higgins's *Experiments and Observations on Cements*), and even offered to send his workman to Mount Vernon. Washington was "incline[d] to do [his new room] in s[t]ucco" but was not too sure about the new style. He asked Vaughan if this decoration was supposed to be painted or left its natural color and if it ever ex-

164. Large dining room. (Courtesy of Mount Vernon Ladies' Association)

*The American Cincinnatus: 1783–1789*

tended below the chair rail. Three days later he ordered "Sieves" from Philadelphia so he could prepare the stucco that would be used by his craftsman. At the same time he ordered "gilded borders . . . [to go] round the Doors & window Casings, surbase &ca." Washington was right in thinking that these ornaments, which he knew from the ballroom at the Governor's Palace in Williamsburg, would give "a plain blew, or green paper a rich & handsome look" (figs. 164, 165).[43]

Samuel Vaughan helped Washington even further by ordering for the room a "marble chimney piece and pair of glass Jarendoles [girandoles]". This gift "made an impression, which never will be forgotten"; Washington tactfully replied that he would value it "more as a monument of your friendship, than as a decoration of my room." When the chimneypiece arrived in February 1785, in ten crates, Washington worried that it was "too elegant & costly by far" for his wooden American house. A year later, Vaughan sent a "picture of a battle in Germany" to go above the porcelain vases on the mantel, thereby finishing what became almost a side chapel. The large painting, which depicts the 1759 Battle of Minden where Lafayette's father was killed, must not have been easy for Washington to view, nor did it match the landscape theme of the other canvases that would hang in the room. Washington later moved it to the lower bedroom, where it remains today.[44]

165. Large dining room chimneypiece. (Courtesy of Richard Bryant, Arcaid)

Washington's concern that the chimneypiece might be too elegant would be answered by his making the rest of the room as handsome as he and Vaughan had initially discussed. That spring Washington engaged Richard Boulton, whom William Fitzhugh had described as "an Excellent Workman, & perfectly Qualify'd to Finish Your Large Room in the most Elegant Manner." But Boulton had a drinking problem, and he never returned to Mount Vernon to begin the work. Three months later, in August 1785, Tench Tilghman located in Maryland a craftsman who would do the job over the following two years. John Rawlins, an English stucco worker, was well versed in the new Adam style and ran a *profitable* Business" in Baltimore. He was highly competent, if a bit overpriced, at least to Washington's thinking. The general negotiated both a design for the stucco decoration of the room and a contract with Rawlins via the mails. Washington gave him the dimensions of the space and identified the location of the "very elegant marble" chimneypiece and the square and tall ("of equal breadth & pitch") Palladian window that Langfier had built for him. This was to let Rawlins "have leisure to think of a design." Washington, writing in August, thought "the season [was too] far advanced" for his workmen to prepare the surfaces and Rawlins to apply the cast stucco decoration before cold weather set in. Rawlins had sent Washington a descriptive letter and a plan that appealed to the general because it was "plain, as I requested." When the work was done, he thought that the friezes Rawlins had devised for the doors and windows were "very pretty".[45] Washington was anxious to display the latest fashion, and he found in Rawlins a craftsman who in England was a member of the London avant-garde, a man who had the latest architectural trends at his fingertips.

In fact, Rawlins devised his scheme for Washington's "New

Room" a year before the publication in late 1786 of William Pain's *British Palladio: Or the Builder's General Assistant,* which was one of the earliest books to showcase Adam design in a comprehensive manner. Pain shows not just motifs but what a whole Adamesque room should look like (fig. 166); his wall elevations in the new style were close to what Rawlins had designed for Mount Vernon. In the nearly two years that passed before his job for Washington was completed, Rawlins may have gotten hold of the new publication because Pain's volume could conceivably have inspired details of the ceiling decoration of the new room (figs. 167, 168). Rawlins altered the specific motifs illustrated in texts such as *British Palladio* in order to create agricultural imagery that was particularly appropriate for a working plantation in America. These would also relate to the agrarian motifs of Samuel Vaughan's mantel.

Washington and Rawlins signed a contract in February 1786, and carpenters at Mount Vernon, many of whom were probably Washington's slaves, were soon at work. They built for Rawlins the coved cornice that curves into the room and prepared that surface and the others where stucco decoration would be used.[46] After the cast pieces were applied, Washington's concern was to find a painter who would be sensitive to the "carved mouldings, to prevent their filling too much with the paint." He advised his estate manager to "try Peales Nephew," apparently Charles Peale Polk, who advertised that year in Philadelphia that he painted houses. Samuel Powel ultimately sent the general a neoclassical "chair which he was so good as to procure . . . as a pattern" of what might look best in the new room. Washington thought it "handsome & neat," though he planned to propose to the furniture maker some

166. William Pain, *British Palladio: Or the Builder's General Assistant* (London, 1786), plate XXVII. (Courtesy of Virginia Historical Society)

167. Large dining room ceiling. (Courtesy of Mount Vernon Ladies' Association)

168. William Pain, *British Palladio: Or the Builder's General Assistant* (London, 1786), plate XXIX. (Courtesy of Virginia Historical Society)

By its neat, handsome design, the architecture of the house suggests that the occupant was a tasteful and temperate citizen. However, due to her advanced age, poor health, and her unhappiness with her financial position, Mary Washington had become, on the contrary, rather eccentric. Ironically, the lifestyle of forced frugality that so displeased her caused future generations to award her praise that she did not earn in life.

George Washington made it clear to his contemporaries that he, his brothers, and his sister took care of their mother in a proper way: "I did, at her request but at my own expense, purchase a commodious house, garden and Lotts (of her own choosing) in Fredericksburg, that she might be near my Sister Lewis, her only daughter; and did moreover agree to take her Land and negroes at a certain yearly rent, to be fixed by Colo. Lewis and others of her own nomination which has been an annual expence to me ever since, as the Estate [Ferry Farm] never raised one half of the rent I was to pay. . . . Confident I am that she has not a child that would not divide the last sixpence to relieve her from *real* distress."[58] This letter, which was written the spring before Yorktown, was sent to the governor of Virginia, Benjamin Harrison, because the state assembly was then considering legislation to provide a pension to Mary Washington, a course of action that would have brought considerable embarrassment to her children. There was no "real distress," as Washington points out. Rather, Mary Washington was in these years an elderly and sickly woman who either perceived that she was in financial jeopardy or simply was unhappy that she was not more affluent.

The problem was unchanged two years later when Washington, still in the field and far from Virginia, had to urge his

173. John Gadsby Chapman, *Residence of Washington's Mother in Fredericksburg, Va.,* 1833, oil on canvas, 21⅝×29⁷⁄₁₆ in. (Courtesy of Homeland Foundation, Incorporated, New York)

*The American Cincinnatus: 1783–1789*

brother to somehow, tactfully, restrain their mother from making public her complaints: "I learn from very good authority that she is upon all occasions, and in all Companies complaining of the hardness of the times, of her wants and distresses; and if not in direct terms, at least by strong innuendos inviting favors. . . . I wish to you to represent to her in delicate terms the impropriety of her complaints and acceptance of favors." During the second retirement Washington periodically traveled the fifty miles to Fredericksburg to offer respect to his mother: "Setting off next Morning for Fredericksburgh to pay my duty to an aged Mother," he wrote to Henry Knox in 1784. A visit three years later, however, would be prompted by urgency. Mary Washington had developed breast cancer and was gravely ill. Betty Lewis had so dutifully nursed her mother that the daughter had become exhausted and her own health was jeopardized. Washington, who arrived in early April, "found both my Mother & Sister better than I expected—the latter out of danger." Mary Washington would not die at this time, but her "extreme low State" promised "little hope of her recovery as she was exceedingly reduced and much debilitated by age and the disorder."[59]

The year 1787 would be difficult for the family. Only two months before the April crisis Washington had sent fifteen guineas to his mother, "in consequence of [her] communication to George [Augustine] Washington, of [her] want of money" and with concern that he was being "considered perhaps by the world as [an] unjust and undutiful son." He reminded his mother that he had already given "between 3 and 4 hundred pounds besides out of my own pocket." Washington's advice was to "break up housekeeping . . . and live with one of your children" but not, he made clear, with him: "My house is at your service, and [I] would press you most sincerely and most devoutly to accept it, but I am sure, and candour requires me to say it will never answer your purposes, in any shape whatsoever—for in truth it may be compared to a well resorted tavern, as scarcely any strangers who are going from north to south, or from south to north do not spend a day or two at it. This would, were you an inhabitant of it, oblige you to do one of 3 things, 1st to be always dressing to appear in company, 2d, to come into [the room] in a dishabille or 3d to be as it were a prisoner in your own chamber." In the summer of 1789, Betty Lewis wrote her brother that the "Breast still Continues bad": "God only knows how it will end; I dread the Consequence. she is sensible of it & is Perfectly resign'd—wishes for nothing more than to keep it Easy—she wishes to here from you, she will not believe you are well till she has it from under your Hand."[60] Mary Washington succumbed on 5 August 1789. George had visited his mother on at least one other documented occasion. This presumably was shortly before Washington left Virginia for New York City in April 1789

174. Jean Leon Gerome Ferris, *Washington's Farewell to His Mother, 1789*, ca. 1923, oil on canvas, 35×24 in. (Courtesy of Virginia Historical Society, Lora Robins Collection of Virginia Art)

to assume the presidency of the United States—or so at least Jared Sparks believed.

Sparks's word was taken by later commentators, including Ferris (fig. 174). Whatever the exact date of his last visit, Washington understood the circumstances, as he later told his sister: "When I was last at Fredericksburg, I took a final leave of my Mother, never expecting to see her more." Washington's "farewell to his mother" is not even mentioned by Weems, who has little to offer about Washington's private life after the war. The incident did not become celebrated until the nineteenth century, when the family unit became venerated as a keystone of respectable society. To honor that theme, Sparks was uncharacteristically inaccurate in his account, which credits Washington's mother with "vigor of mind and body, simplicity of manners, and uprightness of character." He had read the correspondence and must have known of the anxiety she caused her son, but Sparks avoids a discussion of the complexities of Mary Washington's nature and instead suggests that on Washington's visits "she listened to his praises and was silent, or added only that he had been a good son, and she believed he had done his duty as a man."[61]

Possibly inspired by that imaginative account, Ferris prepared a narrative to accompany his image of the last farewell. In his rendering Mary Washington states to her son, "you will see me no more." Washington tells her that the people have elected him president, and he has "come to bid you an affectionate farewell." He will return, he says, but she predicts that by then she will be dead. She gives "a mother's blessing" for Washington to "fulfill the high destinies that heaven appears to have intended for you," and in response, "the great man's frame trembled while a sob burst from his breast." What actually happened during Washington's last visit to his mother can, of course, be only partially reconstructed. She had been anxious to hear from him again according to a July 1789 letter from Betty Lewis, which was written after he had assumed the presidency. On her death she willed to Washington several textiles and pieces of furniture that had no significant monetary value but were valued by the president as "mementos of parental affection." This bequest indicates that the two retained affectionate feelings for one another to the end, as Ferris suggests. Their relationship, though strained, had not been carried to the breaking point. As to Washington's reaction to his mother's fate, he reminded his sister to be appreciative that "Heaven has spared [her] to an age, beyond which few attain, and favored her with the full enjoyment of her mental faculties, and as much bodily strength as usually falls to the lot of four score."[62] Washington probably would not have imagined that his relationship with his mother, who would be sentimentally recalled as a paragon, would actually serve to broaden the parameters of his own repute.

## Improving Nature: Washington as Landscape Gardener

For two weeks in June 1798 Washington hosted Julian Ursyn Niemcewicz, a Polish nobleman who had traveled to America with his countryman and former Washington aide Tadeusz Kościuszko. Kościuszko had himself been the leader of a rebellion in 1794 to free his nation from Russian rule. Niemcewicz was a perceptive visitor who left a long account of much that he saw at Mount Vernon. There is a great deal of detail in many of his descriptions, but Niemcewicz seems to have taken special interest in the garden. He noted that "all the vegetables for the kitchen" were there, and he also listed many of the flowers and trees that Washington had planted, which were well cultivated and kept "neatly." He rightly concluded that in the garden, as in the house, Washington had not merely copied someone else but instead had supplemented his reading with his eye for design to create a scheme that looked good while it served his purposes: "In a word the garden, the plantations, the house, the whole upkeep, proves that a man born with natural taste can divine the beautiful without having seen the model. The G[enera]l has never left America. After seeing his house and his gardens one would say that he had seen the most beautiful examples in England of this style."[63] In his travels in Virginia and the North Washington had seen many colonial gardens based on English models, so he understood how a traditional landscape garden was composed. He also owned an English book about landscape design that showed him other "models," told him what was fashionable, and gave him ideas about how to create the type of garden he envisioned.

The American gardens that Washington knew before 1783 were almost universally rectilinear in their perimeter lines, and often as simple within the parterres as well. In most cases the entire garden, because they tended to be relatively small, was placed to one side of the house. Particularly well known to Washington were those in Virginia and Maryland; in many such instances, if the house was on a river, the garden was often situated between the two and terraced, following the fashion of gardens in England along the Thames River near the villages of Richmond and Twickenham.[64] But the steep terrain at Mount Vernon would not allow a terraced garden falling east to the river, and Washington had seen enough to know that other types of arrangements could be adapted successfully to the Mount Vernon topography.

At the time of the first retirement, when Washington brought his bride home to Mount Vernon, the dependencies he built were placed northwest and southwest of the house, on axes running from it at forty-five-degree angles. The vegetable and flower gardens were situated beyond the dependencies, closer together than they are today. Some of the components of this arrangement, which borrows from the plan at neighboring Belvoir, may even predate Washington's residency at Mount Vernon. These first gardens were relatively small, for they had areas only for vegetables and flowers and were not particularly distinguished for their design.

The general's primary source for his restructuring of the Mount Vernon landscape a decade later would be Batty Langley's *New Principles of Gardening* (1728), which he had ordered from London in 1759 (fig. 175). As with Langley's *Treasury of Designs,* Washington would take from it only a few of the author's ideas and ultimately produce a final product quite different from what Langley had envisioned. Of course his garden book was a half century out of date when Washington began his improvements, but it did offer what still seemed to be "new principles." Langley at the least pointed in the direction of the change in English garden design in the early eighteenth century, which was away from the Continental preference for a rectilinear and mannered landscape toward a more naturalistic one. The naturalistic garden became "picturesque," or like a picture, meaning like a landscape painting by an artist such as Claude Lorrain. In the picturesque garden as in the picturesque painting, the elements are carefully composed to give the appearance of being natural. (See figure 66, a picturesque landscape that Washington installed in the west-parlor chimneypiece.)

As Niemcewicz implied, Washington seems to have known little about the English landscape theories put forward after the publication of Langley's book. The word *picturesque* itself was apparently unknown to him, let alone the theories of its major practitioners, Richard Payne Knight, Humphrey Repton, and Uvedale Price, who argued that not all landscapes of note are sublime or beautiful, as Edmund Burke had suggested; some, in fact, are rough, irregular, and characterized by sudden variation. Those qualities, however, rather than being seen as jarring, are actually pleasing to the eye and mind. Washington had come to much the same conclusion when he surveyed west of the Blue Ridge and traversed the reaches of the Ohio. The kinds of picturesque views that he found pleasing would become evident in some of his landscape designs and would be captured in the landscape paintings by William Winstanley and George Beck that he would hang at Mount Vernon in the 1790s.

In 1799 Uvedale Price politely sent a copy of his new book, *The Picturesque,* to the man who had freed a nation, because the author saw himself as liberating the landscape from unnatural tyranny in much the same way. Washington wrote back, courteously, that "the subject is curious" and that he hoped to read the book when he found some leisure time.[65] If he ever did read it, which is improbable, Washington would have discovered that Price had put into words some of what his "natural taste" had found appealing in the American wilderness. As to bringing this wilderness into the garden, the pages of Langley provided some useful advice that freed Washington to add vistas, variety, and irregularity to the traditional rectilinear grid. Price, of course, had gone much further in removing rectilinear elements from landscape design, and so Washington's garden was transitional, unique, and, in fact, out of date the day it was completed.

Upon looking at *New Principles of Gardening,* Washington may well have been bewildered by the formal and expansive designs diagrammed in Langley's series of plates (see, for example, figure 175). The plates give plans that are so vast in scale as to be without precedent in America, or even in much of England. The reader is prepared for this by the book's subtitle, *The Laying Out and Planting [of] Parterres, Groves, Wildernesses, Labyrinths, Avenues, Parks &c. After a More Grand and Rural Manner, Than Has Been Done Before.* How could Washington utilize these strange designs? The answer would be a radical simplification, which is precisely what had happened with the architecture at Mount Vernon. He would retain Langley's basic elements of a rigid axial plan, with the house at the center of a grid that would be filled by a bowling green and flower and kitchen gardens on one front and a lesser green and flanking groves on the other. The various elements would be linked by a succession of interconnected walks, some broad and others narrow, some of which would curve while others provided relatively straight paths and sight lines. The principal walks would be lined with trees.

Langley's most significant idea was that a garden is a large park encompassing all four sides of a house and containing many elements. It is made up of vegetable and flower gardens, certainly, but there should be as well groves, large parterres of grass, pools of water, wildernesses, and vistas. Admittedly, these elements were almost always arranged in a rectilinear pattern, but there can be variety in their design and in their placement on the grid. A regular garden is "ridiculous," "forbidding," "abominable," and "shocking," Langley tells his readers. "The Pleasure of a Garden depends on the variety of its Parts," and it must present "new and delightful

175. Batty Langley, *New Principles of Gardening* (London, 1728), plate XII. (Courtesy of Virginia Historical Society)

*The American Cincinnatus: 1783–1789*

Scenes to our View at every Step we take." To offer the desired variety, the garden must have a large-enough scale.[66] As Washington expanded the early garden at Mount Vernon into the park that now encircles the mansion, he had to invent schemes for the east, north, and south and drastically revise the existing garden on the west front. He was at work on the new areas in 1776, at which time he devised the radical idea of building open arcades to connect the house to its forecourt dependencies. In the context of the new garden plan, it becomes apparent why he opened those arcades.

In the eastern section of the park Washington already had a vista, one that would answer well Langley's call that "Views in Gardens [should] be as extensive as possible." The Potomac River is spectacular where it passes Mount Vernon, presenting what Niemcewicz called "perhaps the most beautiful view in the world." Thanks to the open design of the connecting quadrants, that vista could be enjoyed even from the western expanse of the park. Between the house and the river, where the terrain is rugged, Washington developed the landscape as best he could; he put a parterre of grass before the house, as Langley advised. Niemcewicz described this as "a lawn of the most beautiful green." He planted and maintained the slope down to the river so that the view would not be blocked by the vegetation but rather framed by it, as was noted by Benjamin Henry Latrobe in 1796: "Down the steep slope trees and shrubs are thickly planted. They are kept so low as not to interrupt the view but merely to furnish an agreeable border to the extensive prospect beyond."[67]

Washington tried to keep deer in this east section of the park. In 1785 and 1786 he asked both George William Fairfax, who was then in England, and his neighbor William Fitzhugh of Chatham to send him deer, and he accumulated a herd of about a dozen. But by 1792 he had turned the deer loose into the woods, in part because his hounds so frightened them. (Fitzhugh had even sent him a doe that he could not use at Chatham because she repeatedly hid in his kitchen when the local hounds chased her.) The deer still roamed the park, however, and apparently spent much of their time eating the shrubs. "I am at a loss," Washington wrote in 1794, "in determining whether to give up the Shrubs or the Deer."[68]

In a way, the view of the Potomac, which is more magnificent than Langley could have imagined, would help to make up for one deficiency that was inevitable in an early-American garden. Imported marble statues were at this point beyond the general's reach and rarely found in any contemporary American landscapes. Although Langley had suggested, "There is

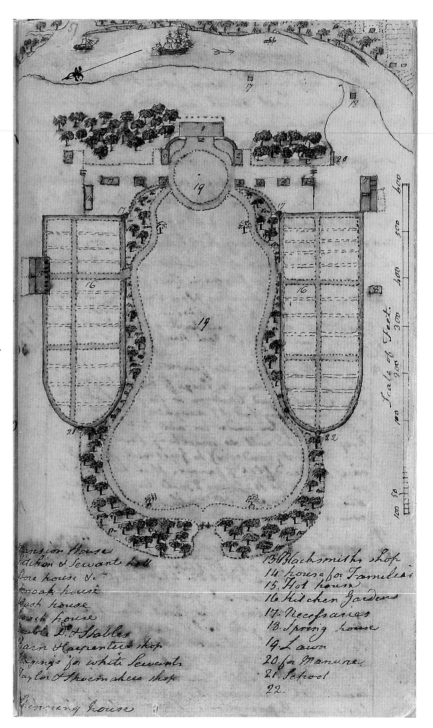

176. Journal of Samuel Vaughan, open to his plan of the Mount Vernon grounds, 1787. (Courtesy of Mount Vernon Ladies' Association)

nothing adds so much to the Beauty and Grandeur of Gardens, as fine Statues," Washington would not be able to provide such elements. Such omissions would identify Washington's park as American, as would the inclusion in it of the dependencies of a working plantation. These small, functional buildings, which were essential for cooking, washing, storage, smoking meat, spinning cloth, and housing people and horses, were so numerous at Mount Vernon that visitors described them as giving the appearance of a village. They had to be placed somewhere, and so, taking his direction from Langley and adding a dash of his own ingenuity, Washington found that such buildings could function to define effectively the major cross axis of his plan, taking the place of the double row of trees that Langley had used to identify principal walks. The prominence of this axis is apparent in the diagram of Washington's estate made by Samuel Vaughan when he visited Mount Vernon in 1787 (fig. 176).[69]

Washington planted trees directly north and south of the house; these helped to give a large scale to the park and to form a portion of the vista through the arcades. The general started this process in 1776 at the same time that the open arcades were planned and built. He had locust trees planted in the area to the north and a variety of species to the south. In 1782 he ordered more "shrubs and ornamental and curious trees" to be planted in both areas, so he could determine, after they had grown, "from circumstances and appearances which shall be the grove and which the wilderness." The trees were arranged almost randomly. Langley had called such a plan "regular irregularity" and had stressed that groves were not to be planted like an orchard but "in a rural Manner, as if they had receiv'd their Situation from Nature itself," because "when we come to copy, or imitate Nature, we should trace her Steps."[70] In Vaughan's drawing we see that both areas seem more like wildernesses than groves because their perimeters are not defined by a geometric shape; we are thereby reminded that although Washington may have had a clear differentiation in his mind, he came to use the terms *grove* and *wilderness* almost interchangeably.

In refiguring the landscape on the west front of the house, the first order of business was to develop an impressive bowling green. In both his text and the accompanying plates, Langley stressed that this "Lawn or Plain of Grass," which he described variously as "grand and beautiful" and "elegant," was essential to the successful design of a park. He recommended various shapes, including the square and the circle. For the lawn on the east front at Mount Vernon, which overlooks the river, the terrain allowed little choice other than a simple rectangle. But for part of the west front Washington selected Langley's circle of grass. Only a small circle would fit, however, between Washington's innermost dependencies, and Langley advised that "open Lawns should be always in Proportion to

the Grandeur of the Building." The general's solution called for the creation of an immense bowling green, some two hundred yards in length, adjoining the small circular lawn. This larger green at least followed Langley in the "regular irregularity" of its unusual form.[71]

Langley added that "no Borders [should] be made . . . in any such Lawn" ("for the Grandeur of those beautiful Carpets consists in their native Plainness"); that "this open Parterre is planted on the Sides . . . with double Lines" of trees; that "open Groves . . . enclose the sides of the plain Parterre"; and that "Shady Walks" should lead from the house to those groves. He repeatedly warned that proper shade from "the scorching Heat of the Sun" must be provided so that one can "with Pleasure pass" through the garden, and he concluded, "there is nothing more agreeable in a Garden than good Shade, and without it a Garden is nothing." Washington followed the advice about the absence of a border around the lawn, but after that he improvised. There was not enough room between the vegetable and flower gardens, if they were to remain roughly where they were, for there to be on each side a double line of trees and a flanking grove. The solution was to intertwine the two. The general devised a serpentine walk shaded by a narrow and seemingly random planting of trees that he described as forming a "wilderness." Langley had provided the geometry that Washington could follow to lay out this curving walkway.[72]

The planning of what trees would shade the serpentine walks had begun by the winter of 1784–85, when Washington asked friends in New York and South Carolina to send him seeds for evergreens, oaks, and magnolias. In January 1785 he "road to my Mill Swamp . . . & to other places in search of the sort of Trees I shall want for my walks, groves, & Wildernesses." Then, from January through March 1785, he was busy "laying out my Serpentine road and Shrubberies adjoining." He put down walks to the necessaries at this time and also laid out some "in my Groves, at each end of the House." In the fall of 1785 Washington "began to level the ground which had been spaded up in the lawn fronting the House."[73]

In February and March of the next year Washington planted trees beside the serpentine walk. A decade later it seemed to Niemcewicz that "a thousand kinds of trees, plants and bushes" were there. The exact scheme was given in a plan drawn by the general that apparently survived at least until 1859, when Benson Lossing reproduced it (fig. 177). Lossing wrote: "I have before me the original plan of these grounds, made by Washington's own hands. It is very carefully drawn. The exact position and name of every tree to be planted, are laid down. With it is a section-drawing, on a larger scale, showing the proposed carriage-way around the lawn, the names of a large number of trees that were to adorn it, and the places of others indicated by letters and numerals, which are explained by a memoran-

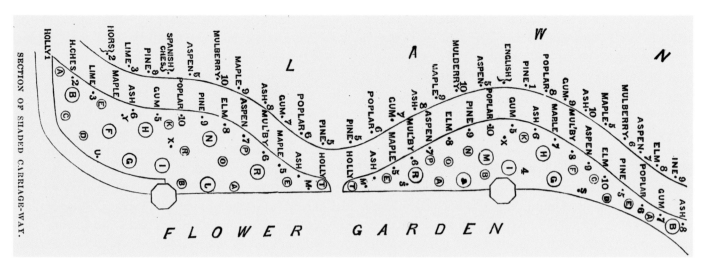

177. Washington's plan for planting the serpentine walk, as reproduced in Benson Lossing, *The Home of Washington* (New York, 1859). (Courtesy of Virginia Historical Society)

dum." Washington left the far-western end of the bowling green open to a width of sixty yards in order to provide what Langley had described as "a boundless View into the Country." The general would have understood this concept in an instant because the garden at the Governor's Palace in Williamsburg was laid out in that fashion. Washington marked the sixty-yard gap at the edge of his bowling green with two mounts, perhaps more to follow Langley than to recall Indian ceremonial mounts that he had seen in the West, as is sometimes suggested. Compared to either those suggested by Langley or the traditional native mounts, those at Mount Vernon are quite small. Langley had envisioned large mounts made from the "Earths cast out of Foundations . . . from which, fine Views may be seen." Washington began to raise the mounts in February 1786, and he planted a weeping willow on each.[74]

The general's vista to the west followed the axis of the passage through the center of the house. In 1792 he thought of opening "another Visto on the West front," and he even considered tapping springs to establish a body of water on the west axis: "I want the water carried on its level to the front of the Mansion house, as it is done in Watered meadows; that I may, if I should hereafter want to water any, or all of that ground or make a pond on the level, directly in front, along the Visto that was opened in a line between the two doors." This was another idea from Langley, who advised that water elements are "the very Life of a delightful rural Garden." It is fortunate, Langley noted, when a park "is so happily situated, as to be bless'd with small Rivulets and purling Streams of clear Water, which generally admit of fine Canals, Fountains, Cascades, &c."[75] Although Washington attempted to develop his park in as proper a manner as he could, some of the designer's suggestions would not come to fruition, in part because the cost of the alterations

would have been prohibitive and also because the demands of the presidency kept Washington away from Mount Vernon for much of the time between 1789 and 1797. His voluminous correspondence with his managers would keep him appraised of the day-to-day operations of the farms but served him less well in the planning and carrying out of his more grandiose plans for the gardens.

Tightly squeezing Washington's wildernesses into their narrow widths are the vegetable and flower gardens, which the general shifted slightly to the north and south of their previous location and then enclosed with brick walls, curved at their westernmost ends in concession to the nearby serpentine walk. The brickwork was under way in the summer of 1785, and in the following February the general "assembled the Men from my Plantations" to physically move the existing garden houses to their new positions. Langley had suggested that "large openings" in the walks of a wilderness might open into fruit and flower gardens to surprise and delight the viewer, but Washington chose to close these gardens to easy entry, perhaps simply to protect their contents from the many animals and people on what was a working farm.[76]

Within the flower garden was a decorative parterre, which did not go unnoticed by Latrobe in 1796: "For the first time again since I left Germany, I saw here a parterre, chipped and trimmed with infinite care into the form of a richly flourished Fleur de Lis: The expiring groans I hope of our Grandfather's pedantry." Washington apparently retained this survivor from old-fashioned Continental geometric gardens in case such an element might still be judged fashionable by some of his European visitors. But most of the garden was given over to living things. Washington indentured a series of professional gardeners to cultivate his many plants. The resident gardener in

1773, Philip Bateman, was ranked by Lund Washington as "the best Kitchen gardener to be met with."[77]

Within the walls of the flower garden Washington built a greenhouse. Some, but not many, of his affluent Maryland and Virginia neighbors enjoyed this luxury, which Washington had appreciated ever since he had traveled to Barbados. The Mount Vernon greenhouse burned in 1835 and was rebuilt in the twentieth century, on the evidence of the ruins and the floor plan drawn by Washington (fig. 178). The general modeled his design on one at Charles Carroll's estate in Baltimore, because "neither myself, nor any person about me is so well skilled in the internal construction as to proceed without a probability at least of running into errors." Baltimore was also the place of residence of his former aide Tench Tilghman, who could answer quickly the general's questions about the dimensions and other details of the Carroll design.[78] The Mount Vernon hothouse is especially impressive because of its size; Washington built it large enough to house the slaves who maintained both the plants within it and those that had been moved outside.

## The First Farmer in America

Upon his retirement Washington turned to farming with a determination to lead there as he had done in the war. He would revolutionize Virginia agriculture and set an example for the state and the nation of how to make a farm productive. John Hunter, an English visitor to Mount Vernon in 1785, explained: "His greatest pride now is, to be thought the first farmer in America. He is quite a Cincinnatus, and often works with his men himself." Farming had become one of Washington's passions before the war, and it quickly became one again. "My principal pursuits are of a rural nature, in which I have great delight," he wrote in 1785. But after the Revolution, he came to see its virtues in a new way: "The more I am acquainted with agricultural affairs the better I am pleased with them. . . . I can no where find so great satisfaction, as in those innocent & useful pursuits. In indulging these feelings, I am led to reflect how much more delightful to an undebauched mind is the task of making improvements on the earth; than all the vain glory which can be acquired from ravaging it, by the most uninterrupted career of conquests."[79]

During Washington's eight-year absence the agricultural operation at Mount Vernon had not prospered. It was difficult enough before the war to turn a profit on the plantation, even with Washington personally directing the enterprise. With him gone, the slim margin for profit fell out of reach. The wheat crop failed in successive years after his departure so that in 1778 he had to ask his manager, "How am I to live[?] I cannot Support myself if I make nothing." At the close of the war he was despondent that his "private concerns . . . do not wear the most smiling countenance": "I shall be more hurt, than at any thing else, to think that an Estate, which I have drawn nothing from, for eight years, and which always enabled me to make any purchase I had in view, should not have been able for the last five years, to pay the manager: And that, worse than going home to empty coffers, and expensive living, I shall be encumbered with debt." Thus, after his return to Mount Vernon Washington was prepared to take a hard look at Virginia farming practices. He considered agriculture to be "of infinite importance to the country" and "the proper source of American wealth & happiness." But his plantation and those of his neighbors were failing. In 1785 Washington would argue to a sympathetic George William Fairfax in England that the American system of farming would have to be overturned: "Our course of Husbandry

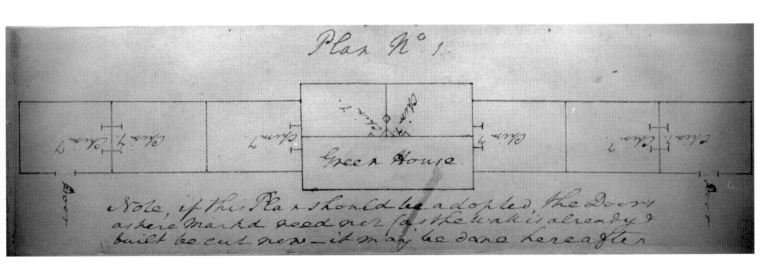

178. George Washington, *Green House Plan,* ca. 1784, pen and ink on paper. (Courtesy of Mount Vernon Ladies' Association)

in this Country, & more especially in this State, is not only exceedingly unprofitable, but so destructive to our Lands, that it is my earnest wish to adopt a better; & as I believe no Country has carried the improvment of Land & the benefits of Agriculture to greater perfection than England, I have asked myself frequently of late, whether a thorough bred *practicaly english Farmer* . . . could not be obtain'd?" In the same letter Washington asks Fairfax to find him "a knowing Farmer, I mean one who understands the best course of Crops; how to plough—to sow—to mow—to hedge—to Ditch & above all, Midas like, one who can convert every thing he touches into manure." This man also had to be able to breed livestock. The general's plan was to institute at Mount Vernon "a compleat course of husbandry as practiced in the best Farming Counties of England."[80] Though a novel idea, his attempt to bring in a knowledgeable English farmer was not so different from indenturing a joiner or mason from England, the talent pool for all these trades.

Washington's plea to his former neighbor brought quick results. Fairfax engaged James Bloxham, who took up residence at Mount Vernon in 1786. The accomplished English agriculturist Arthur Young had also learned of Washington's plans and offered to assist the general:

> The spectacle of a great commander retiring in the manner you have done from the head of a victorious army to the amusements of agriculture, calls all the feelings of my bosom into play & gives me the strongest inclination . . . to contribute to the success of so laudable a pleasure. . . . If you want men, cattle, tools, seeds, or any thing else that may add to yr rural amusement, favour me with your commands, & beleive me I shall take a very sincere pleasure in executing them. . . . Your expression concerning manure being the [f]irst transmutation towards gold, is good, and shews that you may be as great a farmer as a general.

Young would continue to provide what aid he could to the general-turned-farmer; he and Washington would correspond until the general's death in 1799. In writing to Young, Washington described both the vast agricultural operation that he had put together at Mount Vernon and, as important, the state of farming in Virginia as a whole. "Tobacco has been almost the sole object with men of landed property" in Virginia, he explained, "and consequently a regular course of Crops have

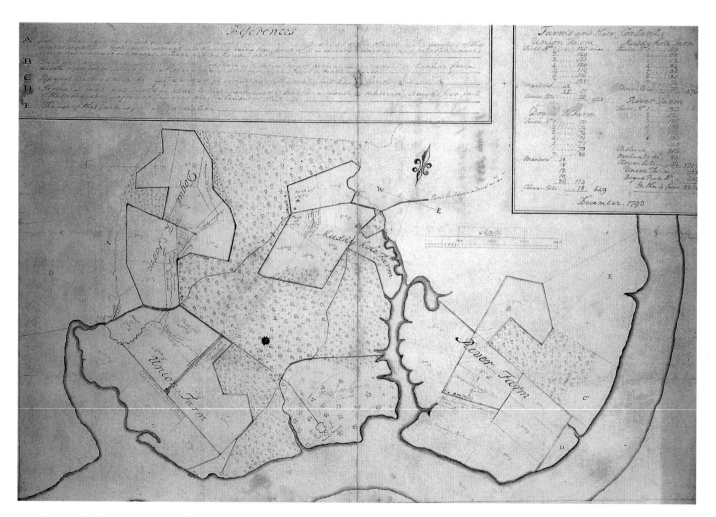

179. George Washington, *Map of the Five Farms at Mount Vernon,* 1793. (Courtesy of Huntington Library, San Marino, Calif.)

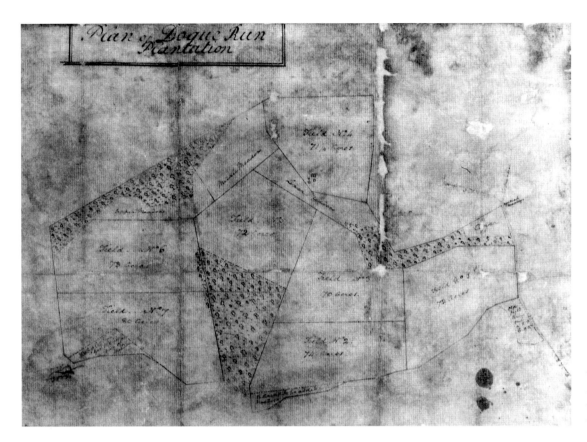

180. George Washington, *Plan of Dogue Run Plantation*, n.d. (Courtesy of Virginia Historical Society)

never been in view." Those who raised crops would simply plant corn, followed by wheat, then rest the land for eighteen months, "and so on, alternately, without any dressing; till the land is exhausted." Few cattle were raised other "than can be supported by lowland meadows, swamps, &ca."[81]

At Mount Vernon Washington had built a complex of five farms that comprised some eight thousand acres, about half of which was cultivable (fig. 179). The acreage fronted several miles of river, which the general valued as "an inexhaustible fund of rich mud" to be used as manure. The land was mostly level, though some of the fields were "washed into gullies" and had "not, as yet, been recovered."[82] There was Union Farm, immediately downriver from the Mansion House (or Home House) Farm, where Washington built a large, rectangular brick barn, "equal perhaps to any in America, and for conveniences of all sorts, particularly for sheltering and feeding horses, cattle, &c, scarcely to be exceeded anywhere." Fifty slaves lived there. Directly west of the mansion house was Dogue Run Farm, manned by forty slaves, where the general built an innovative circular barn for the treading and storage of wheat (fig. 180). Muddy Hole Farm was northwest of the mansion house and home to thirty slaves. Directly upstream was River Farm, the largest of the four and the seat of fifty to sixty slaves. There were several dozen horses, mules, and oxen on the five farms as well as some three hundred black cattle, six hundred

sheep, and a not easily determined number of hogs running loose in the woods. The maintenance of this livestock, especially of the sheep, numbers of which were often reported lost, became problematic for the general, as did his efforts to expand on the number and types of crops.

The general divided each of the farms into seven fields of roughly the same acreage so that he could rotate crops on a seven-year cycle and each year have essentially the same harvest. Instead of the customary rotation of only corn and wheat, Washington planted a variety of other crops, such as rye, barley, peas, and oats, along with grass and clover, which served to rejuvenate fallow fields. He fenced the land and fertilized it, deep-plowed to guard against erosion, and arranged the crops in neat rows. The general immersed himself in the workings of these farms and directed the various operations in extraordinary detail, despite the presence of both a farm manager, who was employed for that purpose, and James Bloxham, who advised about agricultural decisions. Lund Washington, who had served as farm manager for the previous twenty-one years, resigned in 1785. The general's nephew, George Augustine Washington, then took the position, and he was followed by other managers through the 1790s. When Washington was away, he required his manager to submit a weekly report enumerating how the workers were utilized and what was accomplished, and in return he sent detailed instructions concerning the next

*The American Cincinnatus: 1783–1789*

week's endeavors. This highly structured, almost military, regimen, which the general established to govern both crop rotation and work assignments, is evidence of his characteristic sense that in order for there to be efficiency and productivity, he had to maintain control of all aspects of any undertaking.

One occasion when the correspondence system of farm management was put into play was during 1787, when Washington was in Philadelphia presiding over the Constitutional Convention. He had not wanted to leave Mount Vernon but recognized what he described as the need "to revise and correct the defects of the federal System." He worried that the power of state governments would "render the situation of this great country weak, inefficient, and disgraceful" and that they "may ultimately break the band, which holds us together." As early as 1776 Washington had recognized that the drafting of a strong, clear, defining document would be crucial to the success of the new nation. Perhaps not surprisingly, he expressed this understanding in terms borrowed from architecture; he believed that "to form a new Government, requires infinite care, & unbounded attention; for if the foundation is badly laid the superstructure must be bad." If mistakes were made in Philadelphia in 1787, then the efforts of the Revolution would have been in vain, and the general and all his countrymen would ultimately suffer the consequences. More by his presence alone, and by his silence on issues rather than by any forceful actions, Washington guided the convention to a successful conclusion ("so much beyond any thing we had a right to imagine or expect eighteen months ago").[83]

While he was away, however, Washington would not allow the duties of "republicanism" to disrupt the operation of his farms.[84] He wrote lengthy instructions to George Augustine Washington that are useful today as documentation both of the responsibilities of a farm manager and of the general's knowledge of farming and his devotion to its details. They also help explain how he decided what and when to harvest, what and

181. Junius Brutus Stearns, *Washington as a Farmer at Mount Vernon,* 1851, oil on canvas, 37½×54 in. (Courtesy of Virginia Museum of Fine Arts, Richmond, Va., gift of Edgar William and Bernice Chrysler Garbisch)

*The American Cincinnatus: 1783–1789*

when to plant. Washington or his manager would ride daily to attend to matters at the various farms. The general's ardent interest in agricultural pursuits is one of the subjects raised in Junius Brutus Stearns's 1851 painting, *Washington as a Farmer at Mount Vernon,* which celebrates the general's role as "the first farmer in America" (fig. 181). The artist envisions a setting at the Mansion House Farm, with a small group of slaves happily at work. Nelly and Washington Custis enjoy the tranquility of this arcadia. At one side of the painting Washington directs his overseer and, in turn, the whole operation, with an expression that conveys more than a passing interest in what is being accomplished.

Admittedly, there are problems with this image. Washington's fields would have been more clearly defined by both fences and ordered plantings. Also, more than half of the Mount Vernon field hands were females. From our modern point of view, however, perhaps the most disturbing factor is the mythical happiness of the slaves. It is perhaps surprising that on the eve of the Civil War an artist exhibiting in New York City would represent slavery as an essential aspect of his subject's life. Stearns's Washington of course had to be excused for his participation in this system, but his figurative descendants in the South need not be, and so the painting may well have espoused a sectionalist agenda while still honoring the general-turned-planter. By including the grandchildren in the scene Stearns suggests that the general treated the slaves like children and that all the members of his plantation were cared for with kindness; his benevolence and patriarchal affection were available to all.

Stearns probably took his theme from Sparks, who states, "the first year after the war, [Washington] applied himself mainly to farming operations, with the view of restoring his neglected fields and commencing a regular system of practical agriculture." Each morning, Washington "rode to his farms and gave directions for the day to the managers and laborers." Weems had provided a similar account; the postwar Washington "turns all his attentions—bends all his exertions" to farming.[85] All his biographers recognized that farming was important to Washington during the second retirement, but there is no evidence that they knew just what that involved or how much exertion Washington the agriculturist demanded of himself and his workers.

As he made his daily rounds, the general's first concern was that the time of his slaves be utilized to the fullest. He would often remark that lost labor can never be regained. One of the primary tasks was to "direct the Overseers how to apply the labour to advantage"; because one could not spend the entire day observing, that was "all that can be expected." Washington had to be concerned about the productivity of not only the field hands but also the carpenters, coopers, blacksmiths, sta-

blers, and stockkeepers. The general was particularly peeved about the use of wagons: "There is nothing which stands in greater need of regulation than the Waggons and Carts which always whilst I was at home appeared to me to be most wretchedly employed; first in never carrying half a load; 2dly in flying from one thing to another; and thirdly in no person seeming to know what they really did; and oftentimes under pretence of doing this, that, and the other thing, did nothing at all." While in the fields, Washington would daily check the progress of the crops. Is a crop coming up so thickly that it needs to be thinned? How tall and how healthy are some crops, and why are others failing? When he was not in residence he demanded this type of information from his managers. "Inform me in your next how your Grain, particularly the Barley and Oats, stand on the ground—that is, the height of them, whether thick or thin—how branched—how headed—and what the farmer [from England] (who ought to be a judge) thinks of their yield. . . . I am really sorry to hear that the Carro[ts] and Parsnips are so thinly come up. Does this appear to be the effect of bad Seed, unfavourable Seasons, improper ground, or want of proper Culture?" As the crops matured, Washington would determine the best time to harvest. "Begin Harvest as soon as the grain can be cut with Safety" was a general rule. But sometimes the crops were so poor that "all the grass that is fit for Hay" might have to be cut prematurely so that the horses and other livestock would not "be in a bad box next winter." And at other times, a crop of oats, for example, might be so stunted in its growth that it could never be harvested. The call of the marketplace was also a factor governing his decisions about harvesting: "As the first Potatoes at Market will probably sell high, examine now and then your forwardest; and when they are of sufficient size, dispose of them . . . in Alexandria." Money was also to be had from the sale of flour and barley and from the fish netted in the Potomac.[86] In short, decisions had to be made continuously about when and where to sell all the various types of produce from the plantation, and Washington felt the need to be involved in all such commercial dealings.

After Washington had decided when a crop was to be harvested, he would then determine where next to plant it. In his written instructions the general directed his overseers about what crops to sow and when to sow them. "Break up field No. 5 [at Muddy Hole Farm] for Indian Corn," he wrote his manager in 1789 (fig. 182). Then "break up No. 4 for Buck Wheat, which is to be sowed in April and plowed in before harvest, as a manure for the Crop of Wheat which is to be sown therein in the month of August next." Often there was "no more time" to delay, if a crop was to be succeed, and sometimes a new crop had to be planted even before the old one was har-

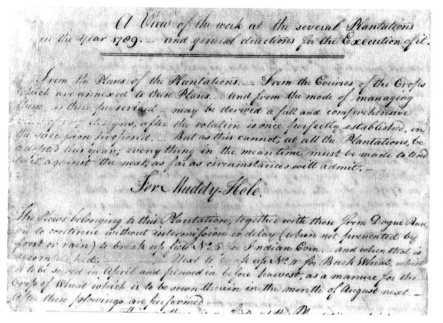

A View of the work at the several Plantations in the year 1789. — and general directions for the Execution of it.

From the Plans of the Plantations. From the Courses of the Crops which are annexed to these Plans. And from the mode of managing them, as there prescribed — may be derived a full and comprehensive ... of ... designs, after the rotation is once perfectly established, in the succession proposed. But as this cannot, at all the Plantations, be adopted this year; every thing in the mean time must be made to tend to it against the next, as far as circumstances will admit. —

**For Muddy-Hole.**

The Plows belonging to this Plantation, together with those from Dogue Run, are to continue without intermission or delay (when not prevented by frost or rain) to break up field No 5 for Indian Corn, and when that is accomplished ... Next to break up No 4 for Buck Wheat, which is to be sowed in April and plowed in before harvest, as a manure for the Crop of Wheat which is to be sown therein in the month of August next. — After these plowings are performed ...

182. George Washington, *A View of the Work at the Several Plantations in the Year 1789. —And General Directions for the Execution of It,* January 1789. (Courtesy of Virginia Historical Society)

vested: "Perceiving you have little chance of sowing much Wheat in Fallow land this Fall . . . it is indispensably necessary (in order that I may have something to depend upon next year) that *all* the Corn ground at *all* the Plantations, should be laid down in either Wheat or rye, . . . and I request it may be done accordingly; and with as little delay as possible. The Season for it is now come, and putting it in, gives the last stirring to the Corn." There was also the matter of seed testing in the botanical beds near the house. Careful records had to be kept. For seeds that had been mailed to Washington, experimental planting was the only way to determine "whether their vegitative properties are good, or are destroyed." Decisions had to be made as to which of these special seeds should be introduced to the farms and when such plantings would be most advantageous.[87]

A sampling of his correspondence from the 1780s suggests that Washington often had much on his mind as he made his rounds of the five farms. The overseers had only to follow his instructions, whereas the general had to make numerous decisions on a daily basis, do what he could to see that his workers would toil from dusk to dawn as he expected, and worry about the weather's cooperation with his ambitious plans. In 1787 it did not. Washington was faced then with "the almost total loss" of his corn crop "by the drought," and he was forced "to purchase upwards of eight hundred Barrels of Corn" to fill the hundreds of human and animal mouths on his farms. Such purchases were particularly galling because they reminded him that even his best efforts could at times end in failure; they also spurred the general to look for better solutions and to consider even more revolutionary agricultural practices.[88]

Washington felt a responsibility to be innovative: "Experiments must be made . . . by Gentlemen who have leizure and abilities to devise and wherewithal to hazard something. The common farmer wil not depart from the *old* road 'till the *new* one is made so plain and easy that he is sure it cannot be mistaken." In this letter to John Beale Bordley, a wealthy neighbor in Maryland, Washington was speaking specifically about his use of seven fields and seven crops. But as "first farmer of America" he also felt compelled to improve the breeds of livestock in the new nation. Indeed, if he was to practice correctly the techniques of English husbandry, Washington had to raise animals as well as plants, because the two are indispensable to one another. (The crops feed the animals, while the manure fertilizes the soil.) The general took a special interest in sheep and mules. He kept anywhere between six hundred and a thousand sheep, "more sheep than is usual in this Country," which was twice the size of his herd of black cattle. During the second retirement, Washington "was proud in being able to produce perhaps the largest mutton and the greatest quantity of Wool from my Sheep that could then be produced." But he "was not satisfied" with that accomplishment, and so before the presidency called him away from Mount Vernon he "contemplated further improvements both in the flesh and wool by the introduction of other breeds." The rearing of hearty sheep would be "most profitable" for the American farmer. But even more significant, from Washington's remarkable perspective, was that this activity was "highly important in a public view, by encouraging extensive establishments of woolen manufactories."[89]

If public duties at times interfered with Washington's ambitious plans for sheep rearing, the general did establish a hearty breed of mules. He received a jackass, which he named "Royal Gift," from the king of Spain and another, named "Knight of Malta," from Lafayette, who also shipped him exotic pheasants and partridges for Mount Vernon's park. "I have a prospect of introducing into this Country a very excellent race of animals," Washington wrote to Arthur Young, who expressed "many doubts" about the effectiveness of mules on a farm, arguing instead that oxen "have no rivals." Undaunted, Washington was able to foresee that the mule could replace the horse, at least for some duties: "mules . . . perform as much labour, with vastly less feeding than horses."[90]

The fishery at Mount Vernon neatly complemented the farming and the raising of livestock. Not only were fresh fish from the Potomac marketable, but they were also a major source of food for the plantation; at times the fishing proved more productive than the farming. The Potomac is "well supplied with various kinds of fish at all Seasons of the year," Washington wrote, and "the whole shore in short is one entire fishery." Niemcewicz said that in April the slave fishermen "caught as many as 100 thousand [herring] with a single draw of the net."[91] In the 1830s, when John Gadsby Chapman visited Mount Vernon, the Potomac apparently still contained an abundance of fish. Black fishermen, as seen in the two boats on the right, as well as white, still cast their nets in hopes of profiting from this bounty (fig. 183). The artist depicts a tranquil river scene that allows the viewer to remember with nostalgia the vast and productive estate that Mount Vernon once had been. There is no way to know if Chapman's black figures are slaves or freedmen, but in either case it is likely that their labor helped to support the plantation shown in the distance, as black labor had done throughout the eighteenth century, making this scene not so idyllic as it might at first appear. While Washington eventually wanted to end slavery at Mount Vernon, the institution had been perpetuated after his death by his heirs; they also hired freedmen at the lowest possible wages. Without the general to conduct the operation with his customary efficiency, however, the plantation that Chapman visited proved so un-productive that eventually one of those heirs would be forced to sell it.

Washington found little time or energy for the hunting that he had enjoyed so much before the war. George Washington Parke Custis wrote how "the hunting establishment" at Mount Vernon "was renewed [in 1785] by the arrival of a pack of French hounds," a gift from Lafayette. When he had visited a year earlier, the Frenchman had observed that the general still enjoyed the pastime of hunting foxes. From the diaries, it is evident that at least during the winter of 1785–86, after Washington had recovered somewhat from his war-induced exhaustion, he attempted to renew this activity. The French hounds, however, were of little help; they showed "no great disposition for Hunting" foxes and needed to "understand more fully the kind of game they are intended to run." The general soon gave up hunting altogether. Custis's statement that "Washington's last hunt with his hounds, was in 1785" is probably close to the truth.[92]

If even the invigorating hunting of foxes could not entice the American Cincinnatus, the thought that the general hunted game during this period is pure fantasy. Nonetheless, the popularity of hunting in the nineteenth century, which accounts for such print images as *Mount Vernon in the Olden Times* (see fig. 84), was sufficient to also inspire the publication in 1868 of a mythical depiction of Washington entertaining a group of distinguished Revolutionary War guests by leading them on a

183. John Gadsby Chapman, *Distant View of Mount Vernon*, 1830s, oil on canvas, 21⁹/₁₆×29 in. (Courtesy of Homeland Foundation, Incorporated, New York)

*The American Cincinnatus: 1783–1789*

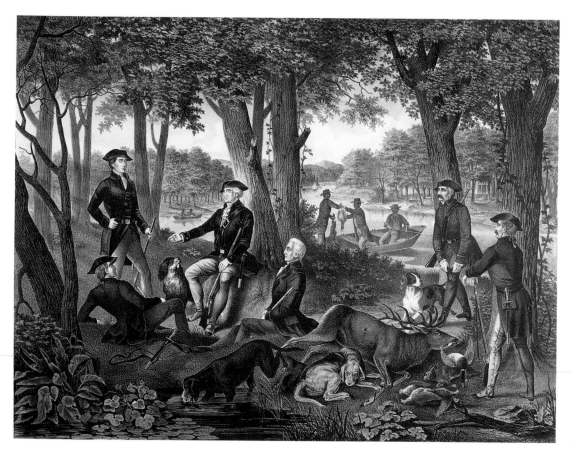

184. Charles P. Tholey, *Washington and Friends After a Day's Hunt in Virginia,* 1868, color lithograph, 21¼×24¼ in., printed by G. Spohni. (Courtesy of Mount Vernon Ladies' Association, gift of Mrs. Douglas Seaman, Vice Regent for Wisconsin, and Mr. Seaman)

deer hunt at Mount Vernon (fig. 184). The artist is Charles Tholey, a minor Philadelphia painter. Almost nothing in the image is factual, making it valuable only as evidence of how much the Washington story could be distorted to meet the demands of the market. The general was more interested in breeding deer for his park than in hunting them. But even more troublesome for twentieth-century viewers, who often search for accuracy in such images, is Tholey's suggestion of an impossible gathering of historical figures. On the print, by their last names only, the artist identifies the five men who listen to Washington's storytelling as Wayne, Lafayette, Green, La Grange, and Pulaski. Gen. "Mad Anthony" Wayne, of Pennsylvania and then Georgia, was a favorite of Washington because of his daring and courage during the Revolutionary War, and the Virginian did stay in touch with him afterward; during the first presidency he would give Wayne command of the army that repulsed Indian insurgents in the Northwest Territory. Green could be Berryman Green, a Virginia neighbor from nearby Westmoreland County who like Wayne had shared the trials of Valley Forge with Washington. Or, more probably, this Green is meant to be the more famous Maj. Gen. Nathanael Greene of Georgia, a wartime friend of Washington who died in 1786. We do not know who "La Grange" would be, but pre-

sumably this name was meant to suggest the stream of French visitors to Mount Vernon. Count Casimir Pulaski was the Polish patriot who had fought valiantly against the British during the American Revolution, but he had been killed at the siege of Savannah in 1779. We have seen that Lafayette was at Mount Vernon in 1784, but there is no evidence to suggest that Wayne or either of the Green(e)s visited, and almost certainly they were never there at the same time.

Tholey's inspiration for this subject may have come from Washington Custis's account of "Washington as a Sportsman," which first appeared in the *American Turf Register and Sporting Magazine* in 1829 and was then published in later editions of his *Recollections of Washington.*[93] Custis states that before the war, the hunting guests would be resident for weeks and that Washington would dress elegantly for the chasing of foxes. He then tells a story, set a decade and a half after the general's own hunting days had ended, of how Washington in 1799 allowed one "old buck" to be killed on his grounds, largely because the neighbors were poaching there. When Custis's party wounded this "patriarch of the herd," the deer, in vain, sought the water "as a refuge from the dogs." There is no evidence other than Custis's word that this hunt ever occurred, and it might well be suspected that the author, who was two generations younger than Washington, told a story that was meant to appeal to his nineteenth-century audience. Tholey improved on Custis's account, making Washington both a hunter of game and a storyteller. Such representations rightly reminded audiences of Washington's skills at woodcraft, but in terms that bear little relation to the general's actual activities.

### What "Imperious Necessity Compels": Washington as a Slaveholder

Stearns's rendering of Washington as a farmer necessarily depicts him as a slaveholder as well. Similarly, Ferdinand Richardt's *East Front of Mount Vernon* remembers not just the house but also the slaves who maintained it (fig. 185). Winslow Homer includes black figures in his Mount Vernon composition (see fig. 108), and Eastman Johnson's painting of the kitchen at Mount Vernon is clearly more about the slaves who worked there than the building itself (fig. 186). Black people were prominent components of the Mount Vernon operation, and all four painters felt the need to recognize and depict their presence.

In Richardt's canvas, the figures of a slave and her two children draw our attention by the way they are silhouetted within the arcade connecting the house to her workplace, the kitchen. In the foreground, white women idly enjoy a game of badminton, while white children behind them are at play and dogs lounge nearby. It is the black people, we discern, who even in Richardt's day still do the work and remain a dominant feature of the Mount Vernon landscape. If painted just after the Civil War, as is believed, this canvas reminds us not only of the impressive estate that George Washington had built, which had recently been saved by the Mount Vernon Ladies' Association, but also of the long history of servitude that had come to an end with the Emancipation Proclamation. Richardt perhaps is also making the additional, bitter point that the status of many black people in the South was in actuality little changed, even after they had been liberated from bondage.

At his death Washington produced his own emancipation proclamation; he freed all the slaves in his name. Nonetheless, the successive heirs to his estate continued to be slaveholders. Of the some 317 slaves who had been controlled by Washing-

185. Ferdinand Richardt, *East Front of Mount Vernon,* ca. 1870, based on a sketch made in 1858, oil on canvas, 18×28 in. (Courtesy of Mount Vernon Ladies' Association)

186. Eastman Johnson, *The Kitchen at Mount Vernon,* ca. 1857, oil on canvas, 12½×20½ in. (Courtesy of Mount Vernon Ladies' Association)

ton at the end of his life, he owned less than half; the others had been inherited by Martha from Daniel Parke Custis and by law remained in her possession. At Martha's death these slaves were passed on to her Custis heirs. However, some may have remained on the plantation because Bushrod Washington, the nephew who inherited Mount Vernon from Martha, put together a slave force there. Later he would sell and transport 54 of these slaves to Louisiana, despite his position as first president of the American Colonization Society and his uncle's resolve not to separate family members.[94] Even after that migration, a black workforce remained in place at Mount Vernon over the years because otherwise the plantation could not operate. Among these workers were free blacks who were hired to do the same work as their ancestors whom Washington had liberated.

Both of Washington's grandfathers had been slaveholders; his fatther had amassed enough of a force to have slaves at each of the farms that he handed to his oldest sons; and the gentlemen of the Fairfax family, in whom Washington found models of appropriate behavior, as well as nearly all other important members of the Virginia aristocracy were slaveholders. It would have been impossible for the young Washington to see slavery as anything but a necessary aspect of gentry life in the colony. However, slavery was an arrangement that Washington eventually came not to care for, because he saw both the evils and the inefficiency of it. But the system was a necessity if

Mount Vernon was to prosper. Though he looked long and hard, the general never found an alternative.

Although we know little about most of Washington's 317 slaves, some accounts survive that describe their working and living conditions. One-third to one-half were too old, too young, or too infirm to do strenuous outdoor labor. Thus, in the mid-1780s, for example, the number of field hands was only 86, of whom 46 were women. These 86 people were in their physical prime, and Washington worked them long and hard. He required that they be "at their work as soon as it is light, work till it is dark, and be diligent while they are at it." They labored seven days a week and were released from that stringent regimen only on holidays. The general reasoned that "every labourer (male or female)" should do as "much in the 24 hours as their strength without endangering the health, or constitution will allow of" (fig. 187).[95] It must be noted, however, that Washington was never one to accept idleness under any circumstances. Throughout his life, he expected every worker or soldier under his command, black or white, to work unremittingly, and he pushed himself the same way. Some of Washington's slaves were actually pushed by other slaves; on three of the five farms during the mid-1780s, the overseers themselves were slaves who had been "promoted."

The general thought that the housing his slaves were allowed to build for themselves provided "sufficient covering," but Niemcewicz said that these "huts" were "more miserable than the most miserable of the cottages of our peasants." He described the conditions with objectivity:

> The husband and wife sleep on a mean pallet, the children on the ground; a very bad fireplace, some utensils for cooking, but in the middle of this poverty some cups and a teapot. . . . A very small garden planted with vegetables was close by, with 5 or 6 hens, each one leading ten to fifteen chickens. It is the only comfort that is permitted them. . . . They allot them each . . . one quart [of maize] a day, and half as much for the children, with 20 herrings each per month. At harvest time those who work in the fields have salt meat; in addition, a jacket and a pair of homespun breeches per year. . . . The condition of our peasants is infinitely happier.[96]

The comparison to the peasants of Europe, which would be made in the nineteenth century by proslavery advocates, is useful because it points to the fact that Washington, like nearly all slaveholders in Virginia, was blind to the possibility of any real upward mobility for the lowest class. Slaves and peasants would always be slaves and peasants. That they were to be treated as such was simply a fact of life.

As to the feelings of the slaves themselves about their forced servitude at Mount Vernon, the clearest record is the evidence of their attempts to escape. When a British sloop of war raided Mount Vernon in the spring of 1781, at least 19 slaves fled. Given their work schedule, living conditions, the few privileges afforded them, and the absence of hope for an improvement in their lot, it is remarkable that more did not leave, and that many of those who remained apparently found the fortitude not to despair. Niemcewicz recorded that he had "never seen the Blacks [at Mount Vernon] sad."[97]

There was even affection between the Washingtons and at least some of the slaves who remained at the plantation. We know of Washington's attachment to his manservant William Lee, one of the mulattoes who Niemcewicz said were "ordinarily chosen for servants" but who by the laws of Virginia were "still slaves." Washington had bought Lee in 1768 from Mrs. Mary Lee of Westmoreland County for sixty-one pounds. Sixteen years later, when Lee's companion, a freedwoman, was in poor health and he requested her removal to Mount Vernon, Washington stated that he "cannot refuse his request" because "he has lived with me so long & followed my fortunes through the War with fidility." In his will the general granted Lee "immediate freedom" and cited again, with appreciation, "his attachment to me" and "faithful services during the Revolutionary War." When the Washingtons left Mount Vernon for the presidency, Martha said farewell to the slaves with no little emotion, according to the report of her nephew Robert Lewis: "The Servants of the House, and a number of the field negros made there appearance—to take leave of their mistress—numbers of these poor wretches seemed greatly *agitated, much affected*—My Aunt equally so."[98]

Though they certainly lived in harsh conditions, the slaves at Mount Vernon were evidently managed with some degree of decency. Niemcewicz reported that Washington "treats his slaves far more humanely than do his fellow citizens of Virginia" (who "give to their Blacks only bread, water and blows"). Apparently, unlike many of his neighbors, Washington made a genuine effort to see that his slaves were not physically and emotionally abused. He was offended that some of his (white) overseers "seem to consider a Negro much in the same light as they do the brute beasts, on the farms" or "view these poor creatures in scarcely any other light than they do a draught horse or Ox." He insisted that the slaves who were sick must be treated "with humanity and tenderness." Admittedly, Washington suffered a financial loss with the death of any slave, and his comments about care for the sick are offered partly in that context. But these statements also carry his conviction about the evils of

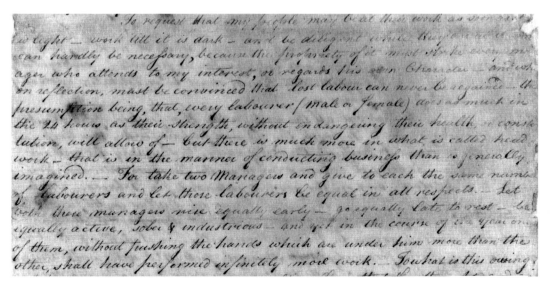

187. George Washington, *A View of the Work at the Several Plantations in the Year 1789.—And General Directions for the Execution of It,* January 1789, instructions for manager John Fairfax. (Courtesy of Virginia Historical Society)

*The American Cincinnatus: 1783–1789*

abusive treatment.[99] Also humane was the general's respect for the sanctity of family relationships among his slaves. Although Washington's patience was never great, and he would in an instant ship a troublemaker to the West Indies, under most circumstances he would not separate families, either by selling slaves or by sending some family members west to settle the lands he owned along the Ohio. Washington's attitudes about slavery, like, one might suggest, his religious beliefs, evolved gradually over the years. The man who freed his slaves at the end of his life was different from the one who in earlier years had purchased them. Even as late as 1773 Washington described slaves crassly as "a very uncertain & precarious Security," and up until the eve of the Revolution he thought little of purchasing them, either locally or from the West Indies in return for flour shipped there.[100] But he did look to end his ownership of slaves as early as 1778.

One factor that came into play as Washington's ideas about slavery evolved was the dramatic growth of the Mount Vernon slave population. In 1758 Washington owned only about twenty slaves. His marriage the next year increased the number who were of working age to about fifty. A quarter century later, by the time of the first complete census of the slaves in 1786, the entire population had risen to 216. The growth during the next decade was almost 50 percent, to 300.[101] The Mount Vernon slaves intermarried and reproduced at a steady pace. By the 1790s Washington owned enough slave families to populate a small town. He had to inventory them continually, and he soon realized that he controlled more people than he could utilize on the plantation (fig. 188). Ownership of so many slaves gave the general another reason to think long and hard about those who were under his dominion.

As early as July 1774, when he served as chairman of the committee that produced the Fairfax County Resolves, Washington took an enlightened stance about the trafficking in slaves. One of the resolves was that "no Slaves ought to be imported into any of the British Colonies on this Continent." That statement was followed by a ringing condemnation of the slave trade: "We take this Opportunity of declaring our most earnest Wishes to see an entire Stop for ever put to such a wicked cruel and unnatural Trade." A month later Washington compared the subjugation of Americans under British tyranny to the status of black slaves on the Virginia plantations. He argued that colonials "must assert our Rights" or become "as tame, & abject Slaves, as the Blacks we Rule over with such arbitrary Sway."[102] For economic as well as philosophical reasons Washington could not carry the comparison a step further and suggest that black slaves in the colonies should also enjoy freedom; he did not want to lose his financial investment. But in this statement, which admittedly has more to do with politics than slaveholding, Washington seems at least to have recognized both the injustice of American slavery and the incompatibility of the new philosophy of independence with the foundation of the southern colonial society that would produce so many of its leading lights.

While by 1774 Washington may have privately acknowledged the existence of a problem, it was not the sort of thing one discussed openly in the South. This is precisely what Eastman Johnson depicts on the eve of the Civil War in *The Kitchen at Mount Vernon* (see fig. 186). Johnson does not show the main house, where the evil of slavery is hidden from sight. Instead, the kitchen stands in his painting as a large and formidable symbol of the people who are enslaved to work on southern plantations. It is a remarkably gloomy, prisonlike space in which all that one views—the people as well as the objects—belong to the master of the house. Johnson demands that his audience see what was often kept at a distance from the eyes of white visitors or obscured in sentimental depictions of the plantation South in an effort to manifest the true cost of a system in which people can be bought and sold.

As we have seen, while the general was in the field fighting the British his plantation had ceased to be profitable. The slaves who toiled in his fields from dawn until dusk, seven days a week, simply had no incentive to work hard, and without Washington present to push them the plantation inevitably failed. The general did complain of the "idleness and deceit" of his field hands when they were supervised by an overseer who did not know how to manage them, but he came to recognize that slavery simply was an inefficient system. As a result, as early as 1778, he considered ending slavery at Mount Vernon. From White Plains, New York, Washington acknowledged that "my Estate in Virginia is scarce able to support itself" so that "I every day long more and more to get clear of [my Negroes]." He would not free them, because the crisis that prompted this line of thought was economic, but he might sell them. Six months later, the general was still wrestling with this issue: "The only points therefore for me to consider, are, first, whether it would be most to my interest, in case of a fortunate determination of the present contest, to have negroes, and the Crops they will make; or the sum they will now fetch and the interest of the money. And, secondly, the critical moment to make this sale. . . . If these poor wretches are to be held in a state of slavery, I do not see that a change of masters will render it more irksome, provided husband and wife, and Parents and children are not separated from each other, which is not my intentions to do."[103]

Four years later, in 1783, the idealistic Lafayette proposed a scheme whereby he and Washington would experiment with emancipation. The example of the general, who was so revered by his countrymen, might inspire all American slaveholders to end the practice: "Let us unite in purchasing a small estate,

188. Inventory of slaves at Mount Vernon, n.d. (Courtesy of Virginia Historical Society)

where we may try the experiment to free the negroes, and use them only as tenants. Such an example as yours might render it a general practice; and if we succeed in America, I will cheerfully devote a part of my time to render the method fashionable in the West Indies. If it be a wild scheme, I had rather be mad this way, than to be thought wise in the other task." Washington responded with interest: "The scheme, my dear Marqs. which you propose as a precedent, to encourage the emancipation of the black people of this Country from that state of Bondage in wch. they are held, is a striking evidence of the benevolence of your Heart. I shall be happy to join you in so laudable a work." Presumably the two talked about their emancipation strategy when Lafayette visited the following year. Nothing further appears in Washington's writings about this subject, and so many observers have concluded that the idea was not pursued. But Niemcewicz records that in 1798 he had a conservation with David Stuart, the stepfather of the Custis children, during which the doctor told him, "they have tried to rent them [the slaves] a piece of land; except for a small number they want neither to work nor to pay their rent."[104] No doubt part of the reason for this failure is tied to the difficulty of anyone turning a profit through agriculture in early Virginia. This incident is significant, however, because it is evidence that Washington not only talked about emancipation but in fact took at least one step in that direction. This was a genuine effort to try to end slavery at Mount Vernon, and, even if one argues that it was attempted for economic reasons, Washington should be given some credit for this effort.

Having failed at his attempt to turn his slaves into tenants, as he had largely failed to rent his Ohio lands, Washington in the mid-1780s looked for a legislative solution to the problems caused by slavery. The institution could be ended, he reasoned, if the state legislatures would simply compensate slaveholders for their financial investment in slaves: "There is not a man living who wishes more sincerely than I do, to see a plan adopted for the abolition of it—but there is only one proper and effectual mode by which it can be accomplished, & that is by Legislative authority." A decade later, in 1796–97, Washington would make the same argument. He called for "gradual abolition, or even . . . an entire emancipation" of slaves, but he thought the former more likely to happen. "I wish from my Soul," he wrote, "that the Legislature of this State could see the policy of a gradual abolition of Slavery." In Virginia, however, not even Washington would be heard on this subject. Without the desired provision for financial compensation Washington felt that he could not push further for abolition. In Philadelphia during the presidencies he had been quick to oppose a Pennsylvania law that might have freed the slaves who served him there because this law provided no remuneration for their loss.[105]

As noted in our discussions of the western lands in chapter 3, in the 1790s, when the agricultural operations at Mount Vernon were again "unproductive," the president tried to sell enough of his holdings to be in an economic position whereby he could not only meet expenses but could also free himself of the institution that "imperious necessity" had compelled him to maintain.[106] The president would free his slaves if he could put himself in a secure-enough financial position to do so. But the proposed sale of 1794 failed. Had a buyer been found, Washington today would be praised for having liberated his slaves.

Six months later, Washington was exasperated by his failure to resolve the problem. "I do not like to even think, much less talk of it," he wrote. The sale of slaves was still out of the question: "Were it not then, that I am principled agt. selling negros, as you would do cattle in the market, I would not, in twelve months from this date, be possessed of one, as a slave. I shall be happily mistaken, if they are not found to be a very troublesome species of property 'ere many years pass." Part of the trouble at Mount Vernon was that so many of the Washingtons' slaves and those on neighboring plantations had intermarried. This made even the rental of slaves impossible if the owner was to be humane and not disassemble family units. In 1796 Washington wrote to David Stuart about the possibility of renting several of his five farms, along with the slaves resident on them: "When it is considered how much the Dower Negros and my own are intermarried, and the former with neighbouring Negros, to part will be an affecting, and trying [event,] happen when it will."[107]

In 1797 Washington's cook escaped, providing evidence that at least some of the slaves at Mount Vernon were unhappy. Washington was thereby forced to become a slave buyer again: "The running off of my Cook, has been a most inconvenient thing to this family; and what renders it more disagreeable, is, that I had resolved never to become the master of another Slave by *purchase;* but this resolution I fear I must break."[108]

Incidents involving the Mount Vernon slave force had been worrisome ever since the former colonists had gained liberty for themselves but had refused to extend it to all residents of the newly formed United States. The irony that the world's greatest liberator and the leader of a free nation was himself a slaveholder was not lost on some European observers. For instance, in 1796 a strong rebuke was offered to the president in a letter written by Edward Rushton, a poet in Liverpool who had briefly participated in the slave trade in Guinea before he came to protest the brutality of the practice. While praising the general's public persona ("the great family of mankind were never more benefited by the military abilities of any individual"), he objects to one aspect of Washington's private life:

> But it is not to the commander in chief of the American forces, nor to the president of the united states, that I have aught to address, my business is with George Washington, of Mount Vernon, in Virginia, a man who, notwithstanding his hatred of oppression and his ardent love of liberty, holds at this moment hundreds of his fellow beings in a state of abject bondage.—Yes! you, who conquered under the banners of freedom—you, who are now the first magistrate of a free people, are, (strange to relate) a slave-holder. That a Liverpool merchant should endeavour to enrich himself by such a business is not a matter of surprise, but that you, an enlightened character, strongly enamoured of your own freedom, you who, if the British forces had succeeded in the eastern states, would have retired with a few congenial spirits to the rude fastnesses of the western wilderness, there to have enjoyed that blessing, without which a paradise would be disgusting, and with which the most savage region is not without its charms; that you, I say, should continue to be a slave-holder, a proprietor of human flesh and blood, creates in many of your British friends both astonishment and regret.

Anticipating the influence that Washington's personal actions might have on his countrymen, as Lafayette had a decade earlier when the marquis encouraged him to take the lead in the liberation of slaves, Rushton continued: "Consider the force of an example like yours, consider how many of the sable race may now be pining in bondage, merely forsooth, because the president of the united states, who has the character of a wise and good man, does not see cause to discontinue the long established practice. Of all the slave-holders under heaven those of the united states appear to me the most reprehensible; for man never is so truly odious as when he inflicts upon others that which he himself abominates." In a stinging conclusion, Rushton emphasized the incongruity of Washington's situation by repeating the refrain "yet you are a slave-holder!" after comments about the successful war for liberty, the exalted position of the first magistrate of a free people, the growing abolitionist movement in America, and the president's widely known religious faith. He ends prophetically with the statement, "Oh! Washington, Ages to come will read with 'astonishment' that the man who was foremost to wrench the rights of America from the tyrannical grasp of Britain, was among the last to relinquish his own oppressive hold of poor and unoffending negroes" and adds that if "pecuniary considerations" have prevented the president from taking the right course of action, then "present reputation, future fame, and all that is estimable among the virtuous, are, for a few thousand pieces of paltry yellow dirt, irremediably renounced." When Rushton's letter to the president was "returned under cover, without a syllable in reply," he decided to publish it the next year in a pamphlet (fig. 189). There is no evidence as to whether or not Rushton's initial letter ever reached Washington's hands and "irritated" him, as its author may have hoped, but it is fair to say that such sentiments about justice and reputation might well have been persuasive to the president and could have influenced his eventual decision not to "continue to be a proprietor of slaves."[109]

Nothing, however, but his own death would solve this dilemma for Washington. Four months before that occurred, in a letter that points to the existing differences between his "farming system" and traditional tobacco plantations, the general again weighed his options, only to come up with no useful alternatives:

> It is demonstratively clear, that on this Estate (Mount Vernon) I have more working Negros by a full moiety, than can be employed to any advantage in the farming system, and I shall never turn Planter [of tobacco] thereon.
>
> To sell the overplus I cannot, because I am principled against this kind of traffic in the human species. To hire them out, is almost as bad, because they could not be disposed of in families to any advantage, and to disperse the families I have an aversion. What is to be done? Something must or I shall be ruined; for all the money (in addition to what I raise by Crops, and rents) that have been *received* for Lands, sold within the last four years, to the amount of Fifty thousand dollars, has scarcely been able to keep me a float.
>
> Under these circumstances, and thorough conviction that half the workers I keep on this Estate, would render me greater *nett* profit than I *now* derive from the whole, has made me resolve, if it can be accomplished, to settle Plantations on one of my other Lands. But where? with going to the Western Country I am unable, as yet to decide; as the *best* if not *all* the Lands I have on the East of the Alliganies, are under Leases.[110]

In his will Washington provided for the liberation and care of his slaves following Martha's death. He excuses this delay by explaining that it was not in his power to emancipate the dower slaves; those people were so intermarried with his people that the freeing of one group before the other would "excite the most painful sensations, if not disagreeable consequences from the latter." We might speculate that Washington hoped that at her death Martha would simultaneously free those slaves who had come to her from the Custis family and thereby solve this problem. The provisions that he made for the slaves were unusual, and can be seen as the result of his genuine determination to resolve fairly a dilemma that he had created as a young man when he had failed to see the problems inherent in the possession of this particular kind of wealth:

> Whereas among [thos]e who will receive freedom ac[cor]ding to this devise, there may b[e] [so]me, who from old age or bodily infi[rm]ities, and others who on account of [thei]r infancy, that will be unable to [su]pport themselves; it is [my] Will a[nd] [de]sire that all who [come under the first] and second descrip[tion] [shall be] [comfor]tably cloathed and [fed by my heirs] while they live; and that such of the latter description as have no parents living, or if living are unable, or unwilling to provide for them, shall be bound by the Court until they shall arrive at the age of twenty five years. . . . The Negroes thus bound, are (by their Masters or Mistresses) to be taught to read and write; and to be brought up to some useful occupation.[111]

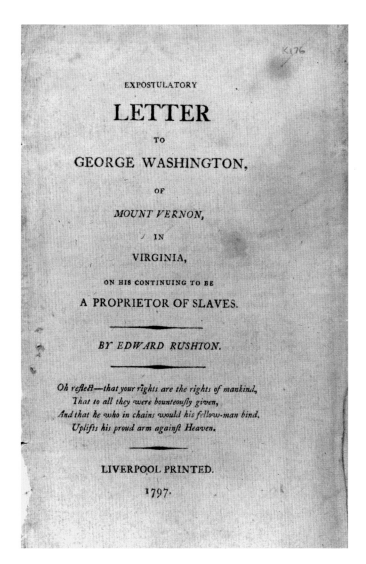

189. Edward Rushton, *Expostulatory Letter to George Washington, of Mount Vernon, in Virginia, on His Continuing to Be a Proprietor of Slaves* (Liverpool, 1797). (Courtesy of Virginia Historical Society)

This discussion of the fate of the slaves appears at the beginning of the will, immediately after Washington awards the entire estate to his widow. He felt passionately about this issue, and to ensure that his wishes would be enacted Washington expressed himself in the strongest of terms: "And I do hereby expressly forbid the Sale, or transportation out of the said Commonwealth, of any Slave I may die possessed of, under any pretence whatsoever. And I do moreover most pointedly, and most solemnly enjoin it upon my Executors . . . to see that *this* [cl]ause respecting Slaves, and every part thereof be religiously fulfilled . . . particularly as it respects the aged and infirm; Seeing that a regular and permanent fund be established for their Support so long as there are subjects requiring it."[112] If he had not been able to award justice to the black people of Mount Vernon during his lifetime, Washington at least attempted to do so after his death.

190. Gilbert Stuart, *George Washington,* Vaughan type, 1795, oil on canvas, 29¼×24 in.
(Courtesy of Homeland Foundation, Incorporated, New York)

## 6

## The First President of the United States
## 1789–1797

### "Concerned Spectator": Washington's Acceptance of the Presidency

THE PORTRAITS of the president by Gilbert Stuart quickly became the best-known images of Washington. Stuart's first attempt to capture the essential Washington, a depiction that revolutionized American painting, has come down to us as the "Vaughan" portrait because the original canvas was sold to Samuel Vaughan, the London merchant who had emigrated to Philadelphia in 1783 and had given Washington the marble mantel for the large dining room at Mount Vernon (see fig. 165). This image of an older, yet still forceful, president quickly eclipsed all other Washington portraits (fig. 190). But the Vaughan would itself soon be pushed into the background by Stuart's next effort. The ascendancy of the "Athenaeum" type would mark Washington's passage into old age in the popular consciousness and look ahead to his final retirement one year later.

Unlike nearly all his successors to the presidency, Washington accepted the position with some degree of reluctance. However, the call of duty was strong because there was a real danger that the new government would fail without Washington at its head. No other American was so universally respected and trusted. Alexander Hamilton, using the most persuasive argument possible to Washington, warned that if the government foundered and Washington had not tried to help, the general's reputation would be in jeopardy.[1] Admittedly, Washington savored his fame—reputation was always of paramount importance to a Virginia gentleman—and so such an appeal would have been difficult to resist. But just as significant was Washington's determination to enjoy at Mount Vernon the just policies of a sound government, which was why he had gone to war in the first place. Hamilton no doubt touched another nerve when he reminded the general of the importance of getting the fledgling government off to a good start: "It is to little purpose to have *introduced* a system if the weightiest influence is not given to its firm *establishment,* in the outset."

Washington was wealthy, at least in terms of property, and he was the most revered man in the Western world. To leave a comfortable position at Mount Vernon for a residency in faraway New York City was not a move he was eager to make. The general was honored, though, by his countrymen's continued trust and perceived the presidency to be yet another obligation to serve his country. This sacrifice of his private life for the public good is the theme of *The Washington Family,* which was painted by Jeremiah Paul, engraved in London, published there and in Philadelphia, and for decades adorned walls in American homes. The popularity of this image is suggested by its appearance in the folk genre of needlework (fig. 191). Paul, a minor Philadelphia artist who lived in that city during the years after the government moved there from New York, probably observed the president and his family at some point, but he borrowed four of the five figures, as well as the grand setting, from Edward Savage's recent painting of the same title (see fig. 223). The fifth figure here is presumably Martha Washington's daughter-in-law, now Mrs. Stuart, the mother of Nelly and Washington Custis. Paul made no attempt to determine what Mount Vernon really looked like. Horse and servant stand waiting in the background, while the newly elected president reluctantly leaves his family. All are sustained at this difficult moment in the spring of 1789 by their knowledge of the importance of the duty that Washington has accepted.

After the conclusion of the Revolutionary War, the general had followed closely the development of the republican government. As commander of a diverse American army he had the perspective to see, perhaps more clearly than most of his contemporaries, the difficulties of combining a disparate citizenry into a single entity and the widely dispersed, once sovereign, geographical units of the nominally "United States" into a single union. Indeed, even before the peace treaty with Britain was signed, he had cautioned the states that "it is yet to be decided, whether the Revolution must ultimately be considered as a blessing or a curse." He had alerted his countrymen then of the need for a strong central government, "a Supreme Power to regulate and govern the general concerns of the Confederated Republic, without which the Union cannot be of long duration." This became the cause he celebrated dura reign of terror that, theoretically at least, was unthinkable in America.

Washington is rarely given enough credit for attracting the best people into the service of the nation and appointing them to the proper positions. His ability to bring together for the common cause the men of greatest talent is perhaps best exemplified by his appointments of the political adversaries Thomas Jefferson and Alexander Hamilton. Having served skillfully as minister to France, Jefferson was the ideal choice for secretary of state.[19] Although Jefferson would later lead an opposition party, he had strongly endorsed the presidency of a man who he knew would never allow a monarchy to emerge out of the chaos that could well have reigned at the start of the Constitution-based union. Hamilton, Washington's brilliant secretary of treasury, had married into the New York gentry and was a staunch Federalist. His importance in the process of bringing the nation to its feet, however, is not as well remembered as that of his colleagues from Virginia. In the aftermath of the panic of 1786, when the problems that confronted the new nation were primarily fiscal, the young and energetic Hamilton devised policies that stabilized the currency, made money available (although not in the West), and established international credit for a nation that had been on the brink of bankruptcy. Perhaps because America was a preponderantly rural nation, Hamilton encouraged infant industries and catered to the mercantile, shipping, and financial interests of the North. Washington, whose outlook, with rare exceptions, was consistently national, prudently endorsed these ideas. It is in part a measure of Hamilton's low popularity with many Americans at the turn of the twentieth century, based primarily on his bad judgment to have participated in the duel with Aaron Burr in which he lost his life, that Hamilton is conspicuously absent in Ferris's scene of the inauguration. This is ironic because Hamilton's genius had much to do with the success of Washington's administrations and therefore was at the root of the very prosperity that the painter celebrates.[20]

Washington's philosophy concerning domestic government consistently looked beyond sectional bias: "In every act of my administration, I have sought the happiness of my fellow-citizens. My system for the attainment of this object has uniformly been to overlook all personal, local and partial considerations: to contemplate the United States, as one great whole." Inevitably he brought this viewpoint to international politics as well. Washington took office empowered to strengthen the nation's weak foreign relations, but by the time of the second inauguration he had made little progress. Among the lingering international problems were the issues of unprotected commerce, the British presence in the American Northwest, and the right of Americans to navigate the Mississippi River to the port of New Orleans. To make matters worse,

France in 1793 was in the aftermath of its own revolution and on a course that might greatly impact American foreign policy. At the moment depicted by Ferris, Washington knew that the French monarchy had been abolished in favor of a republic controlled by "the most mad, wicked and atrocious assembly that was ever collected in any country," according to American diplomat William Short. The president later wrote that "the peculiar situation of our foreign affairs at that epoch" was a major reason he stayed in office for a second term. Washington would not be perceived as displaying "political cowardice."[21] The figures depicted in Ferris's canvas had grave reason in March 1793 to be concerned about the situation abroad. It must have been apparent to them that Washington's second term of office would not be as placid as the first.

One month after the 1793 inauguration Americans learned that the French king and queen had been guillotined and that France had declared war on England, Spain, and Holland. Still technically an ally of France, the United States could have been called upon to protect the French West Indies. The new European war would divide Washington's cabinet and inspire differing opinions among the citizens of the new American nation. Jefferson's Republicans would advocate support for France, and soon they were ready to go to war with Great Britain because of the English seizure of American ships; the New England Federalists, however, who were dependent upon English trade and credit, were pro-British and ready to declare war on France. The president ultimately followed his own earlier advice to his stepson to "determine cooly all great questions."[22] He took no military action but instead declared a policy of neutrality. In 1794 he sent Chief Justice John Jay as envoy extraordinary to Great Britain "to prevent a war," and then, amid pro-French protests, he bravely ratified Jay's treaty that had accomplished Washington's objectives of peace, protection of American commerce, and the evacuation of the British from their posts in the Northwest. A year later Spain, fearful of losing its American colonies, granted navigation of the Mississippi.

If Washington was able to resolve such international crises peacefully, he used force when necessary to settle internal problems brought about by both Indian and white rebels who threatened the sovereignty of the new nation. The Ohio tribes had been agitated by their British allies, whose removal from the Northwest would be a principal accomplishment of Jay's mission. By 1793, following the failed expeditions led by Josiah Harmar in 1790 and Arthur St. Clair in 1791, the advance of these Indians had pushed back the Northwest frontier and made war seem imminent. Washington, who throughout his life was inconsistent at best in response to claims of Native American landownership, sent a reorganized United States Army under the command of Revolutionary War hero An-

194. Attributed to Frederick Kemmelmeyer, *Washington Reviewing the Western Army at Fort Cumberland, Maryland,* after 1794, oil on canvas, 22¾×37¼ in. (Courtesy of Metropolitan Museum of Art, gift of Edgar William and Bernice Chrysler Garbisch, 1963)

thony Wayne to confront the intruders. They rejected Wayne's peace overtures, only to be defeated by his army in the decisive Battle of the Fallen Timbers in August 1794. Little was different from the encounters of nearly four decades earlier in the Ohio Valley, except that the Indians now became the prey of a national army, a force less hindered by the limitations of impermanence and jurisdiction that had governed the colonial militias.[23]

If Washington himself had commanded the army that put down the insurgent Ohio nations, future artists might have depicted that engagement. Instead, German immigrant Frederick Kemmelmeyer created an image of the president reviewing the troops called to disperse the white rebels who would not pay a national tax on whiskey (fig. 194). In the same month that Wayne was victorious over the Indian forces in the Northwest, Washington ordered the militias of four states to the western counties of Pennsylvania. The display of anarchy there, because it was directed at the federal government, annoyed Washington even more than had Shays's Rebellion. The Whiskey Rebellion also inconvenienced him, in the same way that fear of

a possible war with either England or France had cut short a planned trip to his plantation in the days following the second inauguration: "I had it in contemplation to visit that place [Mount Vernon] about the last of September, or beginning of October, but the rebellious conduct of the people in the Western counties of this State renders the journey uncertain, and may defeat it altogether."[24] To add insult to injury, two of the four counties where the unrest festered were named Washington and Lafayette. The Whiskey Rebellion took on historical importance as a significant test case of the power of the federal government. Its successful resolution, therefore, gave Washington particular satisfaction.

The taxes that Alexander Hamilton had levied early in the first administration saved the government from bankruptcy. Most of the incoming revenue was derived from duties on foreign goods and tonnage, which largely came from Britain; not surprisingly, then, many Federalists took a pro-British stance. Of course, none of the taxes were popular, although the "novelty" of imposing "duties on distilled spirits" seems to have been accepted by many southerners. But it was hated in the

203. Gilbert Stuart, *George Washington,* Athenaeum type, 1796, oil on canvas, 29⅞×24½ in. This portrait descended in the Tayloe family of Mount Airy, and the Octagon House, Washington. (Courtesy of Corcoran Gallery of Art, Washington, D.C., bequest of Benjamin Ogle Tayloe)

the point where he eventually discarded them. These facts were known to Rembrandt Peale, who painted the president in 1795.[54] During the remaining years of his life Washington would correspond periodically with Greenwood about repairs and replacements for his sets of false teeth.

Despite the apparent changes in Washington's features, he was still an impressive figure. When he arrived for the second sitting, Charlotte Stuart, the painter's wife, was taken aback by his magnificent appearance, at least according to an account recorded by her daughter: "She saw him as he entered the hall door . . . and she thought him the most superb looking person she had ever seen. He was then dressed in black velvet with white lace ruffles." The resultant image of Washington was the one that appealed most to his nineteenth-century admirers. Barry Schwartz has explained that the portrait became so pop-

ular because it is a depiction of a plain citizen, not a general or president: "it did credit to its subject by reducing rather than enlarging him, by placing him among the people rather than above them." He argues that it is because Americans characteristically disdain ostentation that they have cherished this image.[55] Of course, some of the same could be said about the Vaughan canvas, which in its way also reduces Washington in rank if not in nobility. However, Henry Tuckerman, an early biographer of American artists, suggests that nineteenth-century Americans valued this image not only because it presents citizen Washington, but also because he is additionally shown to be an exceptional human being who can enlighten by his example of determination and virtue. It is the virtue that is so appealing in this canvas, and is perhaps less apparent in the Vaughan image. While it might be attractive to imagine that here Stuart brings Washington down to earth to present the real, necessarily flawed man, we would argue that the face in the best versions of the Athenaeum portrait is actually inspirational. The eyes in particular are so strong and expressive that they invite the viewer to ponder the character of this man who had rejected absolute power and then selflessly continued to serve his country. Nineteenth-century Americans could see in Stuart's canvas the serene "Father of His Country" at the end of a life filled with honor. To their thinking, this individual, who had placed his country above himself, was a figure to revere. Tuckerman explores at some length these aspects of the image of Washington that his contemporaries most cherished:

> The freshness of the color, the studious modeling of the brow, the mingling of clear purpose and benevolence in the eye, and a thorough nobleness and dignity in the whole head, realize all [that] the most intelligent admirer of the original has imagined,—not, indeed, when thinking of him as the intrepid leader of armies, but in the last analysis and complete image of the hero in retirement, in all the consciousness of a sublime career, unimpeachable fidelity to a national trust, and the eternal gratitude of a free people. It is this masterpiece of Stuart that has not only perpetuated, but distributed over the globe, the resemblance of Washington. It has been sometimes lamented that so popular a work does not represent him in the aspect of a successful warrior, or in the flush of youth; but there seems to be a singular harmony between this venerable image—so majestic, benignant and serene—and the absolute character and peculiar example of Washington, separated from what was purely incidental and contingent in his life. Self-control, endurance, dauntless courage, loyalty to a just but sometimes desperate cause, hope through the most hopeless crisis, and a tone of feeling the most exalted, united to habits of candid simplicity, are better embodied in such a calm, magnanimous, mature image, full of dignity and sweetness, than if portrayed in battle array or melodramatic attitude. Let such pictures as David's "Napoleon"—with prancing steed, flashing eye and waving sword—represent the mere victor and military genius; but he who spurned a crown, knew no watchword but duty, no goal but freedom and justice, and no reward but the approval of conscience and the gratitude of a country, lives more appropriately, both to memory and in art, under the aspect of a finished life, crowned with the harvest of honor and peace, and serene in the consummation of disinterested purpose.[56]

While Washington was in fact both driven by the "watchword [of] duty" and "disinterested" in political power, one might argue that there was as well a single, ever present interest in his adult life—the maintenance of the existence that he had created at Mount Vernon—and that all his public endeavors and dutiful acceptances of the will of the people were at heart expressions of his need to provide the freedoms that would make that life possible.

Bingham's call for a full-length portrait must have unnerved Stuart, who had little talent for painting figures and no inclination to study anatomy. Indeed, his full-length portrait of John Foster, the Speaker of the Irish House of Commons, had been such a failure to its Dublin audience that it shook the artist's confidence. To paint his large canvas of Washington, Stuart actually left Philadelphia for the seclusion of the nearby suburb of Germantown (fig. 204). To avoid having to invent a pose and a setting, he turned, predictably, to his collection of prints. In the end he used Pierre Drevet's engraving after Hyacinth Rigaud's baroque portrait of Bishop Bossuet. Stuart's idea was to show the president addressing Congress, empha-

204. By or after Gilbert Stuart (attributed to William Winstanley), *George Washington,* Lansdowne type, oil on canvas, 96×60 in. (Courtesy of Washington and Lee University)

*The First President: 1789–1797*

225

sizing a point through the use of a gesture with his right hand. The Athenaeum head, for which Washington had sat, reappears in the full-length portrait, although the strong, direct gaze has been sacrificed to follow Rigaud. Clearly the president did not pose for the figure Stuart produced. The torso is too small for the head, the limbs are ill proportioned, and none of the parts seem related to the whole. Someone else had stood in for Washington; by various accounts this was either a man named Smith who boarded with Stuart, a man named Keppele who was an alderman in Philadelphia, or the comte de Noailles, who was Lafayette's brother-in-law and had been present at Yorktown.[57] The count is the least likely of those candidates,

but his sword is supposedly the one depicted, which was a gift to Stuart to use in the painting. The sword and the other still-life details, such as the silver inkwell and the Oushak Anatolian carpet, are the best-rendered portions of this canvas.

William Constable, a New York merchant and shipowner, sat for Stuart at the same time that the full-length Washington was in production. He liked what he saw so much that he ordered a version for himself, and asked Stuart to work on the canvas for him simultaneously, so that neither full-length portrait would be the original or the copy. At the same time, Bingham decided to order yet another version of the full-length portrait to give to an English champion of American rights, the mar-

205. Gilbert Stuart, *George Washington,* ca. 1800–01, Monro-Lenox type, oil on canvas, 95½×67 in. (Courtesy of New York Public Library, Astor, Lenox and Tilden Foundations, detail)

*The First President: 1789–1797*

quis of Lansdowne. In England it would serve to demonstrate that Americans, as represented by the universally revered Washington, were the equals of their counterparts in Europe, which was a principal reason that the Federalists had promoted the degree of formality projected by the painting. Another copy was ordered by the American government to be given to France so that the same message could be projected there. However, the French Directory rejected the portrait, and it ended up in the White House, where it was later saved from a fire by Dolly Madison. A number of other versions of the Lansdowne were painted; the quality of these, as with the other portraits, is inconsistent at best.

Lord Lansdowne and the London critics were pleased with Stuart's effort. As was the case concerning the reception of the Houdon sculpture in France, many in England took an interest in the portrait because they had never seen a dependable image of the man whose name they had heard for so many years. The London *Oracle and Public Advertiser* called it one of the best paintings seen there since the death of Joshua Reynolds.[58] All was well until Lansdowne allowed his painting to be engraved by James Heath, thus depriving Stuart of the sizable income the print would earn. Angered, the painter rose to the challenge. He redesigned and improved the Lansdowne portrait so that the pirated image would pale by comparison. Stuart's final version (fig. 205), the original of which is now in the New York Public Library, is a masterpiece truly worthy of the high praise that was generously given to the first version. The figure is that of a powerful and athletic man. The empty gesturing of the first pose is eliminated, while the steady, engaging gaze of the Athenaeum head is returned. The floor of the Drevet engraving is inserted, and the high back wall is lowered to fill the room with light, which better allowed Stuart to demonstrate his mastery of the techniques of the painterly style. In this second version of the Lansdowne, one of the great portraitists of his era produced his greatest painting, suitably, of the greatest man in the Western world. This fact is generally lost, however, because the many replicas of the first full-length image are far better known than this final type.

## The Accoutrements of the President

As was mentioned above, Washington felt obliged to furnish his lodgings with the finest of decorative objects, which would serve to enhance the dignity of the presidency. In making his selections, Washington was governed by a number of factors. First of all, predictably, an item had to be in vogue; if not, it would fail in its mission to impress. For example, plated silver, which had been a favorite type for Washington since the early 1780s, had proved "fashionable and much used in genteel houses in France and England"; he was therefore encouraged

to buy more of it.[59] The next factor was opportunity. Since the time of the Belvoir sale, and particularly after the war's disruption of the flow of commerce, Washington had been an opportunistic purchaser. When quality objects of the type he wanted became available, the president generally bought them without hesitation because the supply of materials in the new nation could be as inconsistent as it had been during the colonial era. Washington the consumer, however, did try to be guided by price. He constantly used the word *cheapest* in his directives and reminded his purchasing agents to look for the best value, although for mail orders he generally had to pay whatever bills were submitted. This is not to say that the president did not have preferences that were factors in his selections of decorative pieces, for he had developed specific tastes concerning the types of objects that attracted his good eye for design. But taste was midway down the list of considerations that governed his purchases.

Even lower was the relationship between the goods that he wished to acquire and the politics of the moment. Beginning in 1783, the general talked about not sending to England for items that he could obtain on tolerable terms elsewhere. Washington liked to encourage American manufacture by his patronage, and he felt an obligation to strengthen economic ties with the French who had made American independence possible. But, as Washington explained in 1783, it was often difficult to place orders with French artisans who did not speak his language or understand the "customs, taste, and manner of living in America."[60]

In the case of silver, which is sturdy and small enough to transport, President Washington could bring many of his own pieces with him from Virginia. In 1789 they had no doubt carried the most suitable pieces to New York; at the close of the presidencies Martha Washington reported that "our plate we brought with us in the carriage" on their return to Mount Vernon.[61] This was another reason that Washington proved a good choice for the presidency; he already owned many of the accoutrements of the aristocracy, which allowed him to entertain in the manner to which his most distinguished visitors would be accustomed. On becoming president Washington had only to add pieces of silver to his own collection. Eight years later when he left the office he made a list of the silver that was "Furnished by the U:States" and the pieces he had purchased. A comparison of that list with objects that descended from the general to Martha Washington's heirs, and with the earlier receipts of purchases for Mount Vernon, shows that the pieces were much the same. Washington simply bought as needed additional flatware as well as items ranging from serving platters to bread baskets.

The silver that makes up the 1797 inventory allowed the president to accommodate the many guests he was obliged to entertain. There were more than twelve dozen spoons as well as a number of urns for punch, tea, and coffee. In 1790 Washington looked to purchase a group of "plated waiters, suitable for carrying tea round to company." He found that those of the "best workmanship" could be had in New York at a "lower" price than in Philadelphia, so this choice was easy for him: "we shall therefore have them made here," he had his secretary write from the first capital.[62]

Washington bought both traditional pieces of silver and the newest, most fashionable goods. New in light fixtures was a better-functioning oil lamp, patented by Aimé Argand, which offered more light and less smoke. Silversmiths in England developed handsome Argand lamp designs in plated ware, which soon made their way to America. The president saw some at Robert Morris's house early in 1790, and later that year he ordered from France some two dozen lamps, specifying that they be "less costly" than Morris's (fig. 206).[63] In 1792 he purchased additional examples from Philadelphia silversmiths, who found it easier to import plated ware from England than to make it themselves. These lamps were both functional and stylish, and the president brought a number of them back to Mount Vernon.

Washington was particularly fond of plated silver. Plating was a relatively new process, developed at midcentury in Sheffield, England. This type of silver, which is layered over sheets of copper for the purpose of lowering costs, changed some aspects of the industry. Larger and more intricate forms were now more affordable and therefore more likely to be found in fashionable American houses. The bargain price of plated ware also appealed to Washington. It should be remembered that his Virginia-bred taste always led him to choose the "plain & neat" over the "extravagant"; he would project a sense of propriety rather than succumb to "the follies of luxury and ostentation."[64]

The story of Washington's purchase of plated-silver plateaux for his dining table, along with other decorative objects to be placed on and around them, says much about his conception of what the accoutrements of the president should be (fig. 207). These pieces, which "ornamented" his "Table, on Public days," were among those that upon his retirement from public service he chose not to keep.[65] Washington had felt almost compelled to follow this new fashion, which had been introduced in the dining rooms of Robert Morris, William Bingham, and the French and Spanish ministers, where porcelain figurines

206. Argand table lamp, ca. 1792, silver plated, English manufacture, possibly purchased from Philadelphia silversmith Joseph Anthony. (Courtesy of Mount Vernon Ladies' Association)

207. Plateau for the center of the dining table, French, 1789–90, silver plated, width 24 inches, shown here with Sèvres porcelain and bisque figures. (Courtesy of Mount Vernon Ladies' Association)

and raised centerpieces were arranged on low mirrored plat-forms made of plated silver. These made the dining room table a focal point, almost like an altarpiece in a chapel. Such a dis-play made an unmistakable social statement in America, where a permanent table for dining had not been a fixture of even many of the better homes before the Revolution.

Although Washington had seen the new fashion in New York and Philadelphia, such plateaux and porcelain figures were not to be found in either city. The president asked Gouverneur Morris, his ambassador to France, to buy for him in either Lon-don or Paris, wherever the price was lowest, "mirrors for a table, with neat and fashionable but not expensive ornaments for them—such as will do credit to your taste." He also asked for "handsome and useful Coolers for wine *at* and *after* dinner." Both the mirrors and the coolers were to be of plated silver. More important to Washington than their specific design was that these objects not be too ornate: "Should my description be defective your imagination is fertile and on this I shall rely. One idea however I must impress you with and that is in whole or part to avoid extravagance. For extravagance would not comport with my own inclination, nor with the example which ought to be set."[66] The president felt that his office de-manded some adherence to current styles, but a line excluding the ostentatious had to be drawn somewhere. Also on his mind was his sense that the chief executive was the American whose model others would aspire to follow. To Washington, the pres-ident had to set a good example for his countrymen. He thought that too much finery was not appropriate for Ameri-can citizens because theirs was a new nation governed by the conditions and opportunities of the New World and in search of its own distinguishing identity. Finally, ostentation would be seen as foreign by much of his constituency. Regardless of what some Federalists might say to him about the need to keep up class boundaries through the use of the most ornate objects available, Washington, after careful consideration, would often fall back on what were clearly the tastes of his youth.

The "surtout of Plateaux &ca." arrived safely in the spring of 1790. Washington reported to Morris that they were "very elegant—much admired—and do great justice to your taste." Three months later he ordered "two more plateaux" because there were so many ornaments to display that the table seemed crowded. The coolers cost more than was expected because they were particularly well made. They inspired Washington to commission bottle holders made of wire for wines that did not need cooling. The wire holders are not known to have sur-vived, although a sketch of them made in the nineteenth cen-tury does exist (fig. 208).[67] They anticipated the popular wine wagons that decades later were made in Sheffield and, like Mount Vernon itself, stand as evidence of Washington's eye for design and his ability to innovate. In this respect he was

208. Joseph Cook, wine coaster, 1790, silver, and Washington's wine coolers, 1789, French, silver plated, as reproduced in Benson Lossing, *The Home of Washington* (New York, 1859). (Courtesy of Virginia Historical Society)

similar to Jefferson, although his talents in this line are rarely credited.

When Washington left the presidency, he tried to sell or give away "two four bottle Coolers—A Plateau in nine pieces. three large groupes with glasses over them, two Vases, and twelve small single figures of Porcelain." The case could be made that one reason he did not care to retain these objects had to do with America's then strained relations with France. Wash-ington wrote to Hamilton in early 1797, "The conduct of France towards the United States, is, according to my ideas of it, outrageous beyond conception: not to be warranted by her treaties with us; by the Law of Nations; by any principle of justice; or even by a regard to decent appearances."[68] But the decision was more than purely political; Washington was happy to keep the set of Sèvres porcelain that he had bought, but he felt that plateaux and figurines were simply too extravagant for Mount Vernon. This decision is further evidence of the mod-erate tastes of much of the colonial-American gentry. Admit-tedly, many table objects were brought back to Mount Vernon, but only because they did not sell. Apparently most of Wash-ington's countrymen agreed that these pieces were too extrav-agant or too ornate for practical use.

The porcelain and furniture at Mount Vernon were respec-tively too fragile and too heavy to be transported back and forth between residences in the way the silver was. However, this did not prove problematic for the president, because in New York the opportunistic Washington was soon able to buy a group of French objects that served well in his formal public rooms. These came, in a sense, with the New York mansion that had been rented by the departing French ambassador, and which Washington in turn took as his residence. The president purchased a number of the comte de Moustier's French-made furnishings, including twelve armchairs, six small chairs, and a sofa. One of the chairs, a "fauteuil," survives at Mount Vernon; by tradition it was kept by Martha Washington for use in her bedroom (fig. 209). This type of furniture is so purposefully ornate and elegant that it made a powerful social statement in the 1790s in a country where for the most part only English furniture design had been known. Again, Washington thought that French furniture was appropriate for the president's mansion primarily because it was on display in the homes of some of the wealthiest Americans. The president also acquired from Moustier 309 pieces of French white-and-gold table porcelain, mostly of Sèvres manufacture (fig. 210). This exquisite china, which is both sophisticated and understated, proved to be a good purchase because it served both the president and, later, the retired planter who had it shipped back to Mount Vernon.

210. Gold-and-white Sèvres porcelain, from the service Washington purchased in 1790 from the comte de Moustier, Paris, ca. 1785. (Courtesy of Mount Vernon Ladies' Association)

211. Plate, Chinese-export porcelain, marked "MW," from a set presented to Mrs. Washington in 1796 by Andreas Everardus van Braam Houckgeest, 1795. (Courtesy of Mount Vernon Ladies' Association)

209. Arm chair, Louis XVI fauteuil type, ca. 1775–90, France, beech (paint not original), 35¼×25¼×19½ in. (Courtesy of Mount Vernon Ladies' Association)

A smaller set of porcelain, which was more personalized in its design, came into Washington's hands with even less effort on his part (fig. 211). This was a gift from an admirer, Andreas van Braam, an agent for the Dutch East India Company. In 1796 he sent it to Martha Washington, whose initials are featured on the china. An expensive gift such as this from a virtual stranger to the president was apparently deemed acceptable because it was in fact given to Washington's wife. Van Braam, a native of Holland, so admired the American political experiment that he had settled in Charleston in 1783. In 1790 the export business took him to Canton, where he remained until 1795. Van Braam designed and commissioned innumerable patterns

212. Vase, Chinese porcelain, for the American market, ca. 1790, height 17½ in.
(Courtesy of Mount Vernon Ladies' Association)

as well as watercolor views, and he amassed a fortune. His gift to the Washingtons served both to enhance the social position of the donor, who had established himself in a pseudo-Chinese palace outside Philadelphia, and to make Chinese porcelain more fashionable in America by its presence on the president's table.

No doubt it was van Braam himself who devised the pattern for the china he presented to Mrs. Washington. From American paper currency that had been issued by the Congress he borrowed the motif of a sunburst and chain. Over that he imposed Martha Washington's initials and the names of the then fifteen American states. To symbolize the American union, they are all bonded together like the links of a chain and encircled with the image of a snake grasping its own tail. Van Braam took the motto "DECUS ET TUTAMEN AB ILLO" ("a glory and a defense from it") from Virgil's *Aeneid,* to make reference to the eminence and strength that are the products of the American union. This "states" china, as it is called, is striking in its design, as was much of what was produced in China for the foreign market. Because of the availability, quality, and reasonable pricing of the porcelain exported from Canton,

Washington purchased Chinese porcelain vases and bowls to ornament his mantels, cabinets, and tables (fig. 212). He also continued to order blue-and-white china for use at Mount Vernon, in part to replace broken pieces. These were to be "handsome, but not the highest price, as they [were] for common use."[69]

Washington purchased Moustier's French-made furniture because he thought it gave dignity to his home and thereby to the presidency. In Philadelphia Washington would eventually add a half-dozen chairs to the Moustier group. He also bought from the ambassador some looking glasses that he later took to Mount Vernon, and he acquired a few French case pieces—a small desk and a dressing table—that he also liked and would keep. Throughout the presidential years, however, Washington also patronized American furniture makers, whose tastes more closely matched his own. From the start of his tenure in New York, the president employed the services of craftsman Thomas Burling. Later, he would buy furniture from a half-dozen other craftsmen in Philadelphia. The items ranged from tables and dressing glasses to knife boxes, corner washstands, and Windsor chairs. He bought these pieces with the intention of shipping

*The First President: 1789–1797*

213. John Aitken, Philadelphia, side chair, Sheraton, ca. 1797, mahogany, 36×20½×17½ in. (Courtesy of Mount Vernon Ladies' Association)

them to Mount Vernon upon his retirement, which he eventually did.[70]

The point here is that well before Washington left the presidency he was thinking about furnishing his expanded plantation house. As early as 1788, the year before he took office, he was looking for a chair model that would work well in his recently completed large dining room, which John Rawlins had decorated in the new neoclassical style. In 1790 he bought two Hepplewhite chairs from Thomas Burling that he later brought to Virginia. On the eve of his retirement he acquired two dozen Sheraton mahogany chairs (fig. 213), which are relatively close in design to the ones by Burling. These were produced by the Philadelphia craftsman John Aitken, from whom Washington also commissioned two sideboards for the new room and a tambour secretary for his study. The two dozen French chairs in his possession could then be placed on the selling block; Washington clearly rejected these pieces for chairs in the more restrained English tradition. Washington's taste for English, neoclassical-style furniture made by American craftsmen was constant throughout the decade. The associations of neoclassicism made objects in that style seem especially appropriate in the American republic, which many saw as the successor to pre-

empire Rome. Nowhere was this vogue more fitting than in the home of the American Cincinnatus.

*Absentee Farmer*

General Washington had sustained himself through the eight long years of the Revolutionary War by monitoring and, when he could, directing the progress of the architectural renovations to Mount Vernon. In the same way, the president bolstered himself during his second eight-year absence from Virginia by engaging in the details of farming on his plantation. He knew well that the agricultural system he had established at Mount Vernon needed his attention if it was not to fail. But more than that, farming was what Washington wanted to be doing. "No pursuit is more congenial with my nature and gratifications, than that of agriculture," he wrote in 1795, "nor none I so much pant after as again to become a tiller of the Earth."[71] This interest in his farm and his attention to its management while he was absent is the subject of Ferris's *News from Mount Vernon, 1796* (fig. 214).

It was disappointing to the president that he had to struggle to find the time to direct his farming operation: "I have

214. Jean Leon Gerome Ferris, *News from Mount Vernon, 1796,* ca. 1930, oil on canvas, 30×24 in. (Courtesy of Virginia Historical Society, Lora Robins Collection of Virginia Art)

to regret that the duties of my public station do not allow me to pay that attention to Agriculture and the objects attached to it (which have ever been my favorite pursuit) that I could wish." Yet, remarkably, Washington was able during the presidencies to devote large blocks of time to farming, if we can judge from a sampling of his correspondence during this period. In 1793, for instance, which admittedly became a time of crisis at Mount Vernon after his farm manager, Anthony Whitting, died, some 40 percent of the surviving pages written by Washington are letters of instruction that he drafted for his caretakers of the estate. While in New York in 1790 the president entered in his diary, "Spent the Afternoon in writing Letters to Mount Vernon."[72] When he complained about presidential protocol, saying that the availability of the chief executive must be curtailed to allow him time to perform his other official duties, he might have added that time was also needed to pursue his private interests.

If the president had been called upon to justify his considerable attention to farming, he would have argued that no "more real and important service can be rendered to any Country, than by improving its agriculture, its breed of useful animals, and other branches of a husbandmans cares." To Washington, this subject was so vital to the nation that he advocated establishing an agricultural institution in America. If modernization did not occur, he feared that the developing situation would be "ruinous . . . to the landed interest" of the East: "A few years more of increased sterility will drive the Inhabitants of the Atlantic States Westwardly for support; whereas if they were taught how to improve the old, instead of going in pursuit of new and productive Soils, they would make those acres which now scarcely yield them any thing, turn out beneficial." As often as possible, the president would "set off for Mount Vernon with Mrs. Washington and the Children . . . to enjoy a few weeks of retirement," particularly between sessions of Congress. Farming and the solace of his plantation offered a respite from what Washington called the "abuse" and "the arrows of malevolence" directed at him by his enemies in the press. And while farming restored his spirits, it also helped him physically, or so he thought. After a severe illness in 1790 that some observers feared might kill the president, he blamed his condition on the "inactivity" of his new job. He even tried to acquire a farm close to Philadelphia by trading parcels of land: "my objects being for the amusement of farming, and for the benefit arising from exercise."[73] Nothing, however, came of this idea, and Washington often had to content himself with directing the affairs of Mount Vernon from afar.

Following Whitting's death in June 1793 the president engaged as a replacement William Pearce, from nearby Kent County, Maryland.[74] In the interim the operation at Mount Vernon had faltered, but with Pearce, who was an experienced and diligent farmer, stability returned. In a contract that Washington drafted for his new manager, the president defined the many procedures and objectives of the Mount Vernon farms. He explained clearly his primary concern, that the land be kept "in an improving instead of a declining state." This was easier said than done, however, so the president added that he wanted Pearce to initiate ideas about how to improve the farms. He also stated the importance of weekly reporting, whereby goals would be set and attempts to meet them measured; he outlined the various seasonal tasks that must be performed; and he described the problem of controlling overseers who lacked motivation. Washington admitted it would be "tedious" and "unnecessary" to tell a competent farmer in further detail how to superintend his operation, but then, perhaps not surprisingly, he goes on to do just that.[75] This document can serve for us, as it did for Pearce, as a primer on how Washington approached farm management.

To the end of his life Washington remained eager to improve the methods of farming at Mount Vernon. He ordered the most recent publications on the subject, such as *The Complete Farmer*, a book on English husbandry that was published in London in 1793 (fig. 215). Having learned as a soldier to value the advice of those who reported to him, Washington consistently urged his farm managers to offer him constructive

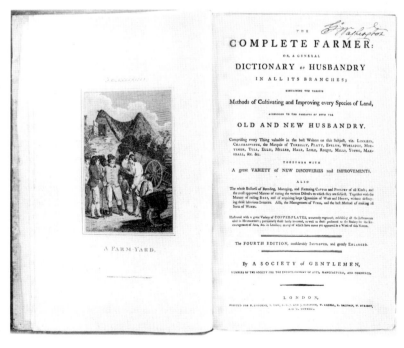

215. Washington's copy of *The Complete Farmer; Or, a General Dictionary of Husbandry* (London, 1793). (Courtesy of Virginia Historical Society)

feedback. If we return to the contract with Pearce, we find that the new manager was urged to share his thinking with the president: "George Washington will always, and with pleasure listen to any suggested alterations which may be offered by him with a view to the advancement of the Crops, increase of the Stocks, and for the general improvement of the Estate." By 1793, it will be remembered, Washington had been a convert to English methods of husbandry for almost a decade. That was the system he expected his farm manager to implement in order to "advance the crops and increase the stocks."

The president already knew much of the information included in *The Complete Farmer* through his correspondence with Arthur Young. By 1787 Washington had received a copy of Young's *Annals of Agriculture,* which also contained a good deal of useful information. This leading agriculturist had taught Washington that "large Crops cannot be raised without large stocks of Cattle and Sheep" and that fallow fields were not to be empty but instead should be planted with "Turnips, Cabbage, Beans Clover, and such like [crops]" that would feed the livestock of the plantation while at the same time conditioning the soil for grains. This was how crops were "advanced"; the soil they grew in had to be prepared by what went in before and by the manure provided by the livestock. Such an operation took years to function properly, but as Washington put it in 1793 when explaining Young's ideas to Whitting, "if it is never begun it can never be executed." He had diagnosed that the Mount Vernon fields had fallen into an "exhausted state" due to the planting of "oppressive crops," and he was determined to restore them "to health and vigour."[76]

Washington also expected Pearce to reverse the losses in his herds of cattle and sheep, which had diminished during his absence from Mount Vernon. The sheep he had bred so carefully in the 1780s were no longer healthy enough to produce the quantity of wool they once did. If the animals were to be kept in "a thriving and healthy state," there would have to be a more "judicious choice of the subjects that are bred from." Washington wanted his livestock to match the best strains found in England; he was informed that good breeding was the basis of "the remarkable quality and sales of . . . Cattle and sheep" that were enjoyed by breeders such as Robert Bakewell of Leicestershire.[77]

When Washington mentioned to Pearce "the general improvement of the estate," he brought up a favorite subject and one that over the next years he "often repeated": "I shall begrudge no reasonable expence that will contribute to the improvement and neatness of my Farms; for nothing pleases me better than to see them in good order,

and every thing trim, handsome, and thriving about them; nor nothing hurts me more than to find them otherwise." The president stated clearly in his contract with Pearce that "weekly reports from each Farm" were a requirement of the job. Washington could thereby control the operation of the farms from Philadelphia. He could define the work that was to be done, and by examining the written reports of his manager he could measure what had been accomplished. As he put it, this meticulous record keeping would not only "[make] the overseers ac-

216. Weekly report from farm manager Anthony Whitting to George Washington, 23 March 1793. (Courtesy of Mount Vernon Ladies' Association)

countable" but also allow him "at any time hereafter [to] shew in what manner the hands have been employed; and the state of the stock and other things at any past period."[78] We have seen that as a child Washington had learned to copy whatever he wanted to better understand or assimilate; as a colonial planter he had made copies of his orders to English merchants so that he would have redress, and as a commander he had kept written records of what he ordered, in readiness to defend his actions if necessary. As president Washington, through his orderly and at times duplicated correspondence, facilitated the complex system of agriculture that he had instituted at Mount Vernon. It made the operation considerably more efficient and turned absentee farming into an almost hands-on enterprise.

The weekly report filed on 23 March 1793 is typical. This would have been one of the last reports written by Anthony Whitting, (fig. 216). An accounting is given for each of the five farms, with available days of labor balanced against various tasks and the days taken to accomplish each. The days are accounted for as if this were a financial record of debts and credits, which is the obvious source from which this system of record keeping is derived. Because the week reviewed here fell in March, there was much hauling, building fences, repairing roads, clearing fields, and plowing recorded. There is also an accounting of how many bushels of the crops were fed to the animals, how many were sent to the mill, and how many bushels of meal came back in return. A count is given of the stock, whose "Decrease" and "Increase" in numbers are also noted. The amount of days lost to sickness are also carefully recorded. The various entries on this weekly report call to mind the sort of accounting that might be made today by a moderately sized business struggling to turn a profit.

We have seen that Pearce's contract outlined the responsibilities of the farm manager as well as what the president expected from the farms and their workforces. These requirements were further defined in minute detail over the next four years in the 127 letters the president sent to Pearce, which were often written in response to the weekly reports.[79] The letter of 13 July 1794 is a fairly typical example (fig. 217). It refers to current activities on the plantation and is filled with instructions. Washington starts by explaining that if a buckwheat crop is to be plowed into the ground, it must be accomplished when it is green or else the advantage of doing so is lost. The president then continues for eleven additional pages that stand as evidence of his interest in agriculture and devotion to the operation at Mount Vernon. He expresses confidence in his manager, crediting him with "good judgment" and "integrity and zeal." He concludes by outlining, as he did repeatedly in the correspondence, his overall objectives of recovering the land, planting hedges, improving the stock, and tending to "the little, as well as the greater concerns of the farms."

These "little" and "greater concerns" are enumerated in many of the letters to Whitting and Pearce. Washington might identify in one as many as two dozen tasks: gravel the walks, plant trees, plant ivy, clean the vineyard, cut wood, plant hedges, grub fields, harvest crops, plow, plant crops, pull down one building, build another, repair the burial vault, paint, ditch, work the carpenters, complete the well, acquire oyster shells, be attentive to the sick slaves—some lists were quite long and generally very detailed. The president apologized to Pearce for "express[ing] my wishes faster than they can be accomplished." He advised both Whitting and Pearce to get a pocket memorandum book in order

217. George Washington to farm manager William Pearce, 13 July 1794. (Courtesy of Mount Vernon Ladies' Association)

not to forget his many directives. When Whitting died, the president described the Mount Vernon enterprise as "a body without a head" because no one was present to monitor the operation and implement his precise instructions. Until Pearce settled in, Washington feared that the proceedings might grind to a halt. At one point he worried that "there will be nothing either for my negroes or horses to eat."[80]

When the president wrote into the contract with Pearce that a "competent" farmer does not need to be told how and when to fence, plow, weed, seed, cut, stack, sell produce, pen and care for cattle, and manure the fields, he was saying in effect that he hoped he had found a manager who knew how to do those things and would not have to be reminded. Pearce answered this description better than had Whitting, and the president was pleased with his competence. Nonetheless, the operation at Mount Vernon was so complex, the profit margin was so slim, and there was so much work to accomplish and so many decisions to be made that even with a diligent manager Wash-

218. Chart of crop rotations for Muddy Hole Farm, from 1789 through 1800, ca. 1789. (Courtesy of Virginia Historical Society)

ington kept writing the long letters. This consistency perhaps also suggests that he did not see this particular type of correspondence as a chore. Washington enjoyed thinking about, managing, and vicariously tending to the needs of his plantation.

The president and Pearce were tireless farmers and therefore unlike the majority of the overseers on the five farms. Their inefficiency was a problem that Washington pointed out to his new manager in the contract. There was a need to keep them "constantly at their posts." In the president's opinion, Whitting had not been able to manage them effectively because he did not set a good example. He "drank freely, kept bad company at my house and in Alexandria, and was a very debauched person." The overseers, in turn, followed Whitting's lead and by their conduct set a bad example for the slaves. The overseer at the River Farm, Washington believed, "never turned out of morning's until the Sun had warmed the Earth" and had "no interest in the Crop." The one at Dogue Run would "frolick" in the evening. The overseer at Ferry and French's Farms was to blame for the "want of care" that accounted for the deaths of too many sheep there. Washington predicted to Pearce that the black overseer, Davy, at Muddy Hole Farm, who "carries on his business as well as the white Overseers," would "give . . . less trouble."[81]

In December 1793, as Pearce was setting up residence at Mount Vernon, Washington was particularly annoyed that three of the overseers had failed to accomplish the fall plowing that was necessary preparation for the spring crops. Washington was "at a loss for words to express [his] vexation and displeasure at [this] neglect," which he called an "irremediable evil" because it would prevent him "from adopting my system of rotation, which I have been preparing to carry into effect for some years past." Another midlevel supervisor, Thomas Green, who oversaw the carpenters, also failed him at this time. Green was so unproductive that Washington was exasperated: "To speak to you is of no more avail, than to speak to a bird that is flying over one's head." He chastised Green, stating he had "no more command of the people over whom you are placed, than I have over the beasts of the forists." Washington's anger is evident in the sarcastic tone of these letters. He advised Pearce to manage these overseers in an almost military fashion. He should present "a steady and firm conduct" and, perhaps not surprisingly, "keep them at a proper distance" in order to maintain authority.[82]

Just as Washington had tried to instill discipline into the ranks and to maintain order in the government, he continued to hope that his farms would function efficiently. He felt strongly that the agricultural practices at Mount Vernon would have to be maintained in a highly ordered regimen if it was to be a successful plantation. There was no place in his operation

for idleness or misuse of time. This was not defined in the contract with Pearce, but in a long letter to his new manager he explained how "method . . . is desirable, and after it is once adopted, and got into a proper train things will work easily." Washington did not want the workers "flying from one thing to another without order or system" or doing a job imperfectly. He was ever issuing maxims to make these points: "A thing but half done is never done, and well done is, in a manner done for ever."[83] These were no mere aphorisms to Washington. Rather, they were the results of a lifetime of experience in positions of authority, written by a man who lived by them to men who had no understanding of his sense of duty or level of dedication.

Washington's fixation on order and system is most visible in the charts he prepared to establish the crop rotations that would be followed for the seven fields of each of the five farms. It will be remembered that in Washington's system of rotation, a crop, at least ideally, was returned to a field only once every seven years; in this way the fields were continually reconstituted. During each year the same seven crops were under cultivation but in different fields. In the example presented, the regular rotation is delayed until 1792 because some of the fields "are much out of heart, & will require time & a coat of grass to recover them" (fig. 218). It was the president's intention to establish in this manner a rigid timetable that would bring structure to the operation and cause it to flourish. By basing his long-range plans on such a schedule he could plan ahead and predict with some accuracy what seeds would be needed for the next planting.

Inevitably, of course, alterations had to be made to these charts because of the weather, the neglect of the overseers, and the president's own reevaluation of his system. A drought could cause too low a yield of the crops that were needed to feed the plantation. Overseers would fail to plow when they should have, either too early and produce a short yield or too late, thereby throwing off the plan. And sometimes crops simply failed, for reasons difficult for anyone to fathom. In 1793 Washington sketched out a series of charts in which he tried different arrangements of corn, potatoes, wheat, buckwheat for manure, clover, grass, and pasture. He then evaluated the merits and disadvantages of each proposed rotation. How would a particular rotation favor the land? What would be its yield of salable crops, and what would be their profit? Would enough food crops be produced to meet the needs of the farm? How much plowing would be required? How much manure would be needed? As he answered these questions, the president readjusted the charts.[84]

In a letter to Pearce of March 1794, Washington engaged his manager's help in developing an extraordinary sixteen-sided barn to be built at Dogue Run Farm (fig. 219). (A similar barn

223. Attributed to Edward Savage, *The Washington Family,* ca. 1789–98, oil on canvas, 26×36 in.
(Courtesy of National Trust Collection, Woodlawn Plantation)

# 7

## Return to Virginia: Washington's Final Retirement to Mount Vernon 1797–1799

### "The Humble and Endearing Scenes of Private Life"

WELL BEFORE the end of his second presidency Washington longed to return to private life. In 1795 he wrote, "I can religiously aver that no man was ever more tired of public life, or more devoutly wished for retirement, than I do." In 1796 he vowed that "after I have retired to Mount Vernon, I shall never go twenty miles beyond the limits of it."[1] The way of life at his plantation was endearing to Washington because his "consort" was "agreeable," as he had first stated in 1759, his second family provided a focus for his paternal inclinations, and the work of managing his farms was, as ever, his first love.

While the fascination with Washington's private life, as with that of any figure who is continually thrust (or thrusts himself) into the spotlight, had ebbed and flowed during his various public endeavors, there was a renewal of interest in the 1790s, perhaps as his countrymen took seriously the new president's comments about his preference for the existence that his duty was again forcing him to abandon. The first painter to capitalize on the need for an image of Washington as head of his own family was Edward Savage, who was active during the final decade of Washington's life. A Massachusetts native, he was commissioned in 1789–90 by the University of Cambridge (later Harvard University) and by Vice President John Adams to take the president's portrait. Savage traveled to New York, where he apparently conceived the idea for his painting *The Washington Family* (fig. 223). From the start his goal may well have been the production of a profitable print; such reproductions were ultimately issued in 1798 and were a huge success. The artist would report to Washington that he had enlisted more than four hundred subscribers, expected more, and anticipated earning "at Least ten thousand Dollars in one twelve-month [period]."[2] Savage actually painted several canvases of *The Washington Family*. One version, which is seven-feet tall and more than nine-feet wide and therefore scaled to fit only a public building, anticipated the large murals that two decades later would begin to fill the rotunda of the U.S. Capitol. (This large rendition is now in the National Gallery of Art in Washington, D.C.)

The artist took the likenesses of the family members in 1789, when Nelly was ten years old and Washington Custis only eight. When the print was issued almost a decade later, Savage apologized to Washington that the "Young people" as he depicted them "are not much Like what they are at present."[3] But this choice was fortuitous because a family scene best conveys domestic bliss when the children are shown at a young age and therefore vulnerable and impressionable. A portrait of the first family taken in 1798, when the children were nearly grown, might well have been a less successful representation of the private Washington. Savage depicts the then new president in a military uniform, but the subject of his service in the army is made subservient to the theme of family life. His pose is relaxed, and his arm rests lovingly on young Washington Custis. The image illustrates a side of Washington with which most men could identify and makes the point that behind even the greatest of heroes exists a domestic life, which both supports him, thereby providing a foundation that allows him to engage in world-historical endeavors, and supplies an intimate reminder of the need for his heroism by serving as a constant example of what might be at stake should he fail.

An accurate portrait of an affluent antebellum Virginia family would be incomplete without the inclusion of a slave, who was often thought to be a necessary appendage to that unit. Shown here, in a rare life portrait, is Washington's faithful personal servant Billy Lee.[4] As in numerous European portraits of the eighteenth century that include a similar black figure, his presence serves primarily to state that the people who control him are uncommonly wealthy. Again, as in Trumbull's 1780 portrait, all of Lee's affection for the family, and the general's well-known affection for him, are put aside. Lee is made to wear livery to accentuate his function and serves in the canvas less as a human being than as an impressive possession.

The Savage painting was pleasing to Washington not only because of its emphasis on his family life but also because it would look to him not only as the model but also as the source of all virtues.

Washington's tomb became a popular site for both pilgrims and artists in the early nineteenth century. In 1815, less than a year after his great victory at New Orleans, the grave was visited by Andrew Jackson, who was surprised and angry at its condition:

> In a small vault at the foot of the hill, overgrown with Cedar, repose the bones of the father of his country. Why is this so! Must the charge of ingratitude ever rest upon Republicks? It is now several sessions since Congress solicited the remains of him whose whole life was devoted to his country's service, in order that some suitable testimonial of a nation's respect might be shewn them. The venerable widow who cherished them as the most precious relict, sacraficed her individual feelings to a nation's wishes, and granted the request. Since then, as though the apparently warm interest they displayed had been a studied mockery, those remains have been permitted to moulder in the "dark, narrow cell" where they were at first deposited.[56]

The tomb's small size and unkempt state, which so annoyed Jackson, at least served well the expressive purposes of Joshua Shaw, whose engraving of it appears in his *Picturesque Views of American Scenery* of 1819–21 (fig. 242). The portfolio is introduced with the statement that America "abounds with Scenery, comprehending all the varieties of the sublime, the beautiful, and the picturesque in nature." Shaw, who borrows the components of his composition from "a drawing by Captain [Joshua Rowley] Watson," sees Washington's sepulchre as the embodiment of the sublime. This is a sanctified site, the holiest of holy places, where nature itself seems to know that it holds the earthly remains of an immortal. The tomb is surrounded by tall trees that writhe and form dark recesses. Parts of the setting are bathed in an electrifying light, while an ominous shadow hangs over the entrance to this gloomy repository. The viewer senses that he dare not intrude farther; he feels insignificant and insecure when even this close to Washington's presence. Shaw produced this book, as he did his *United States Directory for the Use of Travelers* (1822), as a guide so that tourists would know what to look for when traveling to various parts of the country. Of the twenty sites that make up *Picturesque Views,* which purports to include images of the "best and most popular Views" in America, the tomb of Washington is the first on Shaw's list.

John Gadsby Chapman followed his friend Joshua Shaw to the tomb of Washington fifteen years later (fig. 243). In his depiction, the menacing shadow at the entrance to the vault is gone; instead the area is so bathed in light as to call to mind Renaissance scenes of the Resurrection of Christ, which the artist knew well from his recent tour of Italy. The light is intense, to the point where one wonders whether it is sunlight shining down on the grave or a light shining from within. If Washington has not come back to life, his memory at least has survived the grave and now almost radiates, as in the print by Weishaupt. The artist shows through the trees a ship on Washington's beloved Potomac River. Readers of Weems would recall that the parson had made the passing ship a symbol of Washington's figurative survival: "And to this day, often as the ships of war pass that way, they waken up the thunder of their loudest guns, pointed to the spot, as if to tell the sleeping hero,

242. John Hill, after Joshua Shaw, *Washington's Sepulchre, Mount Vernon,* colored aquatint, 14½×9¾ in., from *Picturesque Views of American Scenery* (Philadelphia, 1819–21). (Courtesy of American Antiquarian Society)

that he is not forgotten in his narrow dwelling."[57] The author had told the world that Washington was buried "in his own family vault, near the banks of the great Potomac." In fact, however, in 1831 the bodies of Washington and Martha had been moved to a new vault, the Gothic tomb that still serves that purpose today. As with his scene of Washington's bedchamber, Chapman re-created a setting that had since been changed in order to provide a scene that he hoped his potential patrons might recognize and admire.

Washington had specified in his will that a better tomb be constructed: "I desire that a new one of Brick, and upon a larger Scale, may be built at the foot of what is commonly called the Vineyard Inclosure,—on the ground which is marked out." He thought that the old one was "improperly sit-uated" as well as in disrepair.[58] Perhaps Washington had not gone ahead and constructed the new tomb himself because he anticipated that the nation might one day entomb his body in its Capitol. In any case, Chapman chose to ignore the new burial site and focus his talents on the old family vault, where Jackson, and more recently Lafayette and his son, had paid tribute to Washington. The age and condition of the grave produce feelings of nostalgia for an earlier era when the general's presence was still felt at Mount Vernon; the bright light might well have evoked a similar emotion toward the godlike figure who rested within.

Pilgrims would continue to come to Mount Vernon throughout the antebellum years. One of the most prestigious was the Prince of Wales, whose visit to the new tomb with President

243. John Gadsby Chapman, *Tomb of Washington,* 1834, oil on canvas, 21¾×29⅜ in.
(Courtesy of Homeland Foundation, Incorporated, New York)

248. Horatio Greenough, *George Washington,* 1832–41, marble. (Courtesy of National Museum of American Art, Smithsonian Institution, transfer from the U.S. Capitol)

woman on the right seeks to crown him with one of the laurel wreaths that the women of the family have been making, presumably as part of a special remembrance on the great man's birthday. The young boy on the left, like the boy in *The Image Peddler*, is being taught about Washington, who, when either pictured or standing in a home, provided a constant reminder of the sorts of virtues toward which a young man should aspire.

Baugniet provides a scene of domestic bliss mixed with patriotism that Washington himself would probably have appreciated. Interestingly, the boy seems to be fatherless; indeed, the older woman instructing him, who is presumably his mother, is the only female figure wearing black. Is she in mourning for the boy's father who will not be available to provide the proper guidance or for Washington himself, whose birth is being celebrated? In either case, the only adult male "present" in the room is the president. He will serve as the boy's father, in that he has provided an exemplary life that the boy might emulate. The women may well be able to teach the child a great deal about familial love, but he will need more than that if he is to grow up to participate in the types of climactic moments pictured on the wall. The president's image, and what it had come to mean by the second half of the nineteenth century, will, the viewer hopes, be enough to steer this child in the right direction. One day he will have to become the protector of these women, of the type of happy domestic life that this scene represents, and perhaps even of the country in which it takes place. Only a study of the life of Washington would prepare a boy to assume such responsibilities.

In a letter of January 1834 to Secretary of State Edward Livingston in which he explains his rather remarkable choice to portray Washington in terms that he considers "natural and permanent," Horatio Greenough argues that an attempt to create a sculpture of Washington must take into account the pervasiveness of his story (fig. 248): "I consider my work therefore as addressing itself to a people who are familiar with the facts of Washington's life, with his character and its consequences, who have learned from books and tradition all that is to be known about him and I would fain sculpture an image that shall realize in form that complex of qualities which is our idea of the man, apart from what was common to him with other gentlemen of his day." By 1834 Washington's story was so well known that artists and writers would have to go to great lengths to provide an original representation. Greenough's sculpture of Washington as Zeus, which perhaps owes a bit to Antonio Canova's seated figure that had been destroyed in 1831 when the North Carolina statehouse burned, was such an effort, as were Chapman's serene landscapes and the concurrent publishing of Sparks's biography and edition of Washington's *Writings*. All these attempts to capture something essential about Washington that had not been previously expressed occurred during the 1830s, as Americans celebrated the one hundredth birthday of the man who had been instrumental in providing their freedom. Sparks's effort became popular because it did fill in some gaps in the public's knowledge; Chapman's paintings never achieved great popularity, although one could argue that their inclusion on his résumé had helped him gain one of the Capitol-rotunda commissions; Greenough's work, however, was at best poorly received and in some cases mocked. Washington was still a sainted figure, and Americans recoiled from this image that failed to show him the proper respect. While Greenough may have had the best of intentions, he was forcefully reminded that the American public would not allow anyone to take liberties with its memory of Washington. The available personae—soldier, statesman, and "Father of His Country"—were too well established to allow for any creativity. As such figures as Greenough's Washington disappeared from the public consciousness, however, so did Washington the farmer and family man, and it would not be until the turn of the twentieth century that any room would be made for even these inoffensive aspects of his private life to be again recognized.[64]

249. Matthew Kahle, *George Washington,* mid-nineteenth century, wood, over-life-size,
atop Washington Hall. (Courtesy of Washington and Lee University)

# Afterword: The Legacies of Washington

BEYOND HIS PERSONA as the "Father of His Country," Washington is perhaps best known today because of those aspects of his character that have long been seen as at the core of his being. It would be impossible in a study of this sort to discuss usefully the many exemplary qualities of "the flawless American." As Samuel Tomb put it in 1800, "To mention some of the shining virtues which he displayed both in the field, and in the cabinet; in public, and in private life is all that the present moment will admit." Guthrie Sayen has recently identified what he calls the four "overlapping types" of the "genteel ethos"—"the court gentleman, the virtuous gentleman, the enlightened gentleman, and the warrior gentleman"—and argued convincingly that in a world where it was rare for a man to embody one type successfully, the terms used by his contemporaries to describe Washington suggest that he was perhaps as close to a "compleat gentleman" as one might find. Matthew Spalding and Patrick J. Garrity point to some of his best-known qualities—"courage, integrity, loyalty, dedication"—in their opening discussion of why he was chosen to lead the Continental army. There can be no doubt that such virtues, as well as morality, patriotism (which to him meant putting one's duty to one's country before any private concerns), and, of course, honesty, were important to Washington and have rightly come down to us as characteristics worthy of emulation. As Thomas Jefferson put it in 1814 in a letter in which he also felt free to point out those areas in which he found Washington lacking (fig. 250): "His integrity was most pure, his justice the most inflexible I have ever known. . . . He was indeed, in every sense of the words, a wise, a good, & a great man."[1]

## Mount Vernon and the Mount Vernon Ladies' Association

George Washington had bequeathed Mount Vernon, his papers, and his library to his nephew Bushrod, who was to take possession of the house upon the death of Martha Washington (figs. 251, 252). This eldest son of John Augustine Washington had distinguished himself as a lawyer in Alexandria and Rich-

mond, and in 1799 was appointed to the Supreme Court, not long before Washington wrote his last will. As early as 1794 the uncle had praised his nephew with whom he maintained a close relationship: "It gives me much pleasure to hear, through a variety of Channels, that you are becoming eminent, and respectable in the Law." It would appear that Bushrod Washington was in many ways like his uncle; not only was he ambitious, but reportedly he was also thorough, sound in his reasoning rather than quick, and meticulous in his record keeping.[2] George Washington left part of his farm property to Lawrence and Nelly Lewis as he had promised and another large tract to George Fayette Washington and Charles Augustine Washington, the sons of George Augustine Washington and Fanny Bassett. He gave to George Washington Parke Custis his property in the city of Washington as well as a tract of land "in the vicinity of Alexandria" where his step-grandson would build Arlington House, which would briefly become the home of the Lee family before the outbreak of the Civil War when it was confiscated and ultimately transformed into Arlington National Cemetery.

The president justified his choice of Bushrod to receive the Mount Vernon plantation by citing his affection for the boy's father: "To my Nephew Bushrod Washington and his heirs (partly in consideration of an intimation to his deceased father while we were Bachelors, and he had kindly undertaken to superintend my Estate during my Military Services in the former War between Great Britain and France, that if I should fall therein, Mount Vernon (then less extensive in domain than at present) should become his property) I give and bequeath all that part . . . containing upwards of four thousand Acres, . . . together with the Mansion house and all other buildings and improvemts. thereon."[3]

When Bushrod and his wife, Julia Washington, both died in 1829, the house descended laterally to a nephew, John Augustine Washington. A little more than a decade later it was owned by his son, John Augustine Washington Jr. (fig. 253). This great-grandson and namesake of George Washington's brother had

was dislocated by sudden circumstances, he was slow in re-adjust-
-ment. the consequence was that he often failed in the field, & rarely
against an enemy in station, as at Boston & York. he was incapable
of fear, meeting personal dangers with the calmest unconcern. perhaps
the strongest feature in his character was prudence, never acting until
every circumstance, every consideration was maturely weighed; re-
-fraining if he saw a doubt, but, when once decided, going through with
his purpose whatever obstacles opposed. his integrity was most
pure, his justice the most inflexible I have everknown, no motives of
interest or consanguinity, of friendship or hatred, being able to bias his
decision. ~~his temper was naturally irritable and high toned, but reflection~~
~~his temper was naturally irritable and high toned, but reflection and resolution~~
~~his temper ~~ ~~ ~~

he was indeed, in every sense of the words, a wise, a good, & a great man.
his temper was naturally irritable and high toned; but reflection &
resolution had obtained a firm and habitual ascendancy over it.
if ever however it broke it's bonds he was most tremendous in his wrath.
in his expences he was ~~close~~ honorable, but exact; liberal in contributions to
whatever promised utility; but frowning and unyielding on all vi-
-sionary projects, and all unworthy calls on his charity. his heart was
not warm in it's affections; but he exactly calculated every man's value,
and gave him a solid esteem proportioned to it.   his person, you know,
was fine, his stature exactly what one would wish, his deportment
easy, erect, and noble; the best horseman of his age, and the most grace-
-ful figure that could be seen on horseback. altho' in the circle of
his friends, where he might be unreserved with safety, he took a free
share in conversation, his colloquial talents were not above mediocrity,

250. Thomas Jefferson to Dr. Walter Jones, 2 January 1814. (Courtesy of Virginia Historical Society)

251. C. B. Graham, lithographer, and J. Crutchett, publisher, *Mount Vernon, West Front, 1858,* 1858, lithograph, 10×14¾ in. (Courtesy of Virginia Historical Society)

252. J. B. Longacre, after Chester Harding, *Bushrod Washington,* after 1829, engraving, 13×10½ in. (Courtesy of Virginia Historical Society)

253. John P. Walker, *John Augustine Washington Jr.,* 1909, oil on canvas, 30×25 in. (Courtesy of Virginia Historical Society)

been born in Jefferson County (now West Virginia). He graduated from the University of Virginia in 1841, after which he took up residence at Mount Vernon. Already the estate was "as shabby as possible," according to a French visitor of the year before: "The park is grown over with weeds; the house tumbling down; everything dirty and in a miserable condition." The new owner faced the daunting tasks of restoring and maintaining the property and turning a profit with only a fraction of the former slave force.[4] He would also face the responsibility of entertaining the stream of visitors that had continued to migrate to the house after the president's death.

After a decade of trying to manage the operation, the last Washington owner first offered to sell the house and its acreage to Congress and then to the commonwealth of Virginia, without success. By chance, a woman from South Carolina, Ann Pamela Cunningham, was alerted to Mount Vernon's plight by her mother who in 1853 had viewed the ill-kept property from the deck of a passing steamer (fig. 254). In this sectional age, the mother suggested to the daughter that the women of the South would do themselves and Washington an honor if they would join together to save his house and tomb. Soon the ambitious Miss Cunningham commenced negotiations with John

Augustine Washington Jr., and in 1858 she entered into a contract to provide in a series of installments the selling price of three hundred thousand dollars. Advertising herself in southern newspapers and in a pamphlet (fig. 255) as "A Southern Matron," Cunningham was remarkably successful in garnering support from women in all the states, and the purchase subscription was nearly achieved during the three years prior to the outbreak of the Civil War.[5] John Augustine Washington Jr., his wife, and their seven children left the property in 1860 and set up residence in nearby Fauquier County. Soon he was on active duty in the Confederate army, serving as an aide-de-camp to Gen. Robert E. Lee, his distant relation through marriage. The last Colonel Washington of Mount Vernon was killed in action early in the war, near Cheat Mountain (now West Virginia). We show him in a posthumous portrait wearing his

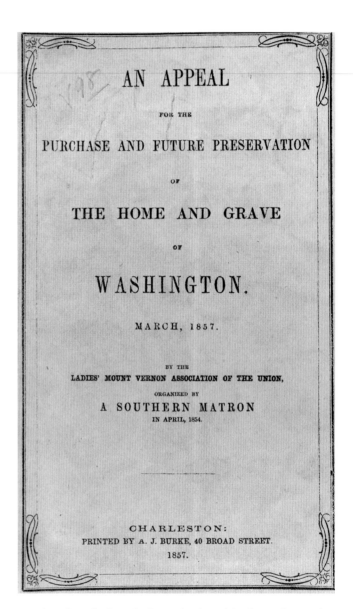

255. Ann Pamela Cunningham, *An Appeal for the Purchase and Future Preservation of the Home and Grave of Washington,* 1857, pamphlet. (Courtesy of Virginia Historical Society)

254. James Reid Lambdin, *Ann Pamela Cunningham,* ca. 1870, oil on canvas, 40×29½ in. (Courtesy of Mount Vernon Ladies' Association)

Confederate uniform in an image that once hung in the R. E. Lee Camp of Confederate Veterans in Richmond (see fig. 253).

In 1845 the *Columbian Magazine* had pointed to Washington's home as the most tangible reminder of his uncommon achievements: "Mount Vernon! While the eye delights in the beauty of the engraving, memory is busy recalling the lofty and manly form that once dwelt there in active life."[6] Beginning in the 1790s, while Washington was still alive, and continuing throughout the nineteenth century, a number of prints depicting the house and grounds were produced, partly to showcase the elevated tastes of the general but mainly to allow their purchasers to remember and celebrate the man and his accomplishments. Some of the prints "improved" the house by masking the evidence of neglect and fixing the slight asymmetry of the land facade (see fig. 251), in the same way that portraitists had "corrected" the face of the owner during the 1780s (see figs. 147 and following). In both cases the goal was to show the subject in the best-possible light. In the example illustrated, which was one of a number produced by the new Mount Vernon Ladies' Association to raise money, the adjustment is subtle; the facade is still asymmetrical but not nearly so

much as in reality, and therefore the imperfection is barely noticeable. One of the more significant of the midcentury prints of Mount Vernon is the lithograph issued in 1859 by Whately and Sinclair to commemorate the rescue of this shrine, which until a few years earlier had been in such disrepair (fig. 256). In this image there is no evidence of the men, women, and children who routinely promenaded across the grounds during the antebellum era; instead emphasis is directed to the many components of this vast property that had been saved by the ladies and that they had assumed the charge to maintain. In this way the print signals a new beginning for Mount Vernon.

Before the outbreak of the war, Ann Pamela Cunningham had assembled from both the northern and the southern states a board of thirty-one vice regents that formed the first Mount Vernon Ladies' Association. During the Civil War years they managed to protect the property by winning approval from both armies that the estate would remain a neutral zone. They first restored the buildings and then began the retrieval of objects that had once been at Mount Vernon. Miss Cunningham set as the goal of her organization the restoration of the property to the state in which Washington had left it: "Ladies, the

256. Whately and Sinclair, *The Two Hundred Acres Purchased by the Mount Vernon Ladies' Association,* 1859, lithograph, 17½×25½ in. (Courtesy of Mount Vernon Ladies' Association, gift of Mrs. Charles Custis Harrison, Vice Regent for Pennsylvania, 1896–1922)

*Afterword*

home of Washington is in your charge—see to it that you keep it the home of Washington! . . . Those who go to the home in which he lived and died wish to see in what he lived and died. Let one spot in this grand country of ours be saved from change. Upon you rests this duty."[7] For nearly a century and a half, in what is perhaps the most successful chapter in the history of the American preservationist movement, the Mount Vernon regents have successfully answered that call. The operation is managed without the aid of government subsidies and is so successful that a million visitors see the house annually and are thereby inspired to consider the contributions of George Washington toward the birth of the American nation.

## Washington Academy (Washington and Lee University)

Ever conscious that his own schooling had been defective, George Washington developed a passion for education. He was prodded to give serious thought to this subject during the Revolutionary War when his troops of the Continental army continually impressed upon him their ignorance and provinciality. A reasonable amount of schooling could correct both of those shortcomings. Before the war was over, and then throughout his later years, the general took an enlightened stance that linked the education of America's citizens to the fulfillment of the nation's destiny.

In late 1781, after the College of William and Mary had sheltered sick and wounded soldiers from the Yorktown campaign, Washington wrote to its president and faculty that he would do all in his power to reestablish the college because "an Institution, important for its Communication of useful Learning . . . [is] conducive to the Diffusion of the true principles of rational Liberty." This was more than polite correspondence; it establishes that Washington was already formulating his ideas about education. His letters of the 1780s give ample evidence of what he called his "heart-felt desire to promote the cause" of education. One of the most significant letters is to a schoolteacher, George Chapman, in which the general first stated a creed he would repeat to the national legislature: "the best means of forming a manly, virtuous and happy people, will be found in the right education of youth." This was the key, he reasoned, to the proper development of the nation as a whole. Education is integral to the understanding of virtue and the pursuit of happiness. But more than that, only an informed citizenry would know how to sustain its liberty, as the president argued in his first annual address to Congress: "There is nothing, which can better deserve your patronage than the promotion of Science and Literature. Knowledge is in every Country the surest basis of public happiness. . . . To the security of a free Constitution it contributes in various ways: By convincing those who are intrusted with the pubic administration, that every valuable end of Government is best answered by the enlightened confidence of the people: And by teaching the people themselves to know and to value their own rights." Five years later Washington perceived yet another danger should America fail to provide adequate institutions of learning. Students sent abroad for their education might become enamored with political systems that were "unfriendly to republican government" and then, "before they are capable of appreciating their own," return home and call for a change in the form of government that he and the other Founding Fathers had determined was the best.[8]

Immediately after the Revolution Washington began to look for ways to contribute to bettering the opportunities for education in the new nation. Because the general knew what it meant to a child to be fatherless and had seen the abject poverty of many of his soldiers, he took a particular interest in schools for children whose parents were either deceased or indigent. In 1785 he made a donation, which was amplified in his will by a bequest of four thousand dollars, to endow the nearby Alexandria Academy "for the purpose of Educating such Orphan children, or the children of such other poor and indigent persons."[9]

Earlier that year he had conceived of an even more ambitious educational scheme. Unexpectedly he had been given by the Virginia legislature a block of stock in the canal companies that had been established to make the James and Potomac Rivers navigable to their headwaters. Ever mindful of his reputation, the general was first embarrassed by the gift, even though it was made with "good wishes" as a token of respect and appreciation. He worried how his receipt of "public money" would be viewed "by the eye of the world." Washington told Lafayette that he could neither accept the gift nor decline it for fear of insulting the donors. He was truly at a loss until several months later, when he saw a way the money might be used to serve the public good. The general wondered if "the product of the Tolls arising from these shares [might be] applied as a fund" that would serve to establish two "charity Schools, one on each river, for the Education & support of the Children of the poor and indigent . . . especially the descendants of those who have fallen in defence of the rights & liberties" of this country.[10] Either from tolls or from the sale of the stock, funding was to be provided for these schools.

A decade later, as the national capital was materializing, "a plan for the establishment of an University in the federal City, [was] frequently . . . the subject of conversation." Accordingly, Washington then adapted his old idea of establishing a charity school on the Potomac River to the more ambitious goal of creating a university there that would attract a national audience and thereby help to diminish the provincialism that he feared was a threat to the union: "By assembling the youth from the different parts of this rising republic, . . . their intercourse, and interchange of information [will contribute] to the removal of prejudices which might perhaps, sometimes arise, from local circumstances." Another advantage would be that young Americans would not have to go abroad for the foreign education that Washington feared might corrupt them. The president would "grant, in perpetuity, fifty shares in the navigation of Potomac River towards the endowment of [this university]." In his lifetime nothing would result from this plan; the anticipated action by Congress was never taken, and in time the canal stocks became worthless. In 1821, however, others would bring to fruition virtually the same idea when they chartered Columbian College, which was renamed George Washington University in 1904.[11]

Two months after announcing his scheme "for establishing so useful a seminary in the federal city," Washington suggested to Thomas Jefferson that he would do the same for the state of Virginia and would ask the governor to consult with the legislature to determine where this second school might be located. The state assembly answered that Washington should appropriate his James River Company canal stock "to a Seminary at such place in the upper Country as [he] should think most convenient to a majority of its Inhabitants." After making "careful enquiries, to ascertain that place" and giving much thought to the matter, the president settled upon Liberty Hall Academy in Rockbridge County.[12]

Washington's gift to this small school, which had been established a half century earlier on the outskirts of the town of Lexington, brought to a fitting close his half-century association with the residents of the valley of Virginia. The young surveyor with aristocratic ambitions, who had been appalled by the appearance, living conditions, and ignorance of these people, had grown to see matters differently when he defended them from their common enemies on the frontier; they, in turn, came to revere him and elected the colonel to the House of Burgesses as their representative. Washington had encountered such people again when they filled the ranks of the Continental army, which inspired both his appreciation for their service and his concern that they be educated so as to function as responsible American citizens. When the trustees of Liberty Hall wrote to Washington to thank him for both the gift and the esteem that accompanied it, and to notify him that they had changed the name of the school to return the honor, the president felt rewarded that at least this part of his educational vision had been realized (fig. 258): "To promote Literature in this rising Empire, and to encourage the Arts, have ever been

257. Matthew Kahle, *George Washington,* mid–nineteenth century, wood, over-life-size, atop Washington Hall. (Courtesy of Washington and Lee University)

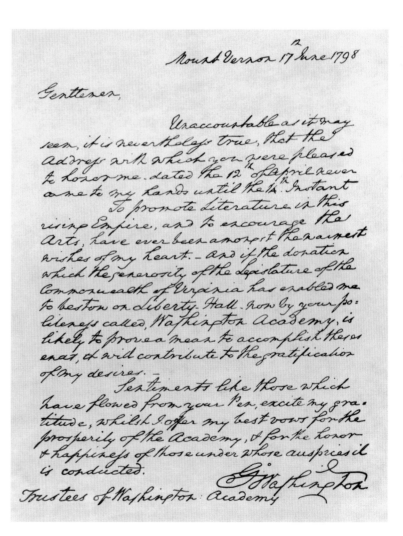

258. George Washington to the Trustees of Washington Academy, 17 June 1798. (Courtesy of Washington and Lee University)

amongst the warmest wishes of my heart. And if the donation which the generosity of the Legislature of the Commonwealth of Virginia has enabled me to bestow on Liberty-Hall, now by your politeness called, Washington Academy, is likely to prove a mean to accomplish these ends, it will contribute to the gratification of my desires."[13] The growth that Washington College enjoyed in the early nineteenth century is evident from the architecture of its lawn, which was erected in stages from the 1820s through the 1840s in the Roman Revival style. The central building, Washington Hall, had its cupola appropriately crowned with a carved wooden figure of the "Pater Patriae," whose image was placed there to inspire students and faculty alike (see figs. 249, 257). The sculptor, a local furniture maker named Matthew Kahle, is known to have traveled for woodworking supplies to Richmond where he would have seen Houdon's marble, which was apparently his inspiration. He replaced Houdon's feeble cane, however, with a mighty sword. In his left hand Washington holds a scroll because he was also a statesman who had guided the framers of America's most important document, the Constitution. Kahle's figure was conceived to be viewed from far below; seeing it close up accentuates the sculpture's appealing folk qualities.

Following the Civil War, former Confederate commanding general Robert E. Lee, the son of "Light-Horse Harry" Lee and son-in-law of George Washington Parke Custis, assumed the presidency of the institution and rejuvenated it in a way that matched what Washington's gift had accomplished seventy years earlier. The academic distinction enjoyed today by Washington and Lee University would no doubt greatly please both of its benefactors as would the institution's policy of recruiting a nationally diverse student body, which to this day works to suppress the "prejudices" that Washington feared.

## The Virginia Historical Society

Washington's accomplishments instilled in the citizens of Virginia a sense of pride in their state's history, which was of greater duration than that of any of the other colonies. Evidence of Virginia's appreciation was first manifested in 1785, when its legislators commissioned a full-length marble statue

259. James Reid Lambdin, *John Marshall*, 1832, oil on canvas, 39¾×32 in. (Courtesy of Virginia Historical Society)

of their victorious native son, which would be prominently displayed in the atrium of the capitol in Richmond (see fig. 145). A lengthy inscription on its base, which was drafted by James Madison and dated 1788, states that the legislators caused the sculpture to be erected "as a monument of affection and gratitude" to Washington. By "uniting to the endowments of the *Hero* the virtues of the *Patriot* and exercising both in establishing the Liberties of his Country," the general had "rendered his name dear to his Fellow Citizens" who clearly reveled in his achievement.[14] Eventually the contributions of all the Virginians who had played a role in the founding of the American nation would be recognized when an institution was established to ensure that what had been accomplished by Virginians, or on Virginia soil, during the struggle for independence would be remembered, and to guarantee that the documents and objects that record that history would be preserved. The Virginia Historical Society was founded in late December 1831, eight weeks before the much anticipated centennial of Washington's birth; its first president was chief justice of the Supreme Court John Marshall (fig. 259).[15]

During the Revolutionary War, Marshall had served with his commander at various engagements, including Brandywine, Germantown, and Monmouth, and with him suffered the privations of Valley Forge. He had run for Congress in 1798 at Washington's urging, and it was Marshall who had offered resolutions in the House of Representatives in late December 1799 that there be erected in the U.S. Capitol a monument to the deceased beneath which the body of Washington was to be deposited, and that the American people should assemble on the following 22 February to testify to their grief at Washington's passing.[16] Marshall had also become an authority on Washington after he had written, at Bushrod's request, the authorized biography of his illustrious uncle. Marshall would give an autographed copy of this work to the Virginia Historical Society's library to begin its collection (fig. 260).

Following Marshall's resolution that Washington's body be removed from Mount Vernon and interred in the Capitol, Martha Washington consented to the idea with "a sacrifice of individual feeling . . . to a sense of public duty." It is reasonable to conclude that the president's widow understood that the placement of his body at the seat of government might serve symbolically to remind future generations of Washington's commitment to the union and thereby help to preserve it. Of course, it would not be possible to put such a plan into effect until the construction of the Capitol was complete; the seat of government was moved there in 1800, but by that year only the north (Senate) wing was finished. In 1815, after peace was restored following the War of 1812, construction of the Capitol, which had been burned during the conflict, was revived, as

was the issue of the interment of Washington's remains. This time, however, the impetus came from Richmond. The intervening years had seen the publication of Marshall's biography, which had renewed the pride of many Virginians in their greatest son. Congress, however, whether because of a lack of funding, nascent sectionalism, or simple inertia, failed to act, and, with a "loss of all hope that Congress would ever act in the matter" and "partly in a spirit of resentment at the neglect which had been suffered," the Virginia legislators resolved in 1816 "to deposit [Washington's remains] beneath a suitable monument in Richmond."[17] A fund was established for this purpose, but Bushrod Washington, the then owner of Mount Vernon where Washington lay entombed, refused the request. A Federalist who longed for the preservation of the union and who understood the merit of the chief justice's resolution of seventeen years earlier, Bushrod may have been holding out for Congress to fulfill its promise. He apparently had good reason to so hope, because following his refusal a congressional com-

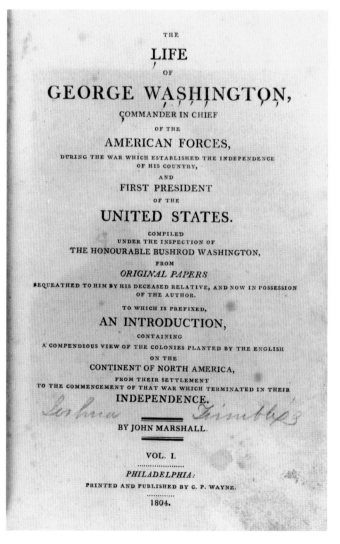

260. John Marshall, *The Life of George Washington* (Philadelphia, 1804–07). (Courtesy of Virginia Historical Society)

mittee was formed to revive the idea of a Capitol entombment. Opposition and lethargy would stall the plan, however, for another eight years.

The saga of a final repository for Washington's remains would span decades and lead to contentious feelings between Virginians and the federal government. In 1824 James Buchanan complained in the House that Washington's "mortal remains have yet been unhonored by that people, who, with justice, call him the father of his country." Buchanan, in words reminiscent of Andrew Jackson's complaint of 1815, found it "difficult to determine" the cause of this "neglect." The resistance that had developed in the years after Washington's death suggests that the nationalist symbolism inherent in the proposed federal-city interment was a volatile issue as early as the late teens and early 1820s. The year 1824 also saw the earliest suggestion that "a Historical and Antiquarian Society [be established] in the Old Dominion." This was in a letter published in the *Virginia Evangelical and Literary Magazine,* a Presbyterian monthly that was edited by the Reverend John Holt Rice. Rice and Jonathan Peter Cushing, a consumptive New Englander whom Rice had hired as a teacher and who ultimately became president of Hampden-Sydney College, established a Literary and Philosophical Society at the school.[18]

It was in anticipation of the centennial of Washington's birth that in 1828, on 22 February, the Virginia assembly passed legislation to invest in high-yield stocks what money had by then accumulated in the state's Washington Monument Fund, which had been established in 1816 but was still "insufficient" to finance the erection of a suitable monument. Only by acting several years in advance of the centennial could the legislators hope to have a monument in place by 1832. Congress apparently saw itself as in a position to wait until closer to the birth date to make its plans for remembering Washington. In 1830, again on 22 February, a committee of the House took up the old subject of interment with George Washington Parke Custis, who responded "with much pleasure and truly much surprise that the Government after the lapse of thirty years has at last determined to give *national* rites of sepulture to the venerated remains of Washington." The committee recommended not only a "national sepulchre" to hold the remains of both George and Martha but also "above this, in the centre of the Rotundo, a full length marble equestrian statue of Washington."[19] This resolution, which perhaps asked for too much, proved to have less chance of passing through Congress than the earlier drafts.

As the centennial neared, the time was finally deemed appropriate for action at both the state and the national levels. The Virginia legislature had begun its session at the beginning of December 1831, and only five days earlier Congress had charged a committee to recommend what it should propose for the centennial. In Richmond, Cushing instigated the organizing of what would first be called the Virginia Philosophical and Historical Society. The founding meeting was held on 29 December 1831, at which Cushing was elected second vice president of the society. The first vice president was Gov. John Floyd, and Marshall was elected president. The purpose of the organization would be "to collect and preserve materials" that would "throw light upon [Virginia's] early history, and especially during the Revolution," because soon "our Revolution would be looked at as the most important event in fixing the destinies of the hundreds of millions who would inhabit this Continent, but also in influencing those of all mankind."[20] It must have seemed necessary to have in place during the centennial year an institution that would serve to recall the accomplishments of the Revolutionary era, particularly since the state's Washington Monument Fund had still failed to mature. It is notable, however, that Washington's name is not mentioned in the newspaper accounts of the society's founding or in the public statement concerning the society's purpose. This is perhaps explained by the fact that most of his papers were already "saved"—in 1827 they had been taken to Boston by Jared Sparks for publication—and because the name "Washington" still commonly resounded in the halls of the Virginia capitol, where the members of the society met in the shadow of Houdon's statue of the general. His importance to Virginia history was obvious; it is difficult to imagine any other impetus that could have powered the founding of the society in the way his centennial did.

If Governor Floyd felt relieved that the new historical society positioned Virginians to celebrate Washington's one hundredth birthday appropriately, he was soon disappointed by the slow-moving machinations of the federal government. The congressional committee that had been charged on 24 December to plan an appropriate celebration on the centennial of the birthday had decided "to do what our predecessors had promised [in 1799]," which is to say, to move his body to the national Capitol. This "excited great feeling" in Virginia. There followed a heated debate in Congress, during which many representatives from the state attempted to block the proposal. Some offered transparent objections, arguing that the city named after Washington was itself enough of a monument to the man, and that the Capitol, which had burned during the last war, was not a safe repository. Finally, William F. Gordon stated bluntly that Washington's bones "belonged to [Virginia's] soil." Richard Coke Jr. argued that the proposed Capitol reinterment put his state "on the verge of losing something in comparison with which all the riches of the world would . . . weigh but as dust"; he "implored [his colleagues] in the name of God not to deprive the land which had given him birth, and which was justly proud of his virtue and renown, of the last consolation of being the depository of his bones." Coke cited the plans already made in Virginia "to transfer [Washington's] honored dust to Richmond" and concluded with what he thought was convincing logic, that "those who knew him best, who most appreciated his worth" had the greater right in this matter. Coke also made the shocking link of this issue to an eventual "severence of this Union"; commenting at this early date on the possibility of the remains being moved, he asked "should Virginia, in offering homage to the memory of the mighty dead, be forced to pay a pilgrimage to the remains of her own son through scenes of blood shed perhaps by kindred hands?"[21]

The objections of the Virginia congressmen were ignored. On behalf of Congress, letters with signatures that included those of Henry Clay and John C. Calhoun were sent to John Marshall, inviting him to speak at the interment in the U.S. Capitol, and to John Augustine Washington, the current resident of Mount Vernon, requesting permission to remove the remains. Governor Floyd informed the Virginia legislature of the latter development, stating that he viewed this scheme to move the resting place to the rotunda with "marked disapprobation" because "it is the province of Virginia to watch over the remains of George Washington"; he then added comments about the "brightness" of Washington's name and the "pride" Virginians held for him. However, just as suddenly as they had emerged, the congressional plans collapsed. First, John Marshall declined the invitation because he was "physically unable to perform the task"; his voice had become "so weak as to be almost inaudible." Then, John Augustine Washington refused to surrender the remains of his grand-uncle, mentioning, as had Martha Washington, the conflict between his "sense of duty" and his "private feelings," but coming to the opposite conclusion, which placed his own interests above any duty to the nation. His decision, which some viewed as selfish, was also influenced by the recent completion of the tomb that George Washington had described in his will. Those instructions, John Augustine said, had "been recently carried into full effect." A week later the Virginia Senate issued what now seems a peculiar resolution that the "decision of John A. Washington, in . . . withholding his assent to the removal of the remains of George Washington, is approved by every Virginian." With its plans for a mausoleum blocked, Congress had to settle for the "full-length pedestrian statue" of Washington that it commissioned two months later from Horatio Greenough for placement in the Capitol rotunda (see fig. 248).[22] The Virginia monument to Washington, which had been proposed in 1816, would not be sufficiently funded until midcentury. This would be an equestrian bronze sculpture by Thomas Crawford (fig. 261); the burial vault provided at its base, however, would never be filled.

During the congressional debates of February 1832 it was argued that disunion "never can happen while the name of Washington is spoken and his memory revered," and that "no act . . . would have so deep and permanent a moral influence in uniting the people and cementing the union" as would the interment of Washington's remains in the Capitol. Perhaps John Augustine Washington had misunderstood the significance of the proposal or perhaps he had failed to realize that Bushrod Washington had refused the request of the state but not the national government. Or possibly, as John Quincy Adams suspected, John Augustine had been converted to sectionalism by his Virginia neighbors. Adams wrote in his diary on 22 February 1832 that the resolution to inter Washington "was connected with an imagination that this federative Union was to last for ages. I now disbelieve its duration for twenty years."[23] In retaining the body, which to this day lies at Mount Vernon in the tomb prepared by John Augustine Washington, Virginians had chosen to ignore Washington's Federalist plea to preserve the union at all costs (see fig. 244). The pride that Washington's example had inspired in his Virginia neighbors had been redirected to assert the doctrine of "states' rights" or "state sovereignty," which would ultimately fuel sectionalism and lead eventually to secession.

In 1832 the new historical society began to collect materials that documented Virginia history. Many examples of the Washingtonia that have been discussed in this catalog are from the collection begun in the centennial year of Washington's birth. In addition to Marshall's autographed volumes of his biography, other donations of the 1830s were the order book kept at Valley Forge by Col. James Meriwether (see fig. 127) and the *Plan of the Investment of Yorktown* (see fig. 135), which was the gift of the soon-to-be secessionist Edmund Ruffin.[24] At midcentury private papers in Washington's hand began to come into the collection, including the diary of 1790–91 (see fig. 198). Following the Civil War the official papers of Gov. Robert Dinwiddie were donated (see figs. 50, 57, 58). When the philanthropist William Wilson Corcoran became a vice president of the society in 1881, he purchased for the institution a number of documents in Washington's hand as well as the famous letter by Thomas Jefferson that records his heartfelt assessment of the first president (fig. 250). Among the objects added to the collection in the 1990s are the dozen scenes by the Colonial Revival painter Jean Leon Gerome Ferris and the deed by which Washington in 1774 purchased several tracts of prime land in Tidewater Virginia on behalf of his ward Jacky Custis (see fig. 86).

*Notes*

*Frequently Cited Sources*

DGW    Donald Jackson and Dorothy Twohig, eds., *The Diaries of George Washington*, 6 vols. (Charlottesville, 1976–1979).

PGW Col.    W. W. Abbot, Dorothy Twohig, and Beverley H. Runge, eds., *The Papers of George Washington, Colonial Series*, 10 vols. (Charlottesville, 1983–1995).

PGW Con.    W. W. Abbot, ed., *The Papers of George Washington, Confederation Series*, 6 vols. (Charlottesville, 1992–97).

PGW Pres.    Dorothy Twohig, Mark A. Mastromarino, and Jack D. Warren, eds., *The Papers of George Washington, Presidential Series*, 6 vols. to date (Charlottesville, 1987– ).

PGW Ret.    W. W. Abbot, ed., *The Papers of George Washington, Retirement Series*, 2 vols. to date (Charlottesville, 1998– ).

PGW Rev.    Philander D. Chase and Frank E. Grizzard Jr., eds., *The Papers of George Washington, Revolutionary War Series*, 7 vols. to date (Charlottesville, 1985– ).

WW    John C. Fitzpatrick, ed., *The Writings of George Washington*, 37 vols. (Washington, D.C., 1931–1940).

## Introduction

1. Paul K. Longmore, *The Invention of George Washington* (Berkeley, Calif., 1988), 204. Longmore explains that this title first appeared in the *Lancaster Almanack* of 1778 and developed out of the perception that King George III was an "unnatural father."

2. If one consults Bartlett, one would think that Lee's phrase was only "First in war, first in peace, first in the hearts of his countrymen" (see Bartlett, *Familiar Quotations* [Boston, 1992], 355).

3. Friedman, "The Flawless American," in *Inventors of the Promised Land* (New York, 1971), 44–78; Marshall, *The Life of George Washington* (Philadelphia, 1804), 1:xi.

4. It must be said that Weems was by far the more blatant of the two. Sparks, who produced his biography to accompany his edition of Washington's writings, was more subtle in his manipulations.

5. In addition to these titles, a useful overview of Washington literature is provided by Don Higginbotham in "The Washington Theme in Recent Historical Literature," *Pennsylvania Magazine of History and Biography* 114:3 (July 1990): 423–37.

6. W. Guthrie Sayen, "George Washington's 'Unmannerly' Behavior," paper presented to the George Washington Symposium, Mount Vernon, 15 Nov. 1997; see also his "'A Compleat Gentleman': The Making of George Washington, 1732–1775" (Ph.D.

diss., Univ. of Connecticut, 1998), 18–47. On what it meant to be a gentleman in early national America, see Richard L. Bushman, *The Refinement of America: Persons, Houses, Cities* (New York, 1992).

7. Longmore, *Invention of Washington*, 32.

8. Washington to Bryan Fairfax, 20 July 1774 (*PGW* Col., 10:128–31).

9. As a sitting president, Jefferson, although revered as an architect of the Revolution, could hardly claim untarnishable status.

## 1. The Early Years

1. John Gadsby Chapman (1808–89) was born in Alexandria, Virginia. Despite his considerable talents, he was unable to support himself as an artist in his native state. During the 1830s and 1840s Chapman achieved notoriety in New York City as the leading American wood engraver, etcher, and illustrator. After 1848 he was active in Italy. Through home-state connections Chapman had won a commission to paint a mural for the rotunda of the U.S. Capitol of *The Baptism of Pocahontas*, another subject from Virginia history.

2. Paulding, *A Life of Washington*, 2 vols. (New York, 1835). Paulding offers the following dedication: "To the pious, retired, domestic MOTHERS OF THE UNITED STATES, this work, designed for the use of their children, is respectfully inscribed by The Author." In the first paragraph of his preface Paulding states his interest in Washington's "private life and domestic habits."

37. See the diary entries for 27 Jan. 1768 ("started a Fox abt. 10 Run him till 3 and lost him") and 13 Aug. 1768 ("we followd & run it after sevl. hours chase into a hold when digging it out it escapd") (*DGW*, 2:32, 84).

38. Sparks, *Writings of Washington*, 1:112.

39. *Maryland Gazette*, 23 April 1761, 2.

40. Schroeder, *Life and Times of Washington* (New York, 1857), 1:124.

41. Sparks, *Writings of Washington*, 1:106. Stearns sold one version of the wedding painting (now at the Butler Art Institute) to the American Art Union, which distributed it by lottery in 1850. He unsuccessfully solicited the Union to purchase three additional Washington paintings, so that there could be a cycle of four scenes from Washington's life. Undaunted, Stearns proceeded on his own to paint the additional canvases. See Thistlethwaite, *Image of Washington*, 31.

42. Custis, *Recollections*, 11; on the contemporary accounts, Harris, *Old New Kent County*, 116–18; see G. W. P. Custis's letter to Benson J. Lossing, 30 Dec. 1852, regarding Stearns's visit to him. Custis describes a new studio fitted up in the south wing, where Stearns made copies of original portraits of Colonel and Mrs. Washington (collection of the Mount Vernon Ladies' Association).

43. George Washington to London merchant Richard Washington, 20 Sept. 1759 (*PGW* Col., 6:358–59); Washington to the marquise de Lafayette, 16 March 1793 (*WW*, 32:389–90).

44. The official appointment took two and a half years to be realized; see "Washington's Appointment as Guardian," 21 Oct. 1761, General Court, Williamsburg (*PGW* Col., 7:84).

45. John Parke Custis to George Washington, 20 Feb. 1774 (*PGW* Col., 9:491). "Nelly" is Eleanor Calvert, the future bride of Jacky Custis.

46. In a letter of 1 June 1760 to her sister Anna Maria, the wife of Burwell Bassett, Martha Washington is confident that "Mr. Bassett will inform you of the mirth and gaietys he has seen . . . in order to induce you to Try Fairfax in a pleasanter season than you did last time" (reprinted in Moore, *The Family Life of George Washington* [Boston, 1926], 85–86).

47. See William Sawitzky, *Matthew Pratt, 1734–1805* (New York, 1942), 76–77. Pratt advertised his services in the *Virginia Gazette* in March 1773, on his return from studying painting in London with Benjamin West. He settled in Philadelphia.

48. This is only hypothesis; there are other possible interpretations of the painting, such as that it does not represent Jacky and Patsy Custis at all but instead was painted a decade later and shows two of the children born to Jacky Custis's widow after her remarriage to David Stuart. There is no evidence that Pratt did not return to the region at a later date or dates.

49. Receipts from William Rumney, 18 Feb. 1769 and 4 June 1772 for medicines, Custis Papers, Virginia Historical Society; *DGW*, 31 July 1769, 2:168; Ledger A, 318–20, in *DGW*, 18 June 1770, 2:247; "Cash Accounts, Aug. 1770" (*PGW* Col., 8:362–63); *DGW*, 31 July 1770, 2:257.

50. Washington to Bassett, 20 June 1773 (*PGW* Col., 9:243–44).

51. Washington to Reverend Jonathan Boucher, a tutor who at this time boarded students in Caroline County, 30 May 1768 (*PGW* Col., 8:89–90).

52. Washington to Jonathan Boucher, 16 Dec. 1770, 5 June 1771, and 7 Jan. 1773; Washington to Benedict Calvert, 3 April 1773 (*PGW* Col., 8:411–12, 476–78, 9:154–55, 209–11).

53. John Vardill to Washington, 20 Sept. 1773 (*PGW* Col., 9:326–27); Custis to Martha Washington, 5 July 1773 (*PGW* Col., 9:266–67 n. 2).

54. George Washington to Lund Washington, 17 Dec. 1778 (*WW*, 13:407–12).

55. *DGW*, 3:436–38; Washington to Jonathan Trumbull Jr., 6 Nov. 1781 (*WW*, 37:554–55); Washington to several inhabitants of Alexandria, 19 Nov. 1781 (*WW*, 23:355–56).

56. On Martha's infertility, *PGW* Con., 4:310 n. 2; George Washington to George Augustine Washington, 25 Oct. 1786 (*PGW* Con., 4:307–10).

57. Entry of 13 March 1748, in "A Journal of my Journey over the Mountains began Fryday the 11th. of March 1747/48" (*DGW*, 1:7); Washington to John Parke Custis, 1 Feb. and 26 May 1778 (*WW*, 10:413–14, 11:456–58); Washington to the states, 8 June 1783 (*WW*, 26:483–96).

58. Washington to David Humphreys, 25 July 1785; Washington wrote much the same in a letter of the same date to Lafayette (*PGW* Con., 3:148–51, 151–55); from the poem of 1884 by Lazarus titled "The New Colossus."

59. Washington to Tobias Lear, 6 May 1794 (*WW*, 33:353–60).

60. Washington to his brother Charles Washington, 31 Jan. 1770 (*PGW* Col., 8:301–4).

61. In November 1772, Washington had to convince the newest governor, Lord Dunmore, that the land should be further surveyed, so that "Rocky" and "Barren" and "Mountain[ous]" sections could be avoided and all the veterans would receive worthwhile bounties. This part of the story has been told above in chapter 2 in our discussion of the portrait of Washington painted in the spring of that year by Charles Willson Peale. See Washington's petition to Botetourt of ca. 15 Dec. 1769 and his petition to Dunmore of ca. 4 Nov. 1772 (*PGW* Col., 8:277–79, 9:118–23).

62. Advertisement of Western Lands, 15 July 1773 (*PGW* Col., 9:278–80).

63. *DGW*, 24 Aug. 1773, 30, 31 March 1774, 7 March 1775, 3:200, 241, 312; Washington to Henry Riddell, 22 Feb. 1774; Valentine Crawford to Washington, 27 July 1774; Washington to James Cleveland, 10 Jan. 1775; William Crawford to Washington, 6 March 1775; Washington to Burwell Bassett, 28 Feb. 1776 (*PGW* Col., 9:493–96, 10:133–36, 230–33, 292–94; *WW*, 4:359–60).

64. Washington to Lafayette, 10 May 1783 (*WW*, 26:421).

65. Washington to John Witherspoon, 10 March 1784 (*WW*, 27:348–52): "It would be a means of connecting friends in a small circle, and making life, in a new and rising Empire . . . pass much more agreeably, than in a mixed, or dispersed situation."

66. Washington to Reverend William Gordon, 3 Nov. 1784 (*WW*, 27:491–92); *DGW*, 4:1–3, 36 n. 4.

67. Washington to Simms, 22 Sept. 1786 (*PGW* Con., 4:254–59); Washington to John Dandridge, 18 Nov. 1788 (*WW*, 30:131–32); Washington to John Cannon, 22 March 1789; Washington to George Clendinen, 25 June 1790 (*WW*, 30:243–45, 31:60–61).

68. Washington to Clendinen, 25 June 1790.

69. Washington to Samuel Washington, 12 July 1797; Washington to Tobias Lear, 6 May 1794; Washington to James Ross, 16

June 1794; Washington to Thomas Law, 2 Oct. 1797 (*WW,* 35:497–98, 33:353–60, 403–5, 36:37).

70. Washington to James Welch, 7 Dec. 1797, 15 Feb. 1799; Washington to Daniel McCarty, 13 Sept. 1798 (*WW,* 36:99–102, 439–41, 37:133); *DGW,* 9 Dec. 1797, 10 May 1799, 6:272–73, 346–47.

71. Washington to the commissioners of the District of Columbia, 5 Sept. 1793 (*WW,* 33:83). Washington acquired the two paintings on 6 April and noted the purchase in his Household Account Book (Library of Congress). The identity of the canvases is given in Alexander Hamilton's letter of 10 April to his wife, Elizabeth: he saw "two views of situations on Hudson's River painted by Mr. Winstanley in the drawing room of Mrs. Washington" in Philadelphia (all cited in J. Hall Pleasants, "Four Late Eighteenth Century Anglo-American Landscape Painters," *Proceedings of the American Antiquarian Society* 52 [Oct. 1942]: 302–3).

72. The *View* paintings were exhibited at the British Institution (Algernon Graves, *British Institution 1806–1867* [London, 1909], 600, cited in Pleasants, "Four Landscape Painters," 318, 320–21). The third and fourth landscapes by Winstanley were purchased on 28 April 1794 (Pleasants, "Four Landscape Painters," 302, 321). *Meeting of the Waters* is owned by the Munson-Williams-Proctor Institute.

73. *Inventory of the Contents of Mount Vernon, 1810,* introduction by Worthington Chauncey Ford (Cambridge, Mass., 1909), 1–2.

74. Frederick Church's later painting of Niagara Falls (Corcoran Gallery of Art) works in this same manner, in that it suggests an entire continent has fed the river with the immense quantity of water that pours over the falls.

75. See Washington to a Participant in the Potomac River Enterprise, ca. 1762; Thomas Johnson to Washington, 18 June 1770; Washington to Johnson, 20 July 1770 (*PGW* Col., 7:175–78, 8:349–53, 357–60); Washington to George William Fairfax, 30 June 1785; Washington to Richard Henry Lee, 22 Aug. 1785 (*PGW* Con., 3:87–92, 195–97). See Washington to Thomas Jefferson, 29 March 1784 (*WW,* 27:373–77): the two agreed about "the practicability of an easy, and short communication between the Waters of the Ohio and Potomac." See also *DGW,* 12 Nov. 1774, 19 Dec. 1774, 26 Jan. 1775, 3–10 Aug. 1785, 21–22 Sept. 1785, 17–18 Oct. 1785, 3:291, 297, 304, 4:171–81, 196–97, 207–8.

76. Washington to the marquis de Chastellux, 12 Oct. 1783 (*WW,* 27:188–90).

77. *DGW,* 4 Oct. 1784, 4:57–71; these same sentiments are expressed in letter of 5 Dec. 1784 to Henry Knox (*WW,* 28:3–5).

78. Washington to Richard Henry Lee, 14 Dec. 1784 (*WW,* 28:9–12); Washington to David Humphreys, 25 July 1785 (*PGW* Con., 3:148–51).

79. Washington to Jefferson, 1 Aug. 1786 (*PGW* Con., 4:183–85); Washington to Buchan, 22 April 1793 (*WW,* 32:427–30). The Potomac Company survived until 1882, when it was incorporated into the Chesapeake and Ohio Canal Company. See *DGW, 6:359 n.*

*80. Washington to James Ross, 16 June 1794* (WW, 33:403–5).

81. For the Mississippi Land Company, see "Articles of Agreement," 3 June 1763 (*PGW* Col., 7:219–25), *DGW,* 1 July 1768, 2:74.

82. Irving, *Life of George Washington,* 1:244–45.

83. For the Dismal Swamp Land Company Articles of Agreement of 3 Nov. 1763, see *PGW* Col., 7:269–74. Washington's trip

to the swamp in October 1763 is mentioned in his diary (*DGW,* 1:319–26); see also Washington's letter to Hugh Williamson, 31 March 1784 (*WW,* 27:377–81). For Washington's comments to Patrick Henry on this subject, see particularly the letter of 24 June 1785 (*PGW* Con., 3:79–80). Washington sold his interest in the Dismal Swamp Company to Henry Lee, thereby contributing to his friend's financial demise; see memorandum of 18 Feb. 1793, and Washington to members of the Dismal Swamp Company, 16 Nov. 1795 (*WW,* 32:349–51, 34:363).

84. Washington to Hugh Williamson, 31 March 1784 (*WW,* 27:377–81); correspondence between Washington and Patrick Henry, 10, 24 June 1785, 30 Nov. 1785 (*PGW* Con., 3:48–49, 79–80, 417–19).

85. See the order from Washington to Robert Cary and Company, London, 1 May 1759; letter from Washington to Cary, 12 June 1759; and invoice from Cary to Washington, 6 Aug. 1759 (*PGW* Col., 6:317–18, 326–27, 332–37). For an identification of all Washington's books in 1764, see *PGW* Col., 7:343–50.

86. Duhamel, *A Practical Treatise of Husbandry* (London, 1762), viii.

87. For the growth of Mount Vernon, see *DGW,* 1:239–42, notes.

88. Washington to George William Fairfax, 19 Jan. 1773 (*PGW* Col., 9:159–60). See also Washington's letter to Fairfax of 10–15 June 1774: "I am now hurrying home, in order, if we have any wheat to Harvest [the crop was injured by a late frost] that I may be present at it" (*PGW* Col., 10:94–101).

89. As early as 1762, Washington was nearly ready to give up on the production of tobacco. "In spite of my utmost care & caution we fail in the Sales of our Tobaccos," he complained to his London merchants. Three years later, sales there still were "pitifully low." This was a matter of "the utmost consequence to our well doing," he wrote. See Washington to Robert Cary and Company, 18 Sept. 1762 and 20 Sept. 1765 (*PGW* Col., 7:153–55, 398–402). Washington to Carlyle and Adam, 15 Feb. 1767 (*PGW* Col., 7:482–91). Washington continued: "The year before last I even attempted to make but very little Tobacco, & last year none." On the mill and fishery, see *DGW,* 5, 10 April, 12 May 1771, 3:24–26.

90. Washington to Robert Cary and Company, 21 July 1766; Washington to George Mason, 5 April 1769 (*PGW* Col., 7:456–57; 8:177–81); Washington to Robert Cary and Company, 25 July 1769 (*PGW* Col., 8:229–31).

91. Washington to B. Fairfax, 20 July 1774 (*PGW* Col., 10:128–31); Washington to G. W. Fairfax, 10–15 June 1774 (*PGW* Col., 10:94–101); Washington to B. Fairfax, 4 July, 24 Aug. 1774 (*PGW* Col., 10:109–11, 154–56). Washington's sentiments on slavery are discussed below.

92. On the resolutions, see *PGW* Col., 10:119–28; Washington to George William Fairfax, 31 May 1775 (*PGW* Col., 10:367–68).

*4. The War Years*

1. John Adams recorded that George Washington was in uniform but added no further details. It is more likely that he was wearing the blue-and-buff uniform of the Fairfax Independent Company that he had recently been training than his old French and Indian War uniform. The wearing of a uniform demonstrated that he was willing to fight for the American cause. It is not known if other delegates were in uniform, but certainly many

"Advertisement"; Fliegelman, *Prodigals and Pilgrims*, 218–19; Motley, *The American Abraham: James Fenimore Cooper and the Frontier Patriarch* (Cambridge, 1987), 106.

67. Washington to Lafayette, 20 Feb. 1781 (*WW*, 21:253–56).

68. Washington to Lafayette, 30 Oct. 1780 (*WW*, 20:266–67).

69. *DGW*, 20 July 1780, 3:397; "Conference at Dobbs Ferry" (*WW*, 22:395–97).

70. Washington to Noah Webster, 31 July 1788 (*WW*, 30:26–28).

71. *DGW*, 20 July, 14, 15 Aug. 1781, 3:397, 409–10; Washington to Lafayette, 21 Aug., 7 Sept. 1781 (*WW*, 23:33–34, 97–98).

72. *DGW*, 3:419 n. 1.

73. Washington to Lund Washington, 31 May 1781 (*WW*, 22:145).

74. Washington to Rochambeau, 8 Jan. 1782 (*WW*, 23:435–36); Moustier and Madame de Bréhan to Thomas Jefferson, 29 Dec. 1788, cited in *DGW*, 5:419.

75. Washington to Lafayette, 2 Sept. 1781 (*WW*, 23:75–78); Freeman, *George Washington: A Biography*, 5:322; Washington to the comte de Grasse, 17 Sept. 1781 (*WW*, 23:122–25).

76. Washington to Lafayette, 15 Nov. 1781 (*WW*, 23:340–42).

77. Washington's General Orders, 20 Oct. 1781 (*WW*, 23:244–47); Washington to the comte de Grasse, 6 Oct. 1781 (*WW*, 23:187).

78. Auguste de Grasse, the son of the comte de Grasse, wrote to Washington: "I have seen in the Saloon of M. de Rochambeau your portrait; I have viewed it a thousand times with a desire to possess [one like] it" (12 June 1789 [*PGW* Pres., 2:475–77]); Washington to Charles Damas, 5 Dec. 1785 (*PGW* Con., 3:114 n. 1).

79. Freeman, *George Washington: A Biography*, 5:377.

80. Washington to Lund Washington, 19 May 1780 (*WW*, 18:391–92).

81. Washington to Nathaniel Green, 4 Oct. 1781 (*WW*, 23:260–61); Edward M. Riley, ed., "St. George Tucker Journal of the Siege of Yorktown, 1781," *William and Mary Quarterly*, 3d ser., 5 (1948), cited in *DGW*, 3:432 n. 1.

82. For the sittings, see, for example, *DGW*, 18, 20, 27 Feb., 22 March, 6 July (and following) 1790, 6:36–38, 51, 86–87. For posing on horseback, see *DGW*, 1 March 1790: "Exercised on horseback this forenoon, attended by Mr. John Trumbull who wanted to see me Mounted" (6:38). For dining, see *DGW*, 14 Jan. 1790, 6:7. For Washington's viewing of Trumbull's art, see *DGW*, 23 Jan. 1790, 6:13. For Washington's endorsement of the prints, see Washington to Lafayette, 22 Nov. 1791; Washington to John Trumbull, 31 Dec. 1795, 25 July 1798; Washington to Governor Jonathan Trumbull, 6 Feb. 1799 (*WW*, 31:425–26, 34:411–12, 36:367–68, 37:124–25).

83. On Tilghman's letter, see Freeman, *George Washington: A Biography*, 5:393; Mitnick, *Ferris*, entry 42.

84. Mary Washington to Washington, 13 March 1782 (Freeman, *George Washington: A Biography*, 5:409).

85. Mitnick, *Ferris*, entry 43.

86. James Tilton to Guinning Bedford, after 25 Dec. 1783, cited in *WW*, 27:285–86, n. 6.

87. Washington to the president and professors of the College of William and Mary, 27 Oct. 1781 (*WW*, 23:276–77); Washington to several inhabitants of Alexandria, 19 Nov. 1781 (*WW*, 23:355–56); Washington to Archibald Cary, 15 June 1782 (*WW*,

24:346–48); Washington to Anne César, Chevalier de la Luzerne, 29 March 1783 (*WW*, 26:264–65).

88. Fryd, *Art and Empire: The Politics of Ethnicity in the United States Capitol, 1815–1860* (New Haven, Conn., 1992), 14.

89. William A. Mercein, printer, *Description of the Four Pictures from Subjects of the Revolution . . . in the Rotunda of the Capitol* (New York, 1827), 24; Circular to the States, 8 June 1783 (*WW*, 26:483–96). (For a discussion of Washington and religion, see Paul F. Bohler Jr., *George Washington and Religion* [Dallas, 1963]).

90. See notice of Truro Parish Vestry Meeting, 20 March 1764, where Washington is listed as a warden (*PGW* Col., 7:296–97); "Sale of the Pews in Alexandria Church" (*DGW*, 3:152–53) and Washington to John Dalton, 15 Feb. 1773 (*PGW* Col., 9:180–83); Washington also buys a pew at the new Pohick Church, for sixteen pounds (*DGW*, 14 July 1773, 3:193 n); the Truro vestry requests Washington to import a "Cushion for the Pulpit and Cloths for the Desks & Communion Table" of Pohick Church (*DGW*, 24 Feb. 1774, 3:234–35 n).

91. Boucher, *Autobiography*, cited in *WW*, 2:486–87 n. 91; Washington to Lund Washington, 26 Nov. 1775 (*PGW* Rev., 2:431–33); Washington's Farewell Address, 19 Sept. 1796 (*WW*, 35:214–38).

92. Washington to Burwell Bassett on the death of his fourteen-year-old daughter, 20 April 1773 (*PGW* Col., 9:219–20); Washington to Martha Washington, on accepting command of the Continental Army, 18 June 1775 (*PGW* Rev., 1:3–6); Washington to Princeton College, 25 Aug. 1783 (*WW*, 27:115–16).

93. Circular to the States, 8 June 1783 (*WW*, 26:483–96); Washington to Benjamin Dulany, 17 Nov. 1781 (*WW*, 23:348–51).

## 5. The American Cincinnatus

1. Washington was apparently interested in purchasing the lands around the springs at Saratoga. See Edward Hotaling, *They're Off! Horse Racing at Saratoga* (Syracuse, 1995), 1–13.

2. See Thomas Fleming, "The Man Who Would Not Be King," *MHQ: The Quarterly Journal of Military History* 10:2 (winter 1998): 96. A number of apocryphal stories about West appeared in the early nineteenth century that parallel the Weemsian legends about Washington. This conversation with George III might well be one of them. For an engaging discussion of the larger implications of Washington as Cincinnatus see Gary Wills, *Cincinnatus: George Washington and the Enlightenment* (Garden City, N.Y., 184). The quotation is taken from page 3.

3. Lafayette to Washington, 6 Feb. 1786 (*PGW* Con., 3:538–47); Washington to Adrienne, marquise de Lafayette, 10 May 1786 (*PGW* Con., 4:39–40).

4. Charles Damas to Washington, undated (*PGW* Con., 3:113–14 n. 1); Benjamin Franklin to Washington, 20 Sept. 1785 (*PGW* Con., 3:266–67); Damas to Washington, undated (*PGW* Con., 3:113–14 n. 1).

5. Jefferson to Washington, 10 July 1785 and Lafayette to Washington, 9 July 1785 (*PGW* Con., 3:111–14); Washington to Houdon, 26 Sept. 1785 (*PGW* Con., 3:279); Washington to David Humphreys, 30 Oct. 1785; Washington to Jefferson, 26 Sept. 1785 (*PGW* Con., 3:328–29, 279–83). Jefferson had told Washington that the empress of Russia had summoned Houdon (10 July 1785), while Lafayette had said that "His Business Here

far Exceeds his leisure" (9 July 1785) (*PGW* Con., 3:111–14, 113 n. 1).

6. Jefferson to Washington (*PGW* Con., 3:111–14); David Humphreys in Paris to Washington, 17 July 1785 (*PGW* Con., 3:131–33).

7. *DGW*, 7, 10 Oct. 1785, 4:202, 204; *DGW*, 9 Oct. 1785, 4:203.

8. John S. Hallam, "Houdon's *Washington* in Richmond: Some New Observations," *American Art Journal* 10 (Nov. 1978): 78–80.

9. Jefferson to Washington, 4 Jan. 1786 (*PGW* Con., 3:490–92); on Harrison, Hallam, "Houdon's *Washington*," 73; Washington to Jefferson, 1 Aug. 1786 (*PGW* Con., 4:183–85).

10. Hallam, "Houdon's *Washington*," 79–80.

11. H. H. Arnason, *The Sculpture of Houdon* (New York, 1975), 80–81; Lafayette to Washington, 26 Oct. 1786 (*PGW* Con., 4:311–13).

12. Clark, *Civilization* (New York, 1969), 266. Washington's physical exhaustion after the war was also noted by his stepgrandson: "From the period of the Revolution, there was an evident bending in that frame so passing straight before, but the stoop is attributable rather to the care and toils of that arduous content than to age" (*Recollections . . . and Notes by Lossing*, 482).

13. Washington to Henry Knox, 20 Feb. 1784 (*PGW* Con., 1:136–38); Washington to Lafayette, 1 Feb. 1784 (*PGW* Con., 1:87–90).

14. Washington to Francis Hopkinson, 16 May 1785 (*PGW* Con., 2:561–62).

15. Monroe H. Fabian, *Joseph Wright, American Artist, 1756–1793* (Washington, D.C., 1985), 91–113; Washington to the comte de Solms, 3 Jan. 1784 (*PGW* Con., 1:8–9); Fabian, *Joseph Wright*, 103–4.

16. Freeman, *George Washington: A Biography*, 3:6, 5:453. The portrait of Washington painted from life by William Williams in 1784 for Alexandria Lodge no. 22, and still owned by the Masons, shows an overweight and weary Washington; this would seem to corroborate Joseph Wright and the written accounts about his physical condition at the end of the war. The portrait by Wright that was owned by Jefferson is now at the Massachusetts Historical Society. Fabian, *Joseph Wright*, 101–2.

17. See Wendy C. Wick, *George Washington, an American Icon: The Eighteenth-Century Graphic Portraits* (Washington, D.C., 1982), 101–2, and Fabian, *Joseph Wright*, 126–27. Wick illustrates the version in the New York Public Library, where Washington looks perhaps the most fatigued; Fabian illustrates the impression in the Metropolitan Museum of Art, which is perhaps the most skillfully etched of the group. Both of these are inscribed, "J. Wright Pinxt. & Ft." Washington and Lee University owns yet another version, with no inscription, which must not be by Wright because the expression in the general's eyes is entirely different, and this handsome figure shows no exhaustion.

18. Catharine Macaulay Graham in England to Washington, 10 Oct. 1786 (*PGW* Con., 4:289–90); George William Fairfax to Washington, 23 June 1785 (*PGW* Con., 3:75–78) and see Washington to Francis Hopkinson, 16 May 1785 (*PGW* Con., 1:561–62); Washington to William Paca, 18 May 1785; see also Washington to Thomas McKean, 16 May 1785 (*PGW* Con., 2:562 n. 1, 567 n. 2).

19. Robert Stuart, *Robert Edge Pine: A British Portrait Painter in America, 1784–1788* (Washington, D.C., 1979), 96; *DGW*, 2 July

1787, 5:173. The statement in Stuart that Washington holds a sword in the Independence Hall portrait is incorrect (*Pine in America*, 96); he holds the same brown, wooden cane that is shown as well in the other versions of the image.

20. *DGW*, 3 July 1787, 5:173; Sellers, *Portraits and Miniatures*, 237–38. See also E. P. Richardson, "Charles Willson Peale's Engravings in the Year of the National Crisis, 1787," *Winterthur Portfolio* 1 (1964): 173–74.

21. "Houdon's Statue of Washington," *Southern Literary Messenger* 18:10 (Oct. 1852): 577.

22. Susan Gray Detweiler, *George Washington's Chinaware* (New York, 1982), 83 (see this source for the Cincinnati and the china in this pattern [81–97]); Washington to Gérard, 29 Oct. 1783 (*WW*, 27:210).

23. John Bigelow, ed., *The Works of Benjamin Franklin* (New York, 1888), 8:439; Louis Gottschalk and Shirley A. Bill, eds., *The Letters of Lafayette to Washington, 1777–1799* (Philadelphia, Memoirs of the American Philosophical Society, CXV, 1976), 273, both cited in Detweiler, *George Washington's Chinaware*, 83; Brown, *Modernization: The Transformation of American Life, 1600–1865* (New York, 1976), 108.

24. 2 Nov. 1783 (*WW*, 27:222–27).

25. Jefferson to Washington, 14 Nov. 1786 (*PGW* Con., 4:363–66); Washington to William Barton, 7 Sept. 1788 (*PGW* Con., 6:501–3); Washington to Madison, 16 Dec. 1786 (*PGW* Con., 4:457–59); Washington to the Society of the Cincinnati, 31 Oct. 1786 (*PGW* Con., 4:316–18).

26. Washington to Lafayette, 28 May 1778 (*WW*, 29:506–8).

27. Washington to Lafayette, 1 Feb. 1784 (*PGW* Con., 1:87–90); Washington to comte de Rochambeau, 1 Feb. 1784 (*PGW* Con., 1:101–2); Washington to Arthur Young, 4 Dec. 1788 (*PGW* Pres., 1:159–63).

28. Washington to Franklin, 26 Sept. 1785 (*PGW* Con., 3:275); Washington to Lafayette, 15 Aug. 1786 (*PGW* Con., 4:214–16). For the certificates of service, see Washington to Tench Tilghman, 23 May 1785 (*PGW* Con., 3:14–15). For the inquiries, letters of compliment, and commonplace business, see Washington to Henry Knox, 5 Jan. 1785 (*PGW* Con., 2:253–56) (one example, admittedly peculiar, was the request "by the Marqs de la Fayette, in behalf of the Empress of Russia, to obtain a vocabulary of the languages of the Ohio Indians," Washington to Richard Butler, 27 Nov. 1786 [*PGW* Con., 4:398–400]; Washington to Tench Tilghman, 23 May 1785 (*PGW* Con., 3:14–15).

29. An affair at Lee Hall is described by the tutor Philip Fithian (Hunter Dickinson Farish, ed., *Journal and Letters of Philip Vickers Fithian, 1773–74: A Plantation Tutor of the Old Dominion* [Williamsburg, 1945], 75–76). Annual balls held at Sabine Hall and Mount Airy took place around New Year's, which is evidence that extreme cold was not allowed to interrupt the social schedule (William M. S. Rasmussen, "Sabine Hall: A Classical Villa in Virginia," *Journal of the Society of Architectural Historians* [Dec. 1980], 286–96).

30. *DGW*, 30 June 1785, 4:157; Washington to Tobias Lear, 31 July 1797 (*Mount Vernon: A Handbook* [Mount Vernon, 1974], 64).

31. Washington to David Stuart, 5 June 1785; Washington to Henry Knox, 18 June 1785 (*PGW* Con., 3:43, 61–64).

32. Washington to Lafayette, 31 Dec. 1777, 30 Sept. 1779 (*WW*, 10:236–37, 16:368–76).

# Illustrations

1. John Gadsby Chapman, *View of the Birthplace of Washington*  2

2. Joseph Berry, survey of Popes Creek Plantation  4

3. Currier and Ives, *The Birth-Place of Washington*  5

4. Excavated ruins of the Washington family house at Popes Creek  6

5. John Gadsby Chapman, *View from the Old Mansion House of the Washington Family Near Fredericksburg, Va.*  7

6. Ferry Farm, Stafford County  8

7. George Washington's *School Exercise Book*  10

8. *Rules of Civility and Decent Behaviour in Company and Conversation,* as copied by George Washington  11

9. Mason Locke Weems, *The Life of Washington,* title page  13

10. Augustus Köllner, *The Frank Confession*  13

11. Grant Wood, *Cartoon for Parson Weems' Fable*  15

12. A. B. Walter, after Henry Inman, *Early Days of Washington*  15

13. Frank Schoonover, *"Now Boys, a Rush Forward and in We Go," Shouted George*  16

14. After Alonzo Chappel, *Washington's Interview with His Mother*  17

15. Jean Leon Gerome Ferris, *The Call of the Sea, 1747*  17

16. Washington family coat of arms  19

17. Unidentified artist, copied by John Hesselius, *William Fitzhugh*  19

18. Letter from William Fitzhugh to Dorothy Fitzhugh, 1686  20

19. Isaac Zane, Belvoir fireback with Fairfax family coat of arms  20

20. Unidentified artist, *Thomas, Sixth Lord Fairfax*  21

21. Thomas, Lord Fairfax to William Fairfax, patent for land, 1737  22

22. Unknown artist, *George William Fairfax*  22

23. Duncan Smith, *Sally Cary Fairfax*  23

24. Letter from George Washington to Sarah Cary Fairfax, 1758  23

25. Belvoir house guest book  24

26. Excavated ruins of Belvoir  25

27. "The Dres[s]ing Chamber," from the Belvoir furniture inventory  27

28. "Account of Sales at Belvoir"  27

29. Unidentified artist, *Ferdinando Fairfax*  28

30. John Gadsby Chapman, *George Washington as a Young Surveyor*  29

31. John Rogers, after John McNevin, *Washington and Fairfax at a War Dance*  30

32. George Washington, survey for Richard Barnes, 1749  31

33. Frank Schoonover, *Whatever He Did He Did Well— So It Followed That His Surveys Were the Best That Could Be Made*  32

34. Herman Moll, map of Barbados  34

35. Charles Willson Peale, *Washington as Colonel of the Virginia Regiment*  36

36. Gorget with the Virginia coat of arms  40

37. Early "Stuart" Virginia coat of arms  40

38. Detail of gorget in Charles Willson Peale, *Washington as Colonel of the Virginia Regiment*  41

39. Gorget with the royal coat of arms  41

40. "Standing Pose to be Used by a Gentleman"  42

41. John Closterman, *Daniel Parke II*  43

42. Charles Willson Peale, *George Washington, 1772* and later  45

43. *The Céleron Plate*  46

44. After Alonzo Chappel, *Washington on His Mission to the Ohio*  47

Parker, Daniel, 172

Patterson, John, 78–79

Paul, Jeremiah, 205, 207

Paulding, James Kirke, xii, 3, 4, 271

Paumunkey River, 81

Peale, Charles Willson, xiv, 3, 14, 37, 38, 39, 42, 43, 44, 45, 64, 85, 92, 94, 96, 113, 123, 137–39, 143–44, 149, 157–59, 163–64, 221–23; *George Washington* (1772 and later), 45; *George Washington* (1787), 164; *Lafayette,* 138; *Martha Parke Custis,* 97; *Martha Washington,* 221; *Washington and His Generals at Yorktown,* 142; *Washington as Colonel of the Virginia Regiment* (1772), 36

Peale, James, 164–65; *George Washington* (1787), 165; *John Parke Custis,* 97

Peale, Rembrandt, 38, 137, 163, 222–24; *Conrad-Alexandre Gérard,* 137

Pearce, William, 233–37, 239, 255, 261

Pendleton, Edmund, 96

Pennsylvania, University of, 251

Peter, Martha Custis, 40, 250

Peter, Thomas, 250

Peter family, 258

Philadelphia College, 98

Philipse, Mary Eliza, 79

Pickett, Joseph, 131; *Coryell's Ferry, 1776,* 130

Pine, Robert Edge, 158, 161–64, 166; *America,* 161; *George Washington* (1785), 162; *George Washington* (1785–87—Independence Hall), 163; *George Washington* (1785–87—Warner Collection), 163; *George Washington Parke Custis,* 180

Pitt, William, 70, 72

Pohick Church, 117

Point Comfort, 118

Polk, Charles Peale, 176

Pope, Anne, 4

Pope, Nathaniel, 4

Popes Creek, 3, 4, 5, 6, 7, 9, 12, 19, 31

Poplar Grove, 81–82

Potomac River, 3, 4, 7, 8, 20, 22, 25, 29, 30, 37, 78, 90, 102–3, 113, 116, 186, 193, 195, 214, 239, 246, 258, 266, 267, 280, 281

Potomac River Canal Company, 103–4

Powel, Samuel, 160, 172, 176

Pratt, Matthew, 96; *The Custis Children,* 96

Price, Uvedale, 185

Prince of Wales (later Edward VII), 268

Princeton, N.J., 133–34, 139, 144

Princeton College (later Princeton University), 98, 115, 153, 251, 252

Prince William County, Va., 21–22, 29

Principio Iron Works, 7

Privy Council, 21, 46

Pulaski, Count Casimir, 196

Ramsey, Allan, 216–17; *King George III,* 216; *Queen Charlotte,* 216

Ramsey, William, 114

Randolph, Anne Harrison (Mrs. William), 85–86

Randolph family, 21

Rappahannock River, 7, 8, 20, 75

Rawlins, John, 175–76, 178, 232

Reagan, Ronald, 136

Redstone Creek, 56

Reed, Anna C., 14

Reeves, Christopher, 90

Repton, Humphrey, 185

Revolutionary War. *See* Washington, George, Revolutionary War, in

Reynolds, Sir Joshua, 134, 226

Rice, John Holt, 284

Richardson, Edgar P., 164

Richardt, Ferdinand, 197; *East Front of Mount Vernon,* 197

Richmond County, Va., 30

Rigaud, Hyacinth, 225–26

Ritchie, A. H. (after Daniel Huntington): *Lady Washington's Reception,* 220

Robinson, John, 57, 96

Rochambeau, comte de, 138, 141, 144–45, 151, 168

Rockbridge County, Va., 281

Rockohoc, 82

Rocky Hill, N.J., 158

Rogers, John: *Washington and Fairfax at a War Dance,* 30

Rossiter, Thomas P., 170, 179, 268; *Visit of the Prince of Wales, President Buchanan and Dignitaries to the Tomb of Washington at Mount Vernon, October 1860,* 268

Rousseau, Jean Jacques, 156

Ruffin, Edmund, 285

"Rules of Civility," xiii, 11–12

Rumney, Dr. William, 97

Rush, Benjamin, 112

Rushton, Edward, 202–3

Ryley, John, 136

Sabine Hall, 75, 116, 118, 127

St. Clair, Arthur, 212

St. John's College (Annapolis), 252

Saint-Simon-Montblérn, General the marquis, 144

Saratoga, N.Y., 134

Savage, Edward, 128, 180, 205, 243, 245; *The Washington Family,* 244

Sayen, W. Guthrie, xii, 12, 275

Schoonover, Frank, 16, 32, 33, 48; *"Now Boys, a Rush Forward and in We Go," Shouted George,* 16; *The Sachems Sat in Silence,* 48; *Whatever He Did He Did Well,* 32

Schroeder, John Frederick, 82, 93

Schwartz, Barry, xii, 224

Sears, William Bernard, 117, 120, 122–23, 125–27

Sellers, Charles Coleman, 38, 164

Seven Years' War, 46, 52. *See also* Washington, George, French and Indian War, in

Sèvres porcelain, 229–30

Shaw, Joshua, 266

Shaw, Samuel, 166

Shaw, William, 180

Shays's Rebellion, 206, 211

Shenandoah River, 31, 103

Shenandoah Valley, 29, 33, 34, 46, 52, 65–66

Shirley, 119, 122

Shirley, Gov. William (Mass.), 75

Short, William, 212

Simms, Charles, 101

Simpson, Stephen, 268

Slavery. *See* Washington, George, Slavery and

Slotkin, Richard, xii

Smith, Duncan: *Sally Cary Fairfax,* 23

Smith, Richard Norton, xii

Smollett, Tobias George, 106

Solms, Count de, 158

*Index*

*Southern Literary Messenger,* 165–66

Spalding, Matthew, xv, 275

Sparks, Jared, xii, 14, 17, 18, 29, 48, 54, 56, 58–60, 63, 80, 91–93, 169–70, 183–84, 193, 222, 273, 284

Spence, William, 254

Stamp Act, 109, 214

Stearns, Junius Brutus, 58–61, 75, 93–94, 193, 197, 254, 260; *The Marriage of Washington to Martha Custis,* 74; *Washington as a Captain in the French and Indian War,* 59; *Washington as a Farmer at Mount Vernon,* 192; *Washington on His Deathbed,* 260

Stony Point, 128

Stratford Hall, 127

Strother, William, 8

Stuart, Charlotte, 224

Stuart, David, 169, 179, 201–2, 207, 250, 252

Stuart, Eleanor. *See* Custis, Eleanor Calvert

Stuart, Gilbert, xv, 14, 82–83, 165, 205, 215–16, 220–27, 243, 248, 249, 250; *George Washington* (Athenaeum portrait), 224; *George Washington* (Lansdowne portrait—type 1, attributed to Winstanley), 225; *George Washington* (Lansdowne portrait—type 2), 227; *George Washington* (Vaughn portrait), 204; *Martha Washington,* 221

Stuart, Jane, 222, 223

Svivin, Pavel, 262

Swan, Abraham, 117, 122, 126


Tanacharison (the "Half King"), 48, 53–54

Tayloe, John, II, 75

Thistlethwaite, Mark Edward, xii

Tholey, Charles P., 196; *Washington and Friends After a Day's Hunt in Virginia,* 196

Thornton, William, 116, 247

Thruston, Charles, 214

Tilghman, Tench, 144, 149, 175, 189

Tilton, Robert S., xii

Titus, James, 65

Tomb, Samuel, 263–64, 275

Toole, John, 140; *The Capture of Major André,* 139

Toulston Manor, 23

Treaty of Paris (1783), 151, 155

Trenton, N.J., Battle of, 131–36

Triplett, William, 78

Trumbull, John, 56, 111, 113, 127–28, 134–35, 145, 146, 149, 151, 221–22, 248–50, 263; *Eleanor Parke Custis,* 249; *Eleanor Parke Custis Lewis* (attributed to Trumbull, after Gilbert Stuart), 249; *General George Washington Resigning His Commission, 23 December 1783,* 152; *George Washington,* 110; *General Washington at Trenton,* 134; *Martha Washington,* 221; sketch for *The Surrender of Lord Cornwallis at Yorktown,* 147; *The Surrender of Lord Cornwallis at Yorktown,* 148

Trumbull, Jonathan, Jr., 141, 146

Truro Parish, Va., 171

Tuckerman, Henry, 130, 224–25

Tudor Place, 250, 258

Tulip Hill, 114

Twain, Mark, 131

Twohig, Dorothy, xii

Tyler, John, 270


Uccello, Paolo, 215

Valley Forge, Pa., 134–37, 170, 180, 196, 283

Van Braam, Andreas, 230–31

Van Braam, Jacob, 47, 49

Vanderlyn, John, 223

Van Dyck, Anthony, 128

Vaughn, Samuel, 174–76, 186–87, 205, 247

Vernon, Admiral Edward, 9, 16, 35

Villiers, Joseph Coulon de, sieur de Jumonville. *See* Jumonville, sieur de

Villiers, Louis Coulon de, 55–56

Virgil, 231

*Virginia Gazette,* 25, 55

Virginia Historical Society (Virginia Philosophical and Historical Society), xv, 282–84

Virginia Regiment, xiii, 37, 38, 39, 41, 42, 44, 52, 62, 64–65, 67–68, 70, 73, 104, 112–13

Voltaire, 158


Walker, John P.: *John Augustine Washington Jr.,* 277

Wall, Charles Cecil, 38

Washington and Lee University, xv, 280, 281, 282

Washington, Augustine (father), xi, 3, 4, 5, 6, 7, 9, 10, 13, 35, 104, 198

Washington, Augustine, Jr. (brother of George), 6, 9, 29, 46, 69, 100

Washington, Bushrod, xv, 113, 172–73, 198, 210, 275, 283

Washington, Charles Augustine, 275

Washington, Charles (brother of George), 261

Washington, Col. John (seventeenth-century ancestor), 4, 18

Washington, George: apotheosis, xv, 261–73; birth place, 3–7; cherry-tree story, 13–14; death, xv, 258–61; Delaware River, crossing of, 50, 130– 34; education, 9–13; "Farewell Address," 240–41; final "call-to-arms," xv, 248; French and Indian War, in, xiv, 33–34, 36–73, 75, 93, 113–14, 214; legacies, xv, 275–87; marriage to Martha Dandridge Custis, 79–88, 93–94; presidency, xv, 204–43, 245; renovations to Mount Vernon, first, 68, 73, 75–79; renovations to Mount Vernon, second, 114–27, 174–78; retirement to Mount Vernon, final, xv, 241–43, 244–58; retirement to Mount Vernon, first, xiv, 74–101, 104, 105–9; retirement to Mount Vernon, second, xv, 154–203; Revolutionary War, in, xiv–xv, 37, 42, 45, 58, 110–14, 127–53, 195, 205, 232, 262, 280, 283; slavery and, xv, 9, 100, 170, 193, 195, 197–203, 254; Valley Forge, 28, 134–37, 170, 180, 196, 283; Yorktown, 99, 116, 139, 141–50, 153, 181, 182, 226, 280; youth, xiv, 3–35, 99

Washington, George Augustine, 99, 180, 183, 191–93, 223, 253, 261, 275

Washington, George Fayette, 275

Washington, George Steptoe, 181

Washington, Harriet, 248

Washington, Jane Butler. *See* Butler, Jane

Washington, John Augustine (brother of George), 20, 59, 111–12, 275

Washington, John Augustine (inherits Mount Vernon from Bushrod), 275, 285

Washington, John (cousin of Augustine), 4

Washington, John Augustine, Jr. (third of that name), xv, 275, 278

Washington, Julia, 275

Washington, Lawrence (brother of George), xi, xiv, 7, 9, 12, 16, 17, 18, 29, 34, 35, 38, 45, 46, 75, 76, 80, 100, 111, 138

Washington, Lawrence (seventeenth-century ancestor), 4, 18

Washington, Lund, xiv, 122, 126–29, 137, 180, 189, 191

Washington, Martha Dandridge Custis, xiv, xv, 9, 20, 23, 25, 37, 42, 45, 68, 73, 75, 78–87, 90, 91, 93–94, 97, 99, 111, 137, 139, 149–51, 169–70, 172, 178–81, 198–99, 203, 205, 219–22, 227, 230, 233, 245–46, 249, 254, 258, 267, 275, 283, 284, 285

Washington, Mary Ball, 7, 9, 17, 18, 149–50, 181–84, 261

Washington, Samuel, 248

Washington, William Augustine, 3, 18

Washington Benevolent Society of Massachusetts, 40

Washington County, 213

Wayne, Gen. "Mad Anthony," 196, 213

Weems, Mason Locke, xii, 10, 13, 16, 17, 18, 50, 54–56, 58–60, 62–63, 65–66, 80, 136–37, 169–70, 183, 193, 260, 266, 287

Weishaupt, H., 264–66; *Apotheosis of Washington,* 264

Welch, James, 102

Wellford, Dr. Robert, 215

West, Benjamin, 127, 146, 149, 155, 157

Westmoreland, England, 9

Westmoreland County, Va., 3–4, 6, 196

Westover, 43, 75, 119

Whately and Sinclair, 279; *The Two Hundred Acres Purchased by the Mount Vernon Ladies' Association,* 279

Wheatley, Phillis, 127

Whiskey Rebellion, 213–15, 222, 262

White, Alexander, 247

White, Edwin, 63; *George Washington Reading the Burial Service Over the Body of Braddock,* 63

White House (home of Martha Custis, New Hope County, Va.), 9, 82, 87, 93

Whitting, Anthony, 233–37

Wilkinson, Maj. James, 133

William and Mary, College of, 280

Williamsburg, Va., 12, 35, 41, 46, 47, 49, 51–52, 75, 81, 97, 109, 115, 123, 175, 188, 216, 217, 220

Wills, Garry, 155

Wilton, 85

Winchester, Va., 66, 68, 72, 76

Winstanley, William, 102–3, 185

Winthrop, John, 207

Wollaston, John, 37, 45, 84–86, 94, 96, 123; *John Parke ( Jacky) Custis and Martha Parke (Patsy) Custis,* 85; *Martha Custis,* 84; *Daniel Parke Custis,* 84; *Mrs. William Randolph III (Anne Harrison Randolph),* 85

Wood, Grant, 14; *Cartoon for Parson Weems' Fable,* 15

Woodlawn Plantation, 250

Wright, Joseph, 158–61, 163–65; *George Washington* (1783), 159; *George Washington* (1784), 160; after Wright, *George Washington* (ca. 1790), 161

York County, Va., 43

York River, 144–45

Yorktown, Va., 99, 116, 139, 141–50, 153, 181, 182, 226, 280

Young, Arthur, 190, 194, 234

Zane, Isaac, 20